Hybrid Warfare

Hybrid Warfare

*Security and Asymmetric Conflict
in International Relations*

Edited by
Mikael Weissmann, Niklas Nilsson,
Björn Palmertz and Per Thunholm

I.B.TAURIS
LONDON • NEW YORK • OXFORD • NEW DELHI • SYDNEY

I.B. TAURIS

Bloomsbury Publishing Plc

50 Bedford Square, London, WC1B 3DP, UK

1385 Broadway, New York, NY 10018, USA

29 Earlsfort Terrace, Dublin 2, Ireland

BLOOMSBURY, I.B. TAURIS and the I.B. Tauris logo are trademarks of Bloomsbury Publishing Plc

First published in Great Britain 2021

Cover design: Holly Bell

A catalogue record for this book is available from the British Library.

A catalog record for this book is available from the Library of Congress.

ISBN: HB: 978-1-7883-1711-5
PB: 978-1-7883-1962-1
ePDF: 978-1-7867-3655-0
eBook: 978-1-7867-2649-0

Typeset by Deanta Global Publishing Services, Chennai, India

To find out more about our authors and books visit www.bloomsbury.com and

Funding for this Open Access publication was provided by the Center for Asymmetric Threat Studies (CATS) and the Swedish Defence University.

Contents

Illustrations

Foreword – Hybrid threats and hybrid warfare

Security and asymmetric conflict in the grey zone

Hybrid threats, as phenomenon and concept, have rapidly placed themselves at the centre of security policy discourse since the Russian aggression against Ukraine in 2014, for good reasons. The nature of antagonistic threats to our open, democratic societies and political decision-making processes has broadened, and the intensity and potential damage of this kind of antagonistic behaviour has increased.

There has been a rapid development of research and analysis as well as practical action over the last years, a natural development considering the worsening security policy situation in Europe and the widened scope of the antagonistic state threats that we are facing.

There is a need to better understand this phenomenon in order to be able to detect and identify it, to build resilience against it and finally to counter it. Theory and practice are now rapidly developing, hand in hand. There is a lively debate between analysts and practitioners in this field. It's not too wild an exaggeration to say that this constitutes the research frontier of security policy right now. We are in a process of developing a new common strategic culture, both nationally and internationally, on specifically how to manage these peacetime antagonistic threats.

There are many issues to be explored and understood, and we need partly new sets of coordinates to orient ourselves in this new landscape of antagonistic threats.

Our traditional conceptual distinctions between external and internal security, military and civilian affairs and between national and international solutions guiding our understanding and bureaucratic; organizational set-up seems less applicable, or may even hinder us, when approaching the subject of hybrid threats.

Sometimes, the question is put whether all the talk (and action) about hybrid threats is just hype, a mere repackaging of something that has always been around. Of course, the methods and a broad toolbox of aggressive instruments to impose one's political will on other states and societies have always existed. Nevertheless, the renewed focus on these issues since the Russian aggression against Ukraine in 2014, and elsewhere, is justified.

A threat can be understood as the combination of capability, intent and opportunity. The capability of certain states to apply a broad range of antagonistic instruments in a coordinated way has certainly increased. Some of these instruments are new, or are being used in new ways. So has the intent: we can observe hostile state activities to an extent not seen in a long time. Over the last decade or so, certain governments have clearly lowered their inhibitions to the use of malign and malicious actions. At the same time, the opportunity presented by our own vulnerabilities has increased, thanks to increased digitalization and dependencies but also under-investment in internal and external security. So yes, hybrid threats exist here and now, and they are not going to go away. Hybrid threats do not constitute a potential risk – something that might happen. They are an actual and present reality, which we need to deal with.

Managing hybrid threats is a rapidly growing subject of discourse nationally and internationally. It requires states, societies and international organizations to understand the threat, build resilience and acquire the capabilities to counter the menace.

Understanding the threat includes developing an awareness of one's vulnerabilities; understanding the motives and modes of action of the antagonistic state; and detecting and identifying the threat, a task that requires a broadened situational awareness. Hybrid threats are coordinated and synchronized actions that can manifest themselves in many ways and in many sectors. We need to connect the dots, often from sensors that have not necessarily been connected before, and assume a holistic approach. Our adversaries certainly do.

Building resilience means reducing the potential gains of the antagonistic state, so-called deterrence by denial. Neither understanding the threat nor building resilience is 'rocket science', although both require targeted efforts and a coordinated whole-of-government approach.

Countering hybrid threats, however, partially means entering unchartered, and challenging, territory. 'Countering' can be divided into applying countermeasures against ongoing antagonistic actions and building deterrence against potential attacks by changing the cost–benefit analysis of the antagonistic state, so-called deterrence by punishment.

Hybrid threats are by nature designed to create confusion and deception and to be difficult to detect and to attribute. They consist of a large number of possible antagonistic means used in a coordinated way, some of which – such as disinformation – do not have to be illegal or contrary to international law. Tit-for-tat symmetric responses are seldom possible or desirable. International law must be upheld. We are in the business of defending our open, democratic societies and the rules-based international order.

Typically, the antagonistic state is an authoritarian government or dictatorship that has little inhibition against aggressive behaviour and that possesses highly centralized, rapid and coordinated decision-making structures. Antagonistic, malicious action is seen – and used – as a political tool to achieve strategic goals, a means to an end. That end may be to influence our decision-making or to undermine our societies, to inflict damage.

Countering hybrid threats, moving beyond building resilience as it were, is a rapidly growing and deepening political and intellectual quest. It is a challenging part of rethinking and redesigning security policy. International cooperation and exchanges between government authorities, think tanks and academia play an important role in this endeavour.

One major challenge in countering hybrid threats is that, on one hand, we face a traditional security and foreign policy issue – a foreign antagonistic state actor, that is, an external threat – yet on the other hand, threats often manifest themselves in the internal security sphere, where many of the possible countermeasures also can be found. The political culture and bureaucratic structures of Cold War or post-Cold War Western states are not necessarily conducive to bridging the gap between what traditionally has been construed as 'internal' and 'external' security challenges. The new hybrid threat environment means that the security policy concept must be widened and partially redefined.

Building resilience does not only imply strengthening infrastructure, be it physical or societal; it is also about strengthening cognitive and legal resilience. The recurring new buzzwords are whole-of-government and whole-of-society approach. Clearly, private business and civil society play an important role in countering hybrid threats. That is a particular strength of our open, liberal democracies.

International cooperation and solidarity are important tools for enhancing deterrence, understanding the threat and building resilience. It is no coincidence that the EU and NATO have developed new toolboxes for addressing hybrid threats.

Addressing this important, but complex and challenging, matter must be a team effort. Academics, analysts and practitioners have much to learn from each other. Sometimes we use different words and conceptual models to address these issues. There are different views about the toolbox and how best to structure our systems to deal with the threats. And there are different perspectives – national/international, internal/external, military/civilian – on this topic. We have much to learn from these different perspectives, sharing best practices and ideas, which are complimentary and can sharpen our minds and actions. This book offers a very rich overview of such views, based on deep knowledge and long experience, and is a very welcome and important contribution to the way forward in dealing with hybrid threats.

Fredrik Löjdquist
Ambassador

Special Envoy for Countering Hybrid Threats at the Ministry for Foreign Affairs of Sweden

Security challenges in the grey zone

Hybrid threats and hybrid warfare[1]

Niklas Nilsson, Mikael Weissmann, Björn Palmertz,
Per Thunholm and Henrik Häggström

The greatest victory is that which requires no battle.
— Sun Tzu, The Art of War

The international security environment has in recent years evolved into a volatile and increasingly grey zone of war and peace. Security challenges arising from hybrid threats and hybrid warfare, henceforth HT&HW, are today high on security agendas across the globe. However, despite the attention, and a growing body of studies on specific issues, there is an imminent need for research bringing attention to how these challenges can be addressed in order to develop a comprehensive approach towards identifying, analysing and countering HT&HW. This volume supports the development of such an approach by bringing together practitioners and scholarly perspectives on HT&HW, by covering the threats themselves as well as the tools and means to counter them together with a number of real-world case studies.

Over time the grey zone between peace and war has grown considerably, underscoring the necessity of understanding hybrid warfare and related threats. Russia's actions in Ukraine have manifested this paradigm, being a good example of the problem in thinking about war and peace as binary categories. How does a country or group of countries deal with threats and aggression in this grey area, such as 'little green men' that appear in uniform but without national denomination and refuse to tell where they come from, election-influenced operations or cyberattacks, to mention but a few possible actions.

By uniting the knowledge of both practitioners and scholars, the volume aims to identify the existing tools for countering HT&HW, as well as experiences from a wide set of empirical contexts. Mirroring this, the project is a cross-sector collaboration between the Department of Military Studies and the Center for Asymmetric Threat Studies (CATS) at the Swedish Defence University. The former represents an academic environment where research and teaching are intertwined in a range of subjects including War Studies, Military Technology and Military History. The latter is a national centre within the Swedish Defence University tasked with developing and disseminating knowledge about asymmetric threats within the context of societal security and resilience.

This volume focuses on the challenge posed by HT&HW to Western democracies, and their ability to address it. Western democracies are not only the type of states most frequently targeted by hybrid measures, but also the most vulnerable. By virtue of being open, pluralistic and liberal societies with freedom of the press and rule of law, Western democracies display both inherent weaknesses that can be targeted and inherent constraints – in particular through the rule of law and basic freedoms – that limit the scope for defensive actions. These vulnerabilities are increasingly recognized by Western governments, which have developed a range of entities to address them, although coordination in many instances remains weak. The later sections outline the growing significance of HT&HW on the security agendas of Western democracies and the challenges they imply, as well as the entities these states have established in response. Although neither list is complete, they provide an overview of the current situation. The final sections provide an outline of the volume's structure and a summary of each chapter.

The rise of HT&HW and the Russia factor

HT&HW are problematic concepts. Contemporary scholarship on these phenomena lacks a common definition and the use of terminology remains contested. In fact, HT&HW are just two of a variety of distinct, but overlapping, concepts employed to describe a similar phenomenon, where 'Asymmetrical Warfare', 'Sixth Generation Warfare', 'Contactless Warfare', 'Grey Wars', 'New warfare', 'Next-generation Warfare', 'Ambiguous Warfare', 'Irregular Warfare' 'Non-linear Warfare', 'Full Spectrum Conflict' and 'Unconventional Warfare' are examples of more or less synonymous terms (see also Chapter 5).[2]

HT&HW – twenty-first-century style – differ from traditional threats and warfare more in intensity and degree than in kind. The exception is the virtual or digital realm, which empowers new tools and lowers the entry cost of using them. HT&HW denote adversaries or antagonists who aim to achieve outcomes without a war, to disrupt, undermine or damage the target's political system and cohesion through a combination of violence, control, subversion, manipulation and dissemination of (mis)information.[3] Hence, they target opposing societies, not combatants.[4] HT&HW imply the simultaneous presence of a range of possible adversarial means, from threats of war to propaganda and everything in between. They therefore include multiple instruments of power and influence, though with an emphasis on threats, non-military as well as military, operating below the threshold of open war. The identification of HT&HW does not allow for a clear-cut distinction between different forms of actors, be they state or non-state; soldiers or civilians; organized violence, terror, crime or war in a traditional sense. Regardless of the actor from which the threat originates, it has become customary for such actors to combine and tailor a mix of conventional and irregular means to achieve maximum effect.[5]

The increased attention paid to HT&HW in current Western strategic thinking is thus foremost a reaction to the innovative behaviour of external antagonists. In particular, Russia has emerged as a dark cloud over Europe and the West through its demonstrated ability to engage in 'a style of warfare that combines the political, economic, social and kinetic in a conflict that recognizes no boundaries between civilian and combatant, covert and overt, war and peace [where] achieving victory – however that may be defined – permits and demands whatever means will be successful: the ethics of total war applied even to the smallest skirmish.'[6]

Indeed, Russia's annexation of Crimea and its subsequent aggression in eastern Ukraine prompted a much broader acceptance of HT&HW as a security challenge (see also Chapter 14). The fact that the Ukraine scenario involved not a militia in the Middle East, but a large state bordering NATO, with substantial conventional military resources, spurred a considerable rethinking of Russia as a potential adversary. It also highlighted the need for a comprehensive view of the various methods, conventional and unconventional, lethal and non-lethal, that Russia proved capable of combining and deploying in Ukraine, which are either already being utilized or could potentially be deployed in a conflict with NATO and the West. In this context, to many Western academics and policymakers, the labelling of threats and warfare as hybrid could fruitfully capture the purportedly complex and comprehensive nature of Russia's ability to combine various levers of state power, from the military and economic to the information space.[7]

The hybrid terminology thus rapidly gained traction in Western public and political debate, where it has evolved into an all-encompassing view of Russia's international behaviour, permeating the strategic, operational and tactical levels. In the meantime, China has gradually risen as not only an economic but also a military power (see also Chapter 7). The fact that the combined military resources of the West remain vastly superior, certainly to those of Russia and for the time being also to those of China, has encouraged these and other actors to develop and combine other, less resource-consuming means for challenging the global hegemony of the West. Due to the asymmetry in military and economic power, these actors seek ways and means to challenge the West by exploiting the vulnerabilities in existing security institutions as well as Western democracies. Thus, HT&HW have become terms commonly used to describe the strategy of challengers to the global hegemony of the West, aside from Russia also including, for example, China, Iran and North Korea, but also of non-state actors, particularly ISIS and Hezbollah.[8]

Yet, as noted earlier, HT&HW remain contested concepts. Regarding Russia and its actions in Ukraine and Syria, several observers have objected to the portrayal of Russian hybrid warfare as a 'new' approach to war fighting, since the combination of military power with, for example, economic means and propaganda has been part of the toolbox of statecraft since ancient times (see also Chapter 6).[9] Moreover, the grouping of a variety of non-kinetic means, including economic and informational means, under the heading of hybrid warfare, it is argued, dangerously stretches the concept of 'war'. Yet other critics point out that the concept of hybrid warfare has become vastly overextended, expanding in scope to cover most of Russian foreign policy, while simultaneously erroneously depicting Russian actions as much more coordinated, strategic and efficient than they actually are.[10] More generally, it has been argued that the extended use of the concept to denote a 'blend' of methods at the strategic, operational and tactical levels, is so vague and all-encompassing that 'hybrid' no longer has analytic utility – rather, current conceptualizations make more sense as a description of contemporary warfare.[11]

In this light, it should be noted that the view presented by Russian officials, representatives of Russia's armed forces and military theorists, is in large part a mirror image of the understanding in the West. Seminal expressions of the Russian armed forces' understanding of the future of warfare can be found in the speeches of General Valery Gerasimov, Chief of Russia's General Staff, to the Russian Academy of Military Science. Gerasimov has presented a picture of increasingly blurred boundaries between war and peace as well as military and non-military means[12] in which Russia must take measures against the 'hybrid methods' employed by its adversaries.[13] Indeed, Russian military thinkers and policymakers seemingly believe that warfare is entering a new era where military force becomes increasingly interchangeable with, and perhaps even secondary to, non-kinetic force.[14] However, these and other Russian assessments regarding the future of war draw on observed twenty-first-century Western warfare in Iraq, Afghanistan and Libya, rather than relevant Russian experiences from its own conduct in, for example, Chechnya, Moldova, Ukraine and the south Caucasus.[15]

Official Russian assessments of the main threats to the country's national security portray the determination of the United States and its allies to retain their global hegemony at all costs and by all means as the fundamental security challenge that Russia is facing. The description of these means is familiar: the West is assumed to deploy overt and covert military resources, along with economic, diplomatic, informational and cultural means in order to contain Russia.[16] In particular, Russia's official security discourse indicates a concern over vulnerabilities implied by an information sphere and a civil society outside the state's control – not least in its interpretation of the string of 'colour' revolutions in post-communist countries and the Arab spring as covert depositions of legitimate governments by Western intelligence services. In this light, the crackdown on Russia's political opposition and civil society, as well as delimiting public access to channels of information, stem from the perceived threat of Western subversion of Russian society, veiled under the liberal norms of market economic principles, human rights and democratization. Although the validity of these conclusions is arguably questionable, and poorly backed by empirical evidence, the fact remains that hybrid warfare, or *gibridnaya voyna*, is a concept that Russia has imported from the West, which in the Russian context denotes the range of threats that Russia purportedly faces from the West.

Yet while acknowledging the ambiguities and weaknesses of HT&HW, as well as other conceptual labels, we maintain its usefulness in the holistic analysis of how a range of actors, state and non-state strategically combine kinetic and non-kinetic means of power to pursue interests and attain objectives in the contemporary globalized world.[17] Given the inherent understanding that the evolution and attractiveness of the idea of HT&HW is connected with asymmetries in power and resources, the conceptualization appears particularly useful as a framework for understanding the methods and conduct of challengers to the West on a global or regional scale, particularly Russia, China and Iran. However, this by no means precludes Western democracies from combining various tools of statecraft in a manner that might be characterized as hybrid warfare. Indeed, with all its flaws and ambiguities, the debate on hybrid warfare has served to challenge Western binary thinking on war and peace as well as conventional and unconventional warfare. It has contributed to a more comprehensive understanding of how adversaries may innovatively combine a range of foreign policy tools to target the particular vulnerabilities of Western societies and circumvent their existing defensive structures. And it has underlined the need for holistic analysis to comprehend and act in the contemporary security environment. From an intelligence perspective, it also underscores the need to fuse intelligence from military and civilian agencies, or even between intelligence and non-intelligence agencies.

This volume neither seeks to resolve the ongoing conceptual discussions, nor lets the lack of a consensus definition and the contested terminology distract from the purpose of the book – to enhance our ability to understand, and in the continuation identify, analyse and counter HT&HW. Because of their diffuse nature, the line between a hybrid threat and ongoing warfare is not always evident. Thus, for the purpose of this volume, unless otherwise specified by the chapter author, HT&HW are considered two synonymous labels for the same type of conceptual phenomenon.

The Western response

The meaning of HT&HW is far from new, but the awareness and work to incorporate its implications into the policy, capacity and capacity implementation in Western democracies have gained momentum in recent years. Some pivotal developments include the activities of ISIS between 2013 and 2019 and, as noted earlier, the Russian annexation of Crimea in early 2014. In addition, the Russian combined influence and cyber operations targeting the US election campaign in 2016, and the French election campaign the following year, clearly exposed the need for political and societal awareness, as well as increased coordination and capabilities in Western democracies to address HT&HW targeting the very core values and processes of such states.

During the last few years, the West has been exposed to continuous media reports of specific actions, for example, disinformation or hack and leak operations aiming to change the course of public debate or diminish the credibility of key societal actors. In such an information environment it is easy to get caught in a problem-oriented sense of a continuous barrage of threats and lose sight of the more subtle long-term developments that bolster the capacity to respond and build resilience against them. It is no doubt easier to describe a threat aimed at a specific event or target delineated in time than more subtle shifts in governments or societies. An extensive literature review in 2018 on information influence activities highlights that more is known about the techniques and conduct of these activities than about how to counter them.[18] Let us therefore outline a few examples of capabilities that have recently come into place and that are relevant in order to understand or diminish the effects of hybrid threats against the West. These include (1) multinational entities and projects, (2) national governmental entities and (3) non-governmental entities.

In 2014 the NATO Wales Summit Final Declaration described 'the specific challenges posed by hybrid warfare threats' and underlined the importance that the alliance develop 'necessary tools and procedures' to enable a response to such threats. They also emphasized that this requires a broad range of efforts related to, but also beyond, traditional military capabilities.[19] The same year saw the initiation of the NATO StratCom Center of Excellence in Riga, Latvia. It is aimed at supporting 'NATO's capability development process, mission effectiveness and interoperability by providing comprehensive and timely expertise in the field of strategic communications'.[20] In addition, the NATO Cooperative Cyber Defence Centre of Excellence, established in 2008, has become another important hub for research, training and exercises for the alliance in terms of hybrid threats. One paper illustrating the overlap between hybrid threats from CCD CoE is Brangetto and Venendaal's 'Influence Cyber Operations: The use of cyberattacks in support of Influence Operations', which examines how influencing the behaviour of a target audience becomes the primary effect of a cyber operation.[21]

Illustrating this need for a comprehensive understanding of the threat environment and joint collaboration, the European Center of Excellence for Countering Hybrid Threats was established in Helsinki in early 2017. It aims to constitute an international platform where governments can share best practices, build capability, test new ideas and exercise defence against hybrid threats, as well as facilitating such activities between the EU and NATO.[22] To date, Hybrid CoE has twenty-seven member states and a structure focused on three key Communities of Interest: (1) hybrid influencing, including a sub-community on non-state actors, (2) strategy and defence and (3) vulnerabilities and resilience.

The EU Intelligence Analysis Centre (INTCEN) is another key actor capable of intelligence collection and collating such contributions from the EU member states. This results in analyses and assessments in order to provide situational insight to the head of the European External Action Service and the EU leadership.[23] As such, it has an important function in ensuring that a number of overlapping areas, such as those found within the realm of hybrid threats, are understood and tracked.

Also, the European Council decided to create the EEAS East StratCom Task Force during a meeting in early 2015.[24] Its task is to develop communication to explain EU policies, as well as support the media environment, in Eastern Partnership Countries. It also analyses and produces reports on disinformation trends and narratives, and actively works to raise awareness of such activities from the Russian state and related actors. This includes maintaining a wide international and member state cooperation to share best practices in strategic communications and enable continued access to objective information.[25]

Another project worth highlighting is the Multinational Capability Development Campaign Countering hybrid warfare project, a joint effort by the EU and a number of additional contributing nations. It is aimed at informing national and multinational policy, enabling cooperation and offer conceptual guidance related to security and defence.[26]

A number of governments, especially in the aftermath of the Russian annexation of Crimea, have amplified their focus on HT&HW and initiated capability development to identify, analyse and counter them. Two examples that illustrate approaches related to influence campaigns are Sweden and Australia.

Sweden has a governmental structure built on very independent agencies, where an annual appropriations bill offers a general direction. However, responsibility for detailed planning and implementation resides with the agency responsible for a specific area. In 2016 the Swedish Civil Contingencies Agency (MSB) was officially tasked to develop capabilities to identify and counter information influence activities, and to support other key societal actors in this area of expertise.[27] This also coincided with an increased Russian influence focus on Sweden, targeting its host nation agreement with NATO and Sweden's further integration with the alliance as a non-member, as well as sowing doubt about the Swedish political system.[28] Since then MSB, in addition to developing their own capacity, has conducted a number of ground-up resilience-building activities. These include visibility via external communication and commentary through various media channels, as well as funding research into state- and non-state-related information influence activities. MSB has also established training and exercise programmes for a large number of public servants, related to election integrity as well as a broader set of influence related challenges. These activities were supported by the 2018 handbook 'Countering information influence activities' developed by Lund University for MSB.[29] Other key state actors include the Office for Crisis Management at the Swedish Department of Justice, the Swedish Security Service, the Armed Forces as well as the Swedish Institute and the Swedish National Defence Radio Establishment.[30] As of 2018 the Swedish Ministry for Foreign Affairs also has an ambassador assigned the portfolio of hybrid threats.[31]

In Australia on the other hand, the growing challenge of foreign interference, especially from China, has resulted in a number of open discussions and actions by the Australian Government. Starting in 2015, the Australian Security Intelligence Organisation (ASIO) issued warnings to domestic political parties regarding monetary contributions from two Chinese businessmen, deemed an attempt by the Chinese Communist Party to attain leverage in Australian politics.[32] Also, since over 1.2 million people of Chinese descent live in Australia and constitute the largest percentage of current migrants, the diaspora is an attractive target for Chinese influence attempts. Compared to Sweden, the Australian response has been a more top-down effort, including legislation and high-level government coordination. For example, Australia decided in 2017 to ban Huawei from participating in its 5G network and introduced the Foreign Influence Transparency Scheme Bill and the Espionage and Foreign Interference Bill the same year.[33] In April 2018, the Australian Government appointed the first National Counter Foreign Interference Coordinator (NCFIC) in the Department of Home Affairs, whose responsibilities include ensuring a whole-of-government effort in this area. This includes drawing on intelligence community capabilities, ensuring the development and implementation of strategy and specific programmes across the government, and interaction to increase the resilience of societal groups or organizations deemed particularly likely targets of for foreign interference. In late 2019 it was announced that the NCFIC would acquire funding to establish a new Counter Foreign Interference Taskforce. In addition, a Foreign Interference Threat Assessment Centre will be established within ASIO.[34]

Aside from the efforts of states and governments, a number of non-governmental entities increasingly provide situational awareness and knowledge concerning the techniques and motivations underlying hybrid threats. Bellingcat, an independent international group of researchers, investigators and citizen journalists using open source and social media investigation, has played a public role in a number of cases. For example, in 2018 they revealed the likely involvement of Russian intelligence operatives in the poisoning of Sergei Skripal in Salisbury, UK. They also identified the Russian air defence system responsible for the downing of Malaysian Airlines flight 17 over eastern Ukraine in 2014.[35]

Another increasingly visible non-governmental resource in recent years has been the Digital Forensic Research Lab at the Atlantic Council. Their aims include identifying, exposing and explaining 'disinformation campaigns, fake news stories, covert military developments, and subversive attempts against democracy'.[36] They have covered a number of areas, including far-right messaging on social media platforms, the conflict in Ukraine, disinformation and influence campaigns during elections, and state crackdowns on public protests in, for example, Russia and Iran.[37]

In sum, the range of entities established in the West to counter HT&HW mirrors a vastly increased awareness of the problem in international, national and domestic settings. Moreover, they also highlight the emergence of numerous cooperative and innovative means for addressing the insecurities implied by HT&HW. Indeed, the multitude of responses are indicative of the increasingly dynamic nature of the present security environment, in which the West is proving capable of not only reacting to the challenges of antagonists, but also of identifying and addressing its own vulnerabilities in this regard as well as devising innovative and creative countermeasures of its own.

Structure of volume

The volume is divided into three parts. Part I presents a practitioner's view on HT&HW, from the perspective of key western actors in this area: NATO, the EU and the United States. Part II focuses on the tools and means employed to conduct and counter HT&HW. It includes chapters taking stock of Russia's military thinking and China's hybrid warfare capabilities, followed by chapters on influence operations and the modern information environment, and multilateral intelligence cooperation. Part II concludes with a chapter on cyberwarfare and the internet. Drawing on the themes identified in Part II, Part III consists of five case studies – the United States, China's political warfare in Taiwan, the Baltics, Ukraine, Iran and Catalonia – demonstrating the employment of these tools and means – how they have been used and countered in practice.

Finally, the conclusion focuses on patterns, practices and implications drawn from the volume. The chapter introduces a dynamic view of HT&HW depicted, presenting what we term 'the Hybridity Blizzard Model'. This model presents a picture of the dynamics of and between HT&HW and responses and countermeasures. The model not only enables a better understanding of the dynamics themselves, but also of how to identify, analyse and counter HT&HW.

Commencing Part I, Chapter 2, 'NATO and hybrid warfare: Seeking a concept to describe the challenge from Russia', is written by Dr G. Alexander Crowther, Research Professor at Florida International University, former Special Assistant to the Supreme Allied Commander, Europe, and former researcher at the Strategic Studies Institute and the US National Defense University. Dr Crowther argues that NATO faced a resurgent Russia that developed its own concept of Hybrid Operations based on the thoughts of Frank Hoffman, Russia's analysis of perceived aggressive actions by the United States and NATO, and Russia's own past of political warfare. NATO, in turn, reacted by conceptualizing the challenge and a response, then used information (in particular diplomacy) in order to minimize support for Russia and maximize support for NATO, collaborated with Allies and other partners, and used NATO's inherent hard power to deter Russia from escalating to violence. Efforts thus far have been necessary but not sufficient, both Russian hybrid operations and NATO efforts to respond to them will continue for the foreseeable future.

Chapter 3, 'An American view: Hybrid threats and intelligence', is written by Dr Gregory F. Treverton, University of Southern California, and former Chair of the US National Intelligence Council (NIC), and draws on lessons from Dr Treverton's experience in government, most recently as Chair of NIC. The first lesson is the value of reaching out to private sector partners for early warning of hybrid threats. The 2016 Russian interventions in US elections came as a surprise but should not have, for a private group looking at jihadist websites had found anomalies, ones indicating that many of those posing as Free Syria on social media were, in fact, Russians, not Syrians. By the same token, the presence of private companies doing their own attribution of cyberattacks complicates the usual government process of intelligence attributing, then passing the attribution to policy officials for action. Yet in the long run, those companies will be valuable allies if government agencies reach out to them, something that does not come naturally, especially for intelligence agencies.

The second lesson is the importance of seeing the world through Russia's eyes, not to excuse Vladimir Putin but to understand what drives his policy, especially in the 'near abroad'. From Russia's perspective, the United States dismissed Russia after the fall of communism, then encircled it, especially by expanding NATO to Russia's borders. That perspective and the desire to be seen as great is the backdrop for Russia's moves into Ukraine, Syria, Libya, Moldova and elsewhere, and will condition Russian responses to future US and NATO actions in Europe. In responding to Russian initiatives in the grey, or hybrid zone, two tactical lessons stand out: don't demean the West's free press by stooping to Putin's level of disinformation, and don't regard the Russians as ten feet tall.

Chapter 4, 'A perspective on EU hybrid threat early warning efforts', shifts focus to the European Union (EU). Here Dr Patrick Cullen, Senior Research Fellow at the Norwegian Institute of International Affairs (NUPI) and a member of the 'Countering Hybrid Warfare' component of the Multinational Capability Development Campaign (MCDC) presents an academic practitioner's perspective on the development of the EU policy engagement with and response to hybrid threats. Special attention is paid to the role of the Russian annexation of Crimea in shaping EU perceptions of a new 'hybrid security environment', its decision to work more closely with NATO, and the development of an EU counter-hybrid security threat niche focused on hybrid threats below the threshold of war. Rather than conducting a survey of all EU counter-hybrid threat efforts, this chapter focuses on the development of its hybrid threat early warning and detection mechanism proposed and implemented by its European External Action Service and its Hybrid Fusion Cell.

Moving on to Part II, in Chapter 5, 'Conceptualizing and countering hybrid threats and hybrid warfare: The role of the military in the grey zone', by Dr Mikael Weissmann, Associate Professor, Head of Research at the Land Operations Section and Co-Convener of the Hybrid Warfare Research Group, Swedish Defence University. After an initial conceptual discussion on HT&HW, Weissmann presents an analytical framework operationalizing hybrid threats and warfare. Asking what role the military can and should play in responding to hybrid threats and warfare today and in the future, the framework is then applied on the official discourse in the Baltic and a case study of Sweden analysing what role the members of the military themselves think it should have.

He is arguing that it is crucial to understand the role of the military in the grey zone, as unless hybrid threats- and warfare can be successfully handled there, the war is likely to have been lost before a conventional war breaks out. The chapter concludes that the role of the military needs to be recognized and utilized in the most efficient way possible across the grey zone while at the same time ensuring that democratic principles and the rule of law are upheld. It is encouraging to see that the role of the military in the grey zone is both recognized and in correlation in the official discourse and in the thinking of military officers. This is a good base to build the resilient society and national defence needed to counter hybrid threats and warfare today and tomorrow. This said, there is today a discrepancy between where we are and where we should be.

In Chapter 6, 'Understanding Russian thinking on *gibridnaya voyna*', Dr Markus Göransson, the project leader of the Russia programme at the Swedish Defence University, analyses the concept of *gibridnaya voyna*, which in recent years has gained ground in Russian military scholarship where it is used as shorthand for multidimensional operations conducted by Western states against non-Western adversaries. It is a direct translation of the Western term 'hybrid warfare' yet is used in a somewhat different sense in parts of the Russian scholarship. Employed not only to designate military action at the tactical and operational levels, *gibridnaya voyna* is used also as a catch-all term for Western non-military subversion against Russia. Because of this difference in meaning, previous research has understood *gibridnaya voyna* as being rooted in a peculiarly Russian understanding of war as a sociopolitical phenomenon that may be waged non-kinetically. Dr. Göransson argues that it is mistaken to view the Russian *gibridnaya voyna* discourse as primarily an academic endeavour. It is conceptually and empirically weak and serves mainly a rhetorical function as it allows for the identification of a vast range of perceived threats to Russia. In other words, it provides an analytical framework that securitizes a range of issues as potential dangers to Russia.

In Chapter 7, 'China and its hybrid warfare spectrum' by Dr Lora Saalman, Associate Senior Fellow with Stockholm International Peace Research Institute and Senior Fellow with EastWest Institute, the focus shifts from Russia to China. Dr Saalman argues that there is a tendency in Western analyses on Chinese hybrid warfare to focus on just a few historical texts, including *The Art of War* from the fifth century BCE and *Unrestricted Warfare* from 1999. Yet this narrow emphasis misses the complexity of views on and employment of hybrid warfare in China. A survey of 192 Chinese-language texts reveals that Chinese writings on hybrid warfare are often so inclusive that it can be difficult to decipher what in effect is 'not' part of their strategic thinking on the subject. To provide greater nuance, this chapter explores Chinese analyses along a spectrum, covering unrestricted warfare, information warfare, cyberwarfare, intelligent warfare and kinetic warfare. In doing so, it seeks to provide a more comprehensive baseline for understanding Chinese perceptions on threat, response and operationalization of hybrid warfare.

The actor-focused chapters on Russia and China are followed by three chapters thematically oriented towards specific tools and means. In Chapter 8, 'Influence operations and the modern information environment', Björn Palmertz, Senior Analyst at CATS at the Swedish Defence University, shows that even though the techniques used by state and non-state actors to conduct influence operations are far from new, the modern information environment has resulted in new opportunities as well as vulnerabilities. An increased availability of data on target audiences, easier access to specific target segments, a rapid speed of information dissemination, and ways of staying anonymous or pretending to be someone else are but a few factors that benefit the employment of influence operations, on their own or in unison with other means, such as cyber operations. This chapter discusses how these relate to targeting, and offer examples illustrating a number of influence techniques that have been employed during recent years. These are hacking, leaking and doxing, distributed denial of service attacks, disinformation, social media advertising, organized trolling and amplification by social bots.

Chapter 9, 'Hybrid threats and new challenges for multilateral intelligence cooperation', is written by Henrik Häggström, Senior Analyst, CATS at the Swedish Defence University. Häggström argues that ever since the 9/11 terror attacks, the range of partners in the intelligence world that share information at the international level has grown exponentially. The change has been both quantitative and qualitative and improved multilateral intelligence cooperation. With a view to effectively address hybrid threats and conducting effective hybrid warfare, multilateral organizations such as NATO, the EU and the UN have launched a number of intelligence initiatives in the past years to improve their capacity. These initiatives have involved structural improvements, policy changes, resource allocation and the establishment of new joint hybrid centres. The extent to which the various new intelligence initiatives within the EU, NATO and the UN will actually enhance methods to combat HT&HW is yet to be determined. Lack of trust, cultural differences and the lack of a functioning leadership in NATO, the EU and the UN are among the troubling trends that could hamper future operations.

Chapter 10 on 'Cyberwarfare and the internet: The Implications of a more digitalized world' is written by Anne-Marie Eklund Löwinder, the Chief Information Security

Officer at the Swedish Internet Foundation and one of Sweden's leading IT-security experts and Anna Djup, an analyst with the CATS at the Swedish Defence University. The creation of the internet has allowed the world to become more interconnected. Government, businesses and organizations alike are now dependent on data flows to conduct their everyday business. This connectivity has made information highly valuable and opened up for new attack vectors, generating a market for hacking and data theft. For the open internet to continue to exist as a platform for social and economic growth, users must be able to trust that organizations can protect the systems governing the society and have the capacity to safeguard personal information. The interdependencies created between the internet and critical infrastructure makes it susceptible to cyberwarfare. Cyberattacks are inherently asymmetric in nature as an actor with few means can do a lot of harm to an individual, organization or nation. The combination of poorly designed systems together with new technologies expands the scope and severity of global cyber threats, and how we tackle these threats will have far-reaching consequences for the future of the internet.

Part III starts with Chapter 11, 'The US and hybrid challenges: Past, present and future', by Jed Willard, director of the Franklin Delano Roosevelt Center for Global Engagement, Harvard University. Willard argues that the United States has the potential to be a powerful hybrid competitor. Various challenges, however, prevent America from bringing its full range of hybrid capacities to bear. This chapter examines the current American capacity for hybrid warfare. The first section covers strategic, definitional, structural and leadership challenges; exploring, for instance, the competing concept of 'grey zone' conflict and the difficulty of explaining and conducting hybrid competition in a large and complex democracy. The second section looks at the history of American hybrid engagement from the Revolution to the Cold War and then examines present and potential future hybrid challenges for the United States.

Chapter 12, 'China's political warfare in Taiwan', is authored by Dr Gulizar Haciyakupoglu of the Centre of Excellence for National Security (CENS) and Dr Michael Raska, who is the Coordinator of the Military Transformations Programme, both at the S. Rajaratnam School of International Studies (RSIS), Nanyang Technological University (NTU) in Singapore. This chapter explores the evolving strategic contours of China's political warfare in Taiwan. Certain aspects of China's political warfare are unique to Taiwan, particularly in the historical, cultural and asymmetric-military context. However, the means through which Beijing allegedly injects influence in Taiwan can emerge as the channels for political warfare in other countries if and when a country's legal, political, social and economic framework permits. These channels include (1) diplomatic and (2) legal pressure, (3) economy and (4) manipulation in the information domain. The diplomatic pressure involves the pressuring of companies to review their identifications of Taiwan, convincing Taiwan's diplomatic allies to switch sides and obstructing Taiwan's participation in international organizations. The means of Legal Pressure include capitalization on laws and restriction of access to international organizations that propose international regulations. The economy emerges as a venue for political warfare with the political implications of cross-straits exchanges and the use of monetary pressure or benefits to influence individuals or groups to act in alignment with Beijing's aims and policies. The information manipulation attempts involve (1) the activities of the agents of influence, information gathering and espionage; (2) spreading influence by way of media; (3) disinformation campaigns and (4) cyberattacks. The chapter concludes with a strategic overview, which situates the question in a global context and suggests that China's political warfare must be viewed in a relative context – through the lens of competitive strategies reflected in the efforts to develop effective countermeasures and responses.

Chapter 13, 'Hybrid warfare in the Baltics' by Dr Dorthe Bach Nyemann, Royal Danish Defence College, pieces together three elements relevant to a possible Russian hybrid operation in the Baltic States; the Russian capability to act as a hybrid actor, the Russian opportunities for success if approaching a hybrid warfare strategy and the Russian priorities and aims towards the Baltic States. The case study shows that Russia does have substantial capabilities as a hybrid actor. Hybrid warfare is a low-cost strategy with potentially high gains, however, the activities by Russia appear scattered, not systematically applied and not well coordinated. An institutional framework for conducting hybrid warfare is present in the Baltic States, but an active continuous 'shaping of the battlefield' is at worst low-key and unambitious. The case study explains this by looking closer at Russian opportunities and interests in the Baltic States. It finds that the combination of traditional military deterrence and broad deterrence by denial below the threshold of an armed attack seems to have decreased the Russian appetite for further engagement. Combined with a rather low priority of the Baltic States in Russian foreign policy, this elucidates the lack of hybrid warfare and the low intensity of hybrid threats. However, we must expect Russia to continue to improve and maintain a broad institutional framework for influence in the region.

In Chapter 14, 'De-hybridization and conflict narration: Ukraine's defence against Russian hybrid warfare', Dr Niklas Nilsson, Co-Convener of the Hybrid Warfare Research Group, Swedish Defence University, observes that Russia's aggression against Ukraine has spurred considerable debate on the resilience and defensive capabilities of Western societies in the face of hybrid warfare as a salient feature of the contemporary security environment. However, Ukraine's responses have received much less attention, despite their importance to the dynamics of the fighting per se as well as perceptions of the conflict. Indeed, Ukraine in this regard constitutes an important case of hybrid warfare defence. This chapter examines two key aspects of Ukraine's response to Russian hybrid warfare after the annexation of Crimea. First, Ukraine's focus on conventional military build-up and its ability to counter the Russian-supported separatist forces in Donbas served to de-hybridize military violence in Donbas. Russia had to deploy regular army and artillery units to prevent the Donetsk and Luhansk 'People's Republics' from caving, displaying its considerable political and military engagement in the conflict. Second, Ukraine has sought to take control of the conflict narrative, both by publicizing a considerable amount of evidence of Russia's military involvement and by devising its own information campaign promoting Ukraine's narrative of the conflict. These responses served to deflect Russia's portrayal of the fighting as a civil war, instead demonstrating that Ukraine is defending itself against an external aggressor. In turn, this has been of immense importance to Ukraine's internal cohesion as well as the sustained support offered to the country from its Western partners.

Chapter 15, 'Iran's hybrid warfare capabilities', is written by Dr Rouzbeh Parsi, Head of the Middle East and North Africa Programme, Swedish Institute of International Affairs. This chapter deals with Iran's understanding of hybrid warfare and its own ability in conducting such operations. The Islamic Republic's military capacity has primarily and historically been geared towards defence and guerrilla-style warfare. It sees the United States as its primary enemy and as it cannot defeat the United States or its allies by means of conventional war (lack of resources and technology), it must develop non-conventional means to maintain a credible deterrence. At the same time, Tehran believes itself to be the victim of hybrid warfare by other actors. The war in Syria constitutes a new stage in Iranian military developments as it is now, somewhat gingerly, trying to develop offensive strategies and control territory.

Finally, in Chapter 16, 'Information influencing in the Catalan illegal referendum and beyond', Dr Rubén Arcos of Rey Juan Carlos University explores hostile information influencing and strategic communication activities in the context of the Catalonian illegal referendum of self-determination and the subsequent unilateral declaration of independence. The Catalonian issue exemplifies how existing vulnerabilities in political and social cohesion can be exploited through disinformation activities. It constitutes a divisive internal political issue that, as such, can be utilized by hybrid actors in information influencing campaigns targeting either foreign or domestic audiences for different aims. These kinds of issues might be utilized for legitimizing political decisions and actions in the domestic arena, or for conveying distorted representations of foreign political systems and societies for different reasons, including weakening the internal cohesion of those targeted societies or transnational political networks. Considering that the holding of the referendum of 1 October 2017 was against the rule of law, it seems more appropriate to speak about pro-Kremlin external/foreign political meddling than of foreign electoral interference. At the same time, domestic actors can also engage in influencing activities, in both legitimate and illegitimate ways, through strategic communication campaigns aiming to manage the perceptions of foreign audiences and produce cognitive, affective and behavioural impacts in domestic stakeholders. Some of the domestic pro-independence actors were proactively seeking to influence the attitudes and behaviours of foreign governments and institutions through strategic communication activities and actions.

The concluding chapter (Chapter 17), Moving out of the blizzard: Towards a comprehensive approach to hybrid threats and hybrid warfare, focuses on patterns, practices and implications drawn from the volume. The chapter introduces the 'Hybridity Blizzard Model'. The model comes in three versions, of which the first presents a simplified picture of the dynamics of and between HT&HW, as well as responses and countermeasures. The second version adds a temporal dimension to this relationship, demonstrating how short-term actions and responses relate to long-term vulnerabilities and resilience. The third version, in contrast, aims to provide a more accurate picture of the complex real-world situation. The aim of the model is to enable not only a better understanding of the dynamics themselves but also how to identify, comprehend and act against HT&HW.

Finally, we conclude that a comprehensive, all-inclusive approach is needed to address HT&HW. There is no one threat, no single solution to countering and responding to HT&HW, nor how to build resilience. Nor is there one actor or structure that can succeed both today and tomorrow. As outlined in the proposed model, there is a blizzard out there that needs to be handled. We have to take it for what it is, and adapt and re-adapt when the opponent and the threat constantly changes. The chapter outlines policy advice on how to manage these challenges. The key is to develop a detection system that is simultaneously aware of false-positives and false-negatives. There is also an essential need for pragmatism, flexibility and inclusiveness of actors, sectors and levels – within and between countries. It is crucial that key international organizations work together with different states both within and outside international organizations, as well as ensuring collaboration across sectors and levels and to avoid allowing traditional borders to hinder collaboration. The latter is never as important as when countering HT&HW, as vulnerabilities tend to exist precisely in the border areas between sectors and levels, and this is what the opponent will target. This requires collaboration between the military, political, economic, civilian and informational spheres, which needs to evolve across the public and private sectors, as well as from the local and regional levels, through the national to the international level.

Notes

1 We would like to acknowledge support received from Riksbankens Jubileumsfond (RJ) (Grant No. F16-1240:1).
2 For a comprehensive discussion on hybrid warfare and its origins, see Ofer Friedman, *Russian 'Hybrid Warfare': Resurgence and Politicisation* (London: Hurst & Company, 2018). Other recommended readings are for example Sean Monaghan, 'Countering Hybrid Warfare: Conceptual Foundations and Implications for Defence Forces', *Multinational Capability Development Campaign (MCDC)*, Information note, March 2019. https://assets.publishing.service.gov.uk/government/uploads/system/uploads/attachment_data/file/840513/20190401-MCDC_CHW_Information_note_-_Conceptual_Foundations.pdf; Mikael Weissmann, 'Hybrid Warfare and Hybrid Threats Today and Tomorrow: Towards an Analytical Framework', *Journal on Baltic Security* 5, no. 1 (2019): 17–26; Rod Thornton, *Asymmetric Warfare: Threat and Response in the Twenty-First Century* (Cambridge: Polity, 2007); Peter R. Mansoor, 'Introduction: Hybrid Warfare in History', in *Hybrid Warfare: Fighting Complex Opponents from the Ancient World to the Present*, eds Williamson Murray and Peter R. Mansoor (Cambridge: Cambridge University Press, 2012); Frank G. Hoffman, 'Hybrid Warfare and Challenges', *JFQ* 52 (1 quarter 2009): 34–9; Frank G. Hoffman, 'Hybrid Threats: Reconceptualizing the Evolving Character of Modern Conflict', *Strategic Forum*, no. 240 (Washington, DC: Institute for National Strategic Studies, National Defense University, April 2009). https://www.comw.org/qdr/fulltext/0904hoffman.pdf.
3 Gregory F. Treverton, Andrew Thvedt, Alicia R. Chen, Kathy Lee and Madeline McCue, *Addressing Hybrid Threats* (Stockholm: Swedish Defence University, 2018), 10 fft.

4   Patryk Pawlak, 'Cyber Security Woes: WannaCry?' (European Union Institute for
    Security Studies (EUISS), 2017), https://www.iss.europa.eu/sites/default/files/EUIS
    SFiles/Alert_13_Cyber.pdf; Försvarsberedningen, 'Motståndskraft: Inriktningen
    av totalförsvaret och utformningen av det civila försvaret 2021–2025', Ds 2017:66
    (Försvarsdepartementet, 2017).
5   See e.g. Keir Giles, 'Missiles Are Not the Only Threat', in *Beyond Bursting Bubbles:
    Understanding the Full Spectrum of the Russian A2/AD Threat and Strategies for
    Counteracting It*, eds Michael Jonsson and Robert Dalsjö (Stockholm: FOI, 2020).
6   Mark Galeotti, 'Hybrid, Ambiguous, and Non-Linear? How New Is Russia's "New Way
    of War"?', *Small Wars & Insurgencies* 27, no. 2 (2016): 7.
7   Michael Kofman and Matthew Rojansky, 'A Closer Look at Russia's "Hybrid War"',
    Kennan Cable 7 (Wilson Center: Kennan Institute, 2015). https://www.files.ethz
    .ch/isn/190090/5-KENNAN%20CABLE-ROJANSKY%20KOFMAN.pdf; Peter
    Pomerantsev, 'How Putin Is Reinventing Warfare', *Foreign Policy*, 5 May 2014. https
    ://foreignpolicy.com/2014/05/05/how-putin-is-reinventing-warfare/; Jānis Bērziņš,
    Russian 'New Generation Warfare': More Democracy Is the Solution (Washington:
    Center for European Policy Analysis, 2014); Heinrich Brauss, Kalev Stoicescu and
    Tony Lawrence, *Capability and Resolve: Deterrence, Security and Stability in the Baltic
    Region* (Tallinn: International Centre for Defence and Security, 2020).
8   Hall Gardner, *Hybrid Warfare: Iranian and Russian Versions of 'Little Green Men' and
    Contemporary Conflict* (Rome: NATO Defence College, Research Division, December
    2015); Frans-Paul van der Putten, Minke Meijnders, Sico van der Meer and Tony van
    der Togt, eds *Hybrid Conflict: The Roles of Russia, North Korea and China* (The Hague:
    Clingendael Institute, 2018); Andrea Beccaro, 'Modern Irregular Warfare: The ISIS
    Case Study', *Small Wars & Insurgencies* 29 no. 2 (2018): 207–28.
9   Nicu Popescu, 'Hybrid Tactics: Neither New nor only Russian' (European Union
    Institute of Security Studies, January 2015). https://www.iss.europa.eu/sites/default/
    files/EUISSFiles/Alert_4_hybrid_warfare.pdf; Keir Giles, 'Russia's "New" Tools for
    Confronting the West: Continuity and Innovation in Moscow's Exercise of Power',
    Chatham House, 21 March 2016. https://www.chathamhouse.org/publication/russias
    -new-tools-confronting-west.
10 Bettina Renz, 'Russia and "Hybrid Warfare"', *Contemporary Politics* 22, no. 3 (2016):
    283–300. See also Samuel Charap, 'The Ghost of Hybrid War', *Survival* 57, no. 6
    (2015): 51–8.
11 Robert Johnson, 'Hybrid War and Its Countermeasures: A Critique of the Literature',
    Small Wars & Insurgencies 29, no. 1 (2018): 143.
12 Valery Gerasimov, 'The Value of Science in Prediction,' *Military-Industrial Kurier*,
    27 February 2013.
13 Valery Gerasimov, 'Hybrid Warfare Requires High-Tech Weapons and a Scientific
    Basis', *Military–Industrial Courier*, 9 March 2016.
14 Galeotti, 'Hybrid, Ambiguous, and Non-Linear?', 287, 291.
15 Timothy Thomas, 'The Evolution of Russian Military Thought: Integrating Hybrid,
    New-Generation and New-Type Thinking', *The Journal of Slavic Military Studies* 29,
    no. 4 (2016): 557–9.
16 2014 Military Strategy, 2015 National Security Strategy, 2016 Foreign Policy Concept;
    Valery Gerasimov, 'Russian General Staff Chief Valery Gerasimov's 2018 Presentation
    to the General Staff Academy: Thoughts on Future Military Conflict-March 2018'.
    Translated by Dr Harold Orenstein. Army University Press, Military Review, January–

February 2019. https://www.armyupress.army.mil/Journals/Military-Review/Eng lish-Edition-Archives/Jan-Feb-2019/Gerasimov-Future/; Sergey Glazyev, advisor to Russian president on issues of economic integration, quoted in RIA Novosti, 8 April 2015.

17 Alexander Lanozska, 'Russian Hybrid Warfare and Extended Deterrence in Eastern Europe', *International Affairs* 92, no. 1 (2016): 178.

18 James Pamment, Howard Nothhaft, Henrik Agardh-Twetman and Alicia Fjällhed, *Countering Information Influence Activities: The State of the Art*, version 1.4 (Lund University, 1 July 2018). https://www.msb.se/RibData/Filer/pdf/28697.pdf, 115.

19 NATO, *Wales Summit Declaration*, 2018. https://www.nato.int/cps/cn/natohq/official _texts_112964.htm.

20 NATO StratCom CoE, Annual Report, 2017. https://www.stratcomcoe.org/audited -annual-report-2017.

21 Pascal Brangetto and Matthijs A. Veenendaal, 'Influence Cyber Operations: The Use of Cyberattacks in Support of Influence Operations', *8th International Conference on Cyber Conflict (CyCon)*, 31 May–3 June 2016, Tallinn, Estonia. https://ieeexplore.ieee .org/abstract/document/7529430.

22 Hybrid CoE, 'What Is Hybrid CoE?'. www.hybridcoe.fi/what-is-hybridcoe/.

23 Rubén Arcos and José-Miguel Palacios, 'EU INTCEN: A Transnational European Culture of Intelligence Analysis?', *Intelligence and National Security* 35, no. 1 (2020): 72–94.

24 European Council (2015-03-20) European Council meeting (19 and 20 March 2015) – Conclusions, Brussels, Paragraph 13.

25 EU EEAS (2018-12-05) Questions and Answers about the East StratCom Task Force. eeas.europa.eu/headquarters/headquarters-homepage/2116/-questions-and-answers -about-the-east-stratcom-task-force_en.

26 MCDC, Countering Hybrid Warfare Project, summary, https://www.gov.uk/govern ment/publications/countering-hybrid-warfare-project-understanding-hybrid-warfare.

27 Swedish Department of Justice, Appropriation Bill for the Swedish Civil Contingencies Agency, 2016.

28 Martin Kragh and Sebastian Åsberg, 'Russia's Strategy for Influence through Public Diplomacy and Active Measures: The Swedish Case', *Journal of Strategic Studies* 40, no. 6 (2017): 35.

29 *Countering Information Influence Activities: A Handbook for Communicators* (Karlstad: Swedish Civil Contingencies Agency (MSB), 2019).

30 Edward Deverell, 'Att identifiera och motstå informationspåverkan: En jämförande studie av hur de nordiska länderna organiserar arbetet', *Kungl Krigsvetenskapsakademiens Handlingar och Tidskrift*, no. 1 (2019): 31–54.

31 Fredrik Löjdquist, 'Commentary: An Ambassador for Countering Hybrid Threats', RUSI, 6 September 2019. https://rusi.org/commentary/ambassador-countering-hybri d-threats.

32 Nick McKenzie, Chris Uhlmann, Richard Baker and Daniel Flitton, 'ASIO Warns Parties that Taking China Cash could Compromise Australia', *The Sydney Morning Herald*, 6 June 2017. https://www.smh.com.au/national/asio-warns-parties-that-taki ng-china-cash-could-compromise-australia-20170602-gwjc8t.html.

33 Jieh-Yung Lo, 'Chinese Australians Are Not a Fifth Column', *Foreign Policy*, 31 May 2019. https://foreignpolicy.com/2019/05/31/chinese-australians-are-not-a-fifth-co lumn-china-ccp-australia-morrison-turnbull-espionage-foreign-interference/.

34 Office of the Prime Minister of Australia, 'Stepping up Australia's Response against Foreign Interference', Media Release, 2 December 2019. www.pm.gov.au/media/stepping-australias-response-against-foreign-interference.

35 Marc Tracy, 'These Reporters Rely on Public Data, Rather Than Secret Sources', *The New York Times*, 1 December 2019. https://www.nytimes.com/2019/12/01/business/media/open-source-journalism-bellingcat.html.

36 www.digitalsherlocks.org.

37 Digital Forensic Research Lab, medium.com/dfrlab.

Part I

The view of practitioners

NATO and hybrid warfare

Seeking a concept to describe the challenge from Russia

G. Alexander Crowther

Introduction

The concepts of 'Hybrid Threats' and 'Hybrid Warfare' have gained increasing prevalence in analyses of the contemporary security environment. Revisionist powers, faced with an ascendant NATO and hyper-powerful United States in the post-Cold War era, have figured out how to confront the West below the threshold of a 'use of force' or 'armed attack' as mentioned in the Charter of the United Nations (UN). The West, used to a binary peace/war paradigm, has struggled to develop a conceptual model within which they could prevent the success of these twenty-first-century operations. NATO has made headway in figuring out how to confront these operations but continues to have trouble with an aggressive Russia that makes use of imaginative approaches to discombobulate the West. NATO has performed the analysis and built the teams that allow them to at least mitigate many Russian operations, regardless of what title that modern pundits seek to use.

To understand NATO and its approach to countering hybrid threats and hybrid warfare, one needs to understand the threat confronting the West. This threat is, as outlined earlier, very much linked to a more aggressive Russia. Thus, Russian behaviour forms the context for NATO's approach to hybrid warfare. This chapter will first outline the threat confronting the West, examining Russian activities in recent years and its approach to hybrid warfare. Thereafter, the chapter shifts focus to NATO's approach to hybrid warfare. Finally, conclusions are drawn.

Understanding Russian hybrid warfare

The Russian Federation in general and President Vladimir Putin in particular see the demise of the Soviet Union as a geostrategic catastrophe. Although Russia was forced to deal with an ascendant West in the wake of the Cold War, once they recovered enough from their economic collapse (aided mainly by buoyant oil prices), they clearly signalled that they would no longer accept the status quo. Although analysts see this trend as starting as early as 2004, it was his address at the 2007 Munich Security Conference where Putin made it clear that they would not tolerate the situation they found themselves in facing in the early 1990s.[1]

One thing they would not tolerate was the loss of what they see as their rightful sphere of influence. The Russian Empire directly ruled the Baltic States, Belarus, Moldova, Ukraine, the states of the Caucasus as well as a variety of states in modern Central Asia. During the Cold War the Soviet Union added their hegemony over a wide swathe of eastern Europe through their domination of the Warsaw Pact. In the wake of the dissolution of the Soviet Union, many of these states sought freedom from Russian rule or influence. Due to their historical role as hegemons, many Russians still feel that eastern European countries should pay attention to what the Russians tell them to do and that former Soviet Republics should obey them.

Although they operate from a position of overall weakness, they can create conditions of local superiority. Additionally, they operate across the entire spectrum of competition and seek to leverage all tools available to the modern state to achieve their goals.

The most recent update of the Russian conceptualization of hybrid warfare is sometimes called the 'Gerasimov Doctrine', named after the Russian General Valery Vasilyevich Gerasimov, the Chief of the General Staff of the Armed Forces of Russia. He says that the West has used hybrid warfare against Russia, citing as evidence the Arab Spring and the 2011 Libya Operation.[2] Although the author Mark Galeotti regrets that he coined the phrase, saying that he 'was just going for a snappy title' and prefers to 'call it non-linear war, or hybrid war, or special war',[3] this is the major phrase used to describe the Russian point of view. The other popular label is 'New Generation Warfare'.

This Russians conceiving hybrid warfare started with Frank Hoffman's writing.[4] They then looked at this through the lens of what they thought that the US was doing to them, in particular the 'Color Revolutions'. They then added significant amounts of information operations to the mix for two reasons. First, as mentioned, Russians have used information as a weapon for centuries. Second, they believe that the USSR collapsed due to a concerted information campaign against themselves and their allies and partners. The mix of these three concepts resulted in what could be called 'Hybrid Warfare with Russian Characteristics'. This, not the Hoffman concept, is what NATO was facing.

According to Jānis Bērziņš, there are ten 'guidelines for developing Russian military capabilities' as part of this approach:

1. from direct destruction to direct influence;
2. from direct annihilation of the opponent to its inner decay;
3. from a war with weapons and technology to a culture war;
4. from a war with conventional forces to specially prepared forces and commercial irregular groupings;

5. from the traditional (3D) battleground to information/psychological warfare and war of perceptions;
6. from direct clash to contactless war;
7. from a superficial and compartmented war to a total war, including the enemy's internal side and base;
8. from war in the physical environment to a war in the human consciousness and in cyberspace;
9. from symmetric to asymmetric warfare by a combination of political, economic, information, technological and ecological campaigns;
10. from war in a defined period of time to a state of permanent war as the natural condition in national life.[5]

Each of these marks the Russian approach: influence operations designed to eat away at the culture of your opponent as part of a total war designed to render the opposition incapable of defeating you. In his book 'Russian Hybrid Warfare', Ofer Fridman identifies a series of characteristics similar to these as coming from the pens of retired Russian Colonels Sergey Chekinov, and Sergey Bogdanov as well as Andrey Kokoshin,[6] all of whom had read 'Unrestricted Warfare' (the Chinese study of how the US-led coalition very effectively defeated Iraq in 1991) as well as previous Russian and Soviet writings on the nature of conflict, reflecting 'on the nature of the concept while integrating existing ideas into their vision and understanding of warfare'.[7]

Figure 2.1 shows us the spectrum of Russian hybrid operations from the very frequent, non-violent information operations they practice on a daily basis up through cyber-enabled conventional military operations that they have only practiced a few times.

Figure 2.1 Russian hybrid operations.

Notable is the integration of information operations, which accompanies every one of these examples. The Russians deploy aggressive rhetoric on a daily basis. For example, Putin has threatened 'to invade Poland, Romania and the Baltic states',[8] Finland[9] and Sweden[10] if they agree to join NATO. Norway has been threatened for hosting more US troops,[11] Poland[12] and Romania[13] for hosting ballistic missile defence facilities. In fact, the threat extends to 'any European countries hosting US missiles'.[14] He has also threatened to exercise the use of nuclear weapons on Denmark,[15] Poland,[16] the Baltics,[17] the United Kingdom,[18] Sweden,[19] Ukraine,[20] the EU[21] and, of course, NATO and the United States.[22]

Information operations do not just stand-alone but are also used in support of other operations. The Russians tout their build-up in Kaliningrad as defensive while NATO deployments to the Baltics are offensive in nature.[23] They lie about the size and intent of their large-scale military manoeuvres to justify non-compliance with the OSCE regulations and the Vienna Agreement.[24] They deny performing cyber operations.[25] They deny that their people have participated in targeted killings, even though the people were caught on video.[26] They say that Crimea was a spontaneous uprising and that Russian troops were not present either in Crimea.[27] That the conflict in the Donbass area of Ukraine was initiated by Ukrainians in the Donbass.[28] These examples show the integration of information from the least- to the most-violent of Russian hybrid operations.

What this discussion shows us is that this type of warfare is hard to understand and master, and that the Russians are very good at it. NATO faced a new reality.

NATO and hybrid warfare

As we have seen, the Russians took Hoffman's ideas on hybrid warfare and looked at them through a Russian lens. NATO took the Russian viewpoint as a start and designed their own in order to confront Russian hybrid techniques. NATO had to do several things in order to respond to this Russian hybrid warfare challenge. First, they had to conceptualize the challenge and then the response. Then NATO had to simultaneously perform a series of actions as part of their response: NATO had to use information (in particular diplomacy) in order to minimize support for Russia and maximize support for NATO, to collaborate with allies and other partners, and to use NATO's inherent hard power to deter Russia.

Continuing operations, conceptualizing problems

As with any problem, the initial requirement is to recognize that you have a problem and think through what that problem is. Although NATO had discussed hybrid threats before 2014, it was the Russian operation that took control of Crimea that really alerted NATO allies to the threat. In the wake of Russian operations in Crimea and the Don River Basin (Donbas) in 2014, NATO allies realized that the Russian approach had changed. From a partner who NATO considered for membership in the 1990s to an antagonist by 2007, Russia had emerged as a spoiler. Because of their inherent economic, demographic and military weaknesses, the Russians could not confront a much stronger NATO alliance directly. Instead, they had to adopt a more indirect approach. They revived concepts from the Russian Empire and the Soviet Union and adapted them to the realities of the twenty-first century as previously described.

NATO had to decide on how to approach the new reality. NATO has a biennial Summit; at the end of each summit, NATO issues a 'declaration'. Each subordinate organization within NATO works very hard to get 'their' subject addressed in the declaration. Therefore, summit declarations are useful to determine what is important within NATO and thereby to NATO. It is illustrative that the 2012 Chicago Declaration does not contain one reference to 'hybrid',[29] whereas the 2014 Wales Declaration opens with a recognition that 'Russia's aggressive actions against Ukraine have fundamentally challenged our vision of a Europe whole, free, and at peace' and also mentions hybrid five times.[30]

Not only did NATO condemn Russian activities in Crimea and the rest of Ukraine, but also came out strongly with the need to face hybrid threats.

> We will ensure that NATO is able to effectively address the specific challenges posed by hybrid warfare threats, where a wide range of overt and covert military, paramilitary, and civilian measures are employed in a highly integrated design. It is essential that the Alliance possesses the necessary tools and procedures required to deter and respond effectively to hybrid warfare threats, and the capabilities to reinforce national forces. This will also include enhancing strategic communications, developing exercise scenarios in light of hybrid threats, and strengthening coordination between NATO and other organisations, in line with relevant decisions taken, with a view to improving information sharing, political consultations, and staff-to-staff coordination. We welcome the establishment of the NATO-accredited Strategic Communications Centre of Excellence in Latvia as a meaningful contribution to NATO's efforts in this area. We have tasked the work on hybrid warfare to be reviewed alongside the implementation of the Readiness Action Plan.[31]

In addition, NATO announced several other initiatives to deal with Russian hybrid operations. These include significantly enhancing the responsiveness of the NATO Response Force (NRF) by developing force packages that can move rapidly and respond to potential challenges and threats and establishing a Very High Readiness Joint Task Force (VJTF). NATO has also established an enhanced exercise program with an increased focus on exercising collective defence, including practicing comprehensive responses to complex civil-military scenarios. Moreover, NATO's decision to suspend all practical civilian and military cooperation between NATO and Russia remains in place (although political channels of communication would remain open).

NATO received plenty of assistance in their mission to conceptualize the threat and propose responses. National security researchers seek issues to develop and responded eagerly and rapidly – NATO has identified over 100 articles published in 2015 alone. This production has remained steady, with over ninety articles published in 2016 and eighty in 2017.[32] A wide variety of actors have published, both from within and without

NATO. NATO has its own capabilities within the NATO Defense College[33] in Rome as well as its Centre of Excellence (COE) program. NATO has twenty-five different COEs. Several of the newer ones focus on aspects of hybrid warfare and include the Cooperative Cyber Defence COE in Tallinn, Estonia, the Strategic Communications COE in Riga, Latvia, the Energy Security COE in Vilnius, Lithuania, and the Hybrid COE in Helsinki, Finland.[34] Organizations in the US and Europe weighed in as well, including the Strategic Studies Institute (the US army's think tank), the Naval War College and the US National Defense University on the government side as well as think tanks such as Center for Strategic and International Studies (CSIS) and the Atlantic Council. Even web-only publications like Small Wars Journal and Small Wars & Insurgencies helped NATO think through hybrid operations. Foreign Affairs and Foreign Policy chimed in. Even mainstream and well-respected organizations like the New York Times and the Washington Post joined the discussion. A variety of European outlets have also thought about hybrid warfare including supra-governmental organizations such as the European Commission, think tanks, defence organizations and different newspapers. This shows that interest in hybrid warfare is wide-ranging. If anything, there may be too much writing about hybrid warfare, which risks confusing the situation by providing several writings by unqualified authors.

The next thing that NATO had to do was to use information (in particular diplomacy) in order to minimize support for Russia and maximize support for NATO. As the NATO web page says, '(NATO) also actively counters propaganda – not with more propaganda, but with facts – online, on air and in print'.[35] NATO has been particularly aggressive about pushing the truth out to the rest of the world. NATO leadership makes regular comments to the press.[36]

The main NATO talking point is the defensive nature of NATO, because Russia says that NATO is aggressive and seeks to attack them. Other subjects include NATO/Russia relations, because Russia claims that NATO spurned Russia in the wake of the Cold War[37] and that NATO refuses to talk to them.[38] NATO puts explanations on the reality of their relationship with Russia on the web.[39] Since exercises are a particular bone of contention between Europe and Russia, NATO also comments on both NATO[40] and Russian exercises. Russia holds large-scale exercises in violation of the Vienna Agreement[41] while claiming that they are too small to trigger Vienna requirements for reporting[42] and then accuses NATO of using exercises to prepare for aggressive moves against Russia,[43] and so NATO responds with press releases emphasizing that they are not preparing to attack Russia.[44] The Russians have two major advantages: they are not constrained by the truth and their decision-making apparatus is much leaner and quicker. Despite those advantages, the West discovered during the Cold War that the truth was more powerful in the long run. This information back and forth is ongoing. The Russians will not stop, so NATO continues their information campaign.

In another part of their response to Russian hybrid operations, NATO had to collaborate with allies and partners. Within the Alliance, NATO

> supports Allies' efforts to identify national vulnerabilities and strengthen their own resilience, if requested. NATO also serves as a hub for expertise, providing support

to Allies in areas such as civil preparedness and chemical, biological, radiological and nuclear (CBRN) incident response; critical infrastructure protection; strategic communications; protection of civilians; cyber defence; energy security; and counter-terrorism.[45]

In particular, NATO coordinates allied responses to Russian efforts via their main tool, hard power, which will be addressed in the next section.

NATO also works closely with partners. At the state level, NATO works with forty-one different countries: twenty-one countries (including Russia) via the Euro-Atlantic Partnership Council (EAPC), seven in the Mediterranean Dialogue, four through the Istanbul Initiative and nine 'Partners Across the Globe'. NATO also works with the United Nations, the European Union and the Organization for Security and Cooperation in Europe.[46]

Some of that collaboration is military in nature, as with the 'NATO plus Two' relationship with Sweden and Finland. The two main tools are the Partnership Interoperability Initiative and the Defence and Related Security Capacity Building Initiative.[47] The overall strategic objectives of partnering include the following:

- Enhance Euro-Atlantic and international security, peace and stability;
- Promote regional security and cooperation;
- Facilitate mutually beneficial cooperation on issues of common interest, including international efforts to meet emerging security challenges;
- Prepare interested eligible nations for NATO membership;
- Promote democratic values and institutional reforms, especially in the defence and security sector;
- Enhance support for NATO-led operations and missions;
- Enhance awareness of security developments including through early warning, with a view to preventing crises;
- Build confidence and achieve better mutual understanding, including about NATO's role and activities, in particular through enhanced public diplomacy.

These are understandable military objectives for partnerships, however, in the twenty-first century, military means alone are insufficient to meet with modern hybrid threats. Perhaps more important for NATO are relationships with other organizations. When one examines who has responsibility for wielding power in Europe, it is obvious that NATO is not able to provide for anything other than hard power, applied externally to Europe. The European Union is responsible for internal hard power (through European Police [EUPOL] and the European Union Military Staff [EUMS]), internal soft power through internal information operations and legislation, and external soft power through diplomacy via the European Union External Action Service (EAS) (Figure 2.2).

The biggest of these issues is military mobility, particularly movement from the US via the ports of northeastern Europe to the Baltic States via the Suwalki Gap on the border between Poland and Lithuania. This is a major issue for NATO and has been

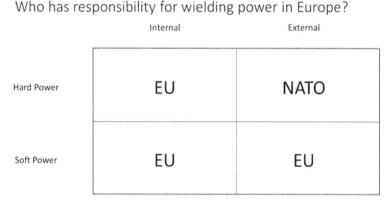

Figure 2.2 Who has responsibility for wielding power in Europe?

discussed in excruciating detail since 2014. Unfortunately, NATO has several problems with military mobility:

- NATO does not own any of the infrastructure necessary for these movements.
- Forces cannot cross borders rapidly with trainloads of arms and munitions in peacetime.
- Foreign ministries control the process of movement across borders.
- Ministries of the interior control the actual movement across borders.
- Private companies control what goes on ships and trains, when and where.
- Infrastructure is not optimized for eastward military movement.
- Rail lines between Warsaw and Tallinn are still a Russian gauge.

For a US armoured unit based in the continental United States to get to the eastern edge of the Alliance, they have to move commercially to a port of embarkation in the United States, move on commercial ships across the Atlantic, debark at a port in western Europe, and move across the heart of Europe to the eastern flank. They have to cross a variety of borders and stop at each one because the ministry of the interior must inspect papers and cargo, especially when the cargo consists of arms and munitions. Although there are agreements for the rapid movement of units across Europe in time of war, there currently are none for the expedited movement of military equipment and munitions quickly in peacetime.

NATO is working with the EU and the Baltics states for transportation infrastructure (in particular the Baltarail project which runs European gauge rail from Warsaw to Tallinn) and with the German government who controls Deutsche Bahn (the German rail system) and, as discussed later, has stood up a logistics headquarters in Ulm, Germany, to assist with this issue.

The other major impediment to this issue is the fact that none of the infrastructure east of the former intra-German border was developed to facilitate eastward movement of military forces. Every river crossing east of that former border was optimized by the Warsaw Pact to move military forces west, not east; indeed, the defensive infrastructure at river crossings was designed to prevent forces from moving east towards the Soviet Union. As NATO does not own any of this infrastructure nor the engineer units that would survey and update them, NATO logisticians have had to work with national forces and governments. As they have been working for years, progress has been made, however. Unfortunately, it appears that the will to spend the requisite amount of money is lacking in parts of Europe.[48]

The last major initiative uses NATO's greatest strength: military power. Military power is necessary but not sufficient to counter, and particularly to deter, hybrid operations. This use of NATO's inherent hard power to deter Russia does not mean that NATO conducts military operations against Russian targets, but that NATO prepares for the defence of allies under article 5 of the Washington Treaty.[49]

NATO's military power waned in the wake of the Cold War. This trend was reversed in the wake of the Russian occupation of Crimea in 2014. At the Wales Summit, NATO announced several changes. The major initiative to develop more readily available forces was the Readiness Action Plan (RAP), which NATO calls 'the most significant reinforcement of NATO's collective defence since the end of the Cold War'.[50] The RAP tripled the size of the NRF and established the VJTF, able to deploy at very short notice. It also enhanced Standing Naval Forces.[51]

In addition to the RAP provisions, NATO also sought to halt decades of declining defence budgets. At Wales the allies promised the following:

> Allies currently meeting the NATO guideline to spend a minimum of 2% of their Gross Domestic Product (GDP) on defence will aim to continue to do so. Likewise, Allies spending more than 20% of their defence budgets on major equipment, including related Research & Development, will continue to do so. Allies whose current proportion of GDP spent on defence is below this level will: halt any decline in defence expenditure; aim to increase defence expenditure in real terms as GDP grows; aim to move towards the 2% guideline within a decade with a view to meeting their NATO Capability Targets and filling NATO's capability shortfalls.[52]

This is probably the most important initiative that NATO has promulgated since agreeing to NATO expansion in the 1990s. All the appropriate rhetoric is useless if the cold reality is that there are no resources for defence. The 2 per cent declaration was designed to boost the defence spending of the twenty-five or so allies who did not spend that much at the time. This spending would meet the intent of article 3 of the Washington Treaty, which calls for 'the Parties, separately and jointly, by means of continuous and effective self-help and mutual aid, will maintain and develop their individual and collective capacity to resist armed attack'.[53]

NATO has continued to improve its capability to deal with hybrid threats through military means. Starting in 2015, they stood up eight NATO Force Integration Units (NFIUs) in Bulgaria, Estonia, Hungary, Latvia, Lithuania, Poland and Romania, and Slovakia to facilitate reception, staging and onward integration (RSOI) for any deploying forces. Additionally, they stood up the Multinational Corps Northeast Headquarters (HQ MNC-NE) as well as Multinational Division Northeast in Poland to provide command and control for any NATO forces deployed into the area. In 2018,

NATO set up counter-hybrid support teams, which provide tailored targeted assistance to allies upon their request.[54]

At the Warsaw Summit in 2016, NATO announced that they would 'establish an enhanced forward presence in Estonia, Latvia, Lithuania and Poland to unambiguously demonstrate, as part of our overall posture'.[55] Starting in 2017, NATO deployed four 1,000 person battle groups to the Baltic States and Poland. As of January 2020. The deployments continue, as depicted in Figure 2.3.[56]

Although NATO allies align national forces against NATO, such as the Enhanced Forward Presence units, these forces are only apportioned to NATO when requested. The vast majority of forces remain under national control. As an example, the US-led EFP battalion in eastern Poland is a US force under NATO command; however, the US Armored Brigade in western Poland remains a US asset, under US command and control, and deployed to Poland under a bilateral agreement. Some forces are dual-hatted. This requires NATO and the owning nation to agree on force structure. Two new major units were stood up in 2018 in order to facilitate military mobility: the US Navy stood up 2d Fleet to command and control US Navy operations in the Atlantic Ocean[57] while the Germans formed the Joint Support and Enabling Command in order to facilitate movement across Europe[58] These two commands are part of the efforts by NATO and NATO allies to safeguard and facilitate movement of forces from their home bases to eastern Europe, where the Russians can achieve local superiority and therefore provide a challenge to the integrity of the territory of several NATO members as discussed earlier.

The most recent NATO improvement is the 'Four 30s' readiness initiative, announced at the Brussels Summit of 2018. In this, NATO promised that 'Allies will offer an additional 30 major naval combatants, 30 heavy or medium maneuver battalions, and 30 kinetic air squadrons, with enabling forces, at 30 days' readiness

Figure 2.3 NATO Enhanced Forward Presence. Source: NATO, *NATO Enhanced Forward Presence*, map, 21 January 2020, https://www.nato.int/nato_static_fl2014/assets/pictures/images_mfu/2020/1/pdf/200121-MAP_eFP-en.pdf.

or less'.[59] This initiative has come to fruition. During the London meeting of the North Atlantic Council in December 2019, the Secretary General announced that 'I can announce that we have delivered on the NATO Readiness Initiative. Allies have committed 30 battalions, 30 air squadrons, and 30 combat ships, available to NATO within 30 days'.[60] We can rest assured that this will not be the last readiness initiative that NATO will produce as part of their attempt to deter the more violent hybrid operations.

Hard power is NATO's strong suit, and therefore the major was for NATO to deter Russian hybrid operations, in particular higher-end, more violent hybrid operations as seen in Georgia and Ukraine. NATO understands both the strengths and weaknesses of the use of that hard power and seeks to use that hard power to prevent the Russians from conducting hybrid operations on NATO territory. Although this has worked so far, it means that the Russians have moved farther into the more non-violent means of challenging NATO, the EU and the rest of the West.

Conclusion

NATO faces a multifaceted threat from Russia. As Russia operates from a position of overall weakness, they seek to operate in the grey zone, below the threshold of armed attack or use of force in order to avoid the strength of their adversaries, in particular the United States and NATO, who are both strong in conventional military capability. Russia took Frank Hoffmans's 2009 concept of Hybrid Warfare and looked at it through two lenses: what they thought the United States was doing to them and how the Russian traditionally compete using wide variety of techniques such as active measures, *dezinformatsia*, political warfare, reflexive control, information warfare, *maskirovka* and others. What they have in common is a strong emphasis on information operations.

Although many discussed hybrid warfare before 2014, it was then that NATO faced the reality of the situation. In the wake of Russian operations in Crimea and the Donbas, NATO reacted quickly at the Wales summit, announcing a variety of measures to counter and deter hybrid warfare. After Wales, they conceptualized the challenge and then the response, began to use information in order to minimize support for Russia and maximize support for NATO, ramped up collaboration with allies and other partners and figured out how to use NATO's inherent hard power to deter Russia.

These measures have had a modicum of success; however, Russia is not going away and will not stop using their traditional methods of competition. NATO must continue to do all of these things into the foreseeable future in order to do their part of guaranteeing a future of a free, secure, just and united Europe.

Efforts thus far have been necessary but not sufficient, both Russian hybrid operations and NATO efforts to respond to them will continue for the foreseeable future. In the end, NATO will consider it a success if they can prevent the Russians from making any violent moves against any NATO countries.

Notes

1 Vladimir Putin, 'Speech and the Following Discussion at the Munich Conference on Security Policy', 10 February 2007. http://en.kremlin.ru/events/president/transcripts/24034.

2 Valery Gerasimov, 'The Value of Science Is in the Foresight: New Challenges Demand Rethinking the Forms and Methods of Carrying out Combat Operations', original in Russian *VPK News*, no. 8 (476) 5 March 2013. https://vpk-news.ru/sites/default/files/pdf/VPK_08_476.pdf. English version in *Military Review*, January–February 2016. https://www.armyupress.army.mil/Portals/7/military-review/Archives/English/MilitaryReview_20160228_art008.pdf.

3 Mark Galeotti, 'The "Gerasimov Doctrine" and Russian Non-Linear War', 6 July 2014. https://inmoscowsshadows.wordpress.com/2014/07/06/the-gerasimov-doctrine-and-russian-non-linear-war/.

4 In 2009, the American Dr Frank Hoffman developed the concept of Hybrid Warfare. He was trying to codify changes that he saw with competition around the world. Hoffman wrote that
Hybrid threats incorporate a full range of different modes of warfare including conventional capabilities, irregular tactics and formations, terrorist acts including indiscriminate violence and coercion, and criminal disorder. Hybrid Wars can be conducted by both states and a variety of non-state actors. These multi-modal activities can be conducted by separate unites, or even by the same unit, but are generally operations and tactically directed and coordinated within the main battlespace to achieve synergistic effects in the physical and psychological dimensions of conflict. The effects can be gained at all levels of war. (Frank Hoffman, *Conflict in the 21st Century: The Rise of Hybrid Wars* (Arlington: Potomac Institute for Policy Studies, 2007), 8. Available at: https://www.potomacinstitute.org/images/stories/publications/potomac_hybridwar_0108.pdf).

5 Jānis Bērziņš, *Russia's New Generation Warfare in Ukraine: Implications for Latvian Defense Policy* (Riga: National Defence Academy of Latvia, Center for Security and Strategic Research, Policy Paper, no. 2, April 2014), 5. https://www.sldinfo.com/wp-content/uploads/2014/05/New-Generation-Warfare.pdf.

6 Ofer Fridman, *Russian 'Hybrid Warfare': Resurgence and Politicisation* (Oxford: Oxford University Press, 2018), 127–8

7 Fridman, *Russian 'Hybrid Warfare'*, 128.

8 Justin Huggler, 'Putin "privately threatened to invade Poland, Romania and the Baltic states"', *The (UK) Telegraph*, 18 September 2014. https://www.telegraph.co.uk/news/worldnews/europe/russia/11106195/Putin-privately-threatened-to-invade-Poland-Romania-and-the-Baltic-states.html.

9 Denis Dyomkin and Tuomas Forsell, 'Putin Hints Russia Will React if Finland Joins NATO', *Reuters*, 1 July 2016. https://www.reuters.com/article/us-russia-finland-nato-putin-idUSKCN0ZH5IV.

10 Thomas Barrabi, 'Russia Threatens Sweden With Military "Consequences" If It Joins NATO Alliance, Report Says', *International Business Times*, 18 June 2015. https://www.ibtimes.com/russia-threatens-sweden-military-consequences-if-it-joins-nato-alliance-report-says-1973905.

11 Jason Lemon, 'Additional U.S. Troops in Norway Could Bring "Destabilizing" Impact, Russia Says', *Newsweek*, 14 June 2018. https://www.newsweek.com/us-troops-norway-destabilizing-russia-977834#slideshow/977827.

12 Harry de Quetteville and Andrew Pierce, 'Russia Threatens Nuclear Attack on Poland over US Missile Shield Deal', *The Telegraph*, 15 August 2008. https://www.telegraph.co.uk/news/worldnews/europe/russia/2566005/Russia-threatens-nuclear-attack-on-Poland-over-US-missile-shield-deal.html.

13 RT, 'Putin: Romania "in crosshairs" after Opening NATO Missile Defense Base', *RT*, 27 May 2016. https://www.rt.com/news/344642-putin-visit-greece-tsipras/.

14 BBC News, 'INF Treaty: Russia "will respond" to New US Missiles in Europe', *BBC News*, 24 October 2018. https://www.bbc.com/news/world-europe-45971537.

15 CBS News, 'NATO Leaders Balk at Russia's Threat to Nuke Warships', *CBS News*, 23 March 2015. https://www.cbsnews.com/news/russia-threat-to-bomb-nato-warships-over-missile-defense-draws-rebuke/.

16 Matthew Day, 'Russia "simulates" Nuclear Attack on Poland', *The Telegraph*, 1 November 2009. https://www.telegraph.co.uk/news/worldnews/europe/poland/6480227/Russia-simulates-nuclear-attack-on-Poland.html.

17 Sten Hankewitz, 'Russia Threatened to Use Nukes against the Baltics', *Estonian World*, 16 September 2018. https://estonianworld.com/security/russia-threatened-to-use-nukes-against-the-baltics-book/.

18 Patrick Christys, 'UK Would be "wiped off face off the earth with ONE STRIKE" – Top Russian Official', *The (UK) Express*, 26 April 2017. https://www.express.co.uk/news/uk/796555/Russia-Britain-nuclear-war-Michael-Fallon-Frants-Klintsevich-Putin-May.

19 Roland Oliphant, 'Russia "simulated a nuclear strike" against Sweden, Nato Admits', *The Telegraph*, 4 February 2016. https://www.telegraph.co.uk/news/worldnews/europe/russia/12139943/Russia-simulated-a-nuclear-strike-against-Sweden-Nato-admits.html.

20 Nathan Francis, 'Russia Threatening To Drop Nuclear Bomb In Ukraine, Defense Minister Claims', *Inquisitr.com*, 2 September 2014. https://www.inquisitr.com/1447008/russia-threatening-to-drop-nuclear-bomb-in-ukraine-defense-minister-claims/#ixzz6HF8yHtfH.

21 Nicole Gallina, 'Putin Threatens to Use Nuclear Warheads against Ukraine, EU', Euromaidan Press, 8 February 2015. http://euromaidanpress.com/2015/02/08/putin-threatens-to-use-nuclear-warheads-against-ukraine-eu/.

22 Arthur Villasanta, 'Putin Threatens To Target US And NATO If Missiles Are Deployed To Europe', *International Business Times*, 20 February 2019. https://www.ibtimes.com/putin-threatens-target-us-nato-if-missiles-are-deployed-europe-2766485.

23 RT, '"Our build-up is defensive, Russia's aggressive," Says NATO after Putin's Remark – but Is that Fair?', *RT*, 22 August 2018. https://www.rt.com/news/436617-nato-russia-military-buildup/.

24 Sputnik, 'Zapad-2017: Why Poland's Media Getting Hysterical over Russia-Belarus Drills', Sputnik, 16 September 2017. https://sputniknews.com/analysis/201709161057444954-russia-belarus-military-drills-media/.

25 Russia Today, 'Another "highly likely"-Style Accusation: Moscow Brushes Aside "evidence-free" Georgia Cyberattack', *Russia Today*, 21 February 2020. https://www.rt.com/news/481374-russia-georgia-cyberattack-blame/.

26 RT, 'RT Editor-in-Chief's Exclusive Interview with Skripal Case Suspects Petrov & Boshirov', *RT*, 13 September 2018. https://www.rt.com/news/438356-rt-petrov-boshirov-full-interview/.

27 John Wight, 'Crimea Is Russian, the Matter Is Finished', *Russia Today*, 13 March 2018. https://www.rt.com/op-ed/421188-crimea-ukraine-russia-putin-uk/.

28	'Kiev launched a military operation in the east of Ukraine in 2014, after local residents refused to recognize the new government that came to power in what they considered a coup'. Sputnik News, 'Conflict in Donbass Cannot Be Resolved Only Through Normandy Format – Kremlin', *Sputnik News*, 10 September 2017. https://sputniknews.com/europe/201710091058067165-conflict-donbass-normandy-format/.

29	NATO, *Chicago Summit Declaration*, 20 May 2012. Available at https://www.nato.int/cps/en/natohq/official_texts_87593.htm?selectedLocale=en.

30	NATO, *Wales Summit Declaration*, 5 September 2014. 'Russia's aggressive actions' in Paragraph 1, 'hybrid' in Paragraph 12. Available at https://www.nato.int/cps/en/natohq/official_texts_112964.htm.

31	NATO, *Wales Summit Declaration*, paragraph 12.

32	NATO Multimedia Library, *Hybrid Warfare Article Archive*. Available at http://www.natolibguides.info/hybridwarfare/articles/archives.

33	NATO Defense College, *Research at the NDC*. Available at http://www.ndc.nato.int/research/research.php?icode=3.

34	NATO Allied Command Transformation (ACT), *2020 COE Catalog*, version 2020 V1, December 2019, https://act.nato.int/images/stories/structure/coe-catalogue-2020.pdf.

35	NATO, 'NATO's Response to Hybrid Threats', 8 August 2019. https://www.nato.int/cps/en/natohq/topics_156338.htm?

36	See, e.g. NATO Secretary General Jens Stoltenberg, *Press Conference Following the Meeting of the North Atlantic Council at the Level of Heads of State and/or Government*, 4 December 2019. https://www.nato.int/cps/en/natohq/opinions_171554.htm; Deputy Secretary General Rose Gottemoeller, *Adapting to a More Dangerous World*, 22 March 2017. https://www.nato.int/cps/en/natohq/opinions_142494.htm?selectedLocale=en; and Chairman of the NATO Military Committee General Petr Pavel, *The Road to Warsaw and Beyond*, 14 October 2015. https://www.nato.int/cps/en/natohq/opinions_123879.htm?selectedLocale=en.

37	Madeline Roache, 'Breaking Down the Complicated Relationship Between Russia and NATO', *Time*, 4 April 2019. https://time.com/5564207/russia-nato-relationship/.

38	RT, '"We used to talk during the Cold War": Top US General Urges Communication with Moscow', *RT*, 15 April 2019. https://www.rt.com/news/456646-usa-nato-russia-talking/.

39	NATO, 'NATO-Russia: Setting the Record Straight', NATO, 9 April 2020. https://www.nato.int/cps/en/natohq/115204.htm.

40	NATO, 'Exercise DEFENDER-Europe 20 Underway', NATO, 6 February 2020. https://shape.nato.int/news-archive/2020/exercise-defendereurope-20-underway.

41	Lee Litzenberger, 'Beyond Zapad 2017: Russia's Destabilizing Approach to Military Exercises', *War on the Rocks*, 28 November 2017. https://warontherocks.com/2017/11/beyond-zapad-2017-russias-destabilizing-approach-military-exercises/.

42	Michael Birnbaum and David Filipov, 'Russia Held a Big Military Exercise this Week: Here's Why the U.S. Is Paying Attention', *Washington Post*, 23 September 2017. https://www.washingtonpost.com/world/europe/russia-held-a-big-military-exercise-this-week-heres-why-the-us-is-paying-attention/2017/09/23/3a0d37ea-9a36-11e7-af6a-6555caaeb8dc_story.html.

43	Mikhail Khodarenok, 'NATO's Defender Europe 2020 Is War against Russia Role-Play, No Matter What they Tell You', *RT*, 4 February 2020. https://www.rt.com/op-ed/480044-nato-defender-europe-russia/.

44	NATO, 'NATO-Russia: Setting the Record Straight'.

45　NATO, 'NATO's Response to Hybrid Threats', 8 August 2017. https://www.nato.int/cps/en/natohq/topics_156338.htm.

46　NATO, 'Partners', NATO, 25 September 2019. https://www.nato.int/cps/en/natohq/51288.htm.

47　NATO, 'Partnerships: Projecting Stability through Cooperation', NATO, 30 August 2018. https://www.nato.int/cps/en/natohq/topics_84336.htm.

48　Alexandra Brzozowski, 'Europe's Military Mobility: Latest Casualty of EU Budget Battle', *EURACTIV.com*, 25 February 2020. https://www.euractiv.com/section/global-europe/news/europes-military-mobility-latest-casualty-of-eu-budget-battle/.

49　*The Washington Treaty*, 4 April 1949. Available at https://www.nato.int/cps/cn/natolive/official_texts_17120.htm.

50　NATO, 'Readiness Action Plan', NATO. https://www.nato.int/cps/en/natohq/topics_119353.htm.

51　NATO, *Wales Summit Declaration*, Paragraph 8.

52　NATO, *Wales Summit Declaration*, Paragraph 14.

53　*Washington Treaty*, Article 3.

54　NATO, 'Readiness Action Plan'.

55　NATO, *Warsaw Summit Declaration*, Paragraph 40, 9 July 2016. https://www.nato.int/cps/en/natohq/official_texts_133169.htm.

56　NATO, *NATO Enhanced Forward Presence*, map, 21 January 2020. https://www.nato.int/nato_static_fl2014/assets/pictures/images_mfu/2020/1/pdf/200121-MAP_eFP-en.pdf.

57　Sam LaGrone, 'Navy Reestablishes U.S. 2nd Fleet to Face Russian Threat; Plan Calls for 250 Person Command in Norfolk', US Naval Institute, 4 May 2018. https://news.usni.org/2018/05/04/navy-reestablishes-2nd-fleet-plan-calls-for-250-person-command-in-norfolk.

58　Reuters, 'Germany Chooses Ulm for New Proposed NATO Logistics Command', *Reuters*, 20 March 2018. https://www.reuters.com/article/us-nato-germany-idUSKBN1GW1QM.

59　NATO, *Brussels Summit Declaration*, Paragraph 40, 30 August 2018. https://www.nato.int/cps/en/natohq/official_texts_156624.htm.

60　NATO Secretary General Jens Stoltenberg, *Press Conference Following the Meeting of the North Atlantic Council at the Level of Heads of State and/or Government*.

3

An American view

Hybrid threats and intelligence

Gregory F. Treverton

Introduction

This chapter thus takes a closer look at the means available in the US context for devising a robust response to the challenges posed by hybrid threats and hybrid warfare. The Russian intervention in the 2016 US elections came as a surprise, but it should not have. There was warning but from an unfamiliar quarter. A group of analysts outside the government was tracking the online dimensions of the jihadists and the Syrian civil war when they came upon interesting anomalies, as early as 2014. When experts criticized the Assad regime online, they were immediately attacked by armies of trolls on Facebook and Twitter. Unrolling the network of the trolls revealed they were a new version of 'honeypots', presenting themselves as attractive young women eager to discuss issues with Americans, especially those involved in national security. The analysts made the connection to Russia but found it impossible, that early, to get anyone in the American government to pay attention, given the crises competing for both policy and intelligence attention. The government was focused on jihadists, not Russians.[1]

I plead innocent: I was then the Chair of the US National Intelligence Council (NIC), and the group looking at jihadists didn't come to me. Yet, in retrospect, the episode underscored two lessons for me. The first was parochial, but one that struck me over and over again while I was at the NIC. I understood the political imperative of combatting terrorism, but the preoccupation deformed our work: when we looked at Nigeria, there was not much Nigeria there; it was all Boko Haram. And when we looked at Boko Haram, there was not much Boko Haram there either. It was all about identifying and unravelling networks and targeting bad guys. To be sure, we worried about the larger questions: Where does Boko Haram come from, and where is it going? But there was scant opportunity to work on those questions given the press of the tactical.

The second lesson is the first theme of this chapter. Especially in the non-kinetic range of hybrid threats, those of us in governments and intelligence services can find partners in civil society – but only if insiders reach out in ways that are novel and often uncomfortable. Those analysts outside the government looking at jihadist websites in 2014 didn't need contracts or grants from the government. They just needed to be listened to.

The Russians are hardly the only ones engaged in hybrid threats, but they are for good reasons as the focal point of concern, and are the focus of this chapter. The new elements in hybrid threats – cyber and social media (SM)-aided propaganda – are both relatively cheap, and so will continue to be attractive to Moscow even as they also appeal to other countries and groups on similar grounds.

The second theme of this chapter, drawing especially on my latest time as a practitioner as Chair of the NIC, is that it is all too easy to respond, tit-for-tat, to the latest Russian misbehaviour. That may be the correct policy but needs to be set in the context of a strategic backdrop beyond reflex responses. That is not to excuse Russia under Vladimir Putin but to understand it in the search for better policy, one with less risk of misunderstanding and inadvertent escalation.[2] This assumption that Russia is now an enemy, whose every action is calculated to confront the United States, now spreads across the political spectrum in the United States. Yet even in the Obama administration, which I last served, there was a kind of visceral hatred for Putin, rooted in the sense that he was a liar who could not be trusted. I occasionally ventured to remind my policy counterparts, ever so gently, that during the Cold War we had also dealt with Soviet liars and cheats but had managed to come to enough agreement to avoid blowing up the planet.

I turn first to the opportunity.

The nature of the threat

Table 3.1 summarizes the range of hybrid threat instruments.

Most of the hybrid toolkit, from money to political parties to proxy combatants ('little green men'), is not new. What is new are cyber tools and SM-aided propaganda, both of which dramatically lower the entry cost: planting an article in a foreign newspaper during the Cold War was hard and expensive; now, trolls can simply post the article, with bots seeking to make it a 'trend', and thus perhaps get picked up by more traditional, quality media.

Hybrid threats are 'wicked' problems, less because they involve new actors interacting in ways we haven't seen, as was the case with terrorists after 9/11. Rather, 'by emphasizing elusiveness, ambiguity, operating outside of and below detection thresholds, and by using non-military tools to attack across all of society, hybrid threats represent a new iteration of the complexity found in wicked problems'.[3] The instruments are used simultaneously, and their target is opposing societies, not armies.

And with virtual tools, geography disappears. That was driven home by the 2016 Houston case. In May, a Facebook page called Heart of Texas encouraged its quarter million followers to demonstrate against an urgent cultural menace – a new library opened by a Houston mosque.[4] 'Stop Islamization of Texas', it cried. But the

Table 3.1 Range of hybrid tools

Tools	Examples
Propaganda	Enabled and made cheaper by social media, also targeted at home
Fake news	'Lisa' was portrayed as a Russian-German raped by migrants[a]
Strategic leaks	Macron emails leaked forty-eight hours before the French election
Funding organizations	China opened Chinese think-tank in Washington
Political parties	Russia supports sympathetic European parties on right and left
Organized protest movements	Russian trolls organized both pro- and anti-protests in Houston mosque case
Cyber tools: • Espionage • Attack • Manipulation	New tool in arsenal: espionage is old tactic with new, cyber means. Attack has targeted critical infrastructure, notably in Estonia in 2007. Manipulation is next frontier, changing information without the holders knowing it.
Economic leverage	China sought to punish South Korea for accepting US anti-missile system
Proxies and unacknowledged war	Hardly new, but covertly deployed Russian military personnel in Ukraine slid into actual combat
Paramilitary organizations	Russian 'Night Wolves' bikers intimidate civilians

[a]Stefan Meister, 'The "Lisa Case": Germany as a Target of Russian Disinformation', *NATO Review,* 25 July 2016. HYPERLINK 'https://www.nato.int/docu/review/articles/2016/07/25/the-lisa-case-germany-as-a-targ et-of-russian-disinformation/index.html' https://www.nato.int/docu/review/articles/2016/07/25/the-lisa-cas e-germany-as-a-target-of-russian-disinformation/index.html.

other side organized as well. A Facebook page linked to the United Muslims of America said that group was planning a counter-protest for the same time and place. In fact, while the United Muslims were a real group, the Facebook page was not its doing. Both the anti- and pro-demonstrations had been organized by Russian trolls.

Crowd sourcing: Changing culture

Opportunities for governments, and for their intelligence services, lie in new media, new networks and new partnerships. However, I know all too well that the culture of intelligence is slow to adapt: when I did a study of the use of SM in intelligence a decade ago, NSA analysts reported getting the question from colleagues, 'what's a hashtag?'[5] Happily, we've come a long way since then. The private citizens looking at jihadi websites in 2014 who found evidence of Russian fakery drive home the possibilities of 'crowd sourcing' around the world, seeking partners in identifying fake news and planted posts. Alas, this kind of openness and reach to private sector runs very much against the grain of intelligence cultures.

Cyber is another great opportunity. In the short run, private actors upset the traditional paradigm of intelligence and policy: if a hack occurred, intelligence would seek to attribute it to its source, then pass that information in secret for policy to take decisions. Now, private companies are doing attribution too and will go public when it suits them. Yet in the longer run, those companies are a great opportunity for partners, and when they go public it might even ease the 'sources and methods' problem for intelligence because to be credible the companies will have to say something about how they came to their conclusion.

The contours of relations between policy and intelligence were on view in one episode when I was chairing the US NIC. When hacks into the US Office of Personnel Management (OPM) in 2015 resulted in the loss of personal data on more than twenty million Americans, the immediate question was: who did it?[6] At this point, forensically, the complexity of hybrid threats had been reduced to a puzzle; attribution had an answer. The OPM hack came soon after the SONY hack. In the case of SONY, good work and good luck let US intelligence attribute it to North Korea quickly and with high confidence. Not so in the OPM case. We were pretty sure the hack came from China, but when policy officials pressed for more detail, we were for some time in the position of having to answer, more or less, 'China is a big place'.

The episode was a reminder that when an intelligence issue becomes a puzzle, policy officials will want – and expect – certainty that often isn't possible. (Taking off my intelligence hat and putting on a policy one, I admit I didn't mind the difficulty of attribution. Not only was it a useful lesson for policy officers, but since, in my view, the retaliatory options for the United States were unpromising, some delay for thought was welcome.[7]) It was also a reminder than attribution, even when good, is seldom quick. For instance, it took Saudi authorities two weeks to assess the damage from the Shamoon attack in 2012 that erased data on 30,000 of Saudi Aramco's computers.

Working with partners is very necessary, and both new partners and forms of partnership abound – a critical point for opportunities. Yet official collaboration is increasingly burdened by fears of leaks and the misuse of shared intelligence. In any case, relationships can rely less and less on the Cold War legacy. The new partnerships necessarily will take intelligence services outside their comfort zones, and underestimating the value of what counterparts, including new ones, provide will be even more counterproductive than in previous periods.

Traditional intelligence collectors will play their roles in new circumstances, but exactly how remains something of an open question. SIGINT, for instance, now uses SM mostly for targeting traditional collection, especially against terrorists: 'terrorists may have good OPSEC but they also have children, and so when I find an email' HUMINT can be critical but will be pushed into a much broader arena, and find itself collaborating with new partners, including some outside government. HUMINT is probably more critical than ever but little easier. To the extent the targets are foreign, especially Russian intelligence services, they are at least known, and perhaps somewhat 'softer' than Al Qaeda.

Penetrating Russian hacker groups, like the Internet Research Agency, would be valuable in the usual ways, providing indications of Russian targets and methods. One of the great successes of US and fellow intelligence services has been following the 'money trail' of terrorists or drug traffickers. It is a question whether and to what extent virtual currencies, like bitcoin, will make that trail harder to follow as, for instance, hybrid threateners fund parties and propaganda in other countries. So far, the effect seems small, but that may be because the currencies have been used more as investments than as media of exchange.

SM are a great source of intelligence – and warning: as one analyst from the US Defense Intelligence Agency put it to me in identifying Russia soldiers in Ukraine, 'selfies are our best friend'. As in that case, cell phones may be geolocated, or the location may be inferred from analysis of the selfie – opening an entire new source for GEOINT. So, too, ubiquitous cameras offer GEOINT new opportunities for identifying people and their movements. Taking advantage of them, however, will also require a change in organizational culture: the world is awash in information, yet in my experience, intelligence agencies still tend to give pride of place to their own secret sources and to ask first what they might collect and how, not what is out there already that might help.

Collection will also require new forms of collaboration between HUMINT and SIGINT, one suggested by the increasing practice of human-aided SIGINT. As microwave transmissions gave way to fibre optics in the 1990s, signals no longer could be gobbled up wholesale by satellites. As encryption became unbreakable, the best ways to intercept signals were before they were encrypted, and that meant getting very close to the signaller. These developments drove a closer partnership between clandestine and SIGINT services.

What is still, slightly weirdly, called 'open source' is very much a work in progress, especially in the United States. Open source gets treated like another INT when it is in fact, in the words of John Gannon, a former director of intelligence at the CIA, 'the air we breathe'. In my last incarnation in government, it was tempted to try to play in the 'big leagues' by showing its worth on 'hard' targets, like proliferation. Those are probably are not its comparative advantage, and compounding the mismatch, the US Open Source Enterprise (OSE) has returned to the CIA, rather than the inter-agency auspices of the director of national Intelligence (DNI). It tends to regard SM as just the latest media to exploit, and it goes about validation in a fairly traditional way, looking at location and numbers of retweets, for instance. Ideally, it would become the focal point for matters virtual but unclassified across the entire government, in particular pushing the artificial intelligence (AI) needed to cope with ubiquitous data.

Hybrid threats will reconfigure counterintelligence. After all, preventing foreign powers from hacking into computers or manipulating public opinion would seem the essence of counterintelligence. The awkwardness, though, is that formulation dramatically expands the institutions to be protected to include both infrastructure and virtual providers that are both in the private sector. As vulnerabilities drive adversaries' targeting, understanding possible target spaces becomes key to channelling resources – online and off. That in turn will require building links inside and outside the government, doing red teaming, and developing fragility indicators and heuristics for potential attack spaces.

An open question for counterintelligence is what role there might be for taking the offensive. In principle, the Western countries could seek to sow conspiracy and doubt in Russia's intelligence cycles. The tactic would draw on their desire to please Putin's world view. The goal would be to widen the chasms between Russian intelligence services, playing them off of each other and draining their limited resources, much as Russia seeks to exacerbate social divisions in the Western countries. If the offensive required covert insertion of misinformation, though, it would risk descending to Putin's level, discrediting both facts and media that seek them – thus making truth still more relative.

Duelling narratives

The second lesson I took away from my time in government is that taking Russia's perspective into account, and considering its possible actions as reactions, not as proactively aggressive, can begin to be strategic in the sense of asking 'what if?' and 'what next?' Russian initiatives have included kinetic force, as in the Ukraine, and may do so again, but the main game is a contest of competing narratives. Our narrative is that of the inevitable victory, as Kennan predicted, of democracy over autocracy, capitalism over communism. Needless to say, Putin's view is very different. He described the fall and breakup of the Soviet Union as the 'greatest geopolitical catastrophe' of the last century.[8] He added, 'Tens of millions of our co-citizens and co-patriots found themselves outside Russian territory . . . The moment we display weakness or spinelessness, our losses will be immeasurably greater.'

From Moscow's perspective, and surely Putin's, in the years after communism's end, the United States and the West dismissed Russia. During the Cold War, we had referred, ruefully, to the Soviet Union as 'Equatorial Guinea with nuclear weapons', but after the Cold War there was some truth to the Russian belief that we treated it that way. The George H. W. Bush administration did a masterful job of handling the Cold War's end, and there was no formal pledge, in the Budapest agreements of 1994 or anywhere else, committing NATO not to expand NATO beyond the unified Germany and or even to Russia's borders. Still, both President Bush and Secretary of State James Baker said things to their counterparties that seemed to imply such commitment.

Surely, NATO expansion during the 1990s is regarded by Russians not just as a 'broken promise' but as an affront to national dignity inflicted on them in a time when Russia was weak, both economically and militarily. The accession of the Baltic States in 2004, which border the Russian Federation, was seen as a threat. The subsequent events in Georgia in 2008 should be viewed in that context. What we regarded as straightforward intervention – but didn't do much about – was for them an attempt to undermine the government of Mikheil Saakashvili, which was very pro-Western and sought to become part of NATO. Russia acted lest another nation on its border defect into the Western alliance.

More generally, after the fall of the Berlin Wall, the Russian people looked to the West for hope and guidance. What they got was a decade of disappointment and economic mismanagement (including by Western advisors). Not just Putin but most Russians felt their dignity as a large country and erstwhile superpower was stripped from them, and that the West, rightly or wrongly, took advantage of them. It was thus understandable that Russians would turn to a strongman nationalist like Putin. His support has dropped in the last years with additional rounds of Russian sanctions and a sagging economy, from 81 per cent in 2018 to under 65 per cent in 2019. Yet his narrative of Russia's again playing a large role on the world stage remains dominant: in 2015, after the annexation of Crimea and the intervention in Ukraine, his approval rating at home reached a stunning 89 per cent.

While the Russians and the Russian leadership are not yearning to go back to creating a Soviet Union, they do care about their position, role and influence in the world and especially in what they call their 'near abroad'. Their influence in the near abroad not only gives them back a sense of status as a large power but also gives them a buffer against what they view as the expansionist West. From the Russian point of view, much of what we regard as aggressive, Russians see as defensive. The West and the United States are the aggressors and since the fall of the Berlin Wall have been pushing a policy of encirclement vis-à-vis the Russian Federation. Taking this perspective into consideration helps explain how Russia has responded to tension and conflict in the Baltics, the Ukraine and Georgia.

The goal should be to avoid misunderstandings and measures that needlessly escalate tension. Think, for instance of reactions to future sanctions, NATO troop build-ups in eastern Europe/Balkans and military exercises or the withdrawal from the INF treaty and the placement of nuclear warheads in Europe. In the case of future sanctions, no matter how much (or little) sanctions have so far hurt Russians, possible additional one, perhaps aimed at excluding Russia from the international banking system, will bite. Those will be viewed much more seriously by the Kremlin and may trigger retaliation in the form of an attack on the US financial system. They also have the unintended side effect of pushing Russia to extract itself from the US-dominated international financial system and transacting in currencies other than dollars – thus insulating itself to some extent from future sanctions. Indeed, Russia has already moved down that road.

On one hand, NATO troop build-ups in Eastern Europe and the Balkans, along with military exercises, demonstrate commitment, and Russia does not see them as an existential threat. On the other hand, they also validate Putin's narrative of NATO militarizing and pushing itself to Russia's borders. The Russians will pocket that validation, and respond by disrupting, pestering, talking of escalation – responses in the grey zone short of conventional conflict.

If the United States' withdrawal from the INF treaty is followed by the placement of nuclear warheads in Europe, that would be seen as an existential threat and would elicit a response by the Russians, which would no doubt start with grey zone measures. And the Balkans remain a key vulnerability in Europe, one over which Russia has tremendous influence. Should events start to suggest that nuclear warheads will be deployed in Europe, Russia could respond by creating havoc starting in the Balkans.

Given that the political stalemate in US politics is likely to continue beyond Trump, this may embolden Russia to make preemptive moves in a number of areas including geopolitical priorities, rhetorical policy and whole of government approach. For instance, given other priorities and disarray, the United States seems to have no time for Libya, and Russia is already stepping into the breach. A stable and Russia-friendly Libya offers huge advantages from an energy security and defence perspective – potential for a naval base in the Mediterranean. Moldova is another country that will be sucked back into the Russian orbit of influence while the United States is distracted and internally focused. Ukraine is tricky, given its upcoming presidential elections. The Russians are already funding various candidates, and in the worst-case scenario, if a pro-Western candidate is elected, they may create enough conflict to maintain the status quo, which is a basket case. The result is a drain on financial resources for the EU and the United States, if also for Russia itself.

Even in rhetoric, the United States has not always been clear that, for instance, interventions in its elections are unacceptable. So, too, its commitment to NATO and article 5 can hardly be restated often enough. And even an organizational change, like creating a Deputy Assistant Secretary of Defense (DASD) for New Generation (grey zone) Warfare, can demonstrate that the Department of Defense is taking these threats seriously, as well as serving as the Defense focal point for a broad approach to hybrid threats.

A 'whole of government approach', on which European states are making progress, seems almost an unnatural act for the United States. At least that is my experience. Being more proactive in countering grey zone threats has a military component, to be sure, but it requires all of government to create a coordinated set of tools and weapons to be deployed. Making sure, for instance, that sanctions do not backfire will require the deep involvement of the departments of Treasury, and State as well. So, too, the various private sectors have an important role to play as both eyes and ears for early warning and for speaking with a credibility that governments, as governments, often lack.

Finally, in being more strategic about Russia, there may be value in more dialogue with Russia. Surely, in the wake of Russia's election meddling, in 2016 and beyond, and the reaction that it stirred in the United States, the dialogue has become very constricted, increasing the risk of misinterpretation and the possibility for escalation. It behooves the United States and its partners to in fact enhance the dialogue on many of the issues and regarding many of these contentious areas so as to reduce the risks of escalation, and perhaps even remove some of the reasons for Russia's disruptive behaviour.

Lessons for intelligence and policy

Finally, it is worth laying out some of the lessons learned so far. Seven lessons stand out to me.

- Recognize that hybrid conflict is war by other means. Cyber and virtual conflict are the wars of the future, society against society.
- Intelligence is best done as a 'whole of society' enterprise, with lots of, in effect, crowd sourcing in both the cyber and virtual realms. Warfighters plainly have a role to play, especially at the end of the spectrum where hybrid shades into kinetic. But the military shouldn't be the dominant element.
- Just as hybrid techniques blur the lines between combatants and citizens, they are another reason why companies and citizens should be wary of cyber threats and manipulated information on SM. Like the rest of us, the US Democratic National Committee was, in 2016, more interested in getting its work done than in protecting its networks. Its mistake made it easier for the Russians to hack into the emails of John Podesta, Hillary Clinton's campaign manager.
- The question of retaliation as an element of deterrence is a complicated one. Surely, there is a growing market of companies offering private companies advice

about how to retaliate, or 'hack back'. And the Macron campaign in France, alert to Russian intervention, mounted a suggestive counterattack, flooding phishing emails with junk to distract the perpetrators.

- For countries, the guidance is probably that of Hippocrates – do no harm. That especially applies especially to the United States, given its dependence on the virtual realm, hence vulnerability. More often than is comfortable, it may have to emulate Lyndon Johnson's line about the mule in the rain, just standing there and taking it. Prevention and defence, then remediation and attribution are critical. Retaliation will most often take the form of naming and shaming, perhaps accompanied by indictments of foreign perpetrators who aren't likely to be extradited.
- In any case, the great strength of the Western democracies is their free media, and so the last thing they should want to do in retaliation is emulate Putin in ways that compromise or discredit those media engaged in telling true news, not fake.
- Finally, while autocracies, like Russia, have advantages in the cyber realm, shamelessness among them, they are hardly ten feet tall. The Russians were sloppy enough in both the American and French elections to raise the question: Did they want us to know what they were doing, perhaps as a demonstration of their capability?

Notes

1   See Andrew Weisburd, Clint Watts and J. M. berger, 'Trolling for Trump: How Russia Is Trying to Destroy Our Democracy', War on the Rocks, 6 November 2016. https://wa rontherocks.com/2016/11/trolling-for-trump-how-russia-is-trying-to-destroy-our-d emocracy/.

2   This paper draws on work by colleagues – commentary by Ydir Vissers and a paper by David Patterson.

3   Patrick Cullen, *Hybrid Threats as a 'Wicked Problem' for Early Warning*, Hybrid COE Strategic Analysis, 4 June 2018. https://www.hybridcoe.fi/publications/strategic-analysi s-may-2018-hybrid-threats-new-wicked-problem-early-warning/.

4   As reported in Manjoo Farhad, 'What Reality TV Teaches Us About Russia's Influence Campaign; State of the Art', *New York Times (international edition)*, 8 November 2017. https://www.nytimes.com/2017/11/08/technology/russia-election-reality-tv.html.

5   The study was, alas, classified. For an unclassified version of part of it, see Gregory F. Treverton, *New Tools for Collaboration: The Experience of the U.S. Intelligence Community*, Center for Strategic and International Studies, 29 January 2016. https:// www.csis.org/analysis/new-tools-collaboration.

6   For details on the hack and how it was discovered, see Brendan I. Koerner, 'Inside the Cyberattack That Shocked the US Government', *Wired*, 18 October 2016. https://www .wired.com/2016/10/inside-cyberattack-shocked-us-government/.

7   On the challenge of formulating a response to major attacks, see Tobias Feakin, *Cyber Brief: Developing a Proportionate Response to a Cyber Incident*, Council on Foreign Relations, August 2015. https://www.cfr.org/sites/default/files/pdf/2015/08/Proporti onate_Response_CyberBrief.pdf.

8   BBC News, 'Putin Deplores Collapse of USSR', *BBC News*, 25 April 2005. http://
    news.bbc.co.uk/2/hi/4480745.stm; and Kattie Sanders, 'Did Vladimir Putin Call the
    Breakup of the USSR "the greatest geopolitical tragedy of the 20th century?"', *PolitiFact*,
    6 March 2014. https://www.politifact.com/factchecks/2014/mar/06/john-bolton/
    did-vladimir-putin-call-breakup-ussr-greatest-geop/. The English version from the
    Kremlin archives uses the word 'disaster'. The Associated Press translation substituted
    'catastrophe'.

4

A perspective on EU hybrid threat early warning efforts

Patrick Cullen

The EU's introduction to hybrid threats

The European understanding and appropriation of the terms 'hybrid threats' and 'hybrid warfare' cannot be understood without reference to the Russian annexation of Crimea in 2014. This aggression in Ukraine – combined with the view that Russia had employed a novel (if not precisely new) style of warfighting – marked a sea-change in the European perceptions of their security environment. NATO applied the moniker hybrid warfare to this event and immediately organized a 'hybrid warfare' deterrence posture built around enhancing its ability to deploy a rapid conventional military response to reassure its eastern members within the Alliance.[1] Others, however, had observed that NATO was ill-equipped to respond to some of the most troubling attributes of what was now being referred to as hybrid warfare; the use of ambiguity, non-attributability, coordinated use of non-military tools (e.g. cyber, economic, financial, information), and the deliberate manipulation of detection, political decision-making and military response thresholds capable of complicating NATO's ability to invoke collective self-defence. Not for the first time,[2] NATO began discussing a need for greater security cooperation between NATO and the European government and civil society actors to address the threats implied by these developments; hybrid threats that could be non-military in nature, that could manifest and cause damage to one's society prior to any military action by the aggressor, and that otherwise fell below or outside the remit of NATO defence responsibilities.[3]

By early 2015 the view that hybrid warfare had exposed a security gap below the threshold of war that could not be filled by NATO and thus required other governmental bodies such as the EU to directly engage in countering this threat was gaining traction. A new European security discourse on 'the changed security environment, often described as hybrid warfare'[4] was being adopted by EU leadership, and it had begun tasking various EU organs like the European Defense Agency and the European External Action Service (EEAS) with developing plans for countering hybrid threats. By March 2015 the EEAS had launched the East StratCom Task Force to counter Russian disinformation campaigns. By May it released a 'Food for thought paper: Countering Hybrid Threats' that explicitly labelled both 'Russia's aggression in Ukraine' and the 'advances and morphing of Da'esh', respectively, as eastern and southern hybrid threats.[5] This document provided a series of proposals that would heavily influence the EU's response to hybrid threats and also informed the EU's collaboration with NATO in the 2016 and 2018 EU-NATO Joint Declarations.

These Joint Declarations essentially institutionalized the vision that each organization could – and should – collaborate more closely in order to close the previously mentioned security gap that allowed adversaries to inflict damage on societies within the EU and its partner nations by deploying hybrid threats in the grey zone between peace and war.[6] Within this context, the EU's 'Joint Framework on countering hybrid threats: a European Union response'[7] and subsequent EU documents on countering hybrid threats outlined twenty-two actions to be undertaken. These efforts focused on early warning and situational awareness, strategic communication, crisis response and resilience building.[8]

Understanding how the EU conceptualized hybrid threats is critical for understanding how and why the EU was tasked with these new responsibilities (and opportunities) to enhance its role in European security-making. The remainder of this chapter is organized as follows. The next section will briefly elaborate EU descriptions of hybrid threats. Thereafter, the focus will move to how the EU has approached early warning/detection of hybrid threats. Specifically, it will address how this security problem created a push for an enhanced EU-wide situational awareness mechanism that was embedded in the newly created EEAS Hybrid Fusion Cell. The chapter concludes with a discussion of joint EU-NATO efforts at enhanced hybrid threat situational awareness.

Describing rather than defining hybrid threats

One can readily find early references to both hybrid *warfare* and hybrid *threats* within various EU speeches, papers and webpages. In the past, the two terms have even been used interchangeably within the same document. For instance, an EEAS paper from 2015 with a section entitled 'defining hybrid threats' began by noting that 'hybrid warfare can be more easily characterized than defined'.[9] Although these terminological hurdles have not yet disappeared, an early political (rather than analytical) consensus has emerged within the EU that it should focus on the less politically charged language of countering of hybrid *threats* while leaving the business of countering hybrid *warfare* to its member states and NATO.[10] In practice, however, the hybrid threat/warfare distinction was left largely unexplored by the EU between 2015 and 2018, although this distinction has been made in a forthcoming document on hybrid threats sponsored by the European Commission.[11] The pragmatic and policy-oriented focus of the EU's approach to its counter-hybrid efforts also explains why the EU has chosen to *describe* rather than *define* hybrid threats. If a precise definition proved divisive or elusive, an adequate description of hybrid threats could facilitate the rapid development of an EU counter-hybrid-threats policy. This focus on political action took precedent over entering a heated definitional debate that was already almost a decade old by 2015 (and that showed no indication of slowing down). Academic and professional military criticism that argued the terms 'hybrid warfare and threats' were too vague and imprecise were considered less important in this context.[12] As a result, the 2016 EU Joint Framework *described* hybrid threats concept as follows:

> While definitions of hybrid threats vary and need to remain flexible to respond to their evolving nature, the concept aims to capture the mixture of coercive and subversive activity, conventional and unconventional methods (i.e diplomatic, military, economic, technological), which can be used in a coordinated manner by state or non-state actors to achieve specific objectives while remaining below the threshold of formally declared warfare. There is usually an emphasis on exploiting the vulnerabilities of the target and on generating ambiguity to hinder decision-making processes. Massive disinformation campaigns, using social media to control the political narrative or to radicalize, recruit and direct proxy actors can be vehicles for hybrid threats.[13]

And this approach seems to be working for the EU. As one EU research centre noted:

> Quite simply: the term 'hybrid threats' is already being used and understood by EU officials and government representatives to capture a range of non-conventional security challenges. Whether in healthcare and/or transport, the 'hybrid' label is encouraging staff in various EU bodies to give more consideration to the security aspects of their respective portfolios than perhaps has been the case in the past.[14]

The next section explores this development in the context of EU hybrid threat detection and early warning.

An EU approach to early warning: Leveraging non-military civilian expertise

The very thing that makes the EU vulnerable to hybrid threats – namely, its position as a governing body with responsibilities over a wide spectrum of civil functions and critical infrastructure across different sectors of the economy and society – also *in principle* provides it with the institutionalized professional expertise that can usefully be applied to counter hybrid threats targeting these same civilian spaces. Properly organized and coordinated into a security mechanism, sector-level expertise – in areas such as transport, health, financial, maritime, energy – held within various civil EU agencies can be exploited in hybrid threat early warning efforts. Importantly, this civilian expertise can be used to supplement the more military-centric early warning and detection efforts of NATO that does not have the same in-house skillset or political mandate to conduct these types of hybrid threat situational awareness measures in civil society.[15] Beyond this civilian skillset, the multinational character of the EU has also been highlighted as a reason why it is natural for it to become a security provider when confronting hybrid threats that have complex 'comprehensive' and transnational characteristics.[16]

In aspirational terms, and as shown later, the EU is slowly re-interpreting a role for itself in leveraging its broad non-military skillset as a compliment to parallel military (e.g. EU member state military/intelligence and NATO) counter-hybrid early warning efforts. It is doing this by using various EU departments and executive agencies to play a role in anticipating (or even identifying) activities or trends with their respective areas of expertise that may be related to hybrid threats that deliberately attempt to use non-military tools and other ambiguous means to damage or otherwise negatively influence targets in the EU. The EEAS has discussed the possibility of this EU-NATO synergy at the strategic level, explaining that '(g)iven the fact that both organizations bring different competencies to bear, there is a rare chance to collaborate on building complimentary and mutually supportive strategies while retaining the autonomy of actions in both organisations'.[17] Thus, even though the EU continues to emphasize that member states have 'the primary responsibility' for countering hybrid threats as a matter of national defence – not least because 'most national vulnerabilities are country-specific'[18] – the EU clearly sees an important and even necessary role for itself in countering hybrid threats that includes hybrid threat identification and early warning. This is no small task. As Fiott and Parks note,

> the major test is to be able to prove with some degree of certainty that the combination of threats facing the EU at any given moment amounts to a hybrid campaign involving an external actor. In other words, when is a disruption to the EU's food supply simply a case of negligence or criminal behaviour and when does it become part of a hybrid campaign.[19]

Some of the earliest publicly available work on the EU approach to building a system of hybrid threat early warning can be found in the EEAS 2015 Food-for-Thought paper.[20] In a section entitled 'Improve Awareness', the paper outlined and recommended a straightforward approach to hybrid threat early warning that can summed up in three steps:

1) Conduct vulnerability assessments to recognize and understand weaknesses to hybrid threats;

2) Acquire and maintain a sufficient level of situational awareness capable of detecting subtle (e.g. nontraditional, convert or ambiguous) hybrid threats;
3) Create an analytical cell within the EU tasked with developing methodologies for monitoring this situational awareness apparatus to 'recognize subtle changes to the threat landscape, which later may turn out to be elements of an (hybrid) adversary's larger campaign'.[21]

Vulnerability assessments

Despite the difficulties involved (addressed later), progress has been made by the EU in each of these three areas. Hybrid threat vulnerability assessments have been pursued through a mechanism called 'Friends of the Presidency Group on hybrid threats (FoP)'. The FoP launched a hybrid risk survey programme tasked with coordinating surveys to identify key vulnerabilities potentially affecting national and pan-European structures and networks and began with a survey in Europe's 'neighbourhood regions'.[22] This work has been extended from 2018 to 2020 to coordinate 'surveys and key vulnerability assessments' of hybrid threats across the EU.[23] The FoP survey relies on national self-reporting, a method that acknowledges that the actual process of vulnerability mapping is itself a highly sensitive process that is best done at the national level. Rather than trying to conduct this work directly, the EU has positioned itself as a resource to assist individual nations with this work, and to act as a conduit to share information from vulnerability assessments provided by states related to hybrid threats. The FoP has also attempted to collect 'specific hybrid related indicators' from EU member and partner states that could potentially be shared across the EU to enhance readiness and early warning.[24]

In practice, this task of collecting vulnerability assessments and indicators has proven difficult, and other EU organizations have also encountered difficulties in this area. For instance, the EU border security organization Frontex was given authority in 2016 to carry out Shengen border threat assessments. Yet its efforts to create a comprehensive picture of Shengen border vulnerabilities were impaired by states' unwillingness to share such information with EU agencies due to concerns over both security leaks of sensitive information, or political embarrassment or censure due to admission of poor national border security practices.[25] Despite progress in EU hybrid threat vulnerability assessment efforts, this problem of states only sharing the most minimally useful information has also negatively impacted FoP efforts.

Hybrid threat situational awareness: Leveraging existing mechanisms

The second key aspect of the EU approach to building hybrid threat situational awareness leverages builds upon institutionalized EU security practices and frameworks that are already in place. The logic underpinning this approach was simple: save time and money while minimizing the impact on EU agencies by embedding hybrid threat early warning tasks and responsibilities into pre-existing strategies, agencies and institutions. This approach was used across the board, and impacted the EU Cybersecurity Strategy, the Energy Security Strategy and the European Union Maritime Security Strategy, among others. The Maritime Security Strategy, for example, was reformulated to enable 'the EU and its member states to tackle maritime security challenges, including countering hybrid threats, through cross-sectoral cooperation between civilian and military actors'.[26] The perceived value-added of the counter-hybrid threat efforts – and a prerequisite for its effectiveness – has been to break down legal, institutional and cultural barriers to information sharing and to create a 'holistic approach' that develops 'synergies' with close cooperation between relevant actors, institutions, strategies and sectors.[27] It was this development of closer coordination and communication between

EU bodies that 'are exposed to or have sight of hybrid threats and indicators' that has been viewed as crucial for building a warning model for hybrid threats. And this is at the core of EU attempts at contributing to hybrid threat situational awareness.[28]

Much of the emphasis on hybrid threat early warning and situational awareness is being operationalized and built into pre-existing EU efforts at critical infrastructure protection. This is driven by an understanding that 'an unconventional attack by perpetrators of hybrid threats on any "soft target" could lead to serious economic or societal disruption'.[29] One example of a pre-existing effort is the European Programme for Critical Infrastructure Protection (EPCIP). This program uses the type of all-hazard and cross-sectoral approach – including a vulnerability analysis that looks for critical interdependencies – that is well-suited to deal with hybrid threats, and as a result to EPCIP is being re-evaluated as a tool to address cross-sectoral hybrid threats.[30] The fact that many of these EU responses to hybrid threats had already existed (or were in the legislative pipeline) prior to and independently of the EU's focus on combatting hybrid threats[31] has also led to some questions regarding what new organizational initiatives, if any, the EU has undertaken to deal with hybrid threat early warning.

EU Hybrid Fusion Cell

The answer to the earlier question of what, if any, new EU organizational initiatives have been dedicated to hybrid threat warning intelligence can be seen in the implementation of the third EEAS recommendation: establishing an analysis unit focusing on hybrid threat situational awareness. The creation of an EU counter-hybrid threat warning intelligence system was born in the shape of the EU Hybrid Fusion Cell that was established in 2016. Located within the EU Intelligence and Situation Centre (EU INTCEN) of the EEAS, it was originally designed to provide 'all source analysis'[32] on hybrid threats and is the designated focal point for intelligence related to potential hybrid threats.[33] Following the pattern of embedding counter-hybrid threat early warning efforts into pre-existing systems already in place within various EU agencies, setting up a hybrid fusion cell located within a pre-existing EU situation centre was described by EEAS as a 'quick win' that could be established without creating a strain on EU resources.

The fundamental purpose of the Cell was based on a perceived need for a fusion of pre-existing knowledge and inefficiently siloed patches of situational awareness into a single pan-EU whole. After an internal review process of EU capacity for early warning/ situational awareness, EEAS originally argued that there already existed 'a good number of indicators and warnings from across the broad range of EU competencies that could support a very effective form of early warning'.[34] What was needed, from their perspective, was the formation of an effective clearinghouse, or 'marketplace' where member states and various other EU bodies and third party institutions, including NATO and the Centre of Excellence for Countering Hybrid Threats, could collaborate and share relevant information and where appropriate, intelligence.[35]

It was thus set up with the aspiration to act as a point of entry for member states and other partners who had experienced hybrid threats in order to shares best practices, warning indicators and lessons learned; raise awareness of vulnerabilities to hybrid threats and promote education related to hybrid threats and early warning. From the outset, EU Member States were encouraged to establish National Contact Points tied to the EU Hybrid Fusion Cell to facilitate outreach and information sharing. This process was repeated internally within the EU itself, with various EU personnel designated as Internal Points of Contact to represent their EU service agency on all matters related to hybrid threats.[36] In this way, the EU Hybrid Fusion Cell was designed to look both internally and externally for hybrid threats. It would receive and analyse information on foreign hybrid threats taken from foreign EU Delegations located in non-EU countries, as well as liaising with EU Commission services to collect and analyse cross-sector information on hybrid threats from an intra-EU perspective.

The EU Hybrid Fusion Cell has thus been designed as the primary hub in a wide multi-actor information-sharing network of counter-hybrid threat nodes (i.e. actors and activities) that span across (and into the organs and capillaries) the EU organization, as well as into partner nations and partner institutions. This role has been both an aspiration and a political responsibility. In aspirational terms, once all this information had been collected into a unified picture, the EU Hybrid Fusion Cell was foreseen to be able to provide hybrid threat warning intelligence to EU leadership. In terms of political responsibility, the director of INTCEN, as the senior Fusion Cell official, had been tasked with rapidly analysing incidents possibly related to a hybrid threat to inform EU strategic decision-making processes, and other policy and operational levels.[37] For instance, when the Fusion Cell's analysis indicates the possible existence of a hybrid threat against either a member state or a partner organization or nation, the director of INTCEN is responsible for using established rapid-reaction protocols to first inform relevant parties at the operational level to urgently respond to the potential threat.[38]

Yet when it comes to a discussion of the methodologies and techniques that the EU Hybrid Fusion Cell is using to identify possible hybrid threats, public details have been (perhaps understandably) limited. One key effort that has been highlighted is the need to train EU staff – including deployed EU staff in delegations, operations and missions – to be able to 'recognize early signs of hybrid threats'.[39] This is a crucial component in any hybrid threat situational awareness effort, because the Fusion Cell will rely on the ability of EU personnel to identify early indications and weak signals of possible hybrid threats affecting their area of responsibility, and then feeding this information to the Fusion Cell for analysis. Arguably, one paradox relating to the EU's recognition that it must train its personnel to 'see' hybrid threats is the EEAS' argument (discussed earlier) that many EU agencies already have the necessary indicators and early warning systems in place and that the only thing required for the Fusion Cell is to act as a clearing house to sync all of them up into an EU-wide, coherent whole. If this observation is accurate, then very little actual training would be required, and the solution for an effective hybrid warfare situational awareness could instead be effectively resolved with a legal-organizational solution. In other words, training analysts in new methodologies designed to detect ambiguous hybrid threats would be irrelevant, since each EU agency already has the early warning indicators needed to detect them. This begs the question as to whether these indicators are standardized in a way that allows for meaningful comparison, and whether they are flexible or creative enough to identify hybrid threats that may be intentionally designed to maximize ambiguity.

However, in at least one area, the EU (i.e. the EEAS specifically) has explained a way in which the EU Hybrid Fusion Cell would be uniquely positioned to identify hybrid threats before any other EU warning system would be able to do so. That is, by using its fused situational awareness to connect the dots into a broader pattern recognition intelligence product, effectively linking a series of low threshold, ambiguous incidents across multiple EU agencies/sectors and thus identifying a (possible) wider hybrid threat campaign. This cross-agency work is facilitated in part by a monthly roundtable meeting at the Hybrid Fusion Cell with representatives from participating EC Directorate Generals. By signalling both a need to achieve this level of situational awareness with concrete plans for the Fusion Cell to work towards it, the Cell's work already transcends a simple collection and fusion of early warning indicators from across the EU. Other discussions of methods related to early warning against hybrid threats within the EU have been rather sparse and piecemeal but give some idea about the kinds of intelligence products they foresee the Fusion Cell providing. For instance, the EEAS has written about using various forms of structured analytic techniques – albeit in very broad language – such as mentioning that 'this virtual fusion cell could include elements such as strategic foresight and early warning and be supported by scientific research',[40] and that 'the cell could catalyze all indicators . . . and then analyze them against a possible hybrid attack scenario both in EU MS and third countries'.[41]

Other warning intelligence efforts undertaken by the EU that fall outside of the efforts of the Hybrid Fusion Cell – but that are clearly central to EU hybrid threat early warning – include work in the strategic communication space. In on example, EEAS STRATCOM EAST does a weekly analysis of Russian disinformation campaigns with one of its key goals as building an improved EU capacity to forecast disinformation activities by external actors.[42]

EU-NATO counter-hybrid early warning: Parallel and coordinated, not joint

NATO secretary Jens Stoltenberg has described the type of pattern recognition required for hybrid threat early warning in order to strip it of its ambiguity when he stated the following:

> To be prepared, we must be able to see and analyze correctly what is happening; to see the patterns behind events which appear isolated and random; and quickly identify who is behind and why. So therefore, we need to sharpen our early warning and improve our situation awareness. This is about intelligence, expert knowledge and analytical capacity. So we know when an attack is an attack.[43]

This emphasis on being able to 'see the patterns behind events which appear isolated and random' is precisely one of the stated goals of the EU Hybrid Fusion Cell.

However, despite the EU-NATO Joint Declaration's calls for closer cooperation, political directives have placed limitations on the degree to which the EU Hybrid Fusion Cell can work with its NATO counterpart, the NATO Hybrid Analysis Branch. The two organizations are not allowed to share intelligence. Instead, they can conduct 'parallel and coordinated assessments' involving discussion of open source materials, the coordination of requests for information (from member state intelligence organizations) and regular meetings.[44]

In this political context, much of the EU-NATO collaboration in countering hybrid threats mirrors the EU's internal process of building on previously existing security programmes. This can be seen in the way EU-NATO collaboration in the realm of cyber defence is being conceptualized and packaged as a counter-hybrid effort. In practical terms senior staff to staff meetings between European Union Military Staff, the EDA and NATO C3 staff held in 2015 helped catalyse regular cooperation at the working level. Cross-briefings on cyber defence took place on a regular basis, and this in turn helped institutionalize collaboration in cyber defence capabilities development. NATO was accepted as an official observer in the EDA cyber ranges project, and NATO reciprocated by inviting the EDA to participate in NATO cyber education, training and exercises.[45] EU-NATO collaboration in early warning and detection in the cyber domain was specifically addressed in 2016 when the EU and NATO completed a technical arrangement between the NATO Computer Incident Response Capability (NCIRC) and the Computer Emergency Response Team – European Union (CERT-EU). Reportedly, this technical information sharing 'will be achieved, for instance, through the sharing of routine information exchange products, (e.g. non-public indicators of compromise, situational awareness, reports) as well as visits to facilities and laboratories'.[46] In the context of formal restrictions on how the EU and NATO can share intelligence, collaboration in countering and detecting hybrid threats will likely be driven by embedding the hybrid problem into already ongoing programmes, as well as by grassroots person-to-person and bottom-up efforts to find practical ways to enhance cooperation between these organizations.

Conclusion

Both the EU's engagement with hybrid threats and its emphasis on early warning and detection have been heavily influenced by Russia's invasion of Ukraine. Not only did this aggression fundamentally realign EU perceptions of Russian intentions as a security threat, but the nature of Russian tactics in Ukraine also revealed it was willing and able to experiment with ambiguous methods of political coercion that threatened Europe in novel ways below the level of actual war (and a NATO Article 5 collective self-defence response). This recognition within the EU and NATO – and their member states – created the impetus for the EU to focus on countering hybrid threats in a newly recognized security gap below the threshold of war that NATO is ill-equipped to respond to.

A significant portion of this EU has focused on identifying hybrid threats in their early stages, and the EU has made considerable progress in these efforts. In the realm of early warning and detection, the EEAS' recommendations made in 2015 focusing on vulnerability assessments, the development of an EU-wide cross-sector situational awareness concept, and the creation of a dedicated fusion cell designed to monitor this joined-up threat landscape have all been implemented. However, these successes have not come without challenges. Creating new information-sharing practices across organizations and cultures is difficult under the best circumstances, and is especially difficult in security matters. With the EEAS and the Hybrid Fusion Cell heavily reliant on the active cooperation of member state intelligence agencies and EU departments for their information, early aspirations for the Cell to be able to provide its clients with actionable intelligence at the tactical or operational level have been replaced with a focus on providing long-term intelligence and trend analysis at the strategic level. Despite some of the practical and political limitations imposed on these EU early warning, the efforts by the Hybrid Fusion Cell represent a significant step in the right direction towards filling the security gap below NATO's Article 5 that hybrid threats seek to exploit.

Notes

1 Atlantic Council, 'Breedlove: NATO Have Begun Shaping Rapid Response Force', *Commanders Series*, 17 September 2014.
2 Michael Aaronson, Sverre Deisen, Yves de Kermabom, Mary Beth Long and Michael Miklaucic, 'NATO: Countering the Hybrid Threat', *PRISM* 2, no. 4 (2011): 111–24.
3 Peter Pindjak, 'Deterring Hybrid Warfare: A Chance for NATO and the EU to Work Together?' *NATO Review*, 18 November 2014.
4 European Defense Agency, 'Hybrid Warfare', 16 July 2015. https://www.eda.europa.eu/what-we-do/activities/activities-search/hybrid-warfare.
5 EEAS, 'Food for Thought Paper "Countering Hybrid Threats"', 13 May 2015. https://www.statewatch.org/news/2015/may/eeas-csdp-hybrid-threats-8887-15.pdf, 2.
6 Daniel Fiott and Roderick Parkes, 'Protecting Europe: The EU's Response to Hybrid Threats', *EUISS Challiot Paper* 151, April 2019, 6.
7 European Commission, 'Joint Framework for Countering Hybrid Threats', 6 April 2016.
8 Hanna Smith, 'Countering Hybrid Threats', in *The EU and NATO: The Essential Partners*', eds Gustav Lindstrom and Thierry Tardy (EUISS: Paris, 2019), 17.
9 EEAS, 'Food for Thought Paper "Countering Hybrid Threats"', 2.
10 Interviews with EU officials working on hybrid threats have stated to the author that the European Commission has 'insisted' on the term threat rather than warfare.
11 This forthcoming publication is a joint product of the EC's Joint Research Centre and the European and the European Centre of Excellence for Countering Hybrid Threats. The author contributed to its development.
12 The Counter Hybrid Warfare project of MCDC, another multinational armed forces initiative, had also adopted this position of describing rather than defining hybrid warfare by 2015. This position has since been replicated by the European Centre of

Excellence for Countering Hybrid Threats and other organizations, including NATO Strategic Communications Centre of Excellence.

13 European Commission, 'Joint Framework for Countering Hybrid Threats', 2.

14 Fiott and Parkes, 'Protecting Europe: The EU's Response to Hybrid Threats', 8.

15 Personnel from numerous EC Directorate Generals participating in the March 2016 EDA Hybrid Threats Table Top Exercise made this point during the exercise. Author participation, 11 March 2016, Brussels.

16 Margriet Drent, Rob Hendriks and Dick Zandee, 'New Threats, New EU and NATO Responses', *Clingendael Report*, July 2015, 38–43.

17 EEAS, 'Food for Thought Paper "Countering Hybrid Threats"', 5.

18 European Commission Fact Sheet, 'FAQ: Joint Framework on Countering Hybrid Threats', 6 April 2016, Brussels, 1.

19 Fiott and Parkes, 'Protecting Europe: The EU's Response to Hybrid Threats', 9.

20 EEAS, 'Food for Thought Paper "Countering Hybrid Threats"'.

21 Parentheses added. EEAS, 'Food for Thought Paper "Countering Hybrid Threats"', 4.

22 Author discussion with EEAS official, also see European Commission, 'Joint Framework for Countering Hybrid Threats', 15.

23 Fiott and Parkes, 'Protecting Europe: The EU's Response to Hybrid Threats', 32.

24 European Commission, 'Joint Framework for Countering Hybrid Threats', 3.

25 Fiott and Parkes, 'Protecting Europe: The EU's Response to Hybrid Threats', 12.

26 Fiott and Parkes, 'Protecting Europe: The EU's Response to Hybrid Threats', 7.

27 Fiott and Parkes, 'Protecting Europe: The EU's Response to Hybrid Threats', 3.

28 EEAS, 'Food for Thought Paper "Countering Hybrid Threats"', 4.

29 European Commission, 'Joint Framework for Countering Hybrid Threats', 6.

30 European Commission, 'Joint Framework for Countering Hybrid Threats'.

31 Jan Jakub uzieblo, 'United in Ambiguity? EU and NATO Approaches to Hybrid Warfare and Hybrid Threats', *EU Diplomacy Paper*, College of Europe, Brugge, May 2017, 22.

32 European Commission, 'Security and Defense: Significant Progress to Enhance Europe's Resilience against Hybrid Threats—More Work Ahead', Press Release, Brussels, 19 July 2017. https://ec.europa.eu/commission/presscorner/detail/en/IP_17_2064.

33 European Commission, 'EU Playbook: Operational Protocol for Countering Hybrid Threats', Brussels, 5 July 2016, 5.

34 EEAS, 'Food for Thought Paper "Countering Hybrid Threats"', 4.

35 EEAS, 'Food for Thought Paper "Countering Hybrid Threats"', 4.

36 European Commission, 'EU Playbook: Operational Protocol for Countering Hybrid Threats', 5.

37 European Commission, 'EU Playbook: Operational Protocol for Countering Hybrid Threats'.

38 European Commission, 'EU Playbook: Operational Protocol for Countering Hybrid Threats', 9.

39 European Commission, 'EU Playbook: Operational Protocol for Countering Hybrid Threats'.

40 EEAS, 'Food for Thought Paper "Countering Hybrid Threats"'. 4.

41 EEAS, 'Food for Thought Paper "Countering Hybrid Threats"'.

42 EEAS, 'Questions and Answers about the East Stratcom Task Force', 26 November 2015. http://collections.internetmemory.org/haeu/content/20160313172652/http://eeas.europa.eu/top_stories/2015/261115_stratcom-east_qanda_en.htm.

43　Jens Stoltenberg, keynote speech, NATO Transformation Seminar, 25 March 2015. https://www.nato.int/cps/ic/natohq/opinions_118435.htm.

44　Interviews with EC and NATO personnel, 27 February 2018.

45　Patryk Pawlak, 'Countering Hybrid Threats: EU-NATO Cooperation', *European Parliamentary Research Service*, March 2017, 10.

46　Pawlak, 'Countering Hybrid Threats: EU-NATO Cooperation'.

Part II

Tools and means

5

Conceptualizing and countering hybrid threats and hybrid warfare

The role of the military in the grey zone

Mikael Weissmann

Introduction[1]

Challenges related to hybrid threats and hybrid warfare (HT&HW) are today something that is high on the security agenda across the world. The need to manage a range of hybrid measures is widely recognized among experts and practitioners,[2] as well as by key international organizations such as NATO and the European Union (EU).[3] It has become clear that the battlefield of the future exists in the grey zone between war and peace. In this grey zone, you will find non-kinetic effects replacing, or mixed with, kinetic effects. There will be a synergistic assortment of military and non-military activities, ranging from different forms of strategic communication, through active measures as intrusions, special operations, sanctions and subversions, through the use of masked soldiers like to so-called green men in Crimea, cyberattacks, sabotage and terror or proxy warfare, before passing the borderline of war. Thus, today there is a need to be able to develop resilience towards, and capabilities to pursue, effective operations and tactics against HT&HW.

To counter HT&HW, there is a need for a range of actors to work together and use the full range of tools at their disposal. This chapter focuses on one part of the toolbox for countering HT&HW: the military. What role, if any, can and should the military play against hybrid scenarios such as the presence of green men, infrastructure and logistics protection, cyber defence, information and influence operations, or simply in support of civil society?

It is crucial to understand the role of the military in the grey zone. Unless HT&HW can be successfully handled there, the war is likely to have been lost before a conventional war breaks out. Sun Zsu's age-old wisdom that '[t]he greatest victory is that which requires no battle' is as true today as it was 2,000 years ago. This is also a wisdom encapsulated in Russia's style of warfare which 'combines the political, economic, social and kinetic in a conflict that recognizes no boundaries between civilian and combatant, covert and overt, war and peace . . . [where] achieving victory – however that may be defined – permits and demands whatever means will be successful'.[4]

In other words, when preparing for a conventional high-intensity conflict towards a qualified opponent, you are preparing for a situation that will not happen if your opponent succeeds with its strategy. Thus, it is of paramount importance to analyse and understand what role the military *can* and *should* play in responding to HT&HW today and in the future. The important thing is not if or how the military should contribute, but to allow for making informed decisions and to know what the consequences are with one's choices. Or lack of choices; not choosing is also a choice. It might be that the sole role for the military is to fight during a conventional war – but then this decision should be taken based on well-informed analysis.

The overarching question guiding this chapter is 'Where do the military fit in when countering HT&HW?' More specifically, it is asked, '*What is the role of the military – if any – to counter* HT&HW?'. This chapter focus on the role of the military in Western democracies in the Baltic Sea region (Sweden, Finland, Denmark, Estonia, Latvia, Lithuania, Poland and Germany). With its focus on the Baltic Sea region, the chapter will focus on analysing HT&HW relating to Russia. The reason for this limitation is that Russia is identified as the main threat in the threat assessments across the countries in the Baltic Sea region.[5] This is not to say there are no other actors active in the region, but the key actor is nevertheless Russia.

The analysis is conducted using a proposed analytical framework outlining seven dimensions of HT&HW. Using this framework, it will first be analysed *what role the military have today and in the future* across the Baltic Sea region. After that, it will be asked what role the military *should have in the future according to the members of the military themselves.* Here Sweden is used as a case study and structured interviews are conducted with senior officers. The latter dimension is important as it allows to better understand what the profession itself thinks about their role and responsibilities. If able to identify possible discrepancies between the officer's perception and the official strategy, it is possible to enhance ones' ability to operationalize and implement the strategy successfully. One should also note that as a collective, the officer corps can be expected to have shared insight and knowledge on their capabilities, or lack of the same, which if taken into consideration may enhance the ability to defence against HT&HW.

The chapter is structured as follows. First, the two concepts in focus – HT&HW – will be presented and defined. In the following section, the concepts will be operationalized, and an analytical framework of HT&HW that draws together existing Western thinking and the understandings in military and policy frameworks is proposed. Thereafter, the proposed framework is discussed and contrasted with the Russian approach to HT&HW. In section three, the existing official discourse on how the military fit in the context of HT&HW among countries in the Baltic Sea region will be analysed. This is followed, in section four, with a case study analysing what role the members of the military themselves think it should have. The case used is Sweden, and the analysis builds on structured interviews with eighty-two senior officers.

Conceptualizing hybrid threats and hybrid warfare

As the introduction sets out, HT&HW are problematic concepts and existing scholarship on these phenomena lacks a common definition and the use of terminology remains contested. The term 'hybrid' itself is associated with 'a blend of conventional and non-conventional warfare where a hostile actor is exploiting the blurred area between peace and war'.[6] When moving away from this basic understanding, there is a lack of consensus about the definition as well as of how terms are used. There is also a problem with the tendency to use hybrid threats and/or hybrid warfare as catch-all phrases. To add to the confusion, these two and other terms tend to be used synonymously. Hybrid threat and hybrid warfare are merely two of a variety of terms used to describe a phenomenon, where 'Asymmetrical warfare', 'Sixth Generation Warfare', 'Contactless warfare', 'New warfare', 'Next-generation warfare', 'Ambiguous warfare', 'Asymmetrical warfare', 'Non-linear warfare', 'Full Spectrum Conflict' are a few examples of more or less synonymous terms.[7]

NATO is a case in point. On the page 'NATO's response to hybrid threats' on the NATO website they use hybrid warfare and threats interchangeably.[8] It is said that 'Hybrid methods of warfare, such as propaganda, deception, sabotage and other non-military tactics have long been used to destabilise adversaries' and that 'NATO has a strategy on its role in countering hybrid warfare and stands ready to defend the Alliance and all Allies against any threat, whether conventional or hybrid'.[9] In the same text, NATO talks about hybrid threats as something that 'combine military and non-military as well as covert and overt means, including disinformation, cyberattacks, economic pressure, deployment of irregular armed groups and use of regular forces'.[10] All this is done under the umbrella of hybrid methods, talking about '[h]ybrid methods of warfare', where hybrid methods are 'used to blur the lines between war and peace, and attempt to sow doubt in the minds of target populations'.[11] Needless to say, NATO does not offer any conceptual clarity.

One way to conceptualize HT&HW is to understand them as being two sides of the same coin, constituting two viewpoints, or phases, of the same phenomenon. Hybrid warfare concerns active hybrid measures by one actor targeting another actor. In contrast, hybrid threats need not be active measures, but can also be passive – being real or perceived threats for possible future actions against oneself. The difference between real and perceived, as well as the question of whether one is subjected to active and ongoing hybrid measures, does not always have a clear answer. Deception and denial are inherent in hybrid methods, and it is sometimes difficult to know for sure that warfare is ongoing, and in the same way, it is inherently difficult to identify if, and when, a perceived threat of future action becomes a reality. Attempts to deny the presence of masked Russian soldiers in Crimea, and the involvement of different actors in influence operations and cyber operations, exemplify this problem (see also discussion on 'Hybrid Blizzard Model' in Chapter 17). There is also a question of perspective, whether you are the target or perpetrator of hybrid measures; among targets there is a tendency to refer to hybrid threats, even if the hybrid warfare label may also be used after identification of said activity. If you are the source of the threat, you know that it is warfare, which is not threatening to yourself. Regardless, whether a certain measure is labelled a threat or warfare is very much a matter of personal preference – threat or warfare depends on the eye of the beholder.[12]

Despite the existing lack of conceptual clarity and consensus, there is still a need for a conceptual starting point when approaching HT&HW. In this chapter, the starting point consists of two understandings of HT&HW developed by the European Centre of Excellence for Countering Hybrid Threats (Hybrid CoE) in Helsinki and the International Institute for Strategic Studies (IISS). Thy Hybrid CoE characterizes hybrid threat as follows:[13]

1) Coordinated and synchronized action, that deliberately targets democratic states' and institutions' systemic vulnerabilities, through a wide range of means (political, economic, military, civil and information),
2) Activities exploit the thresholds of detection and attribution as well as the border between war and peace, and
3) The aim is to influence different forms of decision making at the local (regional), state, or institutional level to favour and/or gain the agent's strategic goals while undermining and/or hurting the target.

While being debated and contested, the Hybrid CoE perspective is arguably a suitable starting point: the Hybrid CoE has been endorsed by both the Council of the European Union and the North Atlantic Council and has a membership that includes the five Western countries in the Baltic Sea region as well as three major external powers (United Kingdom, France and the United States). Their joint framework

> is to serve as a hub of expertise supporting the participating countries' individual and collective efforts to enhance their civil-military capabilities, resilience, and preparedness to counter hybrid threats with a special focus on European security. It is intended that the Centre will offer this collective experience and expertise for the benefit of all participating countries, as well as the EU and NATO. The Centre will follow a comprehensive, multinational, multidisciplinary and academic-based approach.[14]

Thus, Hybrid CoE is the main institution in the Western security architecture tasked to deal with hybrid threats.

For hybrid warfare, this chapter will adopt a definition used by the International Institute for Strategic Studies (IISS), defining hybrid warfare as

> The use of military and non-military tools in an integrated campaign designed to achieve surprise, seize the initiative and gain psychological as well as physical advantages utilising diplomatic means; sophisticated and rapid information, electronic and cyber operations; covert and occasionally overt military and intelligence action; and economic pressure.[15]

Crucial in this definition is the integrated campaign part, which separates the concept from asymmetric warfare.[16]

A number of central features are shared by the two definitions, which will guide this chapter. Hybrid actions are

1) multidimensional, and
2) coordinated and synchronized,
3) being part of an integrated campaign with a strategic goal,
4) They are also deceptive, and
5) exploit the border between war and peace.

In the current debates, HT&HW tend to be linked to states (or in extension their proxies), which has not always been the case. To view HT&HW as of state-centred warfare is a recent development, the concept having its origin as a way to describe and understand the complexity and efficiency of non-state actors on the battlefield.[17] Here there are 'are similarities between Russian actions in Ukraine and previous examples of non-state hybrid warfare – most notably the in the "blurring" of traditional concepts of warfare, its unfamiliarity, the use of non-military means, and the asymmetric relationship to conventional Western warfighting – have all contributed to labelling these Russian actions as HW'.[18]

Analytical framework – the seven dimensions of HT&HW

To be able to trace the role of the military in an area where there lacks a consensus on definition and precise terminology, there is a need for an analytical framework. Utilizing in dimensional understanding of HT&HW, the framework is founded in the understandings of HT&HW as manifested in the IISS, the Hybrid CoE, the Multinational Capability Development Campaign (MCDC) framework, the Swedish Strategic Doctrine, the NATO and the EU perspectives.[19] The IISS and Hybrid CoE definitions have been found to be good definitions as outlined earlier. The MCDC Countering Hybrid Warfare project and the Swedish Strategic Doctrine's understanding of strategic tools and means that can affect and threaten Swedish security have been included as they represent two military-focused frameworks of relevance for the Baltic Sea region. The EU view is included as a representation of the lowest common denominator of the members of the EU as a group, and the NATO view represents the same in the case of the Western military collective.

Analysing the six understandings, a total of seven dimensions can be distilled where HT&HW can be located: (1) diplomatic, (2) economic, (3) cyber (technological), (4) information and influence operations, (5) unconventional methods, (6) civil (non-military) and (7) military (see Table 5.1). The dimensions found in the Hybrid CoE and IISS definitions are present in the NATO and EU thinking on HT&HW, as well as in the frameworks of MCDC and the Swedish Strategic Doctrine. The cyber and unconventional methods are not explicitly part of the five instruments of power in the MCDC framework,[20] nor in the Hybrid CoE definition used here, but the two are present in the two organizations understandings and writing on HT&HW. In the case of the Swedish Strategic Doctrine, civilian (non-military) is not its own category of

Table 5.1 The seven dimensions of hybrid threats and hybrid warfare

Dimension	Definition		Military frameworks		Policy	
	IISS	CoE	MCDC	SWE	EU	NATO
1 Diplomatic	Diplomacy	Political	Political	Diplomatic + political	Diplomatic	n/a
2 Economic	Economic	Economic	Economic	Economic	Economic	Economic pressure
3 Cyber (technological)	Cyber	*Is included*	*Is included*	Cyberattacks	Technological	Cyberattacks
4 Information and influence operations	Info	Information	Information	Psychological	Is included, e.g. Disinformation campaigns	Disinformation, propaganda
5 Unconventional methods	Covert and occasionally military operations	*Is included*	*Is included*	Unconventional	Unconventional	Unconventional (deployment of irregular armed groups + covert means)
6 Civil (non-military)	Non-military	Civil	Civil	*Is included*	Non-military	Non-military
7 Military	Military	Military	Military	Military	Military	Military

Source: Author

strategic tools, but is an integrated part of the total defence idea and also included in the diplomatic, economic, and psychological tools and means.

The threat – bringing Russia back in

The reason for HT&HW becoming of central importance can be linked to the rise of Russia. As outlined in the introduction, this threat is an actor encapsulated in 'a style of warfare that combines the political, economic, social and kinetic in a conflict that recognizes no boundaries between civilian and combatant, covert and overt, war and peace . . . [where] achieving victory – however that may be defined – permits and demands whatever means will be successful: the ethics of total war applied even to the smallest skirmish'.[21] Russia as the main threat has in recent decades become the dominant understanding among Western states, not least in the Baltic Sea region that is the focus of this study.[22]

The Russian paradigm can be seen manifested in Georgia, Ukraine and Syria, all three being a good example of 'wars' where the division into war and peace as traditionally understood in the West is highly problematic. It is clear that the grey one between peace and war has grown considerably, and so has the need to identify and understand how to handle the full range of hybrid threats that may occur. Such an ability is particularly important in the case of Russia, it being a country where the mindset is to perceive security politics as a zero-sum game where the aim always is to win, with the underlying thinking being founded in a perception of an always ongoing state of war.

So what types of HT&HW are to be expected? As outlined in his excellent review on the evolution of Russian military though, Timothy Thomas did in 2016 observe that hybrid warfare and new-generation warfare (NGW) for many years had been at the centre of attention among US and Russian military analysis.[23] In early 2015 a new term was introduced when General-Lieutenant A. V. Kartapolov introduced what he called 'New-type War' (NTW) as an alternative way to understand the Russian view on contemporary war.[24] In his article in *the Journal of the Academy of Military Science*, Kartapolov discussed the way NATO and the United States conducts war and outlined what would be needed for Russia to confront it.[25] NTW is here best understood as 'describing war's evolving character' while the term New-generation warfare 'may more likely be a reference to a method of war', noting that 'the Russian military views "methods" as composed of weapons and military art'.[26]

As argued by Thomas, 'while the term NTW appears to be the "chosen one" at present (until another concept is offered in the evolution of military thought), the term NGW should not disappear from Western consideration. It should be considered as perhaps the major "weapons" aspect of Russia's "methods" of war'.[27] In this chapter, focus will be on the concept NGW as we are here more interested in methods of war than the larger question of the evolving character of war. More specifically, we will here adopt a schematization of NGW as outlined by Tchekinov and Bogdanov.[28] They divide what they call 'new-generation warfare' into eight phases:

First Phase: non-military asymmetric warfare (encompassing information, moral, psychological, ideological, diplomatic, and economic measures as part of a plan to establish a favorable political, economic, and military setup).

Second Phase: special operations to mislead political and military leaders by coordinated measures carried out by diplomatic channels, media, and top government and military agencies by leaking false data, orders, directives, and instructions.

Third Phase: intimidation, deceiving, and bribing government and military officers, with the objective of making them abandon their service duties.

Fourth Phase: destabilizing propaganda to increase discontent among the population, boosted by the arrival of Russian bands of militants, escalating subversion.

Fifth Phase: establishment of no-fly zones over the country to be attacked, imposition of blockades, and extensive use of private military companies in close cooperation with armed opposition units.

Sixth Phase: commencement of military action, immediately preceded by large-scale reconnaissance and subversive missions. All types, forms, methods, and forces, including special operations forces, space, radio, radio engineering, electronic, diplomatic, and secret service intelligence, and industrial espionage.

Seventh Phase: combination of targeted information operation, electronic warfare operation, aerospace operation, continuous airforce harassment, combined with the use of high precision weapons launched from various platforms (long-range artillery, and weapons based on new physical principles, including microwaves, radiation, non-lethal biological weapons).

Eighth Phase: roll over the remaining points of resistance and destroy surviving enemy units by special operations conducted by reconnaissance units to spot which enemy units have survived and transmit their coordinates to the attacker's missile and artillery units; fire barrages to annihilate the defender's resisting army units by effective advanced weapons; airdrop operations to surround points of resistance; and territory mopping-up operations by ground troops. [Bold in original text][29]

As can be seen, Russia strives to utilize the grey zone between peace and war where it is unclear if there has been an attack or not. Furthermore, Russia has also systematically denied acknowledgement when others have tried to pin-point identified attacks to Russia (also see the chapters by Alexander Crowther, Markus Göransson and Niklas Nilsson in this volume.)

The Russian NGW fit well into the here proposed analytical framework, with all seven dimensions included in the eight phases (see Table 5.2). Three patterns stand out. First, while not being explicitly mentioned by name in the schematic presentation, it is clear that the cyber dimension is an integrated tool throughout the eight phases. Rather than being separated into its own phase or as a method, the use of cyber is integrated if to be successful throughout the phases. It important from the first phase of including information, moral, psychological, ideological, diplomatic and economic measures where the cyber dimension will play an important role, to during the commencement of military action and afterwards, with cyber being integrated in today's integrated and networked multidimensional battlefield. Second, the role of information and influence operations is also a crucial aspect in undermining the resilience of its opponent, thereby undermining its society's resilience and the

Table 5.2 The seven dimensions of hybrid threats and hybrid warfare as used in 'new generation warfare'

Dimension	Present in New Generation Warfare?	Phase 1	Phase 2	Phase 3	Phase 4	Phase 5	Phase 6	Phase 7	Phase 8
1 Diplomatic	X	X				X			
2 Economic	X	X		X		X			
3 Cyber (technological)	X	X^*	X^*	X^*	X^*	X^*	X^*	X	X^*
4 Information and influence operations	X	X	X	X	X		X	X	
5 Unconventional methods	X			X	X	X	X	X	X
6 Civil (non-military)	X	X	X	X	X				
7 Military	X					X	X	X	X

*= Is included, though not mentioned explicitly.
Source: Author

countries' ability for national defence. Third, while it sometimes is difficult to draw the exact borders between unconventional-, civil (non-military)-, and military measures, it is clear that all three will be used and hence are to be expected. Here it is important to note that the 'limitation' of Western democracies trying to draw a clear border between war and peace does not encumber Russia; it will simply use the most efficient tool possible to reach its goals without legal constraints.

In conclusion, the seven dimensions do not 'only' fit the Western view of hybrid warfare, but it is also a good fit into the Russian understanding of HT&HW, here represented by Russia's eight-phased 'new generation warfare'.[30] This is of course not surprising, as the Western conceptual understanding has developed in reaction to Russia's perceived behaviour. Or, in the view of the Russians, the other way around.

Sweden can here be used as a good example. The lack of clear threshold is streaming through the Swedish doctrine that is built around the grey-zone idea.[31] Thus, its understanding of reality is very similar to the Russian idea of hybrid warfare. This might not come as a surprise, as what the doctrine does very much is countering a threat from Russia. A reflexive process, the social construction of hybrid warfare and threats, while being very real, are also constructed and continuously reconstructed in the social interaction between actors, here a combination of states, experts, pundit, journalists as well as the public.

Where does the military fit in?

So then, in which dimensions is there a role to be played by the military? That it plays a role in the 'Military' dimension is obvious; this is the raison d'être of the military. It also goes without saying that the military is to play a critical role in the latter phases of in the schematic model of NGW. In contrast, the military is expected to play no or minimal role in the 'Diplomatic' in the case of Western democracies as those studied here. Also in the case of the 'Economic' dimensions its role is expected to be limited. This said, in the context of cooperation with its civilian counterparts there is always a certain role to be played by the military, especially within a 'Total-' or 'Comprehensive' Defence concept.[32] There may also be a role for the military to counter economic pressure or to ensure the societal and infrastructure needs of the economic sphere. One example here could be to safeguard critical infrastructure and energy security.[33] Here 72 per cent of the interviewed Swedish officers thought that the military should play at least a limited role against economic and psychological attacks on critical infrastructure.[34]

As has been outlined earlier, the cyber dimension plays a central role in current discussions on hybrid threats and hybrid warfare. For example, the EU has increased its cooperation on cyber defence to strengthen its capability. The initial EU cyber defence policy framework was adopted in 2014, and in November 2018 the European Council emphasized the need to build strong cybersecurity, referring to in particular the need to be able to respond to and deter cyberattacks.[35] Cyber also plays an important part in the work of NATO. Here the creation of the NATO Cooperative Cyber Defence Centre of Excellence in Tallinn is a good illustration of the importance given to the cyber dimension.[36]

Emphasis on cyber can also be found among the countries in the Baltic Sea region, where cyber defence has become a task where the ministry of defence and the military play an increasingly important role. For example, in the case of Lithuania, its Ministry of National Defence is since 2015 responsible for shaping and implementing the national cybersecurity policy and a National Cyber Security Centre has been established with the task to handle the cybersecurity of state institutions and critical information infrastructure.[37] In Scandinavia, cyber defence is an important and integrated part of the work of the Swedish military,[38] and in Denmark the inter-party defence agreement for the 2018–23 period outlines cybersecurity as one of the particular focus when strengthening the military ability to contribute to national security.[39] There has also been a trend towards developing cyber commands and cyber units. For example, in Poland cyber units 'will be responsible for ensuring cyber security on a continuous basis by coordinating and supervising activities in the cyberspace' and the Polish Armed Forces is to be 'prepared to operate in the dynamic information environment, both proactively and by reacting to hostile actions'.[40] Estonia has developed a Cyber Command, and Latvia has a Cyber Defence Unit linked to its National Guards.[41]

Information and influence operations are a crucial feature of the Russian way to conduct hybrid warfare. The exact role of the military to counter this form of warfare is not absolutely clear as this is a broad category which ultimately is about the overall resilience of the society as a whole. Thus, the role of respective armed force is often linked to the joint efforts of the military and civilian defence such as Total- or Collective Defence concepts. As a consequence, the division of labour between the military and civilian agencies varies between countries. It can be assumed that as the military is a key actor in cyber defence they also by necessity play an important part in countering information and influence operations as those are mainly taking place in the cyber dimension. For example, according to a Lithuanian White Paper, 'Russia conducts deliberate information campaigns targeting Lithuanian society using a broad array of means: from television to social media' and one way its National Defence System take direct actions is in the form of the Lithuanian Armed Forces Communications Department who 'monitors and analyses the information domain to determine the targets, the scale and means of the information attacks'.[42] It should here also be noted that since 2014 there is a NATO Strategic Communications Centre of Excellence in Latvia where all countries in the Baltic Sea region are members.

In the case of supporting civilian authorities, there is an outspoken role for the military to support, including the national police in response to non-military threats. A number of areas stand out where there is a clearly defined role: terrorism, border control, and at times of national emergencies such as natural disasters and large-scale accidents.[43] In, for example, Denmark it is outlined that the armed forces and 'will establish a permanent helicopter response based in the Copenhagen area at very high readiness in support of the police's counter-terrorist preparedness' and that '[r]esources will be reserved for Defence to generate units on high readiness to assist the police in case of terror attacks etc'.[44] There are also provisions for providing support to ensure law, order and security. In Latvia, the military shall provide support to the state police 'ensuring order and security' ('*sabiedriskās kārtības un drošības nodrošināšanā*') and in the case of Finland to 'work with other authorities to maintain law and order and security, prevent and stop terrorists and to secure society in general' to give but two examples.[45]

Moving on to unconventional methods. Not surprisingly, this is together with the cyber dimension, an area where there is a central role for the military. One typical example is the response to Ukraine in Lithuania, who formed a rapid response force in of roughly 2,500 soldiers in 2014 with the task to 'react to local armed incidents or border violations during peacetime, such as actions of irregular armed groups, illegal border crossing, violation of military transit procedures, etc'.[46] Denmark plans to do something similar, planning to establish a Light infantry battalion with up to about 500 troops (1 HQ Company and three standing companies) that can 'be deployed by air or ship and may be part of collective defence, some international operations or nationally, including in support of the police'.[47]

Special Operations Forces (SOF), themselves skilled in unconventional methods, play an important role in confronting unconventional methods in a hybrid context. For example, the Estonian Special Operations Force (ESTSOF) is seen as an essential component for Estonia's defence having the capability to conduct unconventional warfare and handling tasks such as 'special reconnaissance and surveillance, military support and direct action'.[48] In the hybrid context, it is also important to note that the military and SOFs often have a focus on learned lessons from Russia's previous behaviour. The Lithuanian SOF, drawing on lessons from Ukraine, has given special attention to 'the capabilities of the SOF to operate in hybrid scenarios'.[49]

Another actor to be mentioned in the context of unconventional methods is the military security services. For example, in Sweden, they 'follow-up and counters different types of threat; the most common threats being the work of foreign intelligence services, organised crime, subversion, sabotage and terrorism'.[50] Finally, it should here also be recognized that while already been included as part of the cyber dimension, cyberattacks are also a form of unconventional methods where the military plays a central role in the defence.

Responding to hybrid threats and hybrid warfare in the mind of the Swedish officer

How does the official discourse presented earlier fit with the actual thinking among the members of the military? To try to answer this question, structured interviews have been conducted with a total of eighty-two Swedish officers ranging from Captain (OF-2) to Colonel (OF-5) level. Of these, fifty-two were current participants in the Higher Joint Command and Staff Programme (part of either the 2018 or 2019 intake).[51] The question asked was 'How large role do you think the military SHOULD HAVE in meeting the following forms of means and instruments that in different ways may threaten and influence Sweden's security?', asking the respondent to choose on a 5-grade scale where 0 = no role, 1 = small role, 3 = certain role, 4 = large role, 5 = very large role. The same interview guide was used in all three rounds of interviews. The interview guide does not ask about the role of the military in the diplomatic sphere as this is clearly not the role of the military in Sweden.

The role of the military in the military dimension correlates with the findings on the Baltic Sea region as a whole; all respondents think there is a central role to be played by the military. A total of 99 per cent of the respondents thought the military should play a large or very large role against 'Military Intrusions', 'Military Intervention', 'Limited Attack', 'Invasion', and 'Attack by long-range weapons' (average of 99 per cent with the range between the types of measures being 97 and 100 per cent), with 84–100 per cent responding that there should be a very large role (avg. 86 per cent) (Figure 5.1).

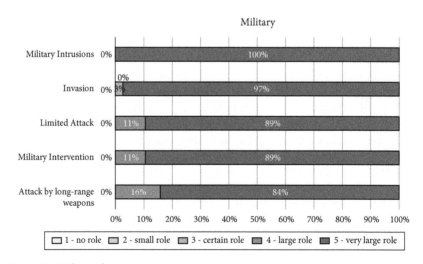

Figure 5.1 Military dimension.

On the other side of the spectrum, in the economic dimension, only one in five saw a large or very large role for the military in meeting 'Attacks by economic and psychological means against critical infrastructure' (Attack Eco + Psy Crit Infra). While 51 per cent did see a certain role for the military in this area, it is nevertheless clear that this area is not perceived as a core task but rather something that should be handled by civilian institutions. However, the certain role aspect leaves space for the military supporting civilian actors (Figure 5.2).

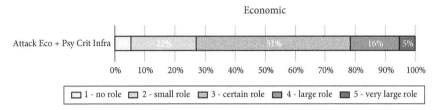

Figure 5.2 Economic dimension.

Moving on to the cyber and technological dimension. Here the perceived role of the military varies between 'Cyberactivism', 'Cyberattacks' and 'Electronic Warfare'. In the case of cyberactivism, about half the respondents think the military should play a large or very large role, with 42 per cent answering a large role. Only 8 per cent think there is a small or no role to be played. These findings are in line with the focus put on the cyber dimension as outlined earlier, with an increasingly large role being played by different parts of the military. In the case of cyberattacks and electronic warfare, the role of the military is higher. For cyberattacks, as many as 77 per cent of the officers do see the military role as central, with 32 per cent answering a very large role and 42 per cent a large role. For electronic warfare, the importance is even higher with 92 per cent thinking that the role should be central, with 54 per cent answering a very large role and 38 per cent a large role. Considering that two forms of hybrid measures are also a form of unconventional warfare, the large role might not come as a surprise (Figure 5.3).

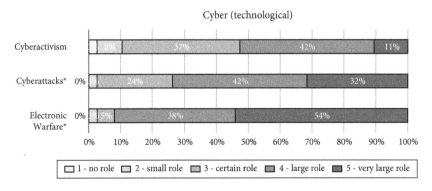

Figure 5.3 Cyber (technological) dimension.

In contrast, in the area of information and influence operations, the role is seen as more limited. While 58 per cent of the respondents see a certain role for the military in meeting 'Propaganda', only 16 per cent saw any larger role to be played. A somewhat larger proportion though there should be a role against 'Influence operations aimed at political and military decision-makers' (Influ Ops Pol+Mil), with four in ten thinking that the military should play a large or very large role. In conclusion, as with the case of cyber the more 'traditional' or 'harder' the threats are, the larger role the officers themselves think that the military should play. Overall, the findings with regard to Swedish officers are in line with the findings on the Baltic Sea region (Figure 5.4).

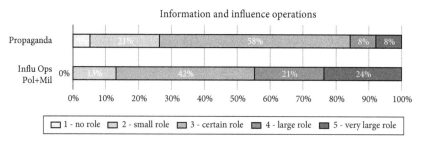

Figure 5.4 Information and influence operation dimension.

When it comes to 'non-military asymmetric warfare' (Non-military Asym Warfare), 'Subversive activities' and 'terror' no more than 5–11 per cent see a very large role and 25–34 per cent a large role. While the officers clearly see a certain role, in particular in the case of terror, it is not seen as a core task. This is not necessarily something that goes against the outspoken role given to the military, but rather a manifestation of an idea that supporting against non-military activities is something that one should do, as long as focus from the main military tasks is not diverted (Figure 5.5).

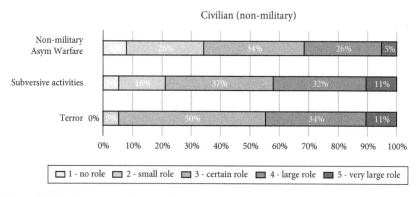

Figure 5.5 Civilian (non-military) dimension.

In the unconventional methods dimensions, which is a very important area in the context of HT&HW and the grey zone, it is clear in the interviews that there should be a central role for the military. About 90 per cent thought there should be a large role in the case of 'warfare through proxies' and cases of 'masked special forces', with roughly half of the respondents answering a very large role. A mere 3 per cent thought there should be a small role and none of the respondents thought there should be no role. Also in the case of cyberattacks and electronic warfare discussed earlier, more than half saw a large or very large role for the military (Figure 5.6).

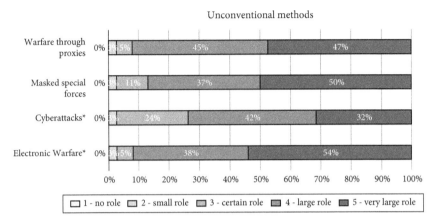

Figure 5.6 Unconventional methods dimension.

In conclusion, according to at least the Swedish officers themselves, there is a large role to be played by the military in the grey zone to respond to different HT&HW. The importance that should be given to the military varies between dimensions and different measures. There is a tendency to be a correlation between how 'hard' the type of threat or warfare is, but at the same time, there is not the understanding that it is only the military dimension that should be the responsibility of the military, nor that it is only in areas of hard security threats that the military should play a role. It can also be concluded that there is also a correlation between what the officers themselves think should be the role of the military and the findings from official documents from countries in the Baltic Sea region. While this might not be surprising, it should not be assumed. It is encouraging to see that the thinking among military officers about where the military fit in when countering HT&HW is corresponding to the official discourse about the same.

Conclusion

The question asked in this chapter was '*What is the role of the military – if any – to counter hybrid threats and -warfare?*' It can be concluded that there, without a doubt, there is a role to be played by the military. How large of a role varies between the different dimensions of HT&HW, the overall picture showed that the military have a crucial role to play in countering HT&HW and building a resilient society.

In the 'military' dimension, the role is obvious; defence against military threats is the core task of the military. In the case of the 'economic' dimension, the analysis shows that there is a certain role for the military though it is limited and can be expected to be played out mainly in the context of collaboration with, and support to, civilian institutions. In the case of the 'civil (non-military)' dimension, there is a shared understanding that the military should support against non-military hybrid measures as well as supporting its civilian counterparts when needed, at least as long as focus from the main military tasks is not jettisoned. In fact, official documents show an increasingly outspoken role for the military in supporting civilian authorities. This trend is also logical considering that HT&HW work across conflict dimensions and sectors targeting the weak points.

In the case of the 'cyber (technological)' and the 'unconventional methods' dimensions, it is found that the military does, and should, play a central role. In the case of cyber, it is clear from the official discourse as well as in the interviews that the military does and should continue to have a central role. Cyber is also an area where much work has been done and is done to facilitate the role of the military in relation to cyber defence and cybersecurity. The role of the military should also be understood in relation to cyberattacks and electronic warfare is a form of unconventional methods. For 'unconventional methods' the picture is similar. This is an area where there is a central role for the military according to official discourse as well as the interviews. This includes the security services which play a central role in the work against HT&HW. Their exact role varies between countries, as different countries both organize their military differently and have differences in how they divide responsibilities between military and civilian institutions.

In the 'information and influence operations' dimension, the role is more unclear, both in regard to what it is and what it should be. This is a broad category, and it is an area that is ultimately about the overall resilience of the society as a whole. Consequently, the role of the military is here embedded in joint efforts of military and civilian actors. Nevertheless, as this dimension is deeply integrated with the cyber dimension, there will, for sure, be a role to be played, if not directly, indirectly.

The way forward

There is evidently a need for a new way of thinking to be able to handle the battlefield of the future that does not recognize either a state peace or of war. This need is particularly true among Western democracies who are embedded in a traditional understanding of international law; in the hybrid era, international law no longer fits with the reality on the ground. Such a need is of course also what is to be expected. The whole idea behind using hybrid methods is to find and exploit your opponent's weaknesses, and the border between peace and war and the limitations and constraints of international law is arguably the Western democracies biggest 'weakness' (and strength?). It is clear from the analysis that there has been, and continues to be, a transformation in the way of thinking surrounding the role of the military. That the mindset is shifting is supported both in the analysis of the official discourse and of the thinking of the officers themselves. There is, of course, a variation between different countries both in regard to how much the thinking has changed, and exactly how it has changed, but the trend is clear.

When deciding on what the role of the military should be, there is a need to strike a balance. If there is too much of pragmatic adaptation to the existing situation, there is at the same time a risk of undermining the democratic principles on which Western democracy is built. Such a path also risks undermining the whole idea of a separation between peace and war, the principles of international law, and in continuation the liberal world order itself. Furthermore, while arguably not something to seek in the first place, neither would such a path necessarily be a recipe for success: the enemy will change and adapt to the new situation, exploiting new weaknesses that over time emerges. In short, warfare is a two-player game with an intelligent opponent. It is essential that the Western countries are flexible, but at the same time, there is a need to ensure to keep to democratic principles and the protection of the existing democratic system. This is the system the military set to defend and if there is no longer a system to defend the question is whether it could be labelled a victory success even if one wins the war. The aim must be to protect our system, not to undermine or destroy the system and become another actor with disregard for democratic principles, international law and the international system as a whole.

In conclusion, the role of the military needs to be recognized and utilized in the most efficient way possible across the grey zone while at the same time ensuring that democratic principles and the rule of law are upheld. It is encouraging to see that the role of the military in the grey zone is both recognized and in correlation in the official discourse and in the thinking of military officers. This is a good base to build the resilient society and national defence needed to counter HT&HW today and tomorrow. This said, there is today a discrepancy between where we are and where we should be. It should also be recognized that there is no set target for where to go, as the target is continuously changing as the use of, and protection against, HT&HW are a two-sided game. The target will change, and it will not change the way we would like. There will be a continuous process of adaptation and change, with all sides trying to out-think and out-smart each other. There is no end-state, only ongoing interactive process of adaptation and change, with multiple actors. There is also the dimension of trying to beat the other's cycle of identifying weaknesses, decisions and actions against them, an area where, unfortunately, the democratic system is inherently slow. To be successful, there is a need to include actors in all sectors in the best way possible, including the military. It is here crucial to learn from each other, across borders and sectors, both inside and outside the Baltic Sea region.

Notes

1   The author wants to acknowledge support from the S. Rajaratnam School of International Studies (RSIS) of Nanyang Technological University where the author was a visiting fellow in the autumn of 2020 hosted by Li Mingjiang. Support has also been received from Riksbankens Jubileumsfond (RJ) (Grant No. F16-1240:1).
2   For example, James J. Wirtz, 'Life in the "Gray Zone": Observations for Contemporary Strategists', *Defense & Security Analysis* 33, no. 2 (2017): 106–14; John Chambers, 'Countering Gray-Zone Hybrid Threats: An Analysis of Russia's "New Generation

Warfare" and Implications for the US Army' (Modern War Institute at West Point, 2016). https://apps.dtic.mil/dtic/tr/fulltext/u2/1020295.pdf; Martin Zapfe, '"Hybrid" Threats and NATO's Forward Presence', *Policy Perspectives* 4, no. 7 (2016). https:// doi.org/10.3929/ethz-a-010717736; Nicholas Barber, 'A Warning from the Crimea: Hybrid Warfare and the Challenge for the ADF', *Australian Defence Force Journal*, no. 198 (2015): 11–22; Fredrik Löjdquist, 'An Ambassador for Countering Hybrid Threats', RUSI. https://www.rusi.org/commentary/ambassador-countering-hybrid-threats; Lyle Morris et al., *Gaining Competitive Advantage in the Gray Zone: Response Options for Coercive Aggression Below the Threshold of Major War* (RAND Corporation, 2019). https://doi.org/10.7249/RR2942; David Carment and Dani Belo, *War's Future: The Risks and Rewards of GreyZone Conflict and Hybrid Warfare,* Policy Paper (Ottawa: Canadian Global Affairs Institute, 2018). https://d3n8a8pro7vhmx.cloudfront.net/cd fai/pages/4059/attachments/original/1539971167/Wars_Future_The_Risks_and_Re wards_of_Grey-Zone_Conflict_and_Hybrid_Warfare.pdf?1539971167; Michael J. Mazarr, *Mastering the Gray Zone: Understanding a Changing Era of Conflict,* SSI monograph (Carlisle Barracks: Strategic Studies Institute and U.S. Army War College Press, 2015).

3   NATO, 'NATO's Response to Hybrid Threats', 8 August 2019. https://www.nato.int/ cps/en/natohq/topics_156338.htm; European External Action Service, 'A Europe That Protects: Countering Hybrid Threats', 13 June 2018. https://eeas.europa.eu/topics/ economic-relations-connectivity-innovation/46393/europe-protects-countering-hybr id-threats_en.

4   Mark Galeotti, *Hybrid War or Gibridnaya Voina? Getting Russia's Non-Linear Military Challenge Right* (Prague: Mayak Intelligence, 2016), 7.

5   See e.g. Ministry of National Defence, 'White Paper Lithuanian Defence Policy' (Vilnius, 2017). https://kam.lt/download/59163/wp-2017-en-el.pdf; Heinrich Brauss, Kalev Stoicescu and Tony Lawrence, *Capability and Resolve: Deterrence, Security and Stability in the Baltic Region* (Tallinn: International Centre for Defence and Security, 2020); Republic of Latvia, 'The National Security Concept', 2016. https://ww w.mod.gov.lv/sites/mod/files/document/NDK_ENG_final.pdf; Ministry of National Defence, 'The Defence Concept of the Republic of Poland', 2017. https://www.gov.pl /attachment/fae62ff2-0471-46e1-95bd-c3c4208234a7, 23–6; Prime Ministers' Office, 'Government's Defence Report', Prime Minister's Office Publications, July 2017. https:/ /www.defmin.fi/files/3688/J07_2017_Governments_Defence_Report_Eng_PLM_160 217.pdf, 8–10; The Danish Government, 'Foreign and Security Policy Strategy: 2019-2020', 2018. https://um.dk/~/media/um/danish-site/documents/udenrigspolitik/ak tuelle%20emner/udenrigs%20og%20sikkerhedspolitik/2019-20/foreign%20and%20se curity%20policy%20strategy%202019-2020.pdf, 11–13.

6   Nupi, 'Multinational Capability Development Campaign 2015-18 (Countering Hybrid Warfare)', Nupi, accessed 17 March 2020. https://www.nupi.no/en/About-NUPI/P rojects-centres-and-programmes/Multinational-Capability-Development-Campaign -2015-18-Countering-Hybrid-Warfare.

7   For a discussion on terminology, see Chapter 1 in this volume. For a comprehensive discussion on hybrid warfare and its origins, see Ofer Friedman, *Russian 'Hybrid Warfare': Resurgence and Politicisation* (London: Hurst & Company, 2018). Other recommended readings includes Mikael Weissmann, 'Hybrid Warfare and Hybrid Threats Today and Tomorrow: Towards an Analytical Framework', *Journal on Baltic Security* 5, no. 1 (2019): 17–26; Sean Monaghan, 'Countering Hybrid Warfare: Conceptual Foundations and Implications for Defence Forces', *Multinational*

Capability Development Campaign (MCDC). https://assets.publishing.service.gov.uk/
government/uploads/system/uploads/attachment_data/file/840513/20190401-MCD
C_CHW_Information_note_-_Conceptual_Foundations.pdf;
Rod Thornton, *Asymmetric Warfare: Threat and Response in the Twenty-First Century*
(Cambridge: Polity, 2007); Peter R. Mansoor, 'Introduction: Hybrid Warfare in
History', in *Hybrid Warfare: Fighting Complex Opponents from the Ancient World to
the Present*, eds Williamson Murray and Peter R. Mansoor (Cambridge: Cambridge
University Press, 2012); Frank G. Hoffman, 'Hybrid Warfare and Challenges'
(National Defense University Washington DC Institute for National Strategic Studies,
2009); Frank G. Hoffman, 'Hybrid Threats: Reconceptualizing the Evolving Character
of Modern Conflict', *Strategic Forum* (Washington, DC: Institute for National Strategic
Studies, National Defense University, 2009).

8 Nato, 'NATO's Response to Hybrid Threats'.
9 Nato, 'NATO's Response to Hybrid Threats'.
10 Nato, 'NATO's Response to Hybrid Threats'.
11 Nato, 'NATO's Response to Hybrid Threats'.
12 One further differentiation between the labels hybrid threats and hybrid warfare
   that has emerged in the authors discussion with public officials is legalistically based,
   arguing that we should talk about hybrid threats as 'warfare' is something that may
   only take place at times of war.
13 The European Centre of Excellence for Countering Hybrid Threats, 'Hybrid Threats:
   Countering Hybrid Threats', *The European Centre of Excellence for Countering Hybrid
   Threats*, accessed 22 March 2019. https://www.hybridcoe.fi/hybrid-threats/. Their
   definition is being altered over time. The version used here originates from 22 March
   2019. At the time of writing (3 March 2020) the explicit listing of the 'wide range of
   means' has been deleted and 'the border between war and peace' has been replaces
   by 'the different interfaces (war-peace, internal-external, local-state, national-
   international, friend-enemy)'. For details see https://web.archive.org/web/*/https://
   www.hybridcoe.fi/hybrid-threats/.
14 The European Centre of Excellence for Countering Hybrid Threats, 'Hybrid CoE - the
   European Centre of Excellence for Countering Hybrid Threats', accessed 5 March
   2020. https://www.hybridcoe.fi/.
15 International Institute for Strategic Studies, *The Military Balance 2015* (Abingdon:
   Routledge for the International Institute for Strategic Studies (IISS), 2015), 5. In *The
   Military Balance* the definition originates in descriptions of Russia's hybrid warfare,
   but the definition itself has a general bearing and need not be limited to Russia but
   can be applied on other actors as well.
16 Hybrid warfare is a concept that is very close to asymmetric warfare. The two may look
   different, but in reality, they are very similar. Hybrid and asymmetric warfare are both
   about compensating for one's own military weakness compared to ones' opponent.
   Simply put, if you have a stronger opponent, you need to find other solutions than
   conventional warfare. However, often asymmetric warfare is used as a broader concept.
   This can for example be seen in how NATO and EU talks about hybrid threat/warfare
   as being 'asymmetrical'. Hybrid warfare is something that is more guided with a clear
   direction and targeted – as seen in the 'integrated campaign' part in the definition used
   in this chapter. Thus hybrid warfare is something that can be linked to an actor and its
   strategic goals, which need not be the case for asymmetric warfare.
   Irregular warfare should also be mentioned. It is similar to asymetrical and hybrid
   warfare, the key difference being that is built on the presence of a non-state actor –

normally in the form of insurgency or terrorist actor with the end goal in obtaining political power to achieve political-, social-, economic and/or religious change (David Jordan et al., *Understanding Modern Warfare* (Cambridge: Cambridge University Press, 2016), ch 13). However, as with the other concepts discussed here irregular warfare is often used as a catch-all phrase referring to a broad range of undefined warfare that is not conventional warfare.

17 Erik Reichborn-Kjennerud and Patrick Cullen, 'What Is Hybrid Warfare?', Norwegian Institute of International Affairs (NUPI), Policy Brief, January 2016. http://hdl.handle .net/11250/2380867, 1–2. Also see Frank G. Hoffman, 'Examining Complex Forms of Conflict: Gray Zone and Hybrid Challenges', *PRISM* 7, no. 4 (2018): esp 36–40; Hoffman, 'Hybrid Threats'; David E. Johnson, *Military Capabilities for Hybrid War: Insights from the Israel Defense Forces in Lebanon and Gaza* (Santa Monica: RAND, 2010); Frank G. Hoffman, *Conflict in the 21st Century: The Rise of Hybrid Wars* (Arlington: Potomac Institute for Policy Studies, 2007) for discussion.

18 Reichborn-Kjennerud and Cullen, 'What Is Hybrid Warfare?', 2.

19 Sean Monaghan, Patrick Cullen and Njord Wegge, *MCDC Countering Hybrid Warfare Project: Countering Hybrid Warfare* (MCDC, March 2019), https://assets.publishing .service.gov.uk/government/uploads/system/uploads/attachment_data/file/784299/co ncepts_mcdc_countering_hybrid_warfare.pdf; Cullen, Patrick; Reichborn-Kjennerud, Erik, 'MCDC Countering Hybrid Warfare Project: Understanding Hybrid Warfare' (MCDC, January 2017), https://assets.publishing.service.gov.uk/government/ uploads/system/uploads/attachment_data/file/647776/dar_mcdc_hybrid_warfare. pdf; Swedish Armed Forces, *Militärstrategisk Doktrin [Military Strategic Doctrine]: MSD 16* (Stockholm: Swedish Armed Forces (Försvarsmakten), 2016); High Representative of the Union for European Commission Foreign Affairs and Security Policy, 'Joint Framework on Countering Hybrid Threats: A European Union Response', European Commission, Brussels, 6 April 2016, JOIN(2016) 18 final. https://eur-lex.europa.eu/legal -content/EN/TXT/PDF/?uri=CELEX:52016JC0018&from=EN; The European Centre of Excellence for Countering Hybrid Threats, 'Hybrid threats: Countering Hybrid Threats' (Also see note 12.); Nato, 'NATO – Official Text: Joint Declaration by the President of the European Council, the President of the European Commission, and the Secretary General of the North Atlantic Treaty Organization, 08-Jul.-2016', https://www.nato.int /cps/en/natohq/official_texts_133163.htm; International Institute for Strategic Studies, *The Military Balance 2015*.

20 The MCDC framework separates between 'Instruments of power' which are the dimensions listed here and 'Target vulnerabilities', that is, what the hybrid actions are targeting at, which are political, military, economic, social, infrastructure and information. (Monaghan, Cullen and Wegge, *MCDC Countering Hybrid Warfare Project: Countering Hybrid Warfare*; Patrick Cullen and Erik Reichborn-Kjennerud, *MCDC Countering Hybrid Warfare Project* (MCDC, January 2017)). https://assets. publishing.service.gov.uk/government/uploads/system/uploads/attachment_data/file /647776/dar_mcdc_hybrid_warfare.pdf.

21 Galeotti, *Hybrid War or Gibridnaya Voina?*, 7

22 On the view of the countries in the Baltic Sea region, see note 5 above. It should be noted that the Russian perspective and narrative about history and what has happened since the end of the Cold War is different from the Western security narrative.

23 Timothy Thomas, 'The Evolution of Russian Military Thought: Integrating Hybrid, New-Generation, and New-Type Thinking', *The Journal of Slavic Military Studies* 29, no. 4 (2016): 554–75.

24 Thomas, 'The Evolution of Russian Military Thought', 570–3.

25 Thomas, 'The Evolution of Russian Military Thought', 570. In his article he outlined a template for NTW which is included as an appendix in Thomas article (p. 575).

26 Thomas, 'The Evolution of Russian Military Thought', 556.

27 Thomas, 'The Evolution of Russian Military Thought', 556.

28 Tchekinov and Bogdanov cited in Jānis Bērziņš, *Russia's New Generation Warfare in Ukraine: Implications for Latvian Defense Policy* (Riga: National Defence Academy of Latvia, Center for Security and Strategic Studies, 2014), 6.

29 Bērziņš, *Russia's New Generation Warfare In Ukraine*, 6 citing Tchekinov and Bogdanov. Bold in original.

30 Bērziņš, *Russia's New Generation Warfare In Ukraine*.

31 The doctrine outlines a wide range of different strategic measures and instruments that may threaten and influence Swedish security divided into six dimensions: diplomatic-, economic-, psychological-, political-, unconventional- and military means. Swedish Armed Forces, *Militärstrategisk Doktrin [Military Strategic Doctrine]: MSD 16*, 35.

32 See e.g. Ministry of Defence, 'Comprehensive National Defence in Latvia', accessed 27 February 2020. https://www.mod.gov.lv/sites/mod/files/document/Comprehensiv e%20National%20Defence%20in%20Latvia.docx; Government of Sweden, 'Sweden's Defence Policy 2016 to 2020', Government Offices of Sweden, 2 June 2015. https:// www.government.se/information-material/2015/06/swedens-defence-policy-2016 -to-2020/; Viljar Veebel and Illimar Ploom, 'Estonia's Comprehensive Approach to National Defence: Origins and Dilemmas', *Journal on Baltic Security* 4, no. 2 (2018): 10–22.

33 See e.g. Nato, 'BRUSSELS SUMMIT DECLARATION: Issued by the Heads of State and Government Participating in the Meeting of the North Atlantic Council in Brussels 11-12 July 2018', Press Release, 11 July 2018. https://www.nato.int/nato_static _fl2014/assets/pdf/pdf_2018_07/20180713_180711-summit-declaration-eng.pdf, §78; Jukka Savolainen, *Hybrid Threats and Vulnerabilities of Modern Critical Infrastructure: Weapons of Mass Disturbance (WMDi)?*, Working Paper, The European Centre of Excellence for Countering Hybrid Threats, November 2019. https://www.hybridcoe.fi/ wp-content/uploads/2019/11/NEW_Working-paper_WMDivers_2019_rgb.pdf.

34 Survey conducted with eighty-two Swedish officers, see section on 'Responding to Hybrid Threats and Warfare in the Mind of the Swedish Officer' for details.

35 Council of the European Union, 'EU Cyber Defence Policy Framework (2018 update)' 14413/18, Brussels, 2018. http://data.consilium.europa.eu/doc/document/ST-14413-2 018-INIT/en/pdf; Council of the European Union, 'OUTCOME OF THE COUNCIL MEETING: 3652nd Council meeting, Foreign Affairs (including Defence)', Brussels, 19 and 20 November 2018 14399/18 (Brussels, 2018). https://www.consilium.europa.e u/media/37952/st14399-en18.pdf.

36 'NATO Centres of Excellence are nationally or multi-nationally funded institutions accredited by NATO. They train and educate leaders and specialists from NATO member and partner countries, assist in doctrine development, identify lessons learned, improve interoperability and capabilities, and test and validate concepts through experimentation. They offer recognized expertise and experience that is of benefit to the Alliance and support the transformation of NATO, while avoiding the duplication of assets, resources and capabilities already present within the NATO command structure.' ('Centres of Excellence: NATO's ACT', accessed 27 February 2020. https://act.nato.int/centres-of-excellence.)

37 Ministry of National Defence, 'White Paper Lithuanian Defence Policy', 55.

38 Ministry of Defence, 'Defence Agreement 2018–2023', accessed 25 February 2020. https://fmn.dk/temaer/forsvarsforlig/Documents/danish-defence-agreement-2 018-2023-pdfa.pdf; Försvarsmakten, 'Cyberförsvar – Försvarsmakten'" accessed 27 February 2020. https://www.forsvarsmakten.se/sv/var-verksamhet/det-har-gor-forsvarsmakten/cyberforsvar/. Also see Government of Sweden, 'Sweden's Defence Policy 2016 to 2020', 5.

39 Ministry of Defence, 'Defence Agreement 2018–2023'.

40 Ministry of National Defence, 'The Defence Concept of the Republic of Poland', 46.

41 Estonian Defence Forces, 'Estonian Defence Forces', Estonian Defence Forces, accessed 24 February 2020. https://mil.ee/en/defence-forces/; Ministry of Defence, 'National Armed Forces Cyber Defence Unit (CDU) Concept', 2013. https://www.zs.mil.lv/sites/zs/files/document/cyberzs_April_2013_EN_final.pdf.

42 Ministry of National Defence, 'White Paper Lithuanian Defence Policy', 54.

43 See e.g Government of Sweden, 'Sweden's Defence Policy 2016 to 2020', 6; Ministry of Defence, 'Defence Agreement 2018–2023'; Estonian Defence Forces, 'Estonian Defence Forces'; National Armed Force, 'Galvenie Uzdevumi [Main Tasks]', accessed 28 February 2020. https://www.mil.lv/index.php/lv/par-mums/par-nbs/galvenie-uz devumi; 'Finnish Defence Forces as Part of the Society – the Finnish Defence Forces', accessed 26 February 2020. https://puolustusvoimat.fi/en/a-part-of-society; Minister of National Defence of the Republic of Lithuania, 'THE MILITARY STRATEGY OF THE REPUBLIC OF LITHUANIA', 17 March 2016. https://kam.lt/download/5 1934/lt%20military%20strategy%202016.pdf; Ministry of National Defence, 'White Paper Lithuanian Defence Policy', 47; German Ministry of Defence, 'Defence Policy Guidelines: Safeguarding National Interests – Assuming International Responsibility – Shaping Security Together', German Ministry of Defence, Berlin, 27 May 2011. https ://www.bmvg.de/resource/blob/16136/0c1b6d8d0c0e6ba0aed5f0feb0af81d8/g-03-11 0527-vpr-engl-data.pdf, 10–11.

44 Ministry of Defence, 'Defence Agreement 2018–2023'.

45 National Armed Force, 'Galvenie uzdevumi [Main tasks]'; Finnish Defence Forces, 'About Us', accessed 26 February 2020. https://puolustusvoimat.fi/en/about-us.

46 Ministry of National Defence, 'White Paper Lithuanian Defence Policy', 31.

47 Ministry of Defence, 'Defence Agreement 2018–2023'.

48 Estonian Defence Forces, 'Special Operations', Estonian Defence Forces, accessed 28 February 2020. https://mil.ee/en/landforces/special-operations/.

49 Ministry of National Defence, 'White Paper Lithuanian Defence Policy', 37.

50 Swedish A. Forces, 'The Intelligence and Security Service – Swedish Armed Forces', accessed 27 February 2020. https://www.forsvarsmakten.se/en/about/organisation/the -intelligence-and-security-service/.

51 Three rounds of interviews were conducted, one in October 2019 and two in February 2020. When controlling for variations between the three datasets, only minor variations were identified. What stands out is a somewhat lower score on the role in the case of 'cyberattack' and 'subversive activities' among the two datasets of army officers (Avg. of 3.74 and 2.72 vs 4.03 and 3.26) and a higher score on 'Subversive actions against Sweden in various areas such as electronically, space, land, and / or in the radio spectrum, including the use of special operations' (Avg. 4.85 vs 4.05). Nevertheless, while there is a substantial difference in the latter case there is still an agreement that there are clearly a role for the armed forces.

6

Understanding Russian thinking on *gibridnaya voyna*

Markus Göransson

Introduction

'Hybrid warfare' has become a staple term in Western military discourse and is used as a shorthand for warfare that combines conventional, unconventional and non-military means.[1] It was coined and elaborated by US researchers including Frank Hoffmann, Nathan Freier and Russel W. Glenn and is often applied to multidimensional challenges by non-Western actors to Western states and militaries. As intelligence scholar Damien Van Puyvelde has noted, it has often been assumed that modern adversaries of Western militaries resort to hybrid means to 'exploit all the dimensions of war to combat the Western superiority in conventional warfare.'[2]

Notwithstanding its Western pedigree, the term has helped to shape military discussions also outside of the West. In Russia, it has been picked up and used in discussions about the changing character of warfare in an age of global connectivity and an enduring nuclear threat. The Russian equivalent of the Western term, *gibridnaya voyna* ('hybrid war'), was first introduced into Russian discussions in the late 2000s after the term gained popularity in the West. Since then it has been used in Russian military scholarship and also (if somewhat reluctantly)[3] by senior Russian military figures such as Chief of the General Staff Valerii Gerasimov. It is generally employed to designate multidimensional warfare that comprises non-military and sometimes conventional military means.[4]

The Russian discussion of *gibridnaya voyna* is something of a carnival mirror image of the Western discussion of *hybrid warfare*. It is different from the latter but bears much that is familiar with it. It operates on an understanding of 'hybrid warfare' that focuses on the combination of military and non-military methods rather than on the reconciling of conventional and non-conventional military means. In a number of ways, Russian military researchers have repurposed the insights of Hoffmann, Freier and Glenn with a mind to security concerns that they believe are pressing for Russia. The primary one of these perceived concerns is the belief that the West is waging a subversive campaign against Russia. Russian researchers have contended that *gibridnaya voyna* is a pertinent concept for explaining the ways in which the West is seeking to undermine Russia.

This chapter provides a survey of recent discussions of *gibridnaya voyna* as they have unfolded in a selection of Russian military and security policy journals and books since 2014. The journals include *Voennaya mysl'* [Military Thought], *Vestnik akademii voyennykh nauk* [Herald of the Academy of Military Sciences] and *Problemy natsional'noi strategii* [Problems of National Strategy]. The books are I. M. Popov and M. M. Khamzatov's *Voyna budushchego. Kontseptual'nye osnovy i prakticheskie vyvody* [The War of the Future. Conceptual Foundations and Practical Conclusions] (2018) and A. I. Vladimirov's three-volume *Osnovy obshchey teorii voyny* [The Foundations of a General Theory of War] (2018). While this selection is by no means exhaustive, it offers a window into Russian academic discussions of *gibridnaya voyna*.

One of the central arguments that will be put forth in this chapter is that *gibridnaya voyna* serves a securitizing rather than an analytical function in Russian academic writing. As such, it should not be understood as a strictly academic endeavour, but one that labels as potential threats phenomena that were previously left out of military analysis and thereby broadens the palette of dangers that are seen to confront Russia. Social protests, NGOs, immigration, religious organizations and special forces are all viewed as potential components of hybrid warfare as waged by the West.[5] As Popov and Khamzatov put it with a note of exasperation, '[in Russia] the term *gibridnaya voyna* began to be understood as everything that did not fit into the notion of traditional armed struggle.'[6]

The Copenhagen school of security studies understands 'securitization' as the process whereby issues that were previously not associated with security are re-framed as matters of security. This is achieved through a securitizing act that is essentially linguistic. It involves (1) a securitizing agent that makes a claim for an issue to be treated as a matter of security; (2) the identification of an alleged threat; (3) the identification of an object that is being threatened; (4) and an audience that needs to be convinced to treat the issue as a threat. The Russian discourse of *gibridnaya voyna* expands the horizon of imagined threats to encompass a range of non-state and foreign actors that are viewed as potentially subversive of the referent object, which is identified variously as the Russian state, Russian sovereignty and even the consciousness of the Russian population.[7] The intended audiences of the *gibridnaya voyna* discourse include the Russian political and military establishments, who, in some publications, are offered recommendations for how to manage Western 'hybrid operations'.

Glaringly, the *gibridnaya voyna* discourse stands on only a limited empirical basis. As will be shown later, Russian researchers provide little empirical support for claims that Western states undertake subversive actions against Russia or indeed have the intention and capacity to coordinate such actions. A key assumption of much of the writing on *gibridnaya voyna* is that there is unity of intention and control in multidimensional operations. Yet this assumption remains largely unsupported in academic writing. It is striking that some of the most careful analyses of Western hybrid warfare are concerned with cases that involve not contemporary Russia but Libya, Yugoslavia and the Soviet Union. They tend to rely on frameworks that are informed by Western conceptualizations of hybrid warfare, not *gibridnaya voyna* in its Russian elaboration.

In this sense, *gibridnaya voyna* seems to be less an attempt to provide an empirically grounded analysis of Western action than an assertion, unscholarly in its scope and securitizing in its effects, that the West is waging multidimensional warfare against Russia. True, Russian analysis is shaped by earlier discourses and experiences, including the memory of Western non-military action against the Soviet Union during the Cold War. But today *gibridnaya voyna* appears to have given a new lease of life to the old Leninist notion of 'constant threats from abroad and within',[8] identifying a near-endless list of threats to Russian sovereignty, while it silently passes over issues of intentionality and capacity and treats empirical evidence with stepmotherly care. Its analytical vagueness may be one reason why the Russian military establishment has at times been reluctant to embrace the term *gibridnaya voyna*.[9] As Popov and Khamzatov have put it, 'The term *"gibridnaya voyna"* in the sense that is imputed to it today by various Russian authors . . . is much too abstract, purely publicistic, and not academic.'[10]

The first part of the chapter considers the origins of the *gibridnaya voyna* discourse and its overlaps with the Western hybrid warfare discourse. The second part of the chapter will discuss the conceptual variation and empirical limitations of *gibridnaya voyna*. The third and final part will explore the term's securitizing function.

The Russian discussion of *gibridnaya voyna*

There is only limited English-language work on *gibridnaya voyna*, but one key publication on the topic is Ofer Fridman's monograph about the term's intellectual pedigree, *Russian 'Hybrid Warfare' – Resurgence and 'Politicization'*. Fridman remarks that he embarked on writing the book after realizing that both Russian and Western military researchers speak about 'hybrid warfare' yet seem to understand the term in markedly different ways. He cites as examples Guillaume Lasconjarias and Jeffrey Larsen's *Nato's Response to Hybrid Threats* and Pavel Tsygankov's *'Gibridnye Voyny' v khaotiziruyushchemsya mire XII veka*, a Western and a Russian book, respectively. When reading these books, Fridman remarks, 'I was surprised to discover that the only mutual ground between them was their titles.'[11]

With this perceived conceptual divergence in mind, Fridman investigates the ways in which the concept of 'hybrid warfare' emerged and evolved in Russia and the West, concluding that the Russian and Western discourses are rooted in different theoretical traditions. He traces the antecedents of the Russian discourse to ideas about non-kinetic warfare put forth by Igor Panarin, Aleksandr Dugin and Evgeny Messner, three Russian thinkers whose writings gained prominence in Russia after the collapse of the Soviet Union (Messner's work was produced during the Cold War but was re-printed and circulated in Russia in the 1990s). In contrast, according to Fridman, the debt that Russian scholars owe to Western theorists, including Frank Hoffman, is much slighter: 'when analysing the works of Russian scholars, strategists and military thinkers, it quickly becomes clear that the only common ground between Hoffman's theory of hybrid warfare and *gibridnaya voyna* is the name.'[12]

Fridman contends that the concept of *gibridnaya voyna* is rooted in a peculiarly Russian understanding of war as a 'sociopolitical phenomenon', which it shares with

Messner's theory of subversion-war, Dugin's theory of net-centric war and Panarin's theory of information war. Both *gibridnaya voyna* and these theories, according to Fridman, understand the aim of non-military warfare as to 'break the spirit of the adversary's nation by a gradual erosion of its culture, values and self-esteem'.[13] It is an objective that can be achieved through political, informational and economic means, not only strictly military ones. Indeed, according to the Russian theorists, military means have become more dangerous in the shadow of the nuclear threat. Fearing nuclear annihilation, countries will seek to impose their will on other states not militarily, which would risk triggering an escalating series of mutual reprisals, but through non-military subversive measures. In other words, the objective of warfare is no longer to achieve military victory over other states but instead to corrupt and weaken adversaries from within, undermining their ability to resist through non-military measures. In Fridman's words, the proponents of *gibridnaya voyna* believe that

> the main purpose of this type of war is to avoid the traditional battlefield and destroy the adversary via a hybrid of ideological, informational, financial, political and economic methods that dismantle the fabric of society, leading to its internal collapse.[14]

There are obvious overlaps between *gibridnaya voyna* and Messner's, Dugin's and Panarin's theories. After all, they share a focus on non-military subversive warfare and an understanding that modern societies are vulnerable to such warfare. Nevertheless, there is little evidence that the theories have informed each other or that researchers of *gibridnaya voyna* actively draw on Messner's, Dugin's and Panarin's ideas. In fact, Fridman himself points out that Dugin's and Panarin's theories were 'conceptualised independently of each other, as well as from Messner's concept of subversion-war'[15] and that Messner's, Dugin's and Panarin's theories are 'independent, but similar theories'.[16] He also remarks that Messner's theory bears close resemblance to Mao Zedong's understanding of insurgency warfare and its stress on demoralizing the enemy, an understanding that is evidently not part of the Russian canon.[17]

Hence, it is problematic to conceive of Messner, Dugin, Panarin and *gibridnaya voyna* as constituting a distinct theoretical tradition in Russian military thought. After all, that states may seek to undermine adversaries by weakening them from within is no novel idea elaborated by Russian theorists. Rather, it may reflect a tendency, which is common in authoritarian states, to exaggerate the scope of internal and external threats. Certainly, the Soviet Union, long before Russian military scholars coined the term *gibridnaya voyna*, accused unregistered Islamic preachers, human rights advocates, unorthodox Communists and a range of other individuals of being supported or manipulated by foreign governments.[18] The Chinese Communist Party's Politburo, similarly, placed the blame for the pro-democracy Tiananmen Square demonstrations in June 1989 on a 'linkup of domestic and foreign counterrevolutionary forces'. One Chinese Politburo member, Vice President Wang Zhen, described them as the culmination of a decades-long American campaign to overthrow the Chinese Communist Party. In words that seem a conceptualization of *gibridnaya voyna* as good as any, Zhen said, 'they'd like to achieve their goal the easy way, by using "peaceful evolution": . . . buying people with money, cultural and ideological subversion, sending spies, stealing intelligence, producing rumors, stimulating turmoil, supporting our internal hostile forces, everything short of direct invasion.'[19]

It also seems erroneous to downplay the Western antecedents to Russian discussions of *gibridnaya voyna*. Numerous Russian scholars cite Western theorists of hybrid warfare even as they omit Messner, Dugin and Panarin. For example, Marina Kuchinskaia, a researcher at the Russian Institute of Strategic Research, who is well-versed in Western writings on hybrid warfare, has written a detailed overview of the Western discussions in '*Voennaya Mysl*'.[20] Another prolific Russian researcher on *gibridnaya voyna* is Aleksandr Bartosh at the Russian Academy of Military Sciences. He explicitly espouses a definition of *gibridnaya voyna* that is based not on Messner or Dugin but on a formulation articulated by the International Institute for Strategic Studies (IISS) in London. Bartosh deems that the ISSI's definition 'precisely expresses the key distinctions between hybrid wars and traditional conflicts'.[21] To be sure, both Kuchinskaia and Bartosh fail to fully operationalize in their research the Western theories that they cite. Nevertheless, their express engagement with these theories shows a theoretical overlap between the Russian and Western discourses.[22]

Interestingly, the influence of Western thinking on the Russian discourse is more visible in passages where Russian scholars discuss countries other than Russia. When Kuchinskaia considers the 2011 Western military intervention in Libya, for example, she talks of hybrid methods in strictly tactical and operational terms, much as is commonly done in the West. She concludes that hybrid methods used at the tactical and operational level by the Western coalition forces in Libya were key to the intervention's success:

The success of the [Libyan] operation was secured first and foremost through the use of armed detachments of the internal opposition coordinated with representatives of the special forces and special operations forces of the United Kingdom, France and the United States, and also through the use of informational-psychological action directed at the local population and the personnel of the government forces.[23]

This goes against Fridman's claim that a focus on 'tactical military and operational activities' is a hallmark of Western conceptualizations of hybrid warfare.[24] In fact, Kuchinskaia is not the only Russian researcher who focuses on the tactical and operational level when discussing *gibridnaya voyna*. Vladimir Kiselyov and Ivan Vorobyov, two retired officers-cum-military researchers, in an article published in *Voyennaya Mysl*', similarly stress the operational advantages that can be derived from deploying hybrid methods in warfare. In a discussion of Nazi Germany's aggression against the Soviet Union during the Second World War,[25] Kiselyov and Vorobyov comment that Nazi Germany attempted to 'blow up the U.S.S.R. from within' by raising '17 subversion and reconnaissance commands, 68 groups, the Brandenburg 800 special forces unit, Kurfürst regiment, and [the] Bergmann battalion' on Soviet territory prior to the invasion.[26] Undeniably, some of the Russian discussions of *gibridnaya voyna* involve references to and ideas imported from Western discussions of hybrid warfare, rendering questionable Fridman's claim that '[Western] hybrid warfare and *gibridnaya voyna* are two completely different things'.[27]

Importantly, however, such attentiveness to Western thinking is all but absent in instances when Kuchinskaia, Kiselyov and Vorobyov and other Russian researchers write about Russia. In those cases, they no longer home in on tactical and operational action but stress strategic covert non-military subversion allegedly conducted by the West against Russia. In her article 'Politika sderzhivaniia Rossii: "novaia norma" (a new normal) dlia NATO', (The Politics of Restraining Russia: 'a new normal' for NATO), Kuchinskaia writes that the United States and NATO are waging a hybrid war against Russia with the use of 'traditional diplomacy and special operations forces, financial bodies, economic sanctions, non-governmental organizations and global mass media'.[28] In other words, Kuchinskaia treats hybrid war against Russia as a different species of hybrid war from the hybrid operation that she described in Libya. This distinction is not made explicit in her text, which moves seamlessly between different conceptualizations of 'hybrid warfare'. Such conceptual ambiguity appears also in other articles and will be considered more closely in the following section.

Gibridnaya voyna as assertion

As in Western scholarship, in Russian research it remains an open question what hybrid warfare/*gibridnaya voyna* actually is. The Russian military theorist Aleksandr Vladimirov views it as a 'struggle over thoughts, morals and codices',[29] while Popov and Khamzatov describe hybrid conflicts as ones waged by 'irregular forces, mixed with regular forces, and characterized by the simultaneous deployment of irregular and regular strategies and tactics'.[30] In the latter example, Popov and Khamzatov use terms that are reminiscent of Western definitions of the concept. Meanwhile, Kuchinskaia believes that hybrid warfare does not need to involve military means,[31] while Bartosh sees hybrid warfare as the very 'integrator of military and non-military forms, means, methods and technologies, used in contemporary multi-dimensional conflicts'.[32] Even the distinction that Chekinov and Bogdanov make between New Generation Warfare and *gibridnaya voyna*, a distinction that Fridman considers to be seminal, is not observed by several other researchers. According to Fridman, New Generation Warfare can be understood as the use of non-military means to weaken the adversary ahead of an attack, while *gibridnaya voyna* is defined as a strategy that involves the employment of non-military measures to weaken and corrupt an adversary and can be implemented without the use of military means. This distinction, which Fridman names the 'main contribution of Chekinov and Bogdanov' to the *gibridnaya voyna* discourse, is brushed aside by Bartosh, Popov and Khamzatov, and Kiselyov and Vorobyov.

Such conceptual variation can be productive and indicates that a range of views on hybrid warfare exist in Russian scholarship. What is less productive is the fact that researchers often fail to substantiate their claims with evidence. This is the case particularly with that segment of the Russian scholarship that understands *gibridnaya voyna* in primarily non-military terms as a Western strategy to undermine Russia.

Kiselyov and Vorobyov's aforementioned article about Nazi Germany's attack on the Soviet Union, for example, contains numerous unqualified assertions about Western subversion against Russia, including that 'several former Soviet republics [. . .] joined NATO in what can really be called a flawless hybrid operation' and that efforts today 'continue to undermine the ethnic Russian people's unity and solidarity of the Slavic spirit today, this time in Ukraine'.[33] Bartosh, with similar confidence and dearth of evidence, asserts that the United States and NATO are supporting 'colour revolutions' and conducting 'hybrid wars' in the Middle East and eastern Europe as substitutes for military involvement.[34] No evidence is put forth to support either of these claims.

In Kiselyov and Vorobyov's piece, there is equally scant evidence to substantiate the assumption that the West possesses the capacity and intention to undertake multidimensional hybrid operations of a kind that would enable it to 'cut off a part of another country's territory by using a combination of coordinated political, diplomatic, information, propaganda, financial, economic, and military measures'.[35] The article provides a detailed overview of the capabilities of US special forces and special operations forces to conduct subversion in wartime but is much less specific in setting out the means whereby an adversary may expose 'the population and authorities where he wants to undertake unlawful operations to political brainwashing'.[36] Unofficial regional political parties, non-profit organizations, migration and private military companies (PMCs) are identified as channels through which foreign adversaries may impose their will on Russia,[37] yet there is no explanation of the mechanisms whereby foreign governments may direct the first three of these or evidence that they have previously done so. In the case of PMCs, such companies belong to the military realm, not to that of political and social subversion. This is true also for the thirty-six Ukrainian volunteer battalions that the article mistakenly refers to as PMCs. There is little discussion of the way in which PMCs may be used to subvert Russia in peacetime.[38] The result is a series of weakly substantiated claims that conjure up a spectre of Western hybrid warfare, identifying new security threats on the basis of limited evidence.

Other articles are similarly weak in evidence. Igor' Aleksandrovich Nikolaychuk, a researcher at the Russian Institute of Strategic Research, writes in *Problemy natsional'noi strategii* that 'even Western specialists say that interference in the internal affairs of foreign states for the purpose of realizing strategic objectives needs to take place in the context of defending national interests with minimal projection of military force'.[39] He supports this claim with a statement from William Courtney at the US-based RAND Corporation, yet if Courtney describes the challenges that the United States faces in responding to Russian actions in Ukraine, contrary to Nikolaychuk's claim he does not say anything about the need to interfere or intervene in other countries' internal affairs. Bartosh, too, leaves several questions unanswered when he writes about NATO's strategy for countering hybrid warfare as it was set out at the alliance's 2016 summit in Warsaw. Noting that NATO's strategy has a defensive slant, Bartosh suggests in a logical leap that the strategy should nevertheless be interpreted as aggressive given NATO's actions 'in the Balkans, the build-up of a military presence in Europe and the deployment of a strategic missile defence'.[40] No better is Bartosh' claim that Western 'politicians and military officials use [the Western conceptual model of hybrid warfare] in practice, first and foremost against Russia and in other places, where it is necessary',[41] an assertion unsupported with empirical evidence.

Such evidential gaps raise questions about *gibridnaya voyna*'s function as an explanatory and analytical tool. It imputes intentionality and coherence to actors and events, but is weakly theorized and largely unsupported empirically. Overall, Russian researchers of *gibridnaya voyna* fail to demonstrate that Western actors possess the capacity and intention to undertake the operations that are ascribed to them.[42] Moreover, several articles on *gibridnaya voyna* operate on dual and conflicting definitions of the term, deploying them opportunistically. As such, the term asserts more than it explains and should be treated with caution.

Gibridnaya voyna as a securitizing act

If *gibridnaya voyna* is of doubtful analytical value, it may serve a rhetorical purpose. It offers a paradigm that allows for the identification of an almost endless series of possible threats to Russia, attributing them to malevolent foreign action. Immigration, disease, NGOs, protesters, special forces and conventional military units are all understood as potential components of a palette of assets that foreign powers, most notably the US and NATO, may deploy in their drive to undermine Russia.[43] Issues that were previously understood in non-security terms are, within the *gibridnaya voyna* framework, elevated to the status of security threats that demand a coordinated state response. No clear definition of hybrid threats or explicit empirical standards for determining whether a hybrid threat is present is provided. As a result, a potentially vast spectrum of organizations, groups, individuals and phenomena can be construed as posing potential hybrid dangers to Russia. In doing so, *gibridnaya voyna* legitimizes an expansion of the reach and control of state bodies to address such dangers.

In this sense, *gibridnaya voyna* fulfils a securitizing function, encouraging state authorities to manage a broader range of phenomena as possible security threats. At times, Russian security and military researchers explicitly recommend to state power holders how to respond to hybrid threats. Aleksandr Bartosh, for example, describes a series of measures that the Russian authorities should take in order to counter the alleged Western hybrid threat. They include stepping up controls on immigration, fighting against corruption, increasing state economic control, undertaking continuous intelligence, bolstering Russia's military power and training personnel in managing hybrid threats.[44] Kiselyov and Vorobyov similarly stress the need to treat migration as a hybrid threat, calling for increased vigilance to 'prevent ill-intentioned individuals from entering' Russia and to 'forestall the spread of terrorist organizations'. They ask that domestic intelligence functions be enhanced while 'all authorities concerned are to keep a close eye on the way in which the situation, political situation, in the first place, is panning out and track it watchfully to detect signs of a brewing hybrid operation in time to frustrate it'.[45] Invoking *gibridnaya voyna*, Bartosh, Kiselyov and Vorobyov present phenomena as varied as economic decentralization, immigration, corruption and Russian military underinvestment as security threats.

One important aspect of the *gibridnaya voyna* discourse is its overlap with other security discourses that are or have been in vogue in Russia. In the 1990s, a central concern of Russian military discussions was whether Russia should prepare for conventional war with NATO or limited wars on its periphery of the kind that occurred in Chechnya, Tajikistan and the south Caucasus. Later, in the 2000s and early 2010s, there was an increased focus on so-called 'Colour Revolutions' in Serbia, Georgia, Ukraine and elsewhere, events for which Russia blamed the West. Conventional war, limited war and colour revolutions pose varied security issues, but scholars of *gibridnaya voyna* consider them within a single framework on the assumption that they represent different stages or aspects of hybrid warfare. Bartosh argues that efforts to subvert adversaries through 'discriminatory sanctions, information warfare . . . the activation of "fifth columns", terrorist actions' and other means are made to pave the way for colour revolutions.[46] In doing so, they may intensify international tensions to a point where these trigger a 'large regional conflict that risks transforming into a global one'.[47] Kuchinskaia similarly understands hybrid warfare as potentially escalatory, noting that the open use of arms belongs to the 'final stage' of hybrid operations.[48] She also writes that it 'is important to consider the possibility that hybrid war is transformed into a conventional one, and by extension into a war where weapons of mass destruction are used'.[49] Thereby, different types of phenomena are weaved into a common threat imaginary. Colour revolutions, limited wars and all-out conflagrations between Russia and NATO are all understood as possible manifestations of an underlying conflict between Russia and the West.

Conclusion

Hybrid warfare, which has become a buzzword in Western military discourse, has made its way into Russian military discussions. It has been imported from Anglo-Saxon theory, translated into Russian and slowly drawn the attention of the Russian military establishment. It purports to capture the essence of modern Western war craft, presenting contemporary war as a multidimensional enterprise that brings together military and non-military means. At times, Russian notions of *gibridnaya voyna* dovetail closely with Western ideas of hybrid warfare. Yet, at other times the Russian and the Western discussions appear to diverge considerably. An important current of thought in the Russian scholarship holds that the West is engaged in a largely non-military subversive campaign designed to effectuate regime change in Russia or reshape Russian national identity for the advancement of Western interests. Constrained by the threat of all-out nuclear war and global economic interdependence, the West, according to Russian theorists like Marina Kuchinskaia and Aleksandr Bartosh, are engaged in hybrid warfare as a low-risk method for undermining Russia.

If there is a long tradition in Russian military scholarship to reflect intellectually on changes in warfare, the *gibridnaya voyna* discourse should not be understood as primarily an academic endeavour. Rather, it seems an undertheorized and empirically weakly supported attempt to broaden the discussion about the threats that confront

Russia. Many of the claims about Western hybrid warfare against Russia rest on scant evidence, while Russian researchers have failed to demonstrate that Western actors possess several of the capabilities that they ascribe to them. There are also numerous examples of conceptual confusion in the Russian discussions, where Russian researchers employ *gibridnaya voyna* in multiple senses to designate as hybrid warfare several types of activity that have very little in common.

Rhetorically, the *gibridnaya voyna* discourse involves a series of securitizing moves that widens the range of issues that are identified as security threats, thereby legitimizing an expansion in the activities of state authorities. Non-governmental organizations, special forces, human rights activists, migrants and epidemics are all viewed as potential components of hybrid warfare. This is rooted in threat perceptions inherited from the Cold War, when Western subversion of Warsaw-Pact countries was rife and well-documented, as well as in a sense of vulnerability in the face of Western preponderance. Yet it is rhetorical more than analytical.

Notes

1 See Damien van Puyvelde, 'Hybrid War – Does It Even Exist?' *NATO Review*, 7 May 2015; Robert Johnson, 'Hybrid Warfare and Its Countermeasures: A Critique of the Literature', *Small Wars & Insurgencies* 29, no. 1 (2018): 141–3.
2 van Puyvelde, 'Hybrid War'.
3 Ofer Fridman, *Russian 'Hybrid Warfare': Resurgence and Politicization* (London: Hurst & Company, 2018), 96.
4 Valery V. Gerasimov, 'Organizatsiia oborony Rossiiskoy federatsii v usloviiakh primeneniia protivnikom "traditsionnykh" i "gibridnykh" metodov vedeniia voyny' [The organization of the defense of the Russian federation under conditions of the employment by the adversary of 'traditional' and 'hybrid' methods of waging war], *Vestnik akademii voyennykh nauk* 2, no. 55 (2016): 19–23. See also Valery. V. Gerasimov, 'Sovremennyie voyny i aktual'nye voprosy oborony strany' [Modern wars and current questions of the country's defense], *Vestnik akademii voyennykh nauk* 2, no. 59 (2017): 9–13.
5 Marina Evgen'evna Kuchinskaia, 'Politika sderzhivaniia Rossii: "novaia norma" [a new normal] dlia NATO', [The politics of deterrence of Russia: 'a new normal' for NATO], *Problemy natsional'noi strategii* 1, no. 40 (2017): 147–62; Aleksandr A. Bartosh, 'Strategy and Counterstrategy in a Hybrid War', *Military Thought* [English edition] 4, no. 27 (2018): 1–18; Aleksandr A. Bartosh, 'Hybrid Warfare: "Friction" and "Wear and Tear"', *Military Thought* [English edition] 1, no. 27 (2018): 1–10.
6 Igor M. Popov and Musa M. Khamzatov, *Voyna budushchego. Kontseptual'nye osnovy i prakticheskie vyvody* (Moscow: Kuchkovo Pole, 2018), 343.
7 Aleksandr A. Bartosh, 'Smysly gibridnoy voyny' [The meanings of hybrid war], *Vestnik akademii voennykh nauk* 59, no. 2 (2017): 165.
8 Stephen J. Blank and Richard Weitz, 'Russian Military Studies: A Call for Action', in *The Russian Military Today and Tomorrow: Essays in Memory of Mary Fitzgerald*, eds Stephen J. Blank and Richard Weitz (Carlisle: Strategic Studies Institute, 2010), 5.
9 Fridman, *Russian 'Hybrid* Warfare', 96.
10 Popov and Khamzatov, *Voyna budushchego*, 344.

11　Fridman, *Russian 'Hybrid Warfare'*, 1.

12　Fridman, *Russian 'Hybrid Warfare'*, 91.

13　Fridman, *Russian 'Hybrid Warfare'*, 92.

14　Fridman, *Russian 'Hybrid Warfare'*, 93.

15　Fridman, *Russian 'Hybrid Warfare'*, 73.

16　Fridman, *Russian 'Hybrid Warfare'*, 92.

17　Fridman, *Russian 'Hybrid Warfare'*, 66.

18　See Vojtech Mastny, *The Cold War and Soviet Insecurity* (Oxford: Oxford University Press, 1997); and Christian Davenport (ed.), *Paths to State Repression: Human Rights Violations and Contentious Politics* (Lanham: Rowman and Littlefield Publishers, 2000).

19　Quoted in Andrew Nathan, 'The New Tiananmen Papers', *Foreign Affairs*, July/August 2019. Available online: https://www.foreignaffairs.com/articles/china/2019-05-30/new-tiananmen-papers (Last accessed 27 June 2019).

20　Marina Evgen'evna Kuchinskaia, 'Fenomen gibridizatsii sovremennykh konfliktov: otechestvennyi i zapadny voenno-politicheskii diskurs', *Problemy natsional'noi strategii* 6, no. 51 (2018): 122–43.

21　The IISS defines hybrid warfare as the 'use of military and nonmilitary tools in an integrated campaign designed to achieve surprise, seize the initiative, and gain psychological as well as physical advantages utilizing diplomatic tools, sophisticated and rapid information, electronic and cyber operations, covert and occasionally overt military and intelligence action, and economic pressure'. See: Bartosh, '"Friction" and "Wear and Tear"', 2–3; Bartosh, 'Smysly gibridnoy voyny', 165–72. Another Russian researcher who explicitly bases himself on a Western definition of 'hybrid warfare' is Yuri Alekseevich Popkov who cites Frank Hoffman's definition of hybrid war as the 'best definition' of the phenomenon (Popkov, 'Tactical Reconnaissance in Hybrid Warfare', *Military Thought* 3, no. 26 (2017): 120.

22　See also: Vakhtang Shotovich Surguladze, '"Setevye", "gibridnye," "novye": sovremennye voyny i politika identichnosti v epokhu globalizatsii' ['Net', 'hybrid', 'new': Contemporary Wars and the Politics of Identity in the Era of Globalization], *Problemy natsional'noi strategii* 3, no. 36 (2016): 248; Igor' A. Nikolaychuk, 'O sushchnosti gibridnoy voyny v kontekste sovremennoy voenno-politicheskoi situatsii', *Problemy natsional'noy strategii* 3, no. 36 (2016): 85–104.

23　Kuchinskaia, 'Fenomen gibridizatsii', 135.

24　Fridman, *Russian 'Hybrid Warfare'*, 92.

25　Vladimir A. Kiselyov and Igor N. Vorobyov, 'Hybrid Operations: A New Type of Warfare', *Military Thought* [English edition] 2, no. 24 (2015): 29.

26　Kiselyov and Vorobyov, 'Hybrid Operations', 29.

27　Fridman, *Russian 'Hybrid Warfare'*, 95.

28　Kuchinskaia, 'Politika sderzhivaniia Rossii', 147–62.

29　Aleksandr Ivanovich Vladimirov, *Osnovy Obshchey Teorii Voyny. Chast' III. Gosudarstvo, Voyna i Armiia: Nekotorye Voprosy Teorii* (Moscow: Universitet Sinergia Izdatel'skiy Dom, 2018), 203.

30　Popov and Khamzatov, *Voyna budushchego*, 344.

31　Kuchinskaia, 'Fenomen gibridizatsii', 122.

32　Bartosh, 'Smysly gibridnoy voyny', 167.

33　Kiselyov and Vorobyov, 'Hybrid Operations', 30.

34　Aleksandr A. Bartosh, 'Kak zakladyvalis' osnovy strategii globalizatsii al'iansa 'Issledovanie o rasshirenii NATO' 20 let spust'ia', *Problemy natsional'noy strategii* 5, no. 32 (2015): 171, 179

35 Kiselyov and Vorobyov, 'Hybrid Operations', 28. Another article by Kiselyov includes outright conspiracy theories, including that 'gunmen from the Kosovo Liberation Army [during the Serbian-Kosovo war] forced Kosovo Albanians out of their homes, on pain of death, and drove them to the border, where Western journalists armed with cameras had already been assembled'. The source for this claim is an article in *Voenno-Promyshlenny Kur'er*. See Vladimir A. Kiselyov, 'What Kind of Warfare should the Russian Armed Forces Be Prepared For?' *Military Thought* 2, no. 26 (2017): 3.

36 Kiselyov and Vorobyov, 'Hybrid Operations', 33.

37 Kiselyov and Vorobyov, 'Hybrid Operations', 33–5.

38 Kiselyov and Vorobyov, 'Hybrid Operations', 33–4.

39 Nikolaychuk, 'O sushchnosti gibridnoy voyny', 87.

40 Bartosh, 'Smysly gibridnoy voyny', 166.

41 Bartosh, 'Smysly gibridnoy voyny', 166.

42 For an article that stresses the confusion, chaos and lack of control that hybrid warfare brings yet explains it as set in motion and managed by a rival actor, see Ivan S. Konyshev, 'Hybrid Warfare: Hygienic and Epidemiological Aspects, and the Role and Place of Information Technologies', *Military Thought* 4, no. 25 (2016): 113–22. See also Bartosh, 'Strategy and Counterstrategy', 5.

43 As Bartosh writes: 'Not all states unconditionally accept attempts to impose the dictatorship of the sole superpower on the whole world, which leads to a sharp intensification of interstate confrontation, the basis of which is made up of nonmilitary measures: political, economic, informational. The confrontation, encompassing many other aspects of the modern society's activity – diplomatic, scientific, sports, and cultural – has actually become total.' Bartosh, 'Strategy and Counterstrategy', 1–18.

44 Bartosh, '"Friction" and "Wear and Tear"', 9.

45 Kiselyov and Vorobyov, 'Hybrid Operations', 35.

46 Aleksandr A. Bartosh, 'Primenenie gibridnykh metodov v sovremennykh konfliktakh', *Problemy natsional'noi strategii* 6, no. 39 (2016): 160.

47 Bartosh, 'Primenenie gibridnykh metodov', 161.

48 Kuchinskaia, 'Fenomen gibridizatsii', 122.

49 Kuchinskaia, 'Fenomen gibridizatsii', 138.

7

China and its hybrid warfare spectrum

Lora Saalman

Introduction

While the Chinese term for 'hybrid warfare' (混合战争) is a derivation of English, its strategic utility against adversaries can be as traced as early as *The Art of War* (孙子兵法) of the fifth century BCE.[1] It was not until the late 1990s, however, that a book written by two Chinese generals entitled *Unrestricted Warfare* (超限战) became the bedrock of Western understanding of Chinese views on hybrid warfare.[2] Still, this narrow emphasis on a few Chinese texts misses the complexity of perspectives on and employment of hybrid warfare in China.[3]

To provide a more comprehensive overview, the author surveyed 192 Chinese-language writings on hybrid warfare.[4] This research on essays by experts from China's military, industrial and academic complexes reveals not only a multiplicity of definitions, but also a wide range of cases of application. Among these, Chinese strategists cite a variety of arenas in which hybrid warfare may be applied, including disruption through trade wars, information manipulation in cyberspace and military integration of advanced technologies.

This survey finds that Chinese writings on hybrid warfare are often so inclusive that it can be difficult to decipher what is effectively *not* factored into their strategic thinking. This chapter seeks to remedy this by evaluating Chinese views hybrid warfare along a spectrum of unrestricted warfare, information warfare, cyber warfare, intelligent warfare and kinetic warfare.[5] Recognizing overlap among these, the author seeks to offer a more nuanced analysis of how each term is applied in Chinese writings on the threat, response and operationalization of hybrid warfare.

To achieve this aim, this chapter begins with an overview of Chinese views on the origins and applications of hybrid warfare. It then examines each element of China's hybrid warfare spectrum to trace cross-domain shifts from soft to hard power. It concludes with an analysis of what this continuum means for political and military planners who seek to understand Chinese trends in the hybridization of warfare.

Origins and applications

While diverse in coverage, there are some points of convergence within Chinese-language texts on hybrid warfare. Central among these is that Chinese strategists place their emphasis on the role of the nation state. In other words, while non-state actors often play a vital role in the execution of hybrid warfare activities, more often than not the force behind them is a foreign power using a wide range of technical, financial and human resources to achieve a desired outcome.[6]

However, there is an important distinction with this Chinese focus on the nation state. It is largely externally directed. When China is alleged to be the country behind hybrid warfare activities, its official and non-official experts deflect such claims citing the difficulty of attribution and the potential of non-state actors and other nation states to have served as the perpetrators.[7] Nonetheless, when citing itself as the victim, the role of the nation state is key.

In tracing this evolution, the majority of Chinese writings cite the United States as the origin point of hybrid warfare during the 1980s and 1990s, through its military operations, colour revolutions,[8] regime change[9] and defence documents[10] impacting such countries as former Czechoslovakia,[11] Iraq,[12] Syria,[13] Iran,[14] Yemen,[15] Libya,[16] Afghanistan,[17] Kosovo,[18] Venezuela[19] and Georgia.[20] They note that it was not until it started to perceive itself as a victim of hybrid warfare, that the United States listed it as a threat in its National Defence Strategy in 2005.[21]

As for Russia, Chinese strategists cite 2013 as its turning point on hybrid warfare. This was the year when the Chief of General Staff of the Russian Armed Forces published an article on the blurring of the boundaries of warfare following large-scale, anti-government demonstrations in Moscow and St. Petersburg.[22] These Chinese writings point to Ukraine and Syria as just a few examples of how Russia has learned from its own victimization to turn hybrid warfare against the United States.[23] In other words, they contend that while Washington originated hybrid warfare, Moscow perfected it.[24]

While Chinese writings concentrate on the actions of other nation states, the ability to correct historical and territorial wrongs through greater adaptability, reaction speed, attack capability, survivability, jointness, flexibility and rapid response has a strong appeal in China.[25] Chinese analysts cite how China faces a range of similar concerns to Russia that include US encirclement and expansion, missile defence deployment, prompt global strike systems, among others.[26] In fact, Moscow's ability to overturn a stronger power's asymmetrical advantage fits perfectly into Beijing's threat environment.[27] This includes a range of challenges that China faces in Hong Kong, Taiwan, Xinjiang, Tibet, the East China Sea and the South China Sea.[28]

In confronting these security threats, Chinese strategists like Major General Tang Yongsheng refer to the Thucydides Trap in which Washington seeks to isolate Beijing on all fronts with a 'new cold war' (新冷战) and 'comprehensive game' (综合博弈) by exploiting their strategic entanglement.[29] In doing so, they detail US use of information penetration and control, economic sanctions and trade wars, support for internal unrest, external ideological pressure as well as destruction of China's strategic capabilities and development.[30]

To counter these trends, Chinese analysts stress the importance of strengthening domestic controls and foreign engagement.[31] While domestically this has contributed to such controversial measures as the social credit system and alleged reeducation camps in Xinjiang,[32] at the international level such pressures have compelled China to improve its relations with Japan, India, the Philippines, the European Union, among others to counteract US attempts to isolate it.[33] Nonetheless, Tokyo's and Canberra's concerns over Beijing's alleged 'grey zone' (灰色地带) activities[34] and influence over political systems[35] demonstrate that these stabilizing trends may have their limits.

Hybrid warfare and unrestricted warfare

As noted at the outset, Chinese concepts underpinning hybrid warfare can be traced back to the fifth century BCE in Sun Zi's *The Art of War*.[36] Strategists like Major General Li Bingyan continue to cite this ancient work to emphasize the butterfly effect of hybrid warfare, in which interdependence can be exploited.[37] Centuries later, General Qiao Liang's and General Wang Xiangshui's book *Unrestricted Warfare* contributed to this discourse by describing an increasingly multilayered technical, political, economic, regional, cultural, diplomatic and military threat surface.[38]

As with many Chinese strategic writings following the first Gulf War, *Unrestricted Warfare* expounds upon how adversaries no longer use 'armed force to compel the enemy to submit to one's will', but rather 'all means, including armed force or non-armed force, military and non-military, and lethal and non-lethal means to compel the enemy to accept one's interests'.[39] The concept of a continuous and comprehensive struggle driven by national core interests, on ground, sea, air, space, and cyberspace, as well as political, economic, cultural and civil society fits well into China's own strategic traditions of continuous revolution at home and abroad.

Yet, an unrelenting campaign also brings risks for Beijing. Chinese strategists have long attributed the United States with the omnipresence required to dominate all of the aforementioned arenas. Even with debates over the reliability of Washington's commitments and alliances overseas,[40] China's broader strategic community continues to lament the outsized strength and role of the United States,[41] arguing that Washington remains positioned to play a 'geopolitical game among great powers' (大国间地缘政治博弈) in which the boundaries of warfare are blurred.[42]

While suggesting hybrid warfare is a Western term, however, Chinese strategists have also shaped the concept into an umbrella for the staged evolution of warfare. Within this, they highlight shifts in four primary spheres: (1) from traditional land, sea and air to multidimensional fields that feature land, sea, air and space electromagnetics; (2) from tangible military geographic space to invisible and intangible networks and virtual space; (3) from country-based exchanges to a complex range of combatants, including regular forces, militia, militants, agents and hackers; and (4) from a narrow conception of combat to an all-inclusive one.[43]

In tracing this progression, Major General Wang Baofu of China's National Defense University argues that 'foreign wars' (外战) have transitioned to 'civil wars' (内战) with the goal of regime change.[44] External interference leads to empowerment, legitimization and arming of domestic organizations comprised of terrorists, extremists, separatists and civil society.[45] Major General Wang emphasizes how foreign-supported domestic rallies and protests provoke the state to respond, thereby opening the door to intervention of other countries in the name of protecting human rights.[46] Much of this explains Chinese narratives of US interference and malfeasance in Hong Kong, Xinjiang, East China Sea, South China Sea and even with the novel coronavirus (2019-nCoV, Covid-19).[47]

However, hybrid warfare is not simply about shaping or manipulating a population. Chinese analysts cite the integration of new combat methods into hybrid warfare with global integrated operations, air and space operations and precision operations.[48] These combine offensive and defensive activities that include conventional and irregular operations, counter-terrorist attacks, counter-armed riots, psychological operations, as well as electronic, information and cyber warfare.[49] In these analyses, the overwhelming Chinese focus remains the manipulation of domestic groups by foreign parties. This leads into the next segment of the spectrum, namely information warfare and cyber warfare.

Information warfare and cyber warfare

More often than not, Chinese analyses cite the centrality of information and cyber operations as part of hybrid warfare. While these terms are at times used interchangeably, there remains a difference. 'Information warfare' or 'informationized warfare' (信息战争、信息化战争) is narrower in scope and largely refers to combat in which information technology is used to obtain or suppress information.[50] By contrast, 'cyber warfare' or 'cyberized warfare' (网络战争、网络化战争) is a broad term that connotes various forms of warfare that are enhanced by information technology.[51] Wang Guifang of China's Academy of Military Sciences has emphasized that the US military places a priority on cyber warfare as a new type of hybrid warfare, strengthening its drills for future integrated cyber operations.[52]

Given US prioritization of the term 'cyber warfare', the concept has also begun to permeate Chinese strategic writings. In part, this stems from China's focus on alleged US and Israeli use of the Stuxnet worm and cyberattacks against Iranian nuclear facilities.[53] Operations as with Russia's alleged BlackEnergy and KillDisk cyberattacks that shut down Ukrainian power facilities also receive Chinese attention, even if less frequent than their coverage of Stuxnet.[54]

Facing the threat of cyberattacks crossing the boundary into kinetic damage, Chinese technical analysts from the Joint Operations College of China's National Defense University provide roadmaps to enhance modelling and simulation of battlefield conditions.[55] These analyses cite cyber means as part of hybrid warfare, emphasizing the importance of China leveraging its position as a major cyber power to improve its cyber capabilities and defences.

Among these, Zhu Xingping of the School of Defense Engineering of China's Army Engineering University advocates strengthening 'civil defence engineering' (人防工程)

to enhance support scaled response and combat of hybrid warfare operations.[56] Further, Xie Suming of China's National Defense Science and Technology Information Center discusses the role of backdoors, viruses and logic bombs in networks tied to intelligence, command and control, government affairs, transportation, energy networks, finance and the internet.[57]

In spite of this shift towards discussion of cyber warfare, there also remains a compelling interest in China in employing information warfare as a force multiplier.[58] This includes manipulation of social media to influence public opinion through information collection, propaganda and psychological tools.[59] In this arena, Zhu Xingping advocates information support forces for all elements of the standing armed forces, as well as state and non-state forces to stand in preparedness to combat colour revolutions, riots, terrorism and counterintelligence.[60]

Operationally, these support forces focus on border and maritime zones through strengthened strategic communications, psychological warfare operations and military-civilian cooperative operations.[61] China's efforts in developing quantum communications to encrypt sensitive information channels and integration of coast guard and naval forces in protecting maritime flows are just a few examples.[62] To facilitate these operations, media propaganda, communication networks, municipal security, civil society, social credit systems, as well as industrial and commercial networks are all to be protected and strengthened.[63]

Recognizing the importance of this information warfare arena, there are a series of Chinese activities that indicate implementation of these concepts not just defensively, but also offensively. These include China's alleged data theft and manipulation targeting the US Office of Personnel Management, Permanent Court of Arbitration at The Hague, and at least seventeen countries in Southeast Asia and South Asia with Advanced Persistent Threat 30 (APT 30).[64] Each of these cases points to China's core national interests and security.

More recently, there have been indications of Chinese information campaigns that both question the origin of Covid-19 and declare China's victory in taming the epidemic as a national and international milestone.[65] However, while successful domestically, the international response has varied. There have been counter-allegations that China seeks to leverage foreign distraction due to the pandemic to conduct more aggressive military actions at the border with India, flyovers of Taiwan, as well as naval and administrative operations in the East China Sea and South China Sea.[66]

As one of the countries impacted by such operations, Japan has developed both official and unofficial writings on grey zone activities that both implicitly and explicitly discuss China's role.[67] Yet, when discussing Japanese views, Chinese analyses on 'grey zone' (灰色地带) incidents demonstrate a marked lack of concern over Japan's response to, much less ability to conduct, such operations.[68] Instead, they argue that grey zone activities are less violent than hybrid warfare and do not rise to the level of those conducted by Russia and the United States.[69]

In essence, Chinese analyses dilute the definition of grey zone operations and dismiss the role of China, arguing that Japan has largely undertaken a 'passive response' (被动应对).[70] Within this narrative, they again shift the blame towards the United States and its use of regional proxies.[71] So while Chinese writings may acknowledge

Japanese concerns over China's advances in space, networking, electromagnetics, anti-access/area-denial (A2/AD), and power projection at sea, they still label Japan as a pawn of the United States.[72]

Thus, when discussing regional hybrid warfare contingencies, Chinese attention continues to focus on Washington. Analysts with the Joint Operations College of China's National Defense University in Beijing train their sights on US conduct of electromagnetic warfare via unmanned expeditionary manoeuvre warfare expendables to combat China's alleged A2/AD operations.[73] They also cite the use of intelligent technology, big data and information technology to design new weapons for subversive cyberspace operations, autonomous intelligent cyber-defence and cyberattacks.[74]

To keep up with these advances and to thwart them, Chinese technical experts emphasize the importance of integrating the high efficiency and low cost of autonomy in unmanned swarm operations for cyber warfare, electromagnetic warfare and even physical combat operations.[75] In other words, these writings move beyond the digital realm to the final part of the spectrum, namely intelligent warfare and kinetic warfare.

Intelligent warfare and kinetic warfare

As the future of hybrid warfare, Chinese analysts have increasingly placed a premium on 'intelligentized' (智能化) tools when combatting and conducting kinetic military operations. In other words, these writings indicate the hybridization of warfare through cross-domain warfare. Early on, discussions of hybrid warfare included dissection of Washington's dispersed targeting and long-range attack weapons systems used in full-depth simultaneous attack, such as the F-22 and Tomahawk cruise missile.[76] More recently, these analyses have focused on how best to counter increasingly artificial intelligence-enabled US air and naval long-range strike forces and forward deployment.[77]

As part of this discourse, Lin Zhiyuan from China's Academy of Military Sciences has sought to understand how the United States is integrating cutting-edge technologies, such as hypersonics, directed energy, space, cyber, advanced autonomous systems, artificial intelligence and biological systems, while enhancing its nuclear triad through modernizing its bomber fleet, developing the next generation of B-21 Raiders and fielding Columbia-class ballistic missile submarines to replace Ohio-class nuclear submarines.[78] Faced with this proliferation of technologies across multiple domains, Chinese strategists highlight the need to defend against conventional, nuclear and biochemical strikes that may be integrated into hybrid warfare of the future.[79]

Among defensive measures, Zhu Xingping from the School of Defense Engineering of the Army Engineering University advocates for the need to effectively counter explosions, network breaches, electromagnetic pulse and nuclear radiation, in part through the introduction of buffer zones around vulnerable information and physical resources.[80] Further, he prioritizes integration of better standards in security inspections, crowd control, ventilation, containment, decontamination, video surveillance, traffic control, power control, water supply systems, drainage systems and fire protection systems.[81]

Again, not all of these measures are defensive in nature.[82] Major General Tang Yongsheng, vice president of the National Security Institute of China's National Defense University, stresses the importance of 'asymmetric' (非对称) hybrid warfare operations, including unmanned systems, hypersonic vehicles and cyber weapons.[83] New hybrid warfare technologies are to be mixed on the battlefield to disrupt interoperability, as well as channels of information employed in command and control. This inclusion of multiple platforms and strategies speaks to larger questions of cross-domain operations and how they are evolving in terms of enhanced accuracy, speed and targeting.[84]

Moreover, a profusion of Chinese analyses on hybrid warfare cite how autonomous systems can assist in frontier warfare, space warfare, precision warfare, paralysis warfare, cluster warfare and cyber warfare. Xie Suming of China's National Defense Science and Technology Information Center notes that autonomous systems can be decisive in facilitating space-based destruction, attack and blockade to achieve the 'commanding heights of battlefield advantage' (夺取战场优势的制高点).[85] He highlights how unmanned intelligent equipment allows for more precise targeting, while enabling 'cloud clusters' (云团), 'swarms' (蜂群) and 'motherships' (母舰) to execute a large number of unmanned swarm attacks.[86]

Further, Chinese analysts with the Department of Vehicle Engineering and Performance Training Center of the Army Armored Forces College and the Joint Equipment Security Department of the United Service College of China's National Defense University examine the central role of unmanned combat aerial vehicles, as well as that of more generic unmanned systems.[87] For counterterrorism and other operations, these platforms are to be used in penetrating hiding areas and urban shelters. They also emphasize swarm and synchronization of command and control of such systems to integrate reconnaissance, targeting and strike capabilities.[88] In fact, these analysts laud the multiplier effect of these systems in enhancing real-time sensing, efficient command, precise strike, rapid manoeuvring, full-dimensional protection, comprehensive support, combined with intelligence.[89]

In integrating these platforms into specific operations, Chinese technical sources cite their utility in combat missions to maintain control and stability, while countering separatism and terrorism.[90] They also discuss the use of unmanned vehicles for reconnaissance and situational awareness, air and ground assault and strike, as well as high-speed information gathering and processing.[91] Thus, while there is discussion of human-machine teaming on target acquisition, there is also discussion of 'autonomous planning ability' (自主规划能力) that suggests greater inclusion of machine learning and autonomy.[92]

Interestingly, Chinese writings in some cases even highlight hypersonic vehicles and their utility in the shifting nature of hybrid warfare. One analyst from Beijing Techxcope Technology Consulting Co Ltd advocates for development of these weapons to be able to engage in the 'strategic game' (战略博弈) among great powers.[93] Pan Letian with Beijing Yuanwang Think Tank Technology Consulting Co., Ltd. further notes that the development of hypersonic technology will deepen integration between military and civilian spheres, through a new generation of space shuttles, reusable space vehicles, as well as hypersonic and aerospace aircraft.[94]

Concerns about blurring the boundaries of warfare still exist within China, even though it has espoused a strategy of 'military-civil fusion' (军民融合).[95] Nonetheless, these cautionary analyses remain trained on US use of unmanned and prompt platforms to intervene in domestic conflicts with impunity.[96] In effect, much like the unmanned platforms, cyberspace tools, and other technologies discussed in the context of hybrid warfare, hypersonic technologies are inherently dual use. As China expands its view of hybrid warfare, which is in effect the hybridization and mixing of tools for combat, there is an ever growing need to evaluate how it intends to employ any range of weapons from cyber warfare algorithms to its unmanned and hypersonic platforms.[97]

Conclusion

Overall, while Chinese analyses on hybrid warfare have historically tended towards abstraction, this survey uncovers signs of increasing granularity. Among these, Chen Hanghui of China's Army Command Academy provides specific foreign cases of hybrid warfare in Syria, Iraq, Yemen and Afghanistan with (1) utilization of interest groups, government and military forces, religious sect militia and tribal armed forces, separatist and terrorist organizations, (2) application of conventional operations, guerrilla warfare, maritime ambush and irregular operations, as well as (3) integration of political, economic and military measures.[98]

As a domestically oriented example, members of the People's Liberation Army in Beijing and Xinjiang – when dissecting Russian hybrid warfare – emphasize the importance of China expanding its advances in special force war fighting, information warfare, non-traditional military power as well as attack capabilities that enhance survivability, flexibility and 'rapid response' (快速反应).[99] Such analyses point not only to the soft elements of hybrid warfare, but also to a series of kinetic platforms that China has also been working to develop, including unmanned combat vehicles.[100]

In mediating between these softer and harder variants of hybrid warfare, Chinese strategic and technical writings tend to encompass nearly every aspect of modern warfare. This hybridization of what is in effect cross-domain warfare makes it difficult to fully understand how it is being applied. However, if hybrid warfare is evaluated along a spectrum and in relation to how other countries are employing it, this can facilitate comprehension of some of the strategic decisions being made by China.

This survey reveals that Chinese views on hybrid warfare are largely vested in the actions of the nation state. When victimized by actions that China deems to be hybrid warfare, Chinese interlocutors attribute these activities to a country, rather than to a non-state actor. Given the prevailing view in China that Washington is the origin point and purveyor of such acts, this means that the United States will be the target of Chinese blame and retaliation. This has already played out repeatedly as China confronts domestic protests, terrorist incidents, pandemics and tensions in Xinjiang, Tibet, Hong Kong, Taiwan, the East China Sea and the South China Sea.

When China becomes the subject of blame, however, the response is the exact opposite. In other words, the role of non-state actors and difficulties of attribution are highlighted. Therefore, it is instructive to observe how Chinese analyses dissect Russia's alleged successes with hybrid warfare in Ukraine and Syria.[101] Given the admiration of Chinese military strategists for Russia's ability to perfect and surpass the United States in hybrid warfare, it is not beyond reason that they may select a similar set of responses when faced with commonly held threats. Given China's strong foundation and aspirations in information, cyber and intelligent warfare, its ability to apply hybrid warfare in multiple domains is destined to expand.

Moreover, when evaluating Chinese responses along a spectrum, there is a move towards integrating kinetic platforms with varying levels of autonomy into strategizing about hybrid warfare. Thus, while information warfare and cyber warfare may continue to dominate, China's future rests with intelligent or AI-enabled warfare. Chinese inclusion of unmanned systems and even hypersonic vehicles into hybrid warfare strategic and technical writings indicates that the emphasis on disinformation is increasingly intertwined with cross-domain applications of hard power.

In sum, while unrestricted warfare, information warfare, and cyber warfare are likely to remain the core of Chinese discussions of hybrid warfare, Chinese military strategists are poised to undertake a future shift towards the intelligent warfare and kinetic warfare end of the continuum. This makes understanding China's hybrid warfare spectrum and its nuances of interpretation and application all the more crucial. Doing so will prepare political and military planners for anticipating how the future hybridization of warfare will evolve and how China will respond and employ it.

Notes

1 Zi Sun, *The Art of War* (Edinburgh: Black & White Classics, 2014).

2 Liang Qiao and Xiangsui Wang, *Unrestricted Warfare* (Beijing: PLA Literature and Arts Publishing House, February 1999). https://archive.org/stream/Unrestricted_ Warfare_Qiao_Liang_and_Wang_Xiangsui/Unrestricted_Warfare_Qiao_Liang_and _Wang_Xiangsui_djvu.txt.

3 Wang Xiangsui is Deputy Secretary-General of CITIC Reform and Development Research Foundation and a professor of Beijing University of Aeronautics and Astronautics. 王湘穗 [Xiangsui Wang], '混合战：前所未有的综合' ['Hybrid Warfare: Unprecedented Synthesis'], *PLA Daily* [解放军报], no. 7 (23 May 2019): 1.

4 This research included Chinese-language coverage of 'hybrid warfare' (混合战争), 'unrestricted warfare' (超限战), and 'grey zones' (灰色地带), which included related analysis on 'information warfare' (信息战), 'cyber warfare' (网络战), among other terms.

5 These come from excerpts from speeches given at the seminar 'Hybrid Warfare in International Political Trade' sponsored by CITIC's Reform and Development Research Foundation. 王湘穗 [Xiangsui Wang], '混合战争是当前国际政治博弈的重要工具' ['Hybrid Warfare Is an Important Tool in Current International Political Games'], 经济导刊 [*Economic Herald*], November 2018, 11–14.

6 Ma Jin is affiliated with the Department of Vehicle Engineering of the Army Armored Forces College and the Graduate Brigade of the United Service

College of China's National Defense University in Beijing. Shu Zhengping is affiliated with the Joint Equipment Security department of the United Service College of China's National Defense University. Zhang Fuxue is affiliated with the Performance Training Center of the Army Armored Forces College. 马瑾、舒正平、穆歌、张富雪 [Jin Ma, Zhengping Shu, Ge Mu and Fuxue Zhang], '混合战争条件下的无人系统作战能力分析' ['Analysis of Unmanned Systematic Combat Capability under Mixed War Conditions'], 第六届中国指挥控制大会论文集 (上册) [*Proceedings of the 6th China Command and Control Conference (Volume 1)*], 2016, 410–14.

7 廖丹子 [Danzi Liao], '"多元性"非传统安全威慑:网络安全挑战与治理' ['"Diversification" of Non-traditional Security Deterrence: Cyber Security Challenges and Governance'], 国际安全研究 [*International Security Studies*], no. 3 (March 2014): 31–4.

8 Huang Zhicheng is affiliated with Beijing Techxcope (possibly [*sic*] Techscope) Technology Consulting Co. Ltd. in Beijing. Ma Jianguang is a professor and director of the Center for International Studies and Li Youren is a postgraduate at China's National Defense University in Changsha. 黄志澄 [Zhicheng Huang], '高超声速武器及其对未来战争的影响' ['Hypersonic Weapons and Their Impact on Future Wars'], 战术导弹技术 [*Tactical Missile Technology*], no. 3 (2018): 1–7; 马建光, 李佑任 [Jianguang Ma and Youren Li], '"出兵-撤兵"与俄罗斯在叙利亚地缘政治目标的实现' ['"Sending Troops-Withdrawing Troops" and the Realization of Russia's Geopolitical Goals in Syria'], 国际安全研究 [*International Security Studies*], no. 3 (2018): 101–16; 李元斌, 何昊宸 [Yuanbin Li and Haochen He], '混合战争视角下的美国极限施压与"颜色革命"' ['U.S. Extreme Pressure and "Color Revolutions" from the Perspective of Hybrid Warfare'], 军事文献 [*Military Literature*], September 2019, 7–10.

9 李元斌, 何昊宸 [Yuanbin Li and Haochen He], '混合战争视角下的美国极限施压与"颜色革命"' ['U.S. Extreme Pressure and "Color Revolutions" from the Perspective of Hybrid Warfare'], 7–10.

10 US Department of Defense, *The National Defense Strategy of the United States of America*, March 2005, https://archive.defense.gov/news/Mar2005/d20050318nds1.pdf.

11 李元斌, 何昊宸 [Yuanbin Li and Haochen He], '混合战争视角下的美国极限施压与"颜色革命"' ['U.S. Extreme Pressure and "Color Revolutions" from the Perspective of Hybrid Warfare'], 7–10.

12 曹永胜 [Yongsheng Cao], '且看"战斗民族"如何打破遏制' ['A Look at How "Combatant Nations" Can Destroy Containment'], 解放军报 [*PLA Daily*], no. 7 (30 March 2017): 1–2.

13 蜜蜡 [La Mi], '从伊尔-20被击落看 "混合战争"' ['A Look at "Hybrid Warfare" from the Shooting Down of the IL-20'], 坦克装甲车辆·新军事 [*Tank and Armored Vehicles - New Military*], no. 11 (2018): 14–21.

14 坦克装甲车辆·新军事 [*Tank and Armored Vehicles -- New Military*], '"撕毁核协定"将激怒伊朗：美国与伊朗中东斗法' ['"Tearing-Up the Nuclear Agreement" Will Anger Iran: US and Iran Fight in the Middle East'], no. 11 (2017): 8–12.

15 陈航辉 [Hanghui Chen], '2017 战火, 摇摆着现代战争模样' ['2017 Flames of War, Swaying the Look of Modern Warfare'], 解放军报 [*PLA Daily*], 21 December 2017, 11.

16 曹永胜 [Yongsheng Cao], '且看"战斗民族"如何打破遏制' ['A Look at How "Combatant Nations" Can Destroy Containment'], 1–2.

17 Qin An is Director of the China Cyberspace Strategy Institute and Director of the Internet Policy and Legal Research Center of the Tianjin University Law School. 秦安 [An Qin], '万物互联时代的网络安全: 本质、态势与对策' ['Cybersecurity in the Internet of Everything Era: Essence, Situation and Countermeasures'], 领导科学论坛 [*The Forum of Leadership Science*], no. 12 (December 2018): 45–60.

18 Zhu Xingping is affiliated with the School of Defense Engineering of the Army Engineering University in Nanjing.朱星平 [Xingping Zhu], '混合战争背景下我国人防工程的使命' ['Mission of China's Civil Air Defense Engineering in the Context of Hybrid Warfare'], 国防科技 [*National Defense Technology*] 40, no. 1 (February 2019): 73–7.

19 李元斌, 何昊宸 [Yuanbin Li and Haochen He], '混合战争视角下的美国极限施压与"颜色革命"' ['U.S. Extreme Pressure and "Color Revolutions" from the Perspective of Hybrid Warfare'], 7–10.

20 朱星平 [Xingping Zhu], '混合战争背景下我国人防工程的使命' ['Mission of China's Civil Air Defense Engineering in the Context of Hybrid Warfare'], 73–7.

21 Chinese analyses argue that this stems in part from US counterterrorism operations in Iraq and Afghanistan that weakened the United States and showed that winning the battle does not equate with winning the overall war. US Department of Defense, *The National Defense Strategy of the United States of America*; 黄志澄 [Zhicheng Huang], '高超声速武器及其对未来战争的影响' ['Hypersonic Weapons and Their Impact on Future Wars'], 1–7; 高凯、赵林 [Kai Gao and Lin Zhao], '"混合战争" 俄罗斯新战略博弈手段' ['"Hybrid Warfare" Russia's New Strategic Game'], 军事文献 [*Military Literature*], July 2019, 10–13.

22 高凯、赵林 [Kai Gao and Lin Zhao], '"混合战争" 俄罗斯新战略博弈手段' ['"Hybrid Warfare" Russia's New Strategic Game'], 10–13; 李元斌, 何昊宸 [Li Yuanbin and He Haochen], '混合战争视角下的美国极限施压与"颜色革命"' ['U.S. Extreme Pressure and "Color Revolutions" from the Perspective of Hybrid Warfare'], 7–10.

23 Lora Saalman, 'Little Grey Men: China and the Ukraine Crisis', *Survival – Global Politics and Strategy* 58, no. 6 (December 2016). http://www.tandfonline.com/doi/abs/10.1080/00396338.2016.1257201?needAccess=true&journalCode=tsur20; Yang Yucai is a professor at the National Security Institute of China's National Defense University. 杨育才 [Yucai Yang], '"新面貌"改革以来俄军的建设与发展' ['Construction and Development of the Russian Army Since the "New Look" Reform'], 俄罗斯东欧中亚研究 [*Russian, East European and Central Asian Studies*], no. 5 (2017): 1–16; 曹永胜 [Yongsheng Cao], '且看 "战斗民族" 如何打破遏制' ['A Look at How "Combatant Nations" Can Destroy Containment'], 1–2.

24 段君泽 [Junze Duan], '俄式"混合战争"实践及其影响' ['Russian-style "Hybrid Warfare" Practice and Impact'], 现代国际关系 [*Modern International Relations*], no. 3 (2017): 31–6; 高凯、赵林 [Kai Gao and Lin Zhao], '"混合战争" 俄罗斯新战略博弈手段' ['"Hybrid Warfare" Russia's New Strategic Game'], 10–13.

25 Liu Jiwei is affiliated with the PLA Torugart Meeting Station of the Xinjiang Military Region in Kizilsu, Xinjiang. Zhang Chang is affiliated with Unit 31001 of the People's Liberation Army in Beijing. 刘纪未、张畅 [Jiwei Liu and Chang Zhang], '"混合战争"理论视阈下：俄罗斯军事战略调整探析' ['Analysis of Russian Military Strategy Adjustment from the Perspective of "Hybrid War" Theory'], 江南社会学院学报 [*Journal of Jinan Social University*] 21, no. 2 (June 2019): 47–52.

26 Major General Wang Baofu is a professor in the Department of Strategic Teaching and Research of China's National Defense University. 王宝付 [Baofu Wang],

'"混合战争": 战争演进的新形态' ['"Hybrid Warfare": A New Form of Warfare Evolution'], 光明日报 [*Guangming Daily*], no. 11 (6 April 2016): 1–3; 王晨阳 [Chenyang Wang], '超越地平线级驱逐舰: 欧盟军事一体化驶向何方' ['Beyond the Common New Generation Destroyer: Where EU Military Integration Is Heading'], 军事文献 [*Military Literature*], July 2018, 53–6; *Agence France Presse*, 'Nato to Formally Recognize China "Challenges" for First Time', In *South China Morning Post*, 4 December 2019. https://www.scmp.com/news/china/article/3040457/nato-formally -recognise-china-challenges-first-time.

27 王宝付 [Baofu Wang], '"混合战争": 战争演进的新形态' ['"Hybrid Warfare": A New Form of Warfare Evolution'].

28 马瑾、舒正平、穆歌、张富雪 [Jin Ma, Zhengping Shu, Ge Mu and Fuxue Zhang], '混合战争条件下的无人系统作战能力分析' ['Analysis of Unmanned Systematic Combat Capability under Mixed War Conditions'], 410–14; 蜜蜡 [La Mi], '从伊尔-20被击落看 "混合战争"' ['A Look at "Hybrid Warfare" from the Shooting Down of the IL-20'], 14–21; 王宝付 [Baofu Wang], '"混合战争": 战争演进的新形态' ['"Hybrid Warfare": A New Form of Warfare Evolution'], 1–3; 刘纪未、张畅 [Jiwei Liu and Chang Zhang], '"混合战争"理论视阈下: 俄罗斯军事战略调整探析' ['Analysis of Russian Military Strategy Adjustment from the Perspective of "Hybrid War" Theory'], 47–52; 政治与国际关系学院 [Politics and International Relations Institute], '第七届国际安全研究论坛暨"百年国际关系学与安全问题研究"学术研讨会在兰州大学召开' ['The 7th International Security Research Forum "A Century of International Relations and Security Studies" Academic Seminar Held at Lanzhou University'], 兰州大学 [Lanzhou University], 18 August 2019. http://news .lzu.edu.cn/c/201908/59068.html.

29 Major General Tang Yongsheng is the vice president of the National Security Institute of China's National Defense University. 唐永胜 [Yongsheng Tang], '以我为主，牵引中美战略竞争发展方向' ['Me First, Driving the Development of China-U.S. Strategic Competition'], 世界观察 [*World Affairs*], November 2019, 13–15.

30 This is part of the China National Social Science Foundation's core project 'Transition of the International System and China's Strategic Choices'. Shen Zhixiong is an associate professor, and Li Wei is a PhD Candidate in the National Security Institute of China's National University of Defense. 唐永胜、李薇、沈志雄 [Yongsheng Tang, Wei Li and Zhixiong Shen], '因势利导: 把握中美竞争的战略主动权' ['Take Advantage of the Situation: Grasping the Strategic Initiative in China-U.S. Competition'], 国际观察 [*International Review*], no. 3 (March 2019): 22–40.

31 唐永胜、李薇、沈志雄 [Yongsheng Tang, Wei Li and Zhixiong Shen], '因势利导: 把握中美竞争的战略主动权' ['Take Advantage of the Situation: Grasping the Strategic Initiative in China-U.S. Competition'], 22–40; 唐永胜 [Yongsheng Tang], '以我为主，牵引中美战略竞争发展方向' ['Me First, Driving the Development of China-U.S. Strategic Competition'], 13–15.

32 Nicole Kobie, 'The Complicated Truth about China's Social Credit System', *Wired*, 7 June 2019. https://www.wired.co.uk/article/china-social-credit-system-e xplained; John Sudworth, 'Searching for Truth in China's Uighur "Re-education" Camps', *BBC News*, 21 June 2019. https://www.bbc.com/news/blogs-china-blog-487 00786.

33 唐永胜、李薇、沈志雄 [Yongsheng Tang, Wei Li and Zhixiong Shen], '因势利导: 把握中美竞争的战略主动权' ['Take Advantage of the Situation: Grasping the Strategic Initiative in China-U.S. Competition'], 22–40.

34 Japan's Ministry of Defense, *National Defense Program Guidelines for FY 2019 and Beyond*, via Cabinet Secretariat, 18 December 2018. http://www.cas.go.jp/jp/siryou/pdf/2019boueikeikaku_e.pdf; Scott W. Harold, Yoshiaki Nakagawa, Junichi Fukuda, John A. Davis, Keiko Kono, Dean Cheng and Kazuto Suzuki, *The U.S.-Japan Alliance and Deterring Gray Zone Coercion in the Maritime, Cyber, and Space Domains* (RAND, 2017). https://www.rand.org/content/dam/rand/pubs/conf_proceedings/CF300/CF379/RAND_CF379.pdf.

35 John Kehoe, 'The Division in Canberra over China', *Financial Review*, 2 December 2019. https://www.afr.com/policy/foreign-affairs/china-power-struggle-in-canberra-20191128-p53f27; Clive Hamilton, 'Australia's Fight Against Chinese Political Interference: What Its New Laws Will Do', *Foreign Affairs*, 26 July 2018. https://www.foreignaffairs.com/articles/australia/2018-07-26/australias-fight-against-chinese-political-interference.

36 Sun, *The Art of War*.

37 Major General Li Bingyan is a senior editor of the *PLA Daily*. 李炳彦 [Bingyan Li], '"智战时代"与东方兵学智慧' ['"Intelligent Warfare Era" and Eastern Military Science Wisdom'], 孙子研究 [*Sun Zi Studies*] 16, no. 4 (April 2017): 81–3; 黄志澄 [Zhicheng Huang], '高超声速武器及其对未来战争的影响' ['Hypersonic Weapons and Their Impact on Future Wars'], 1–7.

38 Qiao and Wang, *Unrestricted Warfare*.

39 Qiao and Wang, *Unrestricted Warfare*

40 Hal Brands, Peter D. Feaver, John J. Mearshimer and Stephen M. Walt, 'Should America Retrench? The Battle Over Offshore Balancing', *Foreign Affairs*, November/December 2016. https://www.foreignaffairs.com/articles/should-america-retrench; Paul K. MacDonald and Joseph M. Parent, 'Trump Didn't Shrink U.S. Military Commitments Abroad—He Expanded Them: The President's False Promise of Retrenchment', *Foreign Affairs*, 3 December 2019. https://www.foreignaffairs.com/articles/2019-12-03/trump-didnt-shrink-us-military-commitments-abroad-he-expanded-them.

41 Based on author's observations at the PLA's Xiangshan Forum in 2018 and 2019. EastWest Institute, 'Dr. Saalman Speaks at 8th Beijing Xiangshan Forum in Beijing', 6 November 2018. https://www.eastwest.ngo/idea/dr-saalman-speaks-%C2%A08th-beijing-xiangshan-forum-beijing; EastWest Institute, 'Dr. Saalman Speaks at 9th Beijing Xiangshan Forum in Beijing', 25 November 2019. https://www.eastwest.ngo/idea/dr-saalman-speaks-9th-beijing-xiangshan-forum-beijing.

42 高凯、赵林 [Kai Gao and Lin Zhao], '"混合战争" 俄罗斯新战略博弈手段' ['"Hybrid Warfare" Russia's New Strategic Game'], 10–13.

43 Hu Xin is affiliated with the Institute of Strategy and Security of the School of International Relations in China's National University of Defense Technology. 胡欣 [Hu, Xin], '"混合战争"终结混乱的方程式?' ['"Hybrid Warfare" The Formula to End Chaos?'], 世界知识 [*World Affairs*], 2 April 2018, 74.

44 王宝付 [Baofu Wang], '"混合战争": 战争演进的新形态' ['"Hybrid Warfare": A New Form of Warfare Evolution'], 1–3.

45 王宝付 [Baofu Wang], '"混合战争": 战争演进的新形态' ['"Hybrid Warfare": A New Form of Warfare Evolution'], 1–3.

46 王宝付 [Baofu Wang], '"混合战争": 战争演进的新形态' ['"Hybrid Warfare": A New Form of Warfare Evolution'], 1–3.

47 Steve Holland, 'In Phone Call with Trump, China's Xi says U.S. Interfering in Internal Affairs', *Reuters*, 20 December 2020. https://www.reuters.com/article/us-

usa-china/in-phone-call-with-trump-chinas-xi-says-u-s-interfering-in-internal-af
fairs-idUSKBN1YO1UN; Melissa Quinn, 'Chinese Ambassador to U.S. Dismisses
Coronavirus Theories as "Absolutely Crazy"', Face the Nation, CBS News, 9 February
2020. https://www.cbsnews.com/news/coronavirus-news-chinese-ambassador-cui
-tiankai-dismisses-coronavirus-theories-as-absolutely-crazy.; Renée DiResta, 'For
China, the "USA Virus" Is a Geopolitical Ploy', *The Atlantic*, 13 May 2020. https://
www.theatlantic.com/ideas/archive/2020/04/chinas-covid-19-conspiracy-theories
/609772; '关于疫情，这10个问题请美国政府回答' ['On the Epidemic, Please US
Government Answer These 10 Questions'], 中国日报网 [*China Daily Online*], 1 May
2020. https://cn.chinadaily.com.cn/a/202005/01/WS5eabc0c8a310eec9c72b6a44
.html. Some of these domestic rumours on 2019-nCoV or Covid-19 in China may
also correlate with an alleged information campaign coming out of Russia. Arthur
Villasanta, 'Coronavirus Update: Russia Blames USA For NCov 2019 Outbreak',
International Business Times, 5 February 2020. https://www.ibtimes.com/coronavirus
-update-russia-blames-usa-ncov-2019-outbreak-2916034.

48 Zhao Shilun is affiliated with the University of International Relations. 赵时轮
[Shilun Zhao], '无人机危害及恐怖行为反制对策研究' ['Countermeasure Research
Against Unmanned Vehicle Harm and Terrorist Acts'], 中国军转民 [*China Military
to Civilian*], Issue Unavailable, Date Unavailable, 15–20.

49 马瑾、舒正平、穆歌、张富雪 [Jin Ma, Zhengping Shu, Ge Mu and Fuxue Zhang],
'混合战争条件下的无人系统作战能力分析' ['Analysis of Unmanned Systematic
Combat Capability under Mixed War Conditions'], 410–14.

50 Qiao and Wang, *Unrestricted Warfare*.

51 Qiao and Wang, *Unrestricted Warfare*.

52 Wang Guifang is affiliated with the War Theory and Strategic Studies
department of China's Academy of Military Sciences. 王桂芳 [Guifang Wang],
'大国网络竞争与中国网络安全战略选择' ['Great Power Cyber Competition and
China's Cyber Security Strategic Choice'], 国际安全研究 [*International Security
Studies*] 35, no. 2 (March/April 2017): 27–46.

53 秦安 [An Qin], '"震网"升级版袭击伊朗，网络毁瘫离我们有多远' ['An Upgraded
Version of "Stuxnet" Hits Iran, How Far Away Is Destruction from Us'], 网路空
间安全 [*Cyberspace Security*] 09, no. 11 (November 2018): 41–3; 秦安 [An Qin],
'万物互联时代的网络安全: 本质、态势与对策' ['Cybersecurity in the Internet of
Everything Era: Essence, Situation and Countermeasures'], 45–60.

54 秦安 [An Qin], '"震网"升级版袭击伊朗，网络毁瘫离我们有多远' ['An Upgraded
Version of "Stuxnet" Hits Iran, How Far Away Is Destruction from Us'], 41–3.

55 Si Guangya, Zhang Yang, and Wang Yanzheng are affiliated with the Joint Operations
College of China's National Defense University in Beijing. 司光亚、张阳、王艳正
[Guangya Si, Yang Zhang and Yanzheng Wang], '网电空间作战建模仿真研究综述'
['Review on Modeling and Simulation in Cyberspace Operations'], 系统仿真学报
[*Journal of System Simulation*] 30, no. 2 (February 2018): 386–97.

56 朱星平 [Xingping Zhu], '混合战争背景下我国人防工程的使命' ['Mission of
China's Civil Air Defense Engineering in the Context of Hybrid Warfare'],
73–7.

57 Xie Suming is affiliated with China's National Defense Science
and Technology Information Center. 谢苏明 [Suming Xie],
'无人化智能化装备技术发展及其影响分析' ['Analysis on the Development of
Unmanned Intelligent Arms Technology and Its Impact'], 现代军事 [*Modern
Military*], no. 3 (March 2017): 51–6.

58 张瑷敏 [Aimin Zhang], '新媒体 "冷战" 渐成 "热战"' ['New Media "Cold War" Is Becoming a "Hot War"'], 军事文献 [*Military Literature*], no. 6 (June 2019): 49–53.

59 张瑷敏 [Aimin Zhang], '新媒体 "冷战" 渐成 "热战"' ['New Media "Cold War" Is Becoming a "Hot War"'], 49–53.

60 朱星平 [Xingping Zhu], '混合战争背景下我国人防工程的使命' ['Mission of China's Civil Air Defense Engineering in the Context of Hybrid Warfare'], 73–7.

61 朱星平 [Xingping Zhu], '混合战争背景下我国人防工程的使命' ['Mission of China's Civil Air Defense Engineering in the Context of Hybrid Warfare'], 73–7.

62 Rafi Letzter, 'China's Quantum-Key Network, the Largest Ever, Is Officially Online', *Live Science*, 19 January 2018. https://www.livescience.com/61474-micius-china-quantum-key-intercontinental.html.

63 朱星平 [Xingping Zhu], '混合战争背景下我国人防工程的使命' ['Mission of China's Civil Air Defense Engineering in the Context of Hybrid Warfare'], 73–7.

64 Saalman, 'Little Grey Men: China and the Ukraine Crisis'; 王聪悦 [Congyue Wang], '特朗普时期美欧网络安全合作的承袭、变局与思考' ['U.S.-European Cyber Security Cooperation Pledges, Changes, and Thinking during the Trump Era'], 国外理论动态 [*Foreign Theoretical Trends*], no. 7 (July 2019): 106–16; FireEye Labs, 'Threat Research: APT 30 and the Mechanics of a Long-Running Cyber Espionage Operation', 12 April 2015, https://www.fireeye.com/blog/threat-research/2015/04/apt_30_and_the_mecha.html.

65 新华社 [*Xinhua News Agency*], '美国关于新冠肺炎疫情的涉华谎言与事实真相' ['U.S. Lies and Truths About the Novel Coronavirus Epidemic'], 9 May 2020. http://www.xinhuanet.com/2020-05/09/c_1125963436.htm; 券商中国 [*Brokerage China*], 'Has the Source of the Virus Been Found? Cambridge Experts Draw a Genetic Map: The World's Three Major Variants' ['病毒源头找到了? 剑桥专家绘出基因图谱: 全球三大变种'], 证券时报网 [*SCTN*], 11 April 2020. http://news.stcn.com/2020/0411/15831620.shtml; 中国日报 [*China Daily*], '"抗击新冠肺炎疫情的中国实践"报告全文' ['The Full Text of the Report "China's Practice in Fighting the Novel Coronavirus Epidemic"'], 21 April 2020. https://cn.chinadaily.com.cn/a/202004/21/WS5e9e45afa310c00b73c786ed.html.

66 Ole Tangen, 'Is China Taking Advantage of COVID-19 to Pursue South China Sea Ambitions?', *Deutsche Welle*, 26 May 2020. https://www.dw.com/en/is-china-taking-advantage-of-covid-19-to-pursue-south-china-sea-ambitions/a-53573918; Foreign Staff, 'China Accuses US of Interfering as Japan says Beijing is Using Pandemic to Push Territorial Claims', *The Telegraph*, 14 July 2020. https://www.telegraph.co.uk/news/2020/07/14/china-accuses-us-interfering-japan-says-beijing-using-pandemic; Helena Legarda, 'The PLA's Mask Diplomacy', *China Global Security Tracker No. 7*, International Institute for Strategic Studies, 12 August 2020. https://www.iiss.org/blogs/research-paper/2020/08/pla-covid-diplomacy.

67 James Kraska, 'Japan's Legal Response in the Gray Zone', *The Diplomat*, 6 August 2020. https://thediplomat.com/2020/08/japans-legal-response-in-the-gray-zone; Japan's Ministry of Defense, *National Defense Program Guidelines for FY 2019 and Beyond*, via Cabinet Secretariat. This is part of the China National Social Science Foundation's core project 'Japan's "Military Rise" and China's Countermeasures'.

68 This is part of the China National Social Science Foundation's core project 'Japan's "Military Rise" and China's Countermeasures'. Gui Yongtao is an assistant professor in the International Relations department at Peking University. Lin Zhiyuan is an analyst in the Military Studies department of China's Academy of Military Sciences. 归泳涛 [Yongtao Gui], '"灰色地带"之争: 美日对华博弈的新态势'

['"Gray Zone" Controversy: New Trends in the U.S.-Japan Game Against China'],
日本学刊 [*Japanese Studies*], no. 1 (January 2019): 45–69; 林治远 [Lin Zhiyuan],
'美国军事战略和作战理论新变化' ['New Changes in U.S. Military Strategy and
Combat Theory'], 军事文献 [*Military Literature*], no. 1 (January 2019): 7–10.

69 归泳涛 [Yongtao Gui], '"灰色地带"之争: 美日对华博弈的新态势' ['"Gray Zone"
Controversy: New Trends in the U.S.-Japan Game Against China'], 45–69.

70 归泳涛 [Yongtao Gui], '"灰色地带"之争: 美日对华博弈的新态势' ['"Gray Zone"
Controversy: New Trends in the U.S.-Japan Game Against China'], 45–69.

71 叶秋玲、王玉琨 [Qiuling Ye and Yukun Wang],
'日本发布新版《防卫计划大纲》寓意为何?' ['What Is the Meaning of Japan's
New Version of Its Defense Plan Guidelines?'], 军事文献 [*Military Literature*], no. 3,
March 2019, 33–5.

72 叶秋玲、王玉琨 [Qiuling Ye and Yukun Wang],
'日本发布新版《防卫计划大纲》寓意为何?' ['What Is the Meaning of Japan's New
Version of its Defense Plan Guidelines?'], 33–5; 司光亚、张阳、王艳正 [Guangya
Si, Yang Zhang and Yanzheng Wang], '网电空间作战建模仿真研究综述' ['Review
on Modeling and Simulation in Cyberspace Operations'], 386–97; Bryan Clark,
Mark Gunzinger and Jesse Sloman, *Winning in the Gray Zone: Using Electromagnetic
Warfare to Regain Escalation Dominance*, Center for Strategic and Budgetary
Assessments, 5 October 2017. https://csbaonline.org/research/publications/winning
-in-the-gray-zone-using-electromagnetic-warfare-to-regain-escalation.

73 司光亚、张阳、王艳正 [Guangya Si, Yang Zhang and Yanzheng Wang],
'网电空间作战建模仿真研究综述' ['Review on Modeling and Simulation in
Cyberspace Operations'], 386–97.

74 司光亚、张阳、王艳正 [Guangya Si, Yang Zhang and Yanzheng Wang],
'网电空间作战建模仿真研究综述' ['Review on Modeling and Simulation in
Cyberspace Operations'], 386–97.

75 Lora Saalman, *The Impact of Artificial Intelligence on Strategic Stability and Nuclear
Risk – Volume II: East Asian Perspectives* (Stockholm: Stockholm International Peace
Research Institute, October 2019), https://www.sipri.org/sites/default/files/2019-10/
the_impact_of_artificial_intelligence_on_strategic_stability_and_nuclear_risk_vo
lume_ii.pdf.

76 Qi Haotian is an assistant professor at the International Relations department
of Peking University. 祁昊天 [Haotian Qi], '威胁迷思、美国角色与能力矛盾:
欧洲防务行动层面的供给与需求' ['Threat Myths, U.S. Role and Capability
Contradictions: Supply and Demand at European Defense Level'], 欧洲研究
[*European Studies*], no. 6 (2018): 25–55; Qiao and Wang, *Unrestricted Warfare*.

77 林治远 [Zhiyuan Lin], '美国军事战略和作战理论新变化' ['New Changes in U.S.
Military Strategy and Combat Theory'], 7–10.

78 林治远 [Zhiyuan Lin], '美国军事战略和作战理论新变化' ['New Changes in U.S.
Military Strategy and Combat Theory'], 7–10.

79 朱星平 [Xingping Zhu], '混合战争背景下我国人防工程的使命' ['Mission of
China's Civil Air Defense Engineering in the Context of Hybrid Warfare'], 73–7.

80 朱星平 [Xingping Zhu], '混合战争背景下我国人防工程的使命' ['Mission of
China's Civil Air Defense Engineering in the Context of Hybrid Warfare'], 73–7.

81 朱星平 [Xingping Zhu], '混合战争背景下我国人防工程的使命' ['Mission of
China's Civil Air Defense Engineering in the Context of Hybrid Warfare'], 73–7.

82 Lora Saalman, 'China's AI-Enabled Offense: Hypersonic Glide Vehicles and Neural
Networks', in *AI, China, Russia, and the Global Order: Technological, Political,*

Global, and Creative Perspectives, Multilayer Assessment (SMA) White Paper, U.S. Department of Defense, January 2019. https://www.airuniversity.af.edu/Portals/10/AUPress/Books/B_0161_WRIGHT_ARTIFICIAL_INTELLIGENCE_CHINA_RUSSIA_AND_THE_GLOBAL_ORDER.PDF; Lora Saalman, 'Fear of False Negatives: AI and China's Nuclear Posture', *Bulletin of the Atomic Scientists*, 24 April 2018. https://thebulletin.org/landing_article/fear-of-false-negatives-ai-and-chinas-nuclear-posture.

83 唐永胜 [Yongsheng Tang], '以我为主，牵引中美战略竞争发展方向' ['Me First, Driving the Development of China-U.S. Strategic Competition'], 13–15.

84 唐永胜 [Yongsheng Tang], '以我为主，牵引中美战略竞争发展方向' ['Me First, Driving the Development of China-U.S. Strategic Competition'], 13–15.

85 谢苏明 [Suming Xie], '无人化智能化装备技术发展及其影响分析' ['Analysis on the Development of Unmanned Intelligent Arms Technology and its Impact'], 51–6.

86 谢苏明 [Suming Xie], '无人化智能化装备技术发展及其影响分析' ['Analysis on the Development of Unmanned Intelligent Arms Technology and Its Impact'], 51–6.

87 马瑾、舒正平、穆歌、张富雪 [Jin Ma, Zhengping Shu, Ge Mu and Fuxue Zhang], '混合战争条件下的无人系统作战能力分析' ['Analysis of Unmanned Systematic Combat Capability under Mixed War Conditions'], 410–14.

88 马瑾、舒正平、穆歌、张富雪 [Jin Ma, Zhengping Shu, Ge Mu and Fuxue Zhang], '混合战争条件下的无人系统作战能力分析' ['Analysis of Unmanned Systematic Combat Capability under Mixed War Conditions'], 410–14.

89 马瑾、舒正平、穆歌、张富雪 [Jin Ma, Zhengping Shu, Ge Mu and Fuxue Zhang], '混合战争条件下的无人系统作战能力分析' ['Analysis of Unmanned Systematic Combat Capability under Mixed War Conditions'], 410–14.

90 马瑾、舒正平、穆歌、张富雪 [Jin Ma, Zhengping Shu, Ge Mu and Fuxue Zhang], '混合战争条件下的无人系统作战能力分析' ['Analysis of Unmanned Systematic Combat Capability under Mixed War Conditions'], 410–14.

91 马瑾、舒正平、穆歌、张富雪 [Jin Ma, Zhengping Shu, Ge Mu and Fuxue Zhang], '混合战争条件下的无人系统作战能力分析' ['Analysis of Unmanned Systematic Combat Capability under Mixed War Conditions'], 410–14.

92 马瑾、舒正平、穆歌、张富雪 [Jin Ma, Zhengping Shu, Ge Mu and Fuxue Zhang], '混合战争条件下的无人系统作战能力分析' ['Analysis of Unmanned Systematic Combat Capability under Mixed War Conditions'], 410–14.

93 黄志澄 [Zhicheng Huang], '高超声速武器及其对未来战争的影响' ['Hypersonic Weapons and Their Impact on Future Wars'], 1–7.

94 Pan Letian is affiliated with the Beijing Yuanwang Think Tank Technology Consulting Co., Ltd in Beijing. 潘乐天 [Letian Pan], '美军"多域战"的实质及启示' ['Substance and Inspiration Behind the U.S. Military's "Multi-Domain" Warfare'], 科技导报 [*Science and Technology Review*] 35, no. 21 (31 May 2017): 125–30; 黄志澄 [Zhicheng Huang], '高超声速武器及其对未来战争的影响' ['Hypersonic Weapons and Their Impact on Future Wars'], 1–7.

95 Lora Saalman, 'Chapter 8: Exploring Artificial Intelligence and Unmanned Platforms in China', in *The Impact of Artificial Intelligence on Strategic Stability and Nuclear Risk – Volume II*, 43–7.

96 Senior Colonel Yuan Yi is Deputy Director of the Research Office and Deputy Researcher in the Institute of War Research of the Academy of Military Sciences. Major Li Zhifei is Deputy Director of the Research Office and Deputy Researcher in the Institute of War Research of the Academy of Military Sciences. Lieutenant Colonel Zhu Feng is an associate researcher at the Academy of Military Sciences. 袁艺、李志飞、朱丰 [Yi Yuan, Zhifei Li and Feng Zhu], '无人机与未来作战刍议'

['Unmanned Vehicles and Future Combat Operations'], 国防 [*National Defense*], no. 5 (May 2019): 36–50.

97 Lora Saalman, 'Factoring Russia into the US-Chinese Equation on Hypersonic Glide Vehicles', SIPRI Insights on Peace and Security, Stockholm International Peace Research Institute, no. 1, January 2017. https://www.sipri.org/sites/default/files/Factoring-Russia-into-US-Chinese-equation-hypersonic-glide-vehicles.pdf; Saalman, 'Fear of False Negatives'.

98 Chen Hanghui is affiliated with China's Army Command Academy. On mixed forces, he details how on the battlefields of Syria and Iraq, interest groups and combatants include US and Russian government and military forces, religious sect militia and tribal armed forces, separatist forces and terrorist organizations. On integration of combat styles, he cites the case of Yemen, in which a series of battles between the Houthi armed forces and the Saudi-led multinational coalition forces occurred around key cities and border areas to include conventional operations within the mountains, air and counter strikes, cross-border guerrilla warfare and maritime ambush, as well as irregular operations with missile attacks against civilian oil fields and airports. On diversification of methods, he notes that US strategy in Afghanistan has led to ever-changing political, economic, and diplomatic measures, while strengthening military strikes. 陈航辉 [Hanghui Chen], '2017 战火, 摇摆着现代战争模样' ['2017 Flames of War, Swaying the Look of Modern Warfare'], 11.

99 刘纪未、张畅 [Jiwei Liu and Chang Zhang], '"混合战争"理论视阈下：俄罗斯军事战略调整探析' ['Analysis of Russian Military Strategy Adjustment from the Perspective of "Hybrid War" Theory'], 47–52.

100 黄志澄 [Zhicheng Huang], '高超声速武器及其对未来战争的影响' ['Hypersonic Weapons and Their Impact on Future Wars'], 1–7.

101 Saalman, 'Little Grey Men: China and the Ukraine Crisis'.

8

Influence operations and the modern information environment

Björn Palmertz

Introduction

The information environment and the vast potential for utilizing it in malicious activities have gained significant attention in the discussion on hybrid threats and hybrid warfare. Since the start of the millennium, the use of influence operations by both state and non-state actors has become increasingly obvious to decision makers and populations alike. The digital revolution affecting information dissemination and social exchange in our communities and the increased connectedness of key societal systems and infrastructure has opened up new opportunities as well as vulnerabilities. In addition, changes to labour markets and the demographic composition of many societies have broadened opportunities and horizons for parts of the public, but left others unsure of their place or representation in the traditional media or political sphere. This has had a direct effect both on national policies and international relations, not the least connected to various referendums and elections in, for example, the United Kingdom and the United States during 2016 and France in 2017. Aiming to clarify the wide range of related terms, Pamment et al. have employed 'information influence activities' to denote 'the targeting of opinion-formation in illegitimate, though not necessarily illegal ways, by foreign actors or their proxies'. [1] They further highlight three terms developed by the Swedish government, forming a hierarchy of influence activities: influence activities (single use of illegitimate techniques); influence operations (multiple coordinated activities); and influence campaigns (multiple coordinated operations across the hybrid spectrum). [2]

The increasing focus as of late can at first glance make it seem as if influence techniques are somewhat new. In reality, such activities have been utilized in situations of peace, conflict and war throughout history. The difference today to a large degree rests with the speed with which dissemination of messaging and information can take place, as well as the capability to hide or obscure the origin or sender of a message. The use of automated accounts and algorithms can also aid both in collecting data, offering more precise target audience analysis, as well as enhance the dissemination so that information seems to engage or be shared by a larger group of people online than is actually the case. In addition, offensive actors have the initiative as well as the advantage of being able to rapidly receive feedback on how information is received. Thus, their efforts can be redirected or withdrawn within a short time frame, depending on whether the perceived effects match their ambitions. The accessibility to target audiences in the modern information environment has also decreased the costs of conducting influence operations and increased the potential effects that can be achieved. Finally, such techniques can also be employed in conjunction with other hybrid threat capabilities. Brangetto and Veenendaal, for example, describe the benefits of combining offensive cyber operations with various influence methodologies: 'they are generally limited in scope and difficult to attribute, thereby limiting the risks of escalation and countermeasures. This is especially reflected in the Russian approach to Information Warfare, which considers it as an instrument of hard power.' They also highlight several illustrative examples such as the hacking of information systems, false flag cyberattacks, distributed denial of service attacks and doxing.[3]

To illustrate a number of techniques utilized in the current information environment Russia will be utilized as a main example, mainly since there are several high-profile actions to draw from that illustrate Russia's use of influence operations in recent years. This does not in any way mean that Russia is the only actor currently directing considerable resources towards this aim. The Chinese Communist Party has actively employed related strategies, as highlighted in a 2018 CSIS report: 'An aggressive strategy has sought to influence political decision-making, pursue unfair advantages in trade and business, suppress criticism of China, facilitate espionage opportunities, and influence overseas Chinese communities.'[4] Other nations such as Iran have also been highlighted as utilizing, for example, 'coordinated inauthentic behaviour' through social media pages, groups and accounts targeting politics and elections in the US and UK.[5] In addition, a number of non-governmental entities have devoted considerable effort to influencing various target audiences, especially through the use of social media and other web-based communication channels.[6]

The following sections first discuss targeting in the modern information environment, and then examine the employment of some prominent combined methodologies that have been observed during the last few years. It is worth noting that the use of these methodologies is in constant shift, in part due to the speed of technological advances, which impacts how users communicate and access information. In addition, the increasing awareness that a certain technique is being utilized reinforces resistance among a target audience and empowers key actors in a society to actively build resilience and counter-narratives. In this craft it is therefore imperative for offensive actors to consistently review their strategies and the means by which they are implemented.

Targeting

One of the key precursors enabling influence operations is targeting. As previously mentioned, information technology and the large amount of data available on social media platforms offer new opportunities to identify target audiences and the most efficient way to reach them. The Cambridge Analytica case is one of the clearest examples of this in recent time. On 17 March 2018, *The New York Times*, along with *The Guardian* and *The Observer*, reported that Cambridge Analytica and its related company, Strategic Communication Laboratories, had harvested data of at least 50 million Facebook users and kept it without consent from the platform.[7] Facebook suspended both Cambridge and SCL, and stated it knew about the breach, but had received legally binding guarantees from the company that all of the data was deleted. The data was used by Cambridge Analytica and SCL to conduct political targeting. More specifically, to build software to analyse personal preferences of voters for their clients which included the Donald Trump campaign team and, according to a whistle-blower, the winning Brexit campaign. In July 2018, British Member of Parliament Damian Collins, heading a parliamentary inquiry into fake news, told CNN that the Information Commissioner's Office (ICO) had found evidence that files from Cambridge Analytica were accessed from Russia.[8]

The data was collected through an app called thisisyourdigitallife, built by academic Aleksandr Kogan who lived in Russia before moving to the United States at age seven. It was developed as a separate project initiated in 2014 apart from his affiliation with Cambridge University. He was also affiliated with St. Petersburg University, which he did not disclose to Cambridge, and received grants from the Russian government to research Facebook users' emotional states.[9] Through his company Global Science Research, in collaboration with Cambridge Analytica, hundreds of thousands of users were paid to take a personality test and agreed to have their data collected for academic use. However, the app also collected the information of the test-takers' Facebook friends, leading to the accumulation of a considerable amount of user data.[10] Facebook stated the collection had not been a data breach since Kogan 'gained access to this information in a legitimate way and through the proper channels' but 'did not subsequently abide by our rules' because he passed the information on to third parties.[11] Two days after the story surfaced, Britain's Channel 4 News released a series of undercover videos showing Cambridge Analytica executives appearing to say they could extort politicians, send women to entrap them and help proliferate propaganda to help their clients.[12] Alexander Nix was suspended from the position as CEO in late March after the videos were broadcasted. In May 2018, Cambridge Analytica and SCL announced they were closing down their business.[13]

Hacking

Gaining unauthorized entry to computer systems can, if exposed, in itself potentially influence the perspectives of certain target audiences and undermine the credibility of key functions in society. It can also serve to provide data and insights benefitting the targeting, timing and design of influence operations. In May 2016, in the lead-up to the US elections later that year, Arizona's voter registration system was taken offline after the FBI issued a warning of a cyber-threat. Investigations revealed that hackers had attempted to penetrate the system, but failed. The state of Illinois, however, was less fortunate and a month later hackers gained access to 90,000 records including the names, dates of birth, gender, driver's licenses and partial social security numbers of registered voters. They had also unsuccessfully attempted to manipulate some of the accessed information.[14] In a US Senate intelligence hearing in June 2017, cyber director at the Department of Homeland Security Sam Liles revealed that Russia had targeted election-related systems in a total of twenty-one states, including those of Arizona and Illinois.[15] The aim of the operation was not entirely clear, but 'the cyber hacking of infrastructure associated with the election, such as voting systems and voter databases, provided the Russians with the techniques, materials, and familiarity with the US election system that can be applied to future Russian influence campaigns – in the US and perhaps elsewhere'.[16]

However, not only state owned systems have been targeted; media organizations are also of interest to Russian hackers. In 2015 a group calling themselves the Cyber Caliphate claimed to be responsible for planting malware with the aim of destroying the transmission system hardware for French channel TV5 Monde. Twelve channels were brought down for nine hours, but the attack could potentially have done much more damage. Thanks to technicians on duty, the infiltrated computer acting as a gate into the channel's network was identified and cut off from the internet.[17] The so called Cyber Caliphate also propagated messages on Twitter expressing support for IS, which struck an especially sensitive chord in France due to the earlier attack on satire magazine Charlie Hebdo in which twelve people were killed and eleven wounded.[18] It was later revealed that the French cyber security agency had found evidence that the real source of the attack was Russian hacker group APT 28. It has not been entirely established why TV5 was seen as an appropriate target, however, it fits with an ongoing trend. In recent years, hacker groups such as APT 28 have extended their actions beyond intelligence collection and espionage to intrusion operations encompassing a wider range of aims, such as enabling future influence activities or disrupting physical infrastructure.[19] These types of hacks are clearly illustrated by two operations conducted against the Ukrainian power grid system in 2015 and 2016. The first left approximately 250,000 inhabitants without power for several hours.[20] The second resulted in a one-hour power outage in the Ukrainian capital region of Kiev.[21] Several investigations have attributed these attacks to a hacker group called Sandworm, also known as Voodoo Bear and Telebots. Cyber security firm FireEye also found connections between Sandworm and Russia based on Russian-language documents found on the command and control servers used by the group – particularly an unaddressed vulnerability that had been presented at a Russian hacker conference, with an explicit Ukraine focus.[22]

As mentioned earlier, collecting large amounts of user data from key platforms can be highly useful for intelligence purposes as well as planning influence campaigns. However, technological information property can be attractive for both state actors and companies seeking a shortcut to increase competitiveness. In September 2018, Facebook experienced a data breach where unknown attackers were able to exploit a core security failure and download the personal data of approximately 50 million users. The data stolen included the user's name, email, phone number, date of birth and posts on the platform.[23] As the information about the breach became public, Facebook in early October acknowledged a second major data leak. This time the Russian company SocialDataHub and its sister firm, Fubutech, had downloaded such a large amount of data from the platform that its marketing materials claimed it essentially had a mirror of the Russian portion of Facebook. In Facebook's assessment, this leak was driven in part by the Russian company's need to mass harvest imagery from Facebook in order to build facial recognition models that could be used by the Russian government for surveillance purposes.[24]

Leaking and doxing

Information accessed through hacking, sometimes complemented by open sources, is not always solely attained for intelligence purposes. It can also be utilized to enhance the effect of influence operations, whereby selected parts of the information are disseminated primarily through web-based platforms. This technique is called doxing – the practice of revealing and publicizing information on an organization or an individual that is private or classified, so as to publically shame or embarrass the target.

The most prominent doxing conducted by Russia occurred during the run-up to the US elections in 2016. In March, Hillary Clinton's campaign manager John Podesta received an email from what seemed to be Google, asking him to immediately change his password. The message was reviewed by the IT department but was, according to later statements, mistakenly assessed as 'legitimate'. The real source of the message, according to investigations by several cyber security firms[25] as well as US intelligence agencies,[26] was the Russian hacker group APT 28. As John Podesta's staff changed the email password, they gave the hackers access to over 50,000 of John Podesta's emails.[27] Two months later, the day after the Democratic National Committee revealed that they had been hacked, an anonymous internet user started releasing the stolen data, accompanied by WikiLeaks a week later. This process carried on until the elections on 8 November. On several occasions, the continuous doxing was timed to maximize its potential media coverage. One example followed the Obama-administration's release of a statement on 7 October, naming the Russian leadership as responsible for the influence campaign against the US elections. *The Washington Post* thirty minutes later released taped recordings by TV-show 'Access Hollywood', where Donald Trump could be heard making denigrating statements about women.[28] Another thirty minutes later, WikiLeaks started releasing email conversations involving Podesta, pointing to presidential candidate Clinton's connections to major banks, an issue which had already been brought up against Clinton in prior debates. Treverton describes how this 'demonstrates the Kremlin's clear preference for candidate Trump and its assistance in helping to increase Trump's electoral chances'.[29] In October 2018, the UK National Cyber Security Centre issued further clarification regarding APT 28, describing in a 'high confidence assessment' the identification of several cyberattacks against political institutions, companies as well as media- and sports organizations orchestrated by the Russian intelligence service GRU. They also stated that, among other groups, APT 28 and its many aliases such as Fancy Bear, Pawnstorm and Cyber Caliphate are associated with the GRU.[30]

Emmanuel Macron's 2017 presidential campaign in France was, like the DNC in the United States, also targeted by a spear-phishing campaign where nine gigabytes of emails and campaign documents were later leaked on the text storage site Pastebin.[31] Within half an hour, discussion threads on the forum site 4chan linked to the material. Soon thereafter, a US journalist working for an alt-right website also linked to the material on Twitter and later told BBC that the 4chan user posting the links had notified him in advance that the material was to be released. The timing was well planned, as the data was published just a few hours before the political reporting ban placed on French media forty-four hours before the voting.[32] The dissemination that followed was considerable and rapid, amounting to 47,000 retweets within a few hours. According to Atlantic Council's Digital Forensic Research Lab, this is an indicator that automated accounts, so called bots, were involved in the process.[33] The Macron team, in part due to the experience of the US elections the year prior, was nevertheless prepared to be targeted. Already a few months before, cybersecurity firm Trend Micro had identified attempts by APT 28 to get into the Macron campaign's computer systems through spear-phishing. The Macron team therefore prepared by hiring cyber security experts, enacting technical as well as psychological defensive procedures, and acted offensively as the spear-phishing attempts started appearing. One method was to deliberately seed fabricated information to the hackers. Mounir Mahjoubi, the IT director for Macron stated: 'You can flood these [phishing] addresses with multiple passwords and log-ins, true ones, false ones, so the people behind them use up a lot of time trying to figure them out.'[34] Five minutes before the reporting ban was activated, the Macron campaign also managed to do a press release condemning the doxing attempt and explaining how they had been targeted by a coordinated hack several weeks before.[35] However, the failure of this influence attempt was also in part based on an incorrect expectation of effect. The resistance from French media to walk into a foreign influence dissemination trap was well established at this point, and the operation lacked a cultural analysis – some fabricated documents inserted into the leaks by the Russian hackers were rather amateurishly forged. Also, a large portion of the dissemination on the internet took place in English, with support from US alt-right actors, which is not ideal when attempting to reach and influence French target audiences.[36]

Distributed denial of service attacks

An indirect signalling method, while potentially creating a sense of vulnerability as well as diminishing the credibility of foreign entities, is the DDoS attack. It refers to disrupting the services of a host computer connected to the internet by flooding it with pointless requests from a distributed network of external machines. The aim is to 'block the entrance' to the server and ensure that none of the legitimate requests get fulfilled. On the spectrum of complexity in the realm of cyberattacks, the technique behind a DDoS attack is rather simple and can be conducted without any major investment in infrastructure, since control over a network can be attained by discreetly renting a botnet or illicitly hijacking the machines of others. These can be computers but also other products connected to the internet. In terms of knowledge there is no shortage of consulting services or even helpful software tools available if someone is willing to pay. During Russia's conflict with Ukraine, DDoS attacks were also part of the package of offensive tools employed by both sides. Baerzner and Robin describe how

> this kind of cyberattack was used multiple times by both parties to the conflict; Ukrainian media websites were targeted by pro-Russian hackers in November 2013, for instance, and Russian media websites were attacked by pro-Ukrainian hackers in December 2013. DDoS attacks can also serve as a distraction in order to monopolize the attention of the emergency team of the targeted institution. While they are busy combating the DDoS attack, the perpetrator(s) can conduct other malicious activities on the relevant network such as installing a backdoor or malware in order to steal data.[37]

In March 2016, a number of Swedish media organizations were similarly targeted by DDoS attacks, leaving some difficult to access for up to five days. At the same time, the amount of data traffic between Sweden and Russia increased, which is not in itself enough to attribute any form of attack.[38] Two years later, however, in a freedom-of-information-act release of an internal US State Department cable from October 2016, the attack against nine Swedish news sites was described as part of a Russian campaign to sow disinformation about NATO. The cable was the first confirmation that Russia was suspected in the March 2016 attacks in Sweden, which came as the Swedish government was debating whether to approve a cooperation treaty with NATO.[39] The agreement was approved by the Swedish parliament in summer 2016.

These operations fall within the methodology of what Cohen and Bar'el refer to as Computer Network Influence (CNI) operations: 'In contrast with standard attacks launched against computer networks, CNI is designed to create the sense of a momentous strike without actually executing one. CNI attacks are meant to instil a sense of insecurity and a lack of control, compromising sovereignty with an inability to safeguard a normative way of life. Examples of such attacks include crippling government sites, sending damaging messages to civilians and shutting down media sites for limited stretches of time.'[40]

Disinformation

Today, social media combine text, images, video and verbal commentary with new and practically instant means of dissemination. These new communication channels also enable a direct line to foreign target audiences without having to consider actors that previously had a stronger role as filters or gatekeepers, for example politicians, academics, experts and established media organizations. The opportunities to utilize disinformation have therefore increased, and they are especially attractive to authoritarian regimes. This also results in an inherent asymmetry. While influence efforts targeting foreign target audiences can benefit from the openness of democratic societies, authoritarian states can implement restrictions in their own domestic information environment, delimiting communication between their own population and external actors. Russia's use of legislation where certain entities are labelled as foreign agents is one example; others include limitations to foreign ownership of media companies, complicating independent journalism and placing limitations on, and actively policing, what can be accessed on the internet within the country.

Giles specifically points out that compared to the time before the internet, seeding information is much easier today. This is partly due to the fact that it is easier for stories to be designed to trend and creep into the reporting of established and credible media sources in natural and legitimate ways.[41]

Such opportunities are especially evident during crises or other situations in democratic societies when there is social unrest or turmoil, and the Covid-19 pandemic is a clear example. Pamment describes that Russia and China have been running image campaigns with disinformation components to frame their handling of the crisis. The communication combines both official and reasonably transparent methods such as public diplomacy and state media reporting, with more covert influence and cyber-related activities. To further complicate the information environment various criminal groups have attempted to benefit from the crisis by spreading clickbait or by running phishing scams. Highlighting the potential effects Pamment states:

> There are profound health and public safety risks associated with the disinformation connected to these campaigns, as well as to the activities of criminal and hacker groups. These campaigns aim to undermine trust in institutions and to poison the climate of debate. Some aspects of these campaigns demonstrate efforts to erode freedom of thought and expression. Some of these activities also pose emerging short-term and long-term risks to personal, organizational, and national security.[42]

A recent report outlines some of the more prominent themes of the Covid-19 pandemic, as identified by independent fact checking organizations in Italy, Spain, Germany, France and the UK. It is important to note that these are not always authored or disseminated with the purpose of causing harm, and would then be seen as misinformation, but could also be injected into the information environment with the intent to cause harm and hence would be labelled as disinformation. The themes include (1) misleading medical advice around supposed cures and remedies for Covid-19, (2) the belief that Covid-19 is caused or worsened by 5G mobile phone technology, (3) advice on how to avoid or prevent infection, at times mixing partially accurate information with unsound medical advice, sometimes falsely attributed to an authority on the subject, (4) claims that the virus was created deliberately, (5) rumours and conspiracy theories related to vaccines such as false claims surrounding mandatory vaccination or vaccines being ready or imminent and (6) a theme centred on face masks and personal protective equipment including claims that masks may be harmful or inaccurate rumours surrounding the logistical supply of personal protective equipment.[43]

Another opportunity utilized during recent years is termed information laundering – how tools of influence operations can be used to penetrate a target media ecosystem and use it as an echo chamber.[44] A report from the Swedish Center for Russian Studies underlines that Russian media narratives are designed by a number of leading national media outlets such as RT, Sputnik and Rossiyskaya Gazeta. Due to the limited impact of these media sources among Western target audiences, they actively utilize social media to increase their exposure. Their most important avenues, however, are Western media outlets that have a larger audience including far-right populist outlets such as Infowars, Breitbart and Voice of Europe. Articles on these sites are also on occasion remarkably similar to those of Sputnik, even if they are not attributed to that source. This enables narratives to reach a target audience without the potentially stigmatizing label of an overt Russian origin. It also makes possible multiple exposures as a reader visits different media sites, even though the origin may be the one and same article authored by Russian media outlets funded by the state. SCRS summarizes the technique and describes how

> both RT and Sputnik often rewrite articles from local sources. They use the domestic tone and level of exaggeration and hatred towards the establishment. This is both easy and cheap and all responsibility lies on the local, primary source, not the Russian outlet. RTs and Sputnik's English-language versions primarily feed Western media outlets with material, rather than the media consumers directly, thereby not showing to the vast majority of the media consumers that Russian media has an important part in the selection, formulation and distribution of the news.[45]

Sometimes mistakes made by established media channels themselves present opportunities that makes this aim easier to attain. On 11 May 2018 Swedish local newspaper Smalandsposten published a news article with a title reading 'Catholic Church were denied ringing church bells – could disturb nearby residents'.[46] The context, which was included in the introduction to the article, was that a Muslim congregation in the town of Vaxjo had been permitted to transmit prayer calls through loudspeaker for three minutes and forty-five seconds each Friday. The information about the previous denial to the catholic congregation came from an employee of the church interviewed in the article. Additional information that the application for ringing church bells was made ten to fifteen years prior was later added to the article. However, when Swedish radio station P4 began researching the issue they could not find records of any such application; the local county office and the police searched their records back to 1996 without result. By then, the topic had nevertheless garnered a substantial dissemination on various anti-immigration focused websites and social media platforms such as Facebook.[47] On 12 May, right-wing populist website Voice of Europe, based in Holland, published a brief article titled 'Sweden: Church calls forbidden in town were mosque is allowed to air 110dB Islamic call to prayer'. On 14 May, Sputnik news followed suit with the headline 'Swedish City Allows 110 DB Muslim Prayer Calls, Rejects Church Clock Ringing'.[48] Sputniks attempt to amplify the propagation of the initial incorrect article through established media sites was, however, superfluous – they did that very well on their own. Well-established Swedish outlets like Expressen, TV4, Metro and The Local all carried rewrites of the Smalandsposten article, lending their credibility to the incorrect story. They thereby indirectly legitimized Russian narratives, including that the Swedish political establishment is guided by political correctness regarding migration and other issues, whereas migrants or Islamists have too much power in society, which affects decision-making and creates problems for Sweden.[49]

Shekhovtsov has conducted a thorough investigation of the relationship between the Russian leadership and Western far-right groups. He explains the historical reasons why a shared information space could develop between the Soviet Union and far-right movements in the cold war era. First, both fascism and communism are revolutionary and totalitarian ideologies – a concurrence in the thrust towards a new civilization, even though the two belief systems have inherently different myths and values. Second, both fascism and communism envision a society that challenges the principles of liberalism. This creates a shared space of perspectives where the 'decadent and degenerate' liberalism poses a threat.[50] A recent report released by the National Endowment for Democracy states that authoritarian states do not use influence operations to attract foreign audiences, but rather to make the societal systems of the West appear less appealing:

> Contrary to some prevailing analysis, the attempt by Beijing and Moscow to wield influence through initiatives in the spheres of media, culture, think tanks, and academia is neither a 'charm offensive' nor an effort to 'win hearts and minds', . . . This authoritarian influence is not principally about attraction or even persuasion; instead, it centres on distraction and manipulation.[51]

One very clear example of a strategy exploiting distrust, polarization and previous political credibility failures in the West occurred in mid-2014. It also points to the asymmetrical opportunities for a Russian media company in the West, versus a Western media company in Russia. The Russian state owned media channel RT, which focuses on foreign audiences, launched a guerrilla advertising campaign in New York and Washington, DC, consisting of 'wild postings' in the words of RT spokesperson Anna Belkina. The core messages of the various posters were tied to an anti-mainstream media narrative proclaiming that people should 'question more' and go to RT.com for the second opinion. Some of the themes used were 'In case they shut us down on TV' and a drawing of former Secretary of State Colin Powell accompanied by the message 'This is what happens when there is no second opinion. Iraq War: No Weapons of Mass Destruction, 141,802 civilian deaths.'[52] A few months later, RT also published a YouTube video featuring interviews with Americans on the street asking them what they thought of the campaign. All comments featured were positive to the campaign and focused on the design of the posters and the anti-establishment message. One man stated, 'You know, all the propaganda that we are being shoved by our political powers. They say one thing on television to try to put us at ease, but in reality, it is not really congruent with the truth', and another 'It is embarrassing that we are such sheep; that's my first reaction. That the messages that we get, we accept without question, and the consequences (points to RT poster) are really serious.'[53] It would be interesting to know if the interviewees were informed in advance that RT is funded by the Russian state, at the time ranked 148th of 180 countries on Reporters without Borders Press Freedom Index, lower than nations such as Zimbabwe, Chad and Cambodia.[54]

A more sophisticated method of generating and spreading disinformation as part of an influence operation is by building networks utilizing unsuspecting individuals or movements in a targeted country. On 1 September 2020 Facebook reported shutting down such a network, after receiving information from the FBI, associated with past activity by the Russian Internet Research Agency (IRA) for violating their policy against foreign interference.[55] The thirteen associated accounts and two pages on Facebook centred on a website domain named PeaceData launched a few months earlier that pretended to be an independent news outlet. The accounts included fictitious personas with AI-generated profile pictures who posed as news editors from various countries. These were then used to recruit a number of freelance journalists who were not aware of the origin of their paid assignments to write on popular topics primarily targeting an audience on the left of the political spectrum. In addition they sought to obtain political advertising authorization to run ads in the US. Some of the topics they focused on were social and racial justice in the United States and the United Kingdom, alleged Western war crimes and corruption, environmental issues, the coronavirus pandemic, the Biden-Harris campaign, the QAnon conspiracy theory and the policies of President Trump. The network was taken down during its early stages and did not garner significant traction in terms of audience or amplification of its content, but according to Nimmo et al. illustrates a development of IRA-influence tactics: (1) the use of AI-generated profile pictures, (2) employing real, but unwitting, authors with a layer of seeming authenticity between the originator and the audience, (3) using a smaller number of well-crafted accounts to target communities and publications rather than the mass audience approach seen during earlier election campaigns and (4) employing a more precise targeting than during prior operations, in this case aiming messages mainly at a limited number of left-leaning political groups.[56]

Social media advertising

An additional technique used by Russia in their influence campaign during the 2016 US election campaign was advertisements coordinated and created by the IRA placed on social media platforms, among others Facebook, Instagram and Google. According to DiResta et al., IRA initiated operations during 2013 in St. Petersburg, Russia. Organized like a marketing agency, they have employed and trained over a thousand people to engage in round-the-clock influence operations. Their target audiences include Russian and Ukrainian citizens, as well as, well before the 2016 US election, Americans. In that operation they reached 126 million people on Facebook, at least 20 million users on Instagram, 1.4 million users on Twitter and uploaded over 1,000 videos to YouTube.[57] A company can advertise on Facebook using its Ads Manager software, which enables them to target users based on interests and behaviours. An analysis conducted by Howard et al. shows that the Russian IRA utilized this information to segment Facebook and Instagram users based on race, ethnicity and identity. Thanks to the functionality of the ad software they could also identify more specific interests within each ethnic group, for example nationalism, immigration or identity. They then put together an online advertising campaign that ran between 2015 and 2017, attracting users to Facebook pages they controlled and posting content they deemed effective for the specific target audience. The campaign consisted of 73 different Facebook pages and Instagram accounts as well as 3,519 ads attempting to get users to like pages, follow Instagram accounts, join events and visit various websites.

Howard et al. identify two communication strategies:

> The first involved appealing to the narratives common within a specific group, such as supporting veterans and police, or pride in race and heritage, as a clickbait strategy to drive traffic to the Facebook and Instagram pages the IRA set up. Based on an analysis of both ads and posts, we find that the IRA posted content on these pages to which they drove traffic with ads. Then the pages posted content that intended to elicit outrage from these groups.

They conclude that the messaging aimed at these target audiences was designed to push and pull them in different ways. The overarching aim, however, was clear: to benefit the Republican Party and presidential candidate Donald Trump. In campaigns targeting conservatives and right-wing voters, the messaging encouraged these groups to support the Trump campaign. For key groups that could challenge Trump, the messaging instead sought to confuse, distract and ultimately discourage members from voting.[58]

Organized trolling and amplification by social bots

The changing patterns of how people communicate, share and consume information through social media platforms and applications utilizing the internet have given rise to a number of techniques. Although not new in terms of their underlying aim and methodological starting point, the use of organized trolling and bots are techniques that have been developed to fit the digital information landscape. Trolling can be utilized to distort perceptions of what public opinion looks like and disrupt or silence key communicators with opposing voices. In combination with this, bots, automated accounts impersonating humans, can amplify specific narratives in a manner that at first glance looks organic, but in reality is artificially generated. Bots can also aid in the dissemination of malware. The term 'social bot' refers to automated software that acts through a social media account. It is important to note that the credibility of bot behaviour varies greatly, since the efforts put into mimicking human behaviour depend on the goals of the operator managing the bots.[59] Bodine-Baron et al. differentiate between bots and trolls. Bot accounts automatically post or share information on social media platforms under the direction of humans.[60] Troll accounts, on the other hand, are operated by humans. It should be underlined that not all trolling activities or bot accounts are connected to influence operations or other organized malign activities. The original definition of a troll was a person that intentionally engaged in polarizing or annoying messaging online in order to get attention or otherwise cause trouble.[61]

In a study of Russian state-sponsored trolls, Zannettou et al. made a number of interesting findings. They used a mathematical method (Hawkes Processes) to model how several communities influenced each other – the Russian troll accounts on Twitter and overall baseline account activity on Twitter as well as social forum platforms Reddit and 4chan. Key observations include that trolls were actively involved in spreading content related to world news and politics, including Russian narratives on topics such as terrorist group IS and Islam. Several troll accounts were also created or repurposed in the weeks leading up to noteworthy world events, including the Republican National Convention or the Charlottesville rally. Accounts in both troll and baseline samples reached a large number of Twitter users with their messages, ranging from 1,000 up to 145,000 followers. This indicates that the amount of followers of the troll accounts is sufficient to share certain narratives with a large number of Twitter users. One behaviour separating the trolls from the baseline was that while random Twitter users mainly tweet from the mobile app, most of the Russian trolls utilized the web client. Zannettou et al. summarize that the influence of the troll accounts studied actually appears quite limited with respect to the baseline platforms: 'With the exception of news originating from the Russian state-sponsored news outlet RT (formerly Russia Today), the troll accounts were generally less influential than other users on Reddit, Twitter, and 4chan.' A plausible explanation is that troll accounts are simply not terribly efficient at spreading news – they are more concerned with causing havoc by pushing ideas, engaging other users, or even taking both sides in controversial online discussions.[62]

Swedish journalists recently examined topics relating to Sweden in a dataset of three million tweets collected by researchers at Clemson University. The data was connected to over 2,800 troll accounts that have been suspended by Twitter. In a comment one of the researchers in the project, professor Darren Linvill, stated that he was surprised by how well organized the troll accounts were. The accounts were of different types and were utilized depending on what happened in the world and what time it was. At 2.00 pm, all the Russian trolls may have been tweeting from left-leaning accounts, then simultaneously switching over to their right-leaning accounts at exactly 3.00 pm. The analysis found 330 English-language accounts that published a total of 1,920 tweets about Sweden. The amount of related messages continuously increased from the time the accounts were activated in 2014 until their peak in 2017. About 1,200 of the tweets were on topics relating to crime, immigration and Muslims. On occasion the accounts took various sides in controversial issues to add fuel to the fire. When President Trump in 2017 exclaimed 'Look at what happened last night in Sweden' in a speech to his followers, he was mocked by troll accounts pretending to have a left-leaning stance, while right-leaning troll accounts claimed that he was correct and that Sweden was in a constant state of crisis due to immigration.[63]

An especially relevant example of research in light of the Covid-19 pandemic and illustrating how a specific subject area can be targeted was presented in a 2018 paper by Broniatowski et al. It is based on Twitter data from 2014 to 2017 which was analysed to see how bots and trolls participated in the online vaccine debate. The findings of the analysis concerning content and number of posts were that

> Russian trolls and sophisticated Twitter bots post content about vaccination at significantly higher rates than does the average user. Content from these sources gives equal attention to pro- and anti-vaccination arguments. This is consistent with a strategy of promoting discord across a range of controversial topics – a known tactic employed by Russian troll accounts.[64]

In a recent paper, Broniatowski et al. presented an example of how a specific subject area can be targeted. Twitter data was collected from 2014 to 2017 to see how bots and trolls participated in the online vaccine debate. Concerning content and number of posts, the analysis found that Russian trolls and sophisticated Twitter bots post content about vaccination at significantly higher rates than does the average user, and that they give equal attention to pro- and anti-vaccination arguments. Actions consistent with a strategy of promoting discord across a range of controversial topics – a known tactic employed by Russian troll accounts.[65] Lazer et al. recently summarized the challenge concerning amplification by bots on social media platforms: by liking, sharing, and searching for information, social bots (automated accounts impersonating humans) can magnify the spread of fake news by orders of magnitude. By one recent estimate – that classified accounts based on observable features such as sharing behaviour, number of ties, and linguistic features – between 9 and 15 per cent of active Twitter accounts are bots. Facebook estimated that as many as 60 million bots may be infesting its platform. They were responsible for a substantial portion of political content posted during the 2016 US campaign, and some of the same bots were later used to attempt to influence the 2017 French election. Bots are also deployed to manipulate algorithms used to predict potential engagement with content by a wider population.[66]

The development of advanced social bot software is moving along at a rapid pace. Today, automatic accounts can scrape the web for information then used to build a credible profile, independently comment on other users' posts, disseminate collected information at specific times and emulate the production of human organic content at a pace that looks lifelike at a glance. Ferrara et al. underline the importance of improved awareness and knowledge in democracies regarding the utilization of social bots. They conclude that bots can 'hinder the advancement of public policy by creating the impression of a grassroots movement of contrarians, or contribute to the strong polarization of political discussion observed in social media. They can alter the perception of social media influence, artificially enlarging the audience of some people, or they can ruin the reputation of a company, for commercial or political purposes.'[67]

Conclusion

Influence operations employ a wide range of methodologies and tools, but they all benefit from the large amount of readily available data, which makes it possible to learn how a foreign information environment works from a distance. The ability to evaluate and realign operations has also increased greatly. With the speed, reach and opportunities for anonymity in today's communication channels, it is also easier to engage or disrupt actors in that environment without revealing your identity and true motivations. The debate, and institutional roles, in Western societies often separate cyber- and influence operations. In reality, Russia and other capable offensive actors combine these capabilities when needed. This includes employing social engineering methods to lure users into opening the door to a system so that data can be extracted. It can also involve hacking into and disrupting critical infrastructure systems potentially affecting government credibility or arousing fear among the population in another country. Disseminating messages that fuel polarization and distort the public debate in another country also serves an important purpose. If a country experiences internal strife and politicians or the public struggle to find common ground, they will have less energy and focus to expend on containing and countering the strategies and actions of the offensive actor.

In light of these challenges, how can key actors in a society then limit the effects of malign influence operations? Public awareness is a first line of defence and proactive strategic communication and transparency from the national leadership and other key communicators is therefore vital. This can sustain focus on the issue and minimize the effect of disinformation, while upholding credibility and long-term communication between decision makers and the population. Communication strategies need to be adapted to an information environment where the number of channels to reach the population is considerably more diverse than just a decade ago. This requires a greater knowledge concerning key target audiences; what are their motivations, concerns and experiences, which channels do they use and how should messages be framed to be understandable and effective? Another key aspect is to incorporate relevant skill sets into security- and intelligence agencies, since the ability to maintain situational awareness is a key precondition for several other response and resilience areas. Since influence operations can take aim at many different situations or actors across the public and private sector, it is also important to close potential responsibility or perception gaps that can be exploited by an opponent. One way of reducing these can be to develop an entity that enables information sharing, training and collaboration for key societal actors, as well as maintaining comprehensive tracking of influence-related threats and an early warning mechanism. This can also facilitate long-term relationships with related core capabilities such as law, cyber security and intelligence. Finally, legal frameworks may need to be revised and developed – an undertaking that needs to be adapted to existing legislation and the current information environment, where data flows freely but under the surface has become a very valuable commodity that is traded globally.

Notes

1   James Pamment, Howard Nothhaft, Henrik Agardh-Twetman and Alicia Fjällhed,
    Countering Information
    Influence Activities: The State of the Art (Lund: Lund University, 2018), 8.

2 Alicia Wanless and James Pamment, 'How Do You Define a Problem Like Influence?' *Journal of Information Warfare* 18, no. 3 (2019): 1–14.

3 Pascal Brangetto and Matthijs Veenendaal, *Influence Cyber Operations: The Use of Cyberattacks in Support of Influence Operations* (NATO CCD COE, 2016).

4 Canadian Security Intelligence Service, *China and the Age of Strategic Rivalry: Highlights from an Academic Outreach Workshop* (2018), 75.

5 Kanishk Karan, Ayushman Kaul and Ben Nimmo, 'Facebook Removes Iran-based Assets. Again', *Atlantic Council Digital Forensic Research Lab*, 30 May 2019. https://medium.com/dfrlab/facebook-removes-iran-based-assets-again-f17358ef21f.

6 Katie Cohen and Lisa Kaati, *Digital Jihad – Propaganda from the Islamic State* (Swedish Defence Research Agency, 2018); Diana Rieger, Lena Frischlich and Gary Bente, *Propaganda 2.0: Psychological Effects of Right-Wing and Islamic Extremist Internet Videos* (Terrorism/Extremism Research Unit of the German Federal Criminal Police Office, 2013); Kate Starbird, *Examining the Alternative Media Ecosystem through the Production of Alternative Narratives of Mass Shooting Events on Twitter* (11th International AAAI Conference on Web and Social Media (ICWSM), 2017).

7 Carole Cadwalladr and Emma Graham-Harrison, 'Revealed: 50 Million Facebook Profiles Harvested for Cambridge Analytica in Major Data Breach', *The Guardian*, 17 March 2018.

8 Donie O'Sullivan, Drew Griffin and Patricia DiCarlo, 'Cambridge Analytica's Facebook Data was Accessed from Russia, MP Says', *CNN*, 17 July 2018.

9 Carole Cadwalladr and Emma Graham-Harrison, 'Cambridge Analytica: Links to Moscow Oil Firm and St Petersburg University', *The Guardian*, 17 March 2018.

10 Paul Lewis and Julia C. Wong, 'Facebook Employs Psychologist Whose Firm Sold Data to Cambridge Analytica', *The Guardian*, 18 March 2018.

11 Paul Grewal, 'Suspending Cambridge Analytica and SCL Group From Facebook', *Facebook Newsroom*, 16 March 2018. https://about.fb.com/news/2018/03/suspending-cambridge-analytica/.

12 Channel 4 News, 'Exposed: Undercover Secrets of Trump's Data Firm', 20 March 2018. https://www.channel4.com/news/exposed-undercover-secrets-of-donald-trump-data-firm-cambridge-analytica.

13 Aliya Ram and Hannah Kuchler, 'Cambridge Analytica Shuts Down and Blames "media siege"', *Financial Times*, 2 May 2018. https://www.ft.com/content/a0345598-4e37-11e8-a7a9-37318e776bab.

14 Michael Riley and Jordan Robertson, 'Russian Cyber Hacks on U.S. Electoral System Far Wider than Previously Known', *Bloomberg*, 13 June 2017.

15 US Senate Select Committee on Intelligence, *Hearing on Russian Interference in the 2016 U.S. Elections*, 21 June 2017. https://www.intelligence.senate.gov/hearings/open-hearing-russian-interference-2016-us-elections#.

16 Gregory F. Treverton, Andrew Thvedt, Alicia R. Chen, Kathy Lee and Madeline McCue, *Addressing Hybrid Threats* (Center for Asymmetric Threat Studies and Hybrid CoE, 2018).

17 BBC News, 'How France's TV5 was Almost Destroyed by "Russian hackers"', 10 October 2015.

18 Feike Hacquebord, *Two Years of Pawn Storm: Examining an Increasingly Relevant Threat* (Trend Micro, 2017). https://blog.trendmicro.com/pawn-storm-power-social-engineering/.

19 Crowdstrike, 'Who Is Fancy Bear (APT28)?', 12 February 2019. https://www.crowdstrike.com/blog/who-is-fancy-bear/.

20 Kim Zetter, 'Inside the Cunning, Unprecedented Hack of Ukraine's Power Grid', *WIRED*, 3 March 2016.

21 Marie Baezner and Patrice Robin, *Cyber and Information Warfare in the Ukrainian Conflict* (Eidgenössische Technische Hochschule Zürich, 2018).

22 Andy Greenberg, 'Your Guide to Russia's Infrastructure Hacking Teams', *WIRED*, 12 July 2017.

23 Mike Isaac and Sheera Frenkel, 'Facebook Security Breach Exposes Accounts of 50 Million Users', *New York Times*, 28 September 2018.

24 Jack Nicas, 'Facebook Says Russian Firms "Scraped" Data, Some for Facial Recognition', *New York Times*, 12 October 2018.

25 Lorenzo Francheski-Bicchierai, 'How Hackers Broke Into John Podesta and Colin Powell's Gmail Accounts', *Motherboard-VICE*, 20 October 2016.

26 Office of the Director of National Intelligence, *Assessing Russian Activities and Intentions in Recent US Elections*, 6 January 2017. https://www.dni.gov/files/docu ments/ICA_2017_01.pdf.

27 Jim Sciutto, 'How One Typo Helped let Russian Hackers In', *CNN*, 28 June 2017.

28 David A. Farenthold, 'Trump Recorded Having Extremely Lewd Conversation about Women in 2005', *Washington Post*, 8 October 2016.

29 Treverton et al., *Addressing Hybrid Threats*.

30 UK National Cyber Security Center, *Reckless Campaign of Cyber Attacks by Russian Military Intelligence Service Exposed*, 4 October 2018.

31 Heather A. Conley and Jean-Baptiste Jeangène Vilmer, *Successfully Countering Russian Electoral Interference* (Center for Strategic & International Studies, 2018).

32 France 24, 'French Media Rules Prohibit Election Coverage over Weekend', 7 May 2017.

33 Ben Nimmo, Naz Durakgolu, Maks Czuperski and Nicholas Yap, 'Hashtag Campaign: #MacronLeaks: Alt-right Attacks Macron in Last Ditch Effort to Sway French Election', *Atlantic Council DFRLab*, 6 May 2017.

34 Christopher Dickey, 'Did Macron Outsmart Campaign Hackers?', *The Daily Beast*, 6 May 2017.

35 BBC News, 'French Election: Emmanuel Macron Condemns "massive" Hack Attack', 6 May 2017.

36 Conley and Jeangène Vilmer, *Successfully Countering*.

37 Baezner and Robin, *Cyber and Information Warfare*.

38 Swedish Defence Research Agency, *DDOS-attack visar behovet av att säkra samhällets infrastruktur*, 21 March 2016.

39 Kevin Collier and Jason Leopold, 'Russian Hackers Targeted Swedish News Sites In 2016, State Department Cable Says', *BuzzFeed*, 8 October 2018.

40 Daniel Cohen and Ofir Bar'el, *The Use of Cyberwarfare in Influence Operations* (Tel Aviv University, Yuval Ne'eman Workshop for Science, Technology and Security, 2017).

41 Keir Giles, *The Next Phase of Russian Information Warfare* (NATO StratCom COE, 2016).

42 J. Pamment, 'The EU's Role in Fighting Disinformation: Taking Back the Initiative' (Carnegie Endowment for International Peace, 2020).

43 AFP, CORRECTIV, Pagella Politica/Facta, Full Fact and Maldita.es (2020) Infodemic Covid-19 in Europe: A Visual Analysis of Disinformation.

44 Biros Toucas, 'Exploring the Information-Laundering Ecosystem: The Russian Case', *Center for Strategic and International Studies*, 31 August 2017.

45 Swedish Center for Russian Studies, *Russian Influence on the Swedish Election 2018* (2018).

46 Per Jodenius, 'Katolska kyrkan vill ringa i klocka', Smålandsposten, 11 May 2018. https://nxt.smp.se/vaxjo/katolska-kyrkan-nekades-klockringning-kunde-stora-villa omrade/

47 Hugo Ewald and Alexandra Carlsson Tenitskaja, 'Faktiskt helt felaktigt att katolska kyrkan nekades ringa klockor', *Dagens Nyheter*, 21 May 2018. https://www.dn.se/nyheter/politik/faktiskt-helt-fel-att-katolska-kyrkan-nekades-ringa -klockor/.

48 Sputnik News, 'Swedish City Allows 110 DB Muslim Prayer Calls, Rejects Church Clock Ringing', 14 May 2018. https://sputniknews.com/europe/201805141064430526- sweden-mosque-loud-prayer-calls/.

49 Swedish Center for Russian Studies, *Russian Narratives on Sweden in 2017* (2018).

50 Anton Shekhovtsov, *Russia and the Western Far Right* (New York: Routledge, 2018).

51 Juan Pablo Cardenal, Jacek Kucharczyk, Grigorij Mesežnikov and Gabriela Pleschová, *Sharp Power: Rising Authoritarian Influence* (Washington, DC: National Endowment for Democracy, 2017).

52 Rosie Gray, 'Russia Today's New Ad Campaign Suggests It Could Have Prevented The Iraq War', *BuzzFeed*, 18 August 2014.

53 RT, 'RT. For the Second Opinion', 6 October 2014. https://www.youtube.com/watch?v =ynBr5AJdZP0.

54 Reporters Without Borders, '2014 World Press Freedom Index'. https://rsf.org/en/ ranking/2014.

55 Facebook (2020) August 2020 Coordinated Inauthentic Behavior Report.

56 B. Nimmo, C. Francois, C. Shawn Eib and L. Ronzaud, *IRA Again: Unlucky Thirteen – Facebook Takes Down Small, Recently Created Network Linked to Internet Research Agency* (Graphika, 2020).

57 Renee DiResta, Kris Shaffer, Becky Ruppel, David Sullivan, Robert Matney, Ryan Fox, Jonathan Albright and Ben Johnson, *The Tactics & Tropes of the Internet Research Agency* (Austin: New Knowledge, 2018).

58 Philip N. Howard, Bharath Ganesh and Dimitra Liotsiou, *The IRA, Social Media and Political Polarization in the United States, 2012-2018* (Oxford: University of Oxford Computational Propaganda Research Project, 2018).

59 Norah Abodokhair, Daisy Yoo and David W. McDonald, 'Dissecting a Social Botnet: Growth, Content and Influence in Twitter', in *Proceedings of the 18th ACM Conference on Computer Supported Cooperative Work & Social Computing*, Vancouver, 2015, 839–51.

60 Elizabeth Bodine-Baron, Todd C. Helmus, Andrew Radin and Elina Treyger, *Countering Russian Social Media Influence* (Santa Monica: RAND Corporation, 2018).

61 'Troll', in Cambridge Dictionary. https://dictionary.cambridge.org/dictionary/english/ troll.

62 Savvas Zannettou, Tristan Caulfield, Emiliano De Cristofaroy, Michael Sirivianos, Gianluca Stringhini and Jeremy Blackburn, *Disinformation Warfare: Understanding State-Sponsored Trolls on Twitter and Their Influence on the Web* (Cyprus University of Technology, University College London & University of Alabama at Birmingham, 2018).

63 Mikael Delin, '2.000 Tweets från Putins Troll Handlar om Sverige – ett land i förfall', *Dagens Nyheter*, 31 August 2018.

64 David A. Broniatowski, Amelia M. Jamison, SiHua Qi, Lulwah AlKulaib, Tao Chen, Adrian Benton, Sandra C. Quinn and Mark Dredze, 'Weaponized Health Communication: Twitter Bots and Russian Trolls Amplify the Vaccine Debate', *American Journal of Public Health* 108, no. 10 (2018): 1378–84.

65 Broniatowski et al., 'Weaponized Health Communication', 1378–84.

66 David M. J. Lazer, Matthew A. Baum, Yochai Benkler, Adam J. Berinsky, Kelly M. Greenhill, Filippo Menczer, Miriam J. Metzger, Brendan Nyhan, Gordon Pennycook, David Rothschild, Michael Schudson, Steven A. Sloman, Cass R. Sunstein, Emily A. Thorson, Duncan J. Watts and Jonathan L. Zittrain, 'The Science of Fake News', *Science* 359, no. 6380 (9 March 2018): 1094–6.

67 Emilio Ferrara, Onur Varol, Clayton Davis, Filippo Menczer and Alessandro Flammini, 'The Rise of Social Bots', *Communications of the ACM* 59, no. 7 (2016): 96–104.

9

Hybrid threats and new challenges for multilateral intelligence cooperation

Henrik Häggström

Introduction

Instability and uncertainty characterize today's security environment and this produces multidimensional challenges when it comes to mitigating hybrid threats. Hybrid threats can arise as a result of anything from changed conditions in the political landscape or shifts in relative power, to technological developments or something as simple as access to the internet. As a result, today a state actor with few resources can achieve great effects in a third country's security environment using a toolbox that combines military and non-military means of power projection. A modern hybrid adversary can use an array of methods simultaneously to achieve its strategic goals, from traditional mechanized combat and cyberattacks, to propaganda wars and funnelling money to terrorist groups, to give just a few examples. An actor – state or non-state – can use assaults, subversion, disinformation, cyber intrusions or any other criminal act, to influence, spread fear or create mayhem.[1] Plausible deniability makes it very difficult to determine who the antagonist is in such an environment.[2]

Today's hybrid conflicts include a spectrum of complex hybrid threats and warfare and require better intelligence than traditional conflicts. Hybrid conflicts are intelligence intensive because they generate considerably larger amounts of information on asymmetric threats.[3] A hybrid warfare operation is based on the intelligence it collects. The boundary between an ordinary military intelligence service and a civil security intelligence service tends to be blurred in hybrid warfare operations. This is a relationship that places special demands on the intelligence service and its practitioners as well as its customers. The aim of this chapter is to analyse bilateral intelligence challenges and the initiatives that have taken place in recent years, both within Europe and in international military operations, to combat the phenomena mentioned earlier.

Before moving on to a discussion on current multilateral intelligence cooperation, however, this chapter first provides an interpretation of the hybrid threat concept and discusses the concept of 'hybrid antagonists'. There then follows a discussion on current multilateral intelligence cooperation to address hybrid threats within the European Union (EU), the North Atlantic Treaty Organization (NATO) and the United Nations

(UN). Finally, the conclusions outline seven challenges facing the international intelligence community in terms of analysis and organization.

What is 'multilateral intelligence collaboration'?

A multilateral agreement is an accord among three or more parties, agencies or national governments.[4]

There is currently no consensus on the definition of multilateral intelligence. For the purpose of this chapter we will use the definition of Walsh (2010) who suggested that it is 'the collection, protection, and analysis of both publicly available and secret information, with the goal of reducing decision makers' uncertainty about a foreign policy problem'.[5]

So multilateral intelligence collaboration is an accord among three or more agencies or national governments working together to collect, protect and analyse information to reduce decision makers uncertainty about a foreign policy.

Hybrid threats and antagonists

Since the concept of hybrid threats was first discussed in the early 2000s, leading scholars such as Major William Nemeth (2002),[6] Nathan Freier (2009)[7] and Jack McCuen (2008)[8] have developed different definitions of hybrid warfare and hybrid threats, and suggested that hybrid warfare might be described as unrestricted warfare where, in principle, anything that might work, goes.[9] There is currently, however, no consensus on the definition of the concepts of hybrid threat and hybrid warfare. The currently most widely accepted and quoted definition of the terms was outlined by Frank Hoffman, one of the leading academic experts on hybrid warfare and hybrid threats:

> Hybrid threats incorporate a full range of different modes of warfare including conventional capabilities, irregular tactics and formations, terrorist acts including indiscriminate violence and coercion, and criminal disorder. Hybrid threats can be conducted by both states and a variety of non-state actors. These multi-modal activities can be conducted by separate units, or even by the same unit, but are generally operationally and tactically directed and coordinated within the main battle space to achieve synergistic effects in the physical and psychological dimensions of the conflict. These effects can be gained at all levels of war.[10]

There are criticisms of the various definitions that exist today. Critics claim, among other things, that the terms are too abstract and unclear.[11] Some claim that they are directly inappropriate as they mix methods that are normally part of conventional warfare and exaggerate their effects.[12]

Antagonists are the source of all hybrid threats. An antagonist is usually described as a threat actor (state or non-state) that intends to attack a society's military/political system and constitution. Modern antagonists comprise an increasing number of professionals, military actors or full-time terrorists, violent extremists, paramilitary groups, self-appointed vigilantes, freedom fighters or criminal gangs and networks.[13] They make the political and security environments more dangerous.[14]

Many antagonists work in virtual communities and on social media platforms where they offer illegal services to the highest bidder. Virtual communities are powerful venues for antagonists to communicate their messages, coordinate their activities in order to exert their influence over parts of the population and carry out hybrid threats. Others finance their activities through the illegal drug trade or other criminal activities. As a result, the interface between organized crime, extremists and state actors has become increasingly blurred.[15] Hybrid conflicts can also be initiated by transnational companies and organizations operating in a globally competitive market. Support in the form of government allocations is sometimes available. Economic profit is a strong driving force for some antagonists, regardless of type or predisposed motives. It can even be a profitable sideline. The digital, virtual cyberspace has created the conditions for a cybereconomy that has provided new opportunities for economic warfare and crime.[16]

Multilateral intelligence cooperation on hybrid threats

Ever since 9/11 the range of partners in the intelligence world that share information at the international level has grown exponentially. The change has been both quantitative and qualitative, and improved intelligence cooperation has changed the way in which agencies work.

Intelligence collaboration occurs when both sides can see potential benefits, be it from gaining information that helps complete the jigsaw, reducing the need for expensive surveillance in other countries, or more recently, less developed nations gaining precious aid resources.[17]

With a view to effectively addressing hybrid threats and conducting effective hybrid warfare, multilateral organizations such as NATO, the EU and the UN have launched a number of intelligence initiatives in the past years to improve their capacity. These initiatives have involved structural improvements, policy changes, resource allocation and the establishment of new joint hybrid centres.

The North Atlantic Treaty Organization

A *NATO Review* video posted on 3 July 2014 was the first official NATO media release to use the term 'hybrid warfare' in the context of the situation in Ukraine.[18] A few months later, during the Wales NATO Summit in September 2014, the term 'hybrid warfare' was used on several occasions to describe Russian aggression in Ukraine that had occurred in March 2014. According to Katie Abbot (2016), 'although currently, there is no Alliance consensus on one single precise definition of the term and no official NATO doctrine or Strategic Concept on hybrid warfare, since the Wales Summit, NATO has used the following definition several times in public statements and practice exercises.'[19]

> Hybrid warfare is where a wide range of overt and covert military, paramilitary and civilian measures are employed in a highly integrated design. The adversary

tries to influence influential policy-makers and key decision makers by combining kinetic operations with subversive effort. The aggressor often resorts to clandestine actions, to avoid attribution or retribution.[20]

Discussion of the concept of hybrid warfare has gained new momentum in military circles, not least within NATO:

Hybrid methods of warfare, such as propaganda, deception, sabotage and other non-military tactics have long been used to destabilize adversaries. What is new about attacks seen in recent years is their speed, scale and intensity, facilitated by rapid technological change and global interconnectivity.[21]

Writing in 2016, Jan Ballast discussed the appointment by NATO on 21 October 2016, of its first Assistant Secretary General for Intelligence and Security (ASG-I&S), Dr Arndt Freiherr Freytag von Loringhoven. The appointment was a result of a meeting of the North Atlantic Council (NAC), NATO's leading political decision-making body, in Warsaw on 8–9 July 2016, where the heads of State and Government reaffirmed the need to strengthen intelligence cooperation within NATO. The organization emphasized that enhanced intelligence cooperation would increase capabilities for early warning, protection and general resilience.[22] Freytag von Loringhoven's mission was to merge NATO's military intelligence and civil intelligence agencies with a view to providing intelligence support to the NAC and the Military Committee (Alliance Military Authority).[23]

At a meeting of NATO Heads of State and Government in Brussels on 25 May 2017, a decision was made to expand the new division by establishing a terrorist intelligence cell. According to the Secretary General, this would 'improve the exchange of information between allies, including on the threat of foreign fighters' to analyse the full spectrum of hybrid measures, including cyber security.[24] NATO had decided in 2015 to adopt a new strategy for dealing with hybrid threats based on three elements: preparing for, deterring and defending against hybrid threats. In July 2018, NATO leaders agreed to set up 'counter-hybrid support teams to counter and combat hybrid threats'. NATO's Joint Intelligence and Security Division has a unit dedicated to analysing and combating various hybrid threats and providing support to member states. It also works on propaganda and information operations.[25] Research into the ongoing conflicts in Afghanistan and Iraq shows that NATO has had difficulty understanding the complex modern warfare fought there. A lack of cultural understanding has also led to weak and sometimes incorrect analyses of hybrid threats, which has negatively affected military efforts.[26]

In the ongoing debate within NATO, it is common to discuss whether future military threats are more likely to be based on conventional or non-conventional methods. It has become increasingly common for analysts and researchers to consider it likely that a future actor will use all available means to conduct warfare against a third country. Hybrid threats are thus deemed to pose the greatest risk to global security in the future, and should serve as the starting point for military planning both nationally and before international operations.[27]

The European Union

The EU and Western armed forces recognize that future conflicts will not be characterized as either conventional or irregular warfare. Future opponents will possess the skills to utilize combinations of traditional, irregular and disruptive methods to achieve operational and strategic aims.[28] A European Commission decision of 2016 set a common regulatory framework for dealing with terrorism and hybrid threats.[29] The framework contains a collection of proposed measures aimed at helping the EU, its member states and partners respond and strengthen their resilience to hybrid threats. The proposal also includes measures to identify and protect important infrastructure in strategic sectors such as transport, energy supply, space and the financial system. Measures to secure industry, energy production, health and food safety are also proposed as well as measures in the field of cybersecurity.[30] The EU has also proposed measures in the defence sector to strengthen capabilities for dealing with hybrid threats. In this area, too, the proposals are covered by the European Security Agenda, which addresses the prevention of radicalization and extremism.[31]

The European Commission and NATO also established a new Center of Excellence in Helsinki on 11 April 2017 to counter hybrid threats. The Center will support EU and NATO member states by providing expertise, support and training, and help with countering future hybrid threats.[32] The new Center of Excellence defines hybrid threats as, 'methods and activities that are targeted towards the vulnerabilities of the opponent'. It warns that 'If the interests and goals of the user of hybrid methods and activity are not achieved, the situation can escalate into hybrid warfare where the role of military and violence will increase significantly'.[33] The aim of such activities is to influence the various forms of decision-making at the local (regional), state or institutional levels to further or achieve the agent's strategic goals while undermining and/or harming the target.[34] This new hybrid threat response within the EU provides a framework for describing the evolution of contemporary threat actors, challenging conventional threat assessment methods and elucidating the dynamics of the contemporary operating environment.[35]

The role of the EU Joint Intelligence Centres (INTCEN) within the EU External Actions Service (EEAS) is to provide intelligence analysis, early warning and awareness of hybrid threats to various EU agencies and to EU member states.[36] The INTCEN does this by monitoring and evaluating hybrid threats and international events, with a particular focus on sensitive geographical areas, terrorism and the proliferation of weapons of mass destruction.[37]

The United Nations

Almost all the UN peace missions since 2000 have been 'Chapter VII missions' with mandates that allow the use of force for peace-making, peacebuilding and peacekeeping purposes. UN efforts have evolved from ceasefire surveillance to include a wide range of tasks such as protecting civilians, supporting the implementation of elections and protecting human rights.[38] A new generation of military peacekeepers has been forced to face the reality of hybrid threats and hybrid warfare, where governments no longer have control, and where law and order no longer function or are about to collapse.[39] Violence directed at UN peacekeepers has become commonplace in these hybrid conflicts. The warring parties are not always military actors, but can be terrorists, violent extremists, paramilitary groups, self-appointed vigilantes, freedom fighters or criminal gangs and networks.[40]

In July 2017, despite fierce protest from some colleagues and UN member states, the UN Secretary-General, Ban Ki Moon, and the Deputy Secretary-General of the Department of Peacekeeping Operations (DPKO), Hervé Ladsous, adopted a new peacekeeping intelligence policy applicable to all UN missions.[41] In 2016, both had argued that the UN must become better at ensuring the security of its own personnel and responding effectively to the complex environments and hybrid threats the UN faces in its various peacekeeping missions.[42] They added that the purpose of the DPKO intelligence policy was to 'provide peacekeeping missions with so much information that they can make the best possible decisions so that their mission can be carried out effectively and safely for UN personnel'.[43] The policy is based, among other things, on the proposals put forward by the UN in its Agenda for Peace, BRAHIMI Report and HIPPO Report, as well as its resolutions, and built on the experience of peacekeeping efforts in which the UN failed to guarantee staff security in, for example, Somalia, Rwanda and Bosnia due to a lack of intelligence.[44]

When in the summer of 2018 the UN DPKO adopted a new handbook on the conduct of intelligence in peacekeeping operations (UNDPKO, 2018), this new direction was consolidated with clear guidelines for methods of intelligence gathering and analysis. The decision was given strong support by the Head of Mission/Special Representative of the Secretary-General (HoM/SRSG) for the peacekeeping operation in Mali (MINUSMA), who has long sought clear directives on the matter.[45] The decision to adopt a new policy and a new handbook on peacekeeping intelligence within the DPKO meant that the UN was openly declaring that it was engaged in intelligence work, rather than just information gathering/analysis, for the first time. The decision marked an institutional change within the UN that fundamentally affected its values and working methods. The UN has, albeit reluctantly, become an actor in the global intelligence community, with the aim of analysing and combating various hybrid threats and providing intelligence support to peacekeeping efforts operating in complex hybrid conflicts.

According to the new intelligence handbook, intelligence work in the field, and in UN peacekeeping missions in the future, must be guided and organized on the basis of a Senior Leadership Team (SLT) led by the SRSG or HoM. The heads of the Joint Mission Analysis Cell (JMAC), the Joint Operations Center (JOC), the Force Headquarters Cell (U2), the Police Component / Criminal Intelligence (CIU) and the UNDSS /Chief Security Advisor would also participate.[46] Under the SLT, intelligence work within each mission is to be led by a coordination function known as the Mission Intelligence Coordination Structure (MICS). Not all MICS will work in the same way, but their main purpose would be to provide strategic advice to the mission's management and to translate this into intelligence needs. They are expected to develop a common intelligence plan for the mission with related intelligence requirements.[47]

Hybrid threats and intelligence challenges

Intelligence studies reveal that work on hybrid threats and hybrid warnings has previously been carried out by personnel from the intelligence and security services, who rely on experience rather than scientific methodology.[48] Surprise and the inability of the intelligence- and security services to anticipate hybrid threats and other antagonistic events have had serious implications for global intelligence cooperation within NATO, the EU and the UN, which, in turn, undermine the security protections provided by these analyses.[49] Previous experience of intelligence services in non-conventional and hybrid conflicts show that the boundaries between military and civilian intelligence often become unclear. This places particular demands on intelligence management and on coordination capacity in international operations.[50]

Hybrid conflicts are often more intelligence intensive at the operational or tactical level than conventional conflicts. They therefore require more intelligence resources. Flight surveillance, human intelligence and surface surveillance are described the literature as particularly effective intelligence methods in hybrid conflicts. Cultural and linguistic competences are also important.[51] Researchers such as Stéphane Lefebvre, Walter Dorn, Olga Abilova, Arthur Boutellis, Alexandra Novosseloff and Sebastian Rietjen argue that multilateral organizations like the EU, the UN and NATO face major challenges in working with intelligence analysis and collaborations designed to counter hybrid threats or combat hybrid antagonists/threat actors.[52]

Seven challenges have been identified as particularly important for future cooperation within these three multilateral organizations:

1. Analysis: The intelligence community has flaws in its ability to conduct relevant hybrid threat analyses. Today's methods are based on traditional threats using customized threat scales, levels and risk analysis matrices. There is significant potential for the development of new models that include non-linear warfare (hybrid threats) and focus on how combining these threats in different ways can harm vital sectors of society. With a working analysis of the hybrid threat environment and a realistic assessment of vulnerabilities in the light of the threat actor's intentions and method of choice, a hybrid threat can be predicted. However, this will require specialist expertise among analysts and managers. A lack of cultural understanding has in the past led to weak and sometimes incorrect analyses of hybrid threats, which has affected, for example, military efforts in Afghanistan.[53]

2. Cultural differences: Multilateral intelligence cooperation within NATO, the EU and the UN is complicated and difficult, as the information sharing concerns sensitive intelligence on national security. It is normal for intelligence cooperation to take place at the bilateral level and for that cooperation to be based on trust and long-term relationships.[54] In the multilateral intelligence cooperation between different member states, cultural differences can affect how classified information is handled and shared. Prior to the 9/11 terrorist attacks, intelligence cooperation in, for example, NATO was primarily focused on the so-called Five Eyes agreement, which comprised the United States, the United Kingdom, Canada, Australia and New Zealand.[55] However, the intelligence information provided by the Five Eyes was not automatically shared with all the NATO member states due to a mistrust of new members and uncertainty about

the robustness of non-proliferation and storage facilities.[56] After 9/11, this approach changed and the United States and the United Kingdom became more pragmatic about intelligence cooperation in NATO in the fight against terrorism. This new pragmatism was also applied to intelligence cooperation in the EU and partially the UN. A key to success in this area is to require member states not to automatically share information as well as intelligence reporting that is at the highest level of confidentiality.

3. Confidential information: Confidentiality in intelligence reporting is reliant on the EU, NATO and the UN establishing functioning information systems that can handle confidential classification, secure relationships and secure document management at all levels, with clearly discernible classification and access levels.[57] Limited resources, unclear mandates and a lack of clear sector boundaries between the intelligence system and other departments/entities affect the confidentiality of information within the EU, NATO and the UN.[58] Today, intelligence material must be handled and filed according to special security procedures based on 'need to know' and 'need to share' principles. These routines probably need to be revised to better align them with the organizations' new requirements. A lack of information transfer technology systems is a problem within the EU, NATO and the UN and restricts the sharing of confidential information.[59]

4. Competence and expertise: Those who are given a mandate to make decisions on issues related to hybrid threats and intelligence services should have the relevant expertise and the ability to perform such work, and must be responsible for their decisions in accordance with the organization's governance and management structures.[60] At the tactical level, in order to be able to provide actionable, close to real time intelligence to operational units on a battlefield, a balanced variety of intelligence assets is needed to both collect and analyse the information required. Apart from their purely military skills, intelligence personnel need to have access to a range of expertise from linguists to regional and sociocultural specialists, as well as legal and political experts, and so on.[61] Organizations will need to arrange training for senior executives in the future on the intelligence resources that are at their disposal and how to formulate intelligence needs, request information and provide feedback.[62]

5. Governance and management: The governance and management of intelligence analysis in multilateral organizations is dependent on the multilateral organizations' staff members being trained and competent, and their understanding the different elements of the intelligence cycle, the demands placed on them and the difference between strategic, operational and tactical intelligence services.[63]

6. Independence: The question of the independence of organizations in relation to other member states with regard to intelligence work places new demands on individual staff. The ambition of the EU, NATO and the UN to be independent of all member states' intelligence and security services in all respects has proved complicated, as intelligence personnel seconded to, for example, the UN from its member states have dual loyalties. Intelligence personnel seconded to the EU, NATO and the UN are dependent on their capitals and home offices for their future career prospects. This can make them more loyal to their capitals than their secondment. The time they work for the EU, NATO and the UN is often limited and most return to their home states after their secondment.

7. Ethical and legal constraints: Ethics and legality are not always perceived as major attributes of intelligence services. In connection with irregular warfare, these two concepts can come to the fore based on how proportionality is treated. Can methods of obtaining intelligence that violate international law, national laws and/or ethics and morals be used and defended in cases where, for example, they might avert a terrorist attack and save a great many lives? In order to answer such questions, multilateral organizations must develop and implement an organizational framework that clearly defines the ethical and legal constraints on intelligence – something that is often currently absent.

The future of hybrid threats and multilateral intelligence collaboration

Instability and uncertainty characterize today's security environment and produce multidimensional challenges for the intelligence community. Complex hybrid threats in Western societies often aim to disrupt, undermine, weaken or damage another state's political system and constitution through a combination of violence, control, subversion, manipulation and dissemination of information in a grey zone between peace and war.[64]

In a globalized world, the shared enemies of democratic nations have shifted from the boundaries of other nations (as was the case during the Cold War) to more amorphous threats such as hybrid warfare, terrorism, extremism and organized crime. Dealing with these international issues realistically requires an international approach – enter multilateral intelligence collaboration.

Several new intelligence initiatives within the EU, NATO and the UN have been created to improve the multilateral collection and dissemination processes of intelligence reporting on hybrid threats. With the help of such intelligence, these multilateral organizations seek to predict the steps an adversary might take and to prepare a military response accordingly.

The extent to which the various new intelligence initiatives within the EU, NATO and the UN will actually enhance methods to combat hybrid threats and hybrid warfare is yet to be determined. Lack of trust, cultural differences and the lack of a functioning leadership in NATO, the EU and the UN are among the troubling trends that could hamper future operations.

The nature of hybrid threats at present should be the starting point for thinking about future intelligence collaboration. The intelligence community will face new combinations of cyber and kinetic operations in the future. Given the fact that the virtual realm has dramatically lowered the cost of hybrid activities such as propaganda and cyber operations, it is conceivable that some of these future threat actors will use proxies to conduct hybrid operations more often than before, in an effort to remain, if not anonymous, then at least difficult to identify.

Multilateral intelligence collaboration can bring a new light to these global hybrid threats by 'bringing diverse perspectives together'.[65]

This gives the nations involved in this type of collaboration a better understanding on how to deal with hybrid threats. Another benefit of multilateral intelligence collaboration is the 'possibility of developing more common vocabularies for thinking about problems with fewer inter-cultural and international misunderstandings'.[66]

It is not possible for one country to effectively cover all the areas of interest that their intelligence collection requirements demand. By dividing up areas of responsibility among partner nations more ground can be covered in more depth than by working in isolation. It is also a fact of the current economic climate that no one nation can afford to pay the bill for comprehensive global intelligence collection.[67]

Notes

1   See, e.g., Benjamin Wittes, 'What Is Hybrid Conflict?', *Lawfare*, 11 September 2015. https://lawfareblog.com/what-hybrid-conflict. See also Damien van Puyvelde, 'Hybrid War – Does It Even Exist?', *NATO Review* 7, 7 May 2015. http://www.nato.int/docu/review/2015/Also-in-2015/hybrid-modern-future-warfare-russia-ukraine/EN/.

2   National Defence Radio Establishment, *Hybridhot,* accessed 7 April 2020. https://www.fra.se/underrattelser/hybridhot.4.60b3f8fa16488d849a54a6.html.

3   Per-Arne Persson, James Nyce, Mats Persson, Minna Räsänen and Jan-Inge Svensson Per-Arne Persson, *Från koncept till öppet system – utveckling av operativ och taktisk underrättelsetjänst i den militära insatsorganisationen, för att verka, synas och respekteras* (Stockholm: Swedish Defence University, 2008).

4   For a definition of multilateral agreements, see http://www.businessdictionary.com/definition/multilateralagreement.html.

5   James Igoe Walsh, *The International Politics of Intelligence Sharing* (New York: Columbia University Press, 2010), 5; and Janine McGruddy, 'Multilateral Intelligence Collaboration and International Oversight', *Journal of Strategic Security* 6, no. 3 (2013): 214–20.

6   William J. Nemeth, *Future War and Chechnya: A Case for Hybrid Warfare* (Monterey: Naval Postgraduate School, 2002); András Racz, *Russia's Hybrid War in Ukraine: Breaking the Enemy's Ability to Resist* (Helsinki: The Finnish Institute of International Affairs, 2015).

7   Nathan Freier, 'Hybrid Threats and Challenges: Describe . . . Don't Define', *Small Wars Journal* 5 (2009): 7–8.

8   John J. McCuen, 'Hybrid Wars', *Military Review* 88, no. 2 (March–April 2008): 10–113.

9   Colin S. Gray, 'Irregular Warfare One Nature, Many Characters', *Strategic Studies Quarterly* 1, no. 2 (2007): 35–57.

10 Frank Hoffmann, *Conflict in the 21st Century: The Rise of Hybrid Wars* (Arlington: Potomac Institute for Policy Studies, December 2007), 14.

11 John Kiszley, 'The Relevance of History to the Military Profession: A British View', in *The Past as a Prologue: The Importance of History to the Military Profession*, eds Williamson Murray and Richard Hart Sinnreich (New York: Cambridge University Press, 2006), 31.

12 See, e.g. Wittes, 'What Is Hybrid Conflict?'; van Puyvelde, 'Hybrid War'.

13 Olga Abilova and Arthur Boutellis, *UN Peace Operations in Violent and Asymmetric Threat Environments* (International Peace Institute, 2016).

14 Henrik Häggström and Filip Ahlin, *Det nya normala – studie om hot mot den kärntekniska industrin* (Swedish Defence University, CATS, 2017).

15 Jörgen Elving and Lars Ulving, *Historiska erfarenheter av underrättelsetjänst i samband med icke konventionella konflikter – ISTAR-förmåga på operativ och taktisk nivå* (Stockholm: Swedish Defence University, 2009).

16 Steven Metz, *Rethinking Insurgency* (Carlisle: Strategic Studies Institute, 2012).

17 McGruddy, 'Multilateral Intelligence Collaboration', 214–20.

18 NATO Review, 'Hybrid War – Hybrid Response?', 1 July 2014. https://www.nato.int/docu/review/articles/2014/07/01/hybrid-war-hybrid-response/index.html.

19 Katie Abbott, *Understanding and Countering Hybrid Warfare: Next Steps for the North Atlantic Treaty Organization* (University of Ottawa, 23 March 2016), 8.

20 North Atlantic Treaty Organization, Wales Summit, 5 September 2014, quoted in Abbott, *Understanding and Countering Hybrid Warfare*, 8.

21 North Atlantic Treaty Organization, 'NATO's Response to Hybrid Threats', 2 July 2018, retrieved 8 maj 2019. https://www.nato.int/cps/en/natohq/topics_156338.htm.

22 Jan Ballast, 'Merging Pillars, Changing Cultures: Nato and the Future of Intelligence Cooperation within the Alliance', *International Journal of Intelligence and CounterIntelligence* 31, no. 4 (2018): 720.

23 Arnt Freytag von Loringhoven, 'Adapting NATO Intelligence in Support of "One NATO"', *NATO Review* 8, September 2017, accessed 31 March 2018. https://www.nato.int/docu/review/2017/Also-in-2017/adapting-nato-intelligence-in-support-of-one-nato-security-military-terrorism/EN/index.htm.

24 Ballast, 'Merging Pillars', 721; North Atlantic Treaty Organization 'NATO Leaders Agree to do More to Fight Terrorism and Ensure Fairer Burden Sharing', 25 May 2017, accessed 25 May 2017. http://www.nato.int/cps/en/natohq/news_144154.htm.

25 North Atlantic Treaty Organization, 'NATO's Response to Hybrid Threats'.

26 Frank G. Hoffman, 'Hybrid Threats: Neither Omnipotent Nor Unbeatable', *Orbis* 54, no. 3 (2010): 441–55.

27 Frank G. Hoffman, 'Hybrid Threats: Reconceptualizing the Evolving Character of Modern Conflict', *Strategic Forum*, no. 240 (Washington, DC: Institute for National Strategic Studies, National Defense University, April 2009).

28 The European Centre of Excellence for Countering Hybrid Threats, 'Countering Hybrid Threats', accessed 7 April 2020. https://www.hybridcoe.fi/hybrid-threats/.

29 Ministry for Foreign Affairs, *Faktapromemoria 2015/16:FPM80: Gemensamt ramverk för att motverka hybridhot*, 11 May 2015.

30 The European Centre of Excellence for Countering Hybrid Threats, 'Countering Hybrid Threats'.

31 Ministry for Foreign Affairs, *Gemensamt ramverk*.

32 The European Centre of Excellence for Countering Hybrid Threats, 'Countering Hybrid Threats'.

33 The European Centre of Excellence for Countering Hybrid Threats, 'Countering Hybrid Threats'.

34 The European Centre of Excellence for Countering Hybrid Threats, 'Countering Hybrid Threats'.

35 Hoffman, 'Neither Omnipotent Nor Unbeatable'.

36 European External Action Service, 'EU Intelligence Analysis Centre (EU INTCEN): Fact Sheet', accessed 20 January 2020. https://www.asktheeu.org/en/request/637/response/2416/attach/html/5/EU%20INTCEN%20Factsheet%20PUBLIC%20120618%201.pdf.html.

37 European External Action Service, 'EU Intelligence Analysis Centre (EU INTCEN): Fact Sheet'.

38 A. Walter Dorn, 'Intelligence at UN Headquarters? The Information and Research Unit and the Intervention in Eastern Zaire 1996', *Intelligence & National Security* 20, no. 3 (September 2005): 440–65.

39 A. Walter Dorn, 'United Nations Peacekeeping Intelligence' in *The Oxford Handbook of National Security Intelligence*, ed. Loch K. Johnson (Oxford: Oxford University Press, 2010), 275–95.

40 Olga Abilova and Alexandra Novosseloff, *Demystifying Intelligence in UN Peace Operations: Toward an Organizational Doctrine* (New York: International Peace Institute, July 2016).

41 United Nations Department of Peacekeeping Operations, *Policy: Peacekeeping Intelligence*, 2 May 2017. https://www.confluxcenter.org/wp-content/uploads/2018/11 /2017.07-Peacekeeping-Intelligence-Policy.pdf.

42 United Nations Department of Peacekeeping Operations, *Policy: Peacekeeping Intelligence*

43 United Nations Department of Peacekeeping Operations, *Policy: Peacekeeping Intelligence*, 10: 3.

44 United Nations General Assembly, Resolution 71/314, *Comprehensive Review of the Whole Question of Peacekeeping Operations in All their Aspects,* adopted 19 July 2017. file:///C:/ Users/mvi17001/Downloads/A_RES_71_314-EN.pdf; United Nations General Assembly, *Identical Letters Dated 21 August 2000 from the Secretary General to the President of the General Assembly and the President of the Security Council, A/55/305-S/2000/809,* 21 August 2000. https://www.refworld.org/docid/49997ae61a.html; United Nations, *Uniting Our Strengths for Peace – Politics, Partnership and People: Report of the High-Level Independent Panel on Peace Operations,* 16 June 2015. https://www.refworld.org/docid /558bb0134.html; United Nations General Assembly, *Report of the High Level Independent Panel on United Nations Peace Operations (HIPPO), A/70/95 S/2015/446,* 17 June 2015. https://www.un.org/en/ga/search/view_doc.asp?symbol=S/2015/446.

45 Interview, Peter Öberg, military advisor, Permanent Mission of Sweden to the United Nations, New York, 17 November 2017.

46 United Nations Department of Peacekeeping Operations, *Policy: Peacekeeping Intelligence*.

47 Abilova and Novosseloff, *Demystifying Intelligence.*

48 Wilhelm Agrell, *The Black Swan and Its Opponents – Early Warning Aspects of the Norway Attacks on 22 July 2011* (Stockholm: National Defence University, CATS, 2013).

49 Stéphane Lefebvre, 'The Difficulties and Dilemmas of International Intelligence Cooperation', *International Journal of Intelligence and CounterIntelligence* 16, no. 4 (2003): 527–42.

50 Elfving and Ulving, *Historiska erfarenheter.*

51 Persson et al., *Från koncept till öppet system.*

52 Sebastiaan Rietjens and A. Walter Dorn, *The Evolution of Peacekeeping Intelligence: The UN's Laboratory in Mali* in *Perspectives on Military Intelligence from the First World War to Mali – Between Learning and Law,* eds Floribert Baudet, Eleni Braat, Jeoffrey van Woensel and Aad Wever (The Hague: Asser Press, 2017).

53 Hoffman, 'Reconceptualizing the Evolving Character'.

54 Adriana N. Seagle, 'Intelligence Sharing Practices Within NATO: An English School Perspective' *International Journal of Intelligence and CounterIntelligence* 28, no. 3 (2015): 560.

55 Ballast, 'Merging Pillars'.
56 John Kriendler, 'NATO Intelligence and Early Warning', *Conflict Studies Research Center Special Series* 06/13 (Swindon: Conflict Studies Research Center, 2006), 3; Friedrich W. Korkisch, *NATO Gets Better Intelligence: New Challenges Require New Answers to Satisfy Intelligence Needs for Headquarters and Deployed/Employed Forces* (Vienna: Center for Foreign and Defense Policy, 2010), 41; Claudia Bernasconi, 'NATO's Fight Against Terrorism: Where Do We Stand?', *Research Paper* no. 66 (Rome: NATO Defense College), 5; Seagle, 'Intelligence Sharing Practices', 558–9.
57 Lefebvre, 'Difficulties and Dilemmas', 527–42.
58 Dorn, *Peacekeeping Intelligence*, 275.
59 A. Walter Dorn, 'The Cloak and the Blue Beret: limitations on Intelligence in UN Peacekeeping', *International Journal of Intelligence and CounterIntelligence* 12, no. 4 (1999): 417–47; Dorn, 'Intelligence at UN Headquarters', 440–65.
60 Abilova and Novosseloff, *Demystifying Intelligence*; Abilova and Boutellis, *UN Peace Operations*.
61 Rainer Glatz, 'ISAF Lessons Learned: A German Perspective', *PRISM* 2, no. 2 (March 2011): 169–76.
62 Erik D. Jens, 'Human Intelligence Operations in ISAF', *American Intelligence Journal* 13, no. 1 (2013): 21–8.
63 Abilova and Novosseloff, *Demystifying Intelligence*.
64 Sofia Hedenstierna, Bo Johansson Gilljam, Mats Hartmann, Camilla Andersson, Joakim Storck, Matilda Ågren, Charlie Hagerman, Rolf Jarlås, Niklas Johansson, Peter Alvå and Johan Pelo, *Metoder för sårbarhets- och verkansvärdering – Sammanfattande slutrapport för perioden 2017-2019* (Swedish Defence Research Agency, 2019).
65 Roger Z. George, *Meeting 21st Century Transnational Challenges: Building a Global Intelligence Paradigm* (Washington, DC: CIA Center for the Study of Intelligence, 2007), 151. https://www.cia.gov/library/center-for-thestudy-of-intelligence/csi-publications/csi-studies/studies/vol51no3/building-a-global-intelligenceparadigm.html.
66 George, *Meeting 21st Century Transnational Challenges*.
67 McGruddy, 'Multilateral Intelligence Collaboration', 214–20.

Cyberwarfare and the internet

The implications of a more digitalized world

Anne-Marie Eklund Löwinder and Anna Djup

Introduction

The creation of the internet has allowed the world to become more globalized and interconnected, producing an environment where organizations are dependent on data flows to conduct their everyday business, affecting everything from operability to business models. In an article from *The Economist* in 2017, it was argued that data is becoming as crucial to the society as oil[1] since the growing reliance on interconnected information makes it impossible to disconnect. This connectivity has in turn made information highly valuable and opened up for new attack vectors, generating a market for hacking and data theft.

If 'data is the new oil',[2] the growing market for cyber theft could potentially jeopardize the future digital society. For the open internet to continue to exist as a platform for social and economic growth, users must be able to trust that organizations can protect the systems governing the society and have the capacity to safeguard personal information. However, several cases over the years have proved that neither governments nor businesses possess the ability to mitigate imminent cyber threats.

Due to the nature of cyberattacks, it is difficult to ascertain who the actor is and what their intentions are. Cyberattacks are inherently asymmetric in nature as an actor with few means can do much harm to a single individual, organization or nation. Fuelled by the continued trend of organizations and companies connecting to the internet, actors can now easily exploit existing bugs and vulnerabilities in connected devices and networks to achieve their goals.

The much-feared cyber havoc or digital Pearl Harbor[3] becomes possible as critical infrastructure is accommodating to the needs of a more digitalized society. To create a digital Pearl Harbor, threat actors will direct an attack against industrial control systems responsible for critical infrastructure. The systems are suitable targets given that the systems were not designed for a digital world, are often out of date, inadequately maintained and difficult to patch. The situation gets even direr as threat actors are using digital tools such as targeted advertising and deep fakes to conduct invisible manipulation of public opinion and election outcomes.

The combination of poorly designed systems, together with new technologies, expands the scope and severity of global cyber threats, and how to tackle these threats will have far-reaching consequences for the future of the internet.

The internet architecture and its vulnerabilities

The internet consists of a layered and distributed architecture, starting at the physical level and then ending with users and applications. At the most fundamental level, the infrastructure includes hardware, physical infrastructure, interconnection, software, protocols, information services and human resources.

Networks, or autonomous systems, connect to components in the physical layers, carrying data via a set of protocols to the desired destination through logical addressing schemes. This enables operators to troubleshoot and take immediate action if problems arise as a delayed response could cause disruptions and severely affect the functionality of the internet. Between those layers, the internet is comprised of various components needed to ensure reliability, resilience and robustness.

At each level, various risks and vulnerabilities become apparent, which different actors can exploit to their advantage. These include, among others routing threats or attacks against the Domain Name System (DNS). The DNS-system represents one of the cornerstones of the internet as the system enables the translation of URLs into IP-addresses, creating a directory for every connected node, device, computer or resources available on the internet.

An attacker can exploit the system through DNS-hijacking or DNS-spoofing, whereby an attacker intercepts a user's DNS-request and redirects them to a compromised DNS-server or infects the user's device with malicious code through a phishing mail, infested link or other malicious activity. The malware then changes the victim's settings and redirects DNS-requests to the attacker's DNS-server. One such case was Roaming Mantis, which infected Android-based tablets and smartphones globally in 2018.[4] Routing threats are just severe DNS-attacks as routers provide the basis for the robustness of the internet. An attacker can hi-jack, re-configure or intercept assigned numbers, addresses or namespaces to influence or undermine the operation of one or several interconnected networks.[5]

Moreover, threat actors can execute denial-of-service (DoS) attacks. DoS attacks are characterized by an explicit attempt by attackers to prevent legitimate use of a service. There are two general forms of DoS attacks, those that crash services and those that flood services. The most serious attacks are distributed (DDoS). In order to execute a DDoS attack, you need control of a large number of connected devices, which can be managed by a command and control centre (C&C). In a DDoS attack the goal is to make a device or network unavailable to its intended users. Attackers usually target sites or services hosted by high-profile web servers such as banks, credit card gateways, DNS name servers or root name servers. Targets of recent DDoS attacks include the DNS providers Cloudflare and Akamai, resulting in disrupted operability for the providers and all their customers. The biggest DDoS attack to date happened in

February 2018 when threat actors targeted GitHub, a platform popular for online code management and used by millions of developers. At its peak, the platform experienced 1.35 terabytes of traffic per second,[6] which indicates what enormous power some threat actors can wield at any given time.

Furthermore, as the complexity and scale of the internet architecture deepen, so does the dependencies between open source, software development kits, scripting and programming frameworks, resulting in additional risks and vulnerabilities. What previously needed to be a complex, intensive and highly targeted operation by a threat actor can now be done with much less effort. Historically, you needed some type of insider to create a backdoor for an actor to gain access to an organization's network, which meant that each operation was labour intensive and very costly. Only nation-states had that capability and resources to execute such operation and, therefore, carefully selected their targets. One example is Backdoor Reign, which was an extremely complex backdoor Trojan used by nation-states to conduct surveillance activities against selected targets.[7]

In a recent report published by the company Synopsys, researchers discovered that approximately 77 per cent of the code-base in IoT-devices came from open-source components with an average of 677 vulnerabilities per application.[8] As most software now is a mash-up of code from different libraries, and continuously being updated by developers via delivery models, it becomes difficult to audit and allows threat actors to insert malicious code into the environment. However, the positive effects of open-source software are the application of the 'many-eyes'-principles, which reduces the risk of security by obscurity in comparison with proprietary code, that is, closed source software.

As most software now is a mash-up of code from different libraries and is continuously being updated by developers via delivery models, it becomes difficult to audit and allows threat actors to insert malicious code into the environment.

Moreover, the threat of backdoors keeps expanding and now presents a real danger to organizations, businesses and governments alike. During the first half of 2018, 3.1 per cent of all attacks directed at industrial automation systems stemmed from backdoors, which was a 50 per cent increase from the previous year,[9] and businesses saw a 173 per cent increase year-on-year for backdoor detections.[10] Worrying examples of backdoor vulnerabilities had become particularly apparent since 2017 when WannaCry and NotPetya emerged and raised havoc around the world.

A hacker group named Shadow Brokers was taking advantage of hitting unpatched systems all over the globe with the WannaCry attack, which used an exploit known as 'EternalBlue', spread across 150 countries. The threat actors exploited vulnerabilities in Microsoft's SMBv1 server protocol, which affected not only Microsoft's operating systems such as Windows XP and Windows 10 but other systems running on Microsoft's SMBv1 server protocol.[11] The vulnerability allowed for an attacker to remotely execute arbitrary code on a targeted system by sending crafted messages to an SMBv1 server. Microsoft patched a number of the vulnerabilities in 2017, but patching was not performed as quickly as needed. And then the world was hit by NonPetya.[12]

As of yet, the majority of the world's governments have not spent enough time evaluating the security and risks of the internet infrastructure, leading to different approaches and levels of security. Many governments are currently selling off or outsourcing large parts of their critical infrastructure without a thorough risk analysis of third parties and private actors, leaving them vulnerable to attacks that may disrupt critical societal services. This could potentially create a situation of uncertainty when assessing third parties and private actors as their goals and interests may not be aligned with the host country.

The fragility of the system becomes apparent when looking at the last two decades. Between the 1980s and the 1990s, the development of fibre-optic technologies and deregulation of the telecommunications market significantly changed how networks operated. As many fibre-optic cable projects became deregulated and privatized, the ventures focused on making a profit rather than meeting forecasted demand, affecting the resilience and robustness of providing an internet connection. If an undersea communication cable were to be tampered with, it could severely cripple a nation or an entire region's access to the World Wide Web and hamper their information warfare capability.[13]

Although it appears to be a redundancy of physical fibre-optic cables according to the Infrapedia's Network Atlas,[14] they are usually hard to protect and prone to disruptions due to their visibility and coverage of large geographical areas. This vulnerability can be illustrated with the case of a Georgian woman accidentally cutting off the main fibre-optic cable connecting Armenia to the rest of the world when she was scavenging for scrap metal.[15] As Georgia provides around 90 per cent of Armenia's internet, the consequences of this unintentional disruption were disastrous.

The interdependencies created between the internet and critical infrastructure make it susceptible to cyberwarfare. One example is the dependency between the internet and electrical power. The internet is dependent on electrical power for its functioning, and electrical power grids are dependent on the internet for their operability. Modernizing and automating electrical power grid networks via the internet produces a more efficient and cost-effective way of distributing power; however, it introduces several new vulnerabilities and risks that were non-existent decades ago. Several governments globally are now worried about cyberattacks targeting their power grids. According to a Wired article from 2009,[16] China and Russia have successfully infiltrated the US electrical grid and implemented malicious software that could create massive outages and disrupt the US economy. One example of how devastating it can be was the blackout in Ukraine in 2015 and 2016.

We will most certainly need a new paradigm: We are all hacked. And act accordingly.

Cyberwarfare as a mean

The definition of cyberwarfare is highly contested internationally, as no single concept has been widely accepted. Several definitions have been proposed over the years, such as the 'actions by a nation-state to penetrate another nation's computer or networks for the purposes of causing damage or disruption'[17] by Richard A. Clarke, a former US government official and National Coordinator for Security, Infrastructure Protection and Counter-terrorism. Martin C. Libicki[18] offers another explanation and defines it as two types, strategic and operational, where the strategic type is 'a campaign of cyberattacks one entity carries out on another', while the operational type 'involves the use of cyberattacks on the other side's military in the context of a physical war'. It can also be explained as the actions made by an actor to attack or attempt to damage an adversary's computer or information network through malicious code, targeting online control systems governing logical and physical networks.

As the internet becomes intertwined with states' national security, offensive and defence cyber strategies will shape the future internet for users and industry alike. Cyberspace is now considered to be the fifth domain of warfare, joining land, sea, air and space, but unlike the other domains, the conflicts in cyberspace will not be like traditional warfare. Instead, nation-states, criminal organizations, hacktivists[19] and terrorist groups will utilize existing vulnerabilities in computer and network systems governing civilian populations and society as a whole. Actors will target all aspects of the internet infrastructure, including physical and logical infrastructure, internet service providers, to different platforms, data communication mediums and network equipment. As a result, nation-states around the globe have been developing cyber capabilities and engaged in cyber conflicts, including the United States, China, Russia, Israel, the United Kingdom, Iran and North Korea, making cyberwarfare an integrated part of their overall military strategy.

As societies become more digitalized, cyberwarfare as a means to achieve strategic goals has never been easier. Nation-states and criminal organizations alike can potentially use clandestine means within the cyberspace to attain secret information as exhibited by the United States' National Security Agency (NSA) tracking of cell phone conversations made in the Bahamas without the permission of the Bahamian government or the data breach against the US Office of Personnel, which was allegedly done by China.

Cyberspace also provides an excellent venue for sabotage, economic disruption and influence campaigns. The asymmetric nature of internet-based attacks makes it difficult to determine motivating factors and attribute the attack to a specific actor, producing an environment of uncertainty and whether a specific act can be considered as an act of war.

In mid-July 2010, security experts discovered a malicious software programme named Stuxnet, which had infiltrated computers at an Iranian nuclear facility delaying Iran's ability to develop a nuclear capability. The *New York Times* regarded the attack to be 'the first attack on critical infrastructure that sits at the foundation of modern economies'.[20] In 2017, the world experienced WannaCry and NotPetya, two cases of malicious code masquerading as ransomware, which severely affected the UK's National Health Service and the shipping company Maersk.[21]

Examples of influence campaigns with underlying cyberwarfare components can be seen in 2008 when Russia attacked the Georgian government website or when the Chinese attackers targeted the media company CNN as the company reported on Chinese repression in Tibet.

Stuxnet, WannaCry and NotPetya highlight not only the vulnerabilities of connecting critical infrastructure to the cyberspace but also how malware developers effectively can influence global politics and governments by sharing exploits and developments to others. This allows lesser hackers to become proficient in executing large-scale attacks, which only a few were able to do previously. The sharing of information has also created a form of online arms proliferation as techniques and malware are being sold to the highest bidder through black markets.

According to Clarke, the civilian population is also at risk of being exposed to cyberattacks, noting that attackers have gone beyond stealing credit card numbers to also include attacks against for societal services or the stock market.[22] Cyberwarfare represents a multitude of threats as cyberattacks can have a supporting role in traditional warfare. Considering 'hard threats' and 'soft threats', a well-executed cyberattack can either enable the tampering with a country's air defence systems in order to facilitate an attack from the sky, cut off all power to a country or facilitate cyber espionage activities and influence campaigns.

Conclusion

With the increased threat of cyberattacks from nation-states, hackers and criminal organizations alike, it has started to affect the way the world views the internet. Inadequate management of cyber threats puts users at risk, erodes the trust in the platform and jeopardizes its ability to be a driver for economic and social innovation.

Misinformed and disproportionate government responses can potentially threaten internet freedom and create a climate of fear, uncertainty and doubt. The future of the internet and the continued growth of the platform will be determined by how governments and organizations collectively respond to the volume and scale of cyberattacks. As governments come under pressure to mitigate the effects of cyberattacks, there is a growing risk that online freedoms and global connectivity will be severely restricted in favour of national security. New models for incentives, accountability and liability are urgently needed to increase cybersecurity readiness, reduce vulnerabilities and to ensure end-user security. The complexity and scope of cyberattacks necessitate multi-stakeholder and expert-driven responses for the digital economy to continue to thrive and for the trust in the internet to be rebuilt.

Neither governments nor the private sector have the ability to deal with the scope and the scale of cyber threats alone. Due to the interconnected nature of the internet, actions made by lone stakeholders will do little to mitigate or eliminate cyber threats. Driven by the need to be seen as 'doing something' in the face of increasingly complex cyberattacks, it is expected that government responses to emerging cyber threats will be increasingly reactive. However, such reactive responses will not effectively mitigate the threat, but rather result in excessive overregulation. Effective action and network resilience against cyber threats can only emerge through information sharing, strategic thinking and collaborative efforts among stakeholders.

It is also important to emphasize that the way stakeholders adapt to future cyberattacks may change the internet from being a platform of openness and collaboration to a fragmented, closed and secure network environment. A fundamental change to the architecture and the underlying principles of the internet could deliver a dystopian future of a secured walled garden, filtering access and with no encryption, anonymity or privacy. The national security of national states would overshadow the freedoms and rights we now take for granted, causing a struggle between perceived national security interests and end-user security measures.

The long-discussed need for a global culture on cybersecurity will take on new relevance and urgency as cybersecurity becomes the responsibility of everyone. No system will be immune to cyberattacks and cybercrime in the future, and these threats will affect all aspects of society. The idea that a 'network is only as strong as its weakest link' will take on a new meaning in a hyper-connected world, as connected devices can undermine an entire nation. It will become imperative to raise the awareness of the importance of security on all levels, either through security literacy or by developing secure connected devices. To meet the future needs, a market for security needs to be established in order to ensure overall network and device security. This can be done by either implementing liability models or improving governments' procurement practices.

Cyber governance can no longer remain solely in the hands of governments as the risk of being exposed to a cyberattack continuously increases. Much of the global internet infrastructure today are being developed, owned and maintained by private actors, and because of the complexity and scope of cyberattacks, governments alone are unable to provide inclusive and expert-driven regulatory responses, and thus need to encourage private actors to join the discussions on the future of the internet.

As cyberattacks become more advanced and a tool for nation-states to extract information, influence elections and disrupt critical infrastructure, the threat has grown to immense proportions. Private actors are now calling on governments to implement norms that would protect civilians in times of peace and are trying to encourage the international community to establish an international organization with the mandate to investigate state-sponsored cyberattacks. There are also calls for private tech-companies to pledge to protect their users from all cyberattacks regardless of origin and never assist a nation-state in carrying out offensive operations in cyberspace. Governments around the world will need to work together to fix software vulnerabilities – not stockpile them to use against each other.

Notes

1   Economist, 'The World's Most Valuable Source Is No Longer Oil, but Data', *The Economist,* 6 May 2019. https://www.economist.com/leaders/2017/05/06/the-worlds -most-valuable-resource-is-no-longer-oil-but-data.

2   Samuel Flender, 'Data Is Not the New Oil: About the Reality of Working with Data', *Towards Data Science,* 10 February 2019. https://towardsdatascience.com/data-is-not -the-new-oil-bdb31f61bc2d.

3   Dave Weinstein, 'Stop Saying "Digital Pearl Harbor"', *DARKReading,* 2 October 2018. https://www.darkreading.com/threat-intelligence/stop-saying-digital-pearl-harbor/a /d-id/1332932.

4   Suguru Ishimaru, 'Roaming Mantis Uses DNS Hacking to Infect Android Smartphones', *Kapersky*, 16 April 2018. https://securelist.com/roaming-mantis-uses -dns-hijacking-to-infect-android-smartphones/85178/; Suguru Ishimaru, 'Roaming Mantis Dabbles in Mining and Phishing Multilingually',*Kaspersky*, 18 May 2018. https ://securelist.com/roaming-mantis-dabbles-in-mining-and-phishing-multilingually/8 5607/; National Cyber Security Center, 'DNS Hacking Activity', 25 January 2019. https ://www.ncsc.gov.uk/news/alert-dns-hijacking-activity.

5   RFC 4593, Generic threats to routing protocols. https://tools.ietf.org/html/rfc4593.

6   Lily Newman Hay, 'GitHub Survived the Biggest DDOS Attack Ever Recorded', *The Wired*, 1 March 2018. https://www.wired.com/story/github-ddos-memcached/.

7   Symantec Security Response, 'Reign: Top-Tier Espionage Tool Enables Stealthy Surveillance', 23 November 2014. https://www.symantec.com/connect/blogs/regin-top -tier-espionage-tool-enables-stealthy-surveillance.

8   Taylor Armerding, 'The Future of Open Source Software: More of Everything', Synopsys, 24 January 2019. https://www.synopsys.com/blogs/software-security/future -of-open-source-predictions/.

9   Kaspersky Labs ICS-CERT, *Threat Landscape for Industrial Automation Systems H1 2019,* 30 September 2019. https://ics-cert.kaspersky.com/reports/2019/09/30/threat -landscape-for-industrial-automation-systems-h1-2019/.

10 Malwarebytes Labs, *2019 State of Malware,* 2019. https://resources.malwarebytes.com/ files/2019/01/Malwarebytes-Labs-2019-State-of-Malware-Report-2.pdf.

11 SentinelOne, 'EternalBlue: The NSA-Developed Exploit that Just Won't Die',*SentinelOne*, 27 May 2019. https://www.sentinelone.com/blog/eternalblue-nsa-d eveloped-exploit-just-wont-die/.

12 Pradeep Kulkarni, Sameer Patil, Prashant Kadam and Aniruddha Dolas, 'EternalBlue: A Prominent Threat Actor of 2017–2018', *Virus Bulletin*. https://www.virusbulletin .com/virusbulletin/2018/06/eternalblue-prominent-threat-actor-20172018/.

13 Nicole Starosielski, *The Undersea Network* (Durham: Duke University Press, 2015). See also NATO CCDCOE, 'Strategic Importance of, and Dependence on, Undersea Cables', November 2019; John Filitz, 'Undersea Fiber-Optic Cable Security – Threats from Below', *Stable Sea*, 27 March 2019.

14 Infrapedia, https://www.infrapedia.com/.

15 Tom Parfitt, 'Georgian Woman Cuts Off Web Access to Whole of Armenia', *The Guardian,* 6 April 2011. https://www.theguardian.com/world/2011/apr/06/georgian- woman-cuts-web-access.

16 Wired, 'China and Russia vs. US Grid!', *Wired*, 4 August 2009. https://www.wired.com /2009/04/china-and-russi/.

17 Richard A. Clarke, *Cyber War* (New York: HarperCollins, 2010), 6. See also Adam Segal, *The Hacked World Order: How Nations Fight, Trade, Maneuver, and Manipulate in the Digital Age* (New York: PublicAffairs, 2017); Kaplan Fred, *Dark Territory: The Secret History of Cyber War* (New York: Simon and Schuster, 2017); Robert Clarke and Robert E. Knake, *The Fifth Domain: Defending Our Country, Our Companies, and Ourselves in the Age of Cyber Threats* (New York: Penguin Press, 2019).

18 Martin C. Libicki, *Cyberdeterrence and Cyberwar* (Santa Monica: RAND Corporation, 2009), 8. See also Jonathan William Welburn et al., 'Cyber Deterrence: How We Learned to Stop Worrying and Love the Signal', *Rand National Security Research Division*, July 2019; Jaspar Scott, *Strategic Cyber Deterrence: The Active Cyber Defense Option* (Lanham: Rowman and Littlefield, 2017).

19 Hacktivists use cyberattacks to promote a certain political or societal agenda. These attacks can easily be mistaken as cyberwarfare as they utilize their knowledge of computers and software tools to gain unauthorized access to computer systems to sabotage, manipulate or destroy information, in order to draw attention to their cause. Hacktivist groups such as Anonymous are often labelled as cyber-terrorists by the media as they deface websites, post sensitive information and threat to conduct further attacks if their demands are not met.

20 Riva Richmond, 'Malware Hits Computerized Industrial Equipment', *New York Times,* 24 September 2010. https://bits.blogs.nytimes.com/2010/09/24/malware-hits-compu terized-industrial-equipment/.

21 Andy Greenberg, 'The Untold Story of NotPetya, the Most Devastating Cyberattack in History', 22 August 2018. https://www.wired.com/story/notpetya-cyberattack-ukraine -russia-code-crashed-the-world/.

22 Clarke, *Cyber War.*

Part III

Cases

11

The US and hybrid challenges

Past, present and future

Jed Willard

Introduction

It has been said, judgmentally, that the United States plays risk, with a near-worldwide forward presence; while Russia plays chess, sometimes responding far away from the immediate zone of tension. But as a maritime power benefiting greatly from the post-Second World War global order, the United States arguably has no choice but to play risk. While Russia, as a continental power par excellence, for which threats to its periphery are always existential, has no choice but to play chess.[1]

Sometimes, however, the United States must play chess. There are many levels of warfare, from tactical to operational to strategic to political to existential. The United States does not need to always respond directly to tactical operations. Rather, America could respond strategically, in chess-like manner, using pressure points far away from the theatre at hand. In contests between a maritime power and a continental power, it's important to recognize both games, and not to be confined to playing only one game well.

China, for example, is a continental power with sea lanes to the outside. They need access and influence in a series of concentric circles radiating from Beijing. The inner circle is essentially the Han world, from which emperors used to keep the barbarians at bay. Beyond that circle are the sometime vassal states of Korea and Vietnam and the old rival, Japan. Further out are the weak land borders, beyond which China does not seek wars of conquest or colonies, but rather way-stations to get to resources needed at the centre. Last is the periphery: again, a source of resources rather than colonies. China, an imperial power within the inner circle but not a colonial power, has no need to take over these outer circles, only to use them for supplies. To maintain access to these resources, China has a long-developed bag of tricks, many of which resemble what in this book we call 'hybrid warfare'.

Some argue that America, and the West in general, is always engaging in offensive political warfare, but that our tools are so different from those of our adversaries that it is challenging to describe them both with the same word, 'hybrid'. The argument runs that the tools are different because authoritarian countries' weaknesses are different, and therefore our methods of influencing them, if we're going to be successful, must be different from their methods of influencing us. But while viewing Western behaviour through the same lens as authoritarian behaviour is arguably problematic, the notion that our methods are so different as to be unrelated seems to be a minority viewpoint.

States such as Russia, China and Iran have hybrid warfare incorporated into their military doctrine, says Professor Alina Polyakova of the Brookings Institution, and they assume the US does as well. When Russia uses the term 'hybrid', she says, they are describing what they perceive to be standard American tactics: 'they see themselves as on the defensive . . . [and] use hybrid [warfare] to contest US power.'[2] Some European officials agree, suggesting the Russian view is that America habitually wages hybrid war against post-Soviet regimes via colour revolutions.

'We [Americans] are weak in our understanding of [the low end of] full-spectrum warfare', Polyakova says, 'and especially don't understand Russia's ability to use different tools in combination'. The way the United States thinks about warfare is 'not how our adversaries think', she continues, it's not 'either/or' for them.[3] The United States needs other ways to hit back at China's posturing in its near-abroad, for example, not in a tit-for-tat manner, but rather by using non-kinetic 'munitions' such as points of economic leverage and diplomatic manoeuvring alongside our friends in ASEAN.

While Polyakova believes the United States should be prepared to respond in-kind to the chess-like moves of hybrid warfare, she recognizes that developing such a capability is 'uncomfortable territory right now', and that debate and self-criticism are well-warranted.[4]

The 'grey zone'

The US does not operate in either the gray zone or as a hybrid force
                                                    – Taylor Fravel, MIT University[5]

The US Defense department recognizes traditional and irregular warfare as separate modes of conflict that can and should be used in combination. So while defence leadership has not formally defined 'hybrid', it considers all war, waged effectively, to be hybrid in this particular sense.[6] Both traditional and irregular warfare were used, for example, in Operation Iraqi Freedom (2003–), and irregular operations were carried out by the United States throughout the Cold War. Participants in the irregular components of these operations describe them as tactically similar to standard irregular tactics, though strategically different in that they were local aspects of a larger struggle.

'Grey zone' is an unofficial, sometimes loathed term that is not used in American military doctrine. Nonetheless, in some American military circles it is a more popular term than 'hybrid', and is important to consider when examining the US approach to hybrid conflict.

Meaning, roughly, 'the zone of competition below the level of armed conflict', the grey zone represents an environment in between war and peace: a challenging setting for the United States to operate within. General Joseph Dunford, Chairman of America's Joint Chiefs of Staff and America's highest-ranking officer, describes the challenge this way:

> So I'm trying to shy away from the gray space hybrid because it's kind of – it doesn't really do justice to what we're talking about. We're talking about, you know, a competition with an adversary that has a military dimension, but the adversary knows exactly what the threshold is for us to take decisive military action. So they operate below that level. They continue to advance their interests and we lose competitive advantage. And, frankly, our interests are adversely affected. And for me it's actually one of the most significant challenges that we're dealing with right now.[7]

Or, as a Center for Strategic and International Studies report summarizes:

> The United States faces an array of challenges from adversaries that blend all tools of statecraft while also operating below the threshold of conventional war. The United States lacks clearly defined strategies to address these challenges.[8]

On the other side of the Atlantic, the terms 'hybrid' and 'grey zone' have both sometimes raised hackles. Some European officials insist that 'hybrid' is pejorative: that it is what Russia does, that it means 'warfare by sneaky people', a shadow policy when regular policy is not achieving desired goals. Others consider 'grey zone' to be a useless new term. 'If you put everything in there it becomes blurry', says one Council of the European Union official commenting anonymously,

> [these tactics are] often not part of a grand, strategic objective . . . Everyone does 'influence', [which] is seen as more-or-less legitimate. The US is very good at exporting its culture, economic model, companies, and technology. Is this a hybrid campaign? Or must it be malicious to be hybrid? Must hybrid warfare involve a wedge strategy, [or otherwise] be meant to be nefarious? Overt and transparent influence campaigns probably aren't hybrid warfare.

There is an understanding, however, that the ability to create faits accomplis by getting inside – or staying outside – an adversary's decision loop is a potent capability. Andrea Dew, Associate Professor of Strategy and Policy at the US Naval War College, clarifies: a strategy that 'gets you to your political goals, under the threshold of acceptable risk, is not ambiguous'.[9]

Others see 'Hybrid' as a useful term. For them the scope of hybrid is not a problem: hybrid warfare incorporates real but explicitly non-military capabilities such as cultural and educational exchanges, yet also extends the other end of the spectrum further into the kinetic.

'My understanding', writes Atlantic Council Senior Fellow Jakub Kalenský,

> is that 'hybrid' means a combination of traditional warfare, irregular units, information operations and political / diplomatic / economic pressure to achieve

both military and political goals. It might frequently describe similar activities we would describe when we talk about what's happening in the gray zone, it is just that in one case [gray zone], we are talking about where the conflict is happening, whereas in the other case [hybrid], we are rather describing what are the methods and tools that are being used in this conflict. That might be the most important distinction.[10]

Structural challenges

Unlike many of its adversaries, the United States largely continues to conceptualize conflict through the traditional black-and-white model of war and peace, fixating on conventional military warfare, while marginalizing the other critical instruments of national power

– Deterring Russia in the Gray Zone, Strategic Studies Institute[11]

The larger the administration, the tougher it is to execute whole-of-government responses. For small countries, countering hybrid threats is a survival strategy. For a country the size of the United States, hybrid threats are often perceived as non-critical. With less need to think in terms of national survival, the United States can focus on parochial interests. And when the United States plans policy based on parochial interests, information sharing across agencies is difficult. This is partially by design: coordination, when perceived as unnecessary, can be easily seen as cumbersome. There is simply a different culture of threat perception in smaller countries. This difference may be partially behind America's over-emphasis on military solutions to hybrid threats.

One of the most difficult aspects of hybrid warfare for the United States is defining the responsibilities of civilian assets versus the responsibilities of the military. The US military, which has enormous assets on the ground worldwide, is often first to 'see' hybrid tactics deployed. Yet without declared hostilities, they have no authority to strike back. Civilian agencies, which lack equivalent assets on the ground, can sometimes be guided by the military to, for example, make appropriate arrests and seizures, but these agencies aren't tasked with engaging in 'warfare' of any sort and therefore measuring the effectiveness of such cooperation in the 'grey zone' is problematic.

But countering hybrid threats is a policy-side effort, and some at the US Defense department find it frustrating to see regular military assets used in conflicts that are more suited to irregular or more delicate operations. The armed forces can sometimes be seen as an 'easy button' for American policy makers; a better approach might be to use defence assets and expertise to inform civilian agencies.

'Winning wars, as well as hearts and minds require[s] a combination of hard and soft power', notes David Phillips, Program Director on Peace-building and Rights at Columbia University,

This balance is especially important when countering or preventing violent extremism. The US has overwhelming military capacity, but it cannot hope to drain the swamp of support for radical extremism without soft power tools: economic development, education for all, women's empowerment and good governance. These soft power tools are also essential during Phase IV stability operations in order to consolidate peace and prevent spoilers from resuming their attacks.[12]

America's size creates other vulnerabilities, as well. The federal system allows state and local entities some detachment from the country's unitary systems, allowing for hybrid competitors to gain access and influence beneath the federal level. Allocating more freedom and power to the lower levels of government creates a major weakness for the United States in terms of lowering the difficulty level of attacks, though it arguably also builds resilience by spreading risk over fifty states.

'We need to create better defensive infrastructure' in the information space, writes Brett Bruen, president of Global Situation Room. 'Not just the ability to counter disinformation, but support and services that allow campaigns, companies, and citizens to tap into more resources that help them protect themselves, their organisations, their messages, from manipulation.'[13]

Broadly, this defensive infrastructure could take three forms: awareness, attention and alternative narratives.

Awareness refers to the American public's general knowledge of who the bad actors are and the tactics they use. This should not take the form of fact-checking, but of general warnings about which divisive or hot-button issues are likely to be selected for interference. Warnings such as 'if a post makes you angry, double check the source', or 'be aware that false information is being circulated about topics x, y, and z' are more effective than labelling disinformation, and far better than repeating disinformation in the form or fact-checking.

Attention means attention from American entities with a responsibility to understand, communicate about and respond to active measures. These include political campaigns at all levels of government, corporate communicators (including financial communications), journalists and media platforms. Fact-checking and details of specific campaigns and threats are useful for these types of responsible entities.

Alternative narratives are the most important form of defence against information operations. False stories spread to sow confusion and disunion cannot simply be corrected, they must be replaced. Political voices at all levels should understand that only positive visions of America's future can counter the narratives of division and dystopia sown by the United States' hybrid opponents.

Looking beyond the information space, some in the US defence establishment agree that America has more to learn from our European friends and allies than we do from them. Strategic patience, for instance: the United States, could use a longer attention span. America could also use a structure for waging hybrid warfare across agencies.

Professor Hy Rothstein, director of the DoD IO Center for Research at the US Naval Postgraduate School, agrees that America needs a separate structure for hybrid engagement. 'Irregular warfare capabilities should [have] a separate entity' from which the full array of tools in America's military toolkit can be deployed. Irregular 'gets squashed and conventionalised' in the regular military, he adds, since it's seen as inconsistent with the American way of war.[14]

Such an entity would need to be subject to strategic oversight. This would be essential since mistakes can and will happen, and America needs to be able to self-police. Overreaction to hybrid threats is already a vulnerability, and with America a global military super power, even the perception of abuse can be targeted.

Leadership challenges

Embracing a narrow conventional conception of conflict does not prepare future leaders for the range of emerging threats we face, nor is it conducive to developing doctrine and training

– Frank Hoffman, National Defense University[15]

America is better at waging offensive hybrid war, especially when the United States sets the tempo, than at defending against hybrid threats. One reason defence is challenging is that America's political leadership does not seem to care that much about hybrid warfare. Hybrid, being all about perceptions, legitimacy and relevance, is more challenging to explain to the public than, for example, kinetic warfare or threats to physical infrastructure. Adversaries can make hybrid look like a game, or at least unlike a potent threat. For American leaders to frame for the American people why they are in this fight for the long term is a real challenge.

Frank Hoffman, Distinguished Research Fellow at the US National Defense University, describes three consequences of this conundrum:

- Unreasonable political and public expectations for quick wins at low cost,
- An overly simplistic grasp of the application of blunt military power and what it will supposedly achieve and
- Naïve views of both adversaries and the context for conflict.[16]

Meanwhile, the American military itself, argues the US Naval Postgraduate School's Rothstein, is able to do irregular warfare successfully only when regular forces do not care about the conflict at hand or are distracted. In the 1980s, for example, America's regular forces were distracted in Europe, and the US had to engage in irregular warfare in El Salvador. It turned out successful; whereas American regular forces, suggests Rothstein, would have been much more of a magnet for insurgent attacks.[17]

The US military is 'allergic to irregular options', says Rothstein, and will try all other options first and perhaps fail. This is because mass firepower and attrition have worked so well for the United States in the past – and, in terms of great power conflict, present. Rothstein notes that great powers have not recently fought, and still will not fight today, with the United States conventionally. But adversaries know that they can operate in the grey zone without triggering a regular US response: America 'will not be propelled to war without a significant trigger', he points out, leaving the United States 'preparing for great power competition in an age when rival powers are preparing for irregular'.[18]

Just as in the post-America-Vietnam war era, Rothstein continues, the United States is ceasing large-scale training for irregular warfare. He predicts that this will be taken advantage of by adversaries: 'we will either over-militarise, or not respond, because of the way we think.' Rothstein mostly holds America's military leadership responsible for the failure to prepare for an effective hybrid response. 'Senior military leaders have a duty' to change the way defence thinks about warfare and to prepare for a full range of threats, he says, 'but [they] are not doing so'.[19]

'The larger problem', writes the National Defense University's Hoffman,

> is that the U.S. has a strategic culture that does not appreciate history or strategy, nor does it devote sufficient attention to the breadth of adversaries facing it and the many different forms that human conflict can take . . . While there are deficiencies in U.S. planning and strategy processes, the larger intellectual challenge is a blinkered conception of conflict that frequently quotes the great Prussian soldier Clausewitz without realizing the true essence of his theory and how it applies to the ever evolving, interactive phenomenon we call 'war.' Moreover, the U.S. national security establishment too often fails to understand opponents, their strategic cultures, and their own unique conceptions of victory and war.[20]

In his quest for a solution, Rothstein is dismissive of looking to the 'Global War on Terror' and USSOCOM's (Special Operations Command) current approach. 'I've nothing against killing terrorists', he explains, 'that's very therapeutic'. But there is 'nothing strategic about killing terrorists'. USSOCOM, he argues, has the capability to operate in the grey zone but lacks the willingness to consider using such options, for example, in Venezuela today.[21]

'There are places in the world that will be problems in the future', Rothstein predicts, 'and someone needs to be monitoring [them] and engaged'. He wishes that USSOCOM intelligence was focused on the threats of the future, including which third-parties could potentially 'fall under the spell' of 'Russia, China, or Iran'. 'This should be a full-time job for them', he declares, adding that we should be studying how to 'force our will on our opponents' without spending 'two billion dollars a week like in Iraq'. Special Operations Forces should be 'global scouts' in combination with local sources, he continues, 'you've got to be there' or you 'can't influence squat'. US allies, he predicts, would be quite willing to sign on and assist in a hybrid effort if America created the blueprint.[22]

Brookings' Polyakova agrees that America is too often 'absent from the game', for instance in the Balkans where 'Russia is getting a lot for a little' and 'the US is not there'. She also agrees that while the US does have to think about hybrid approaches, a 'Global War on Terror'-style response is not the solution. 'At least [regarding cyber threats] we are thinking about it . . . both defence and offence', she says. On cyber the United States is working well with our allies, she continues, and she is optimistic in that realm, especially with regard to infrastructure.[23]

When it comes to the information aspects of hybrid warfare, the Atlantic Council's Jakub Kalenský believes the US reaction to interference in the 2016 elections gives America an advantage. 'It might be partly due to the fact that Americans are investigating this malicious activity (unlike Europeans, who seem not to react to [the] Kremlin's information operations)', he writes, 'but given the scale of [the] Kremlin's operations, it very much seems that apart from Ukraine and the Baltic states, the US might have the biggest experience with [the] Kremlin's information operations.'[24]

A Council of the European Union official agrees with Kalenský, pointing out that the Mueller probe was impressively done, though he believes that at least some EU member states are equally good at reacting to information operations deployed against them. He also believes that the US is quite good at hybrid offence, writ large, especially in cyber, but also in terms of intelligence, strategic communication, economy, trade, PsyOps and cultural tools. This last, the export of culture, may seem transparent, though may also simultaneously prepare the human terrain for future intervention. The US may also have some advantage on defence, thanks to its top end intelligence techniques. Entities such as IARPA (Intelligence Advanced Research Projects Activity) are constantly improving the American ability to create forecasts and linkages, which is very important in hybrid warfare, since seeing the links between seemingly unrelated events is key to understanding when hybrid engagements are actually happening and what they mean.

'We are good at experimentation', in the disinformation space, adds Brett Bruen of Global Situation Room,

> We are through GEC [Global Engagement Center, US State Department] and other programs piloting, seeding, testing some ideas, albeit far too few. This at least may germinate into technology or techniques that will have utility, if not for us immediately, perhaps for other nations or the private sector.[25]

Polyakova is less sanguine, however, especially regarding the information contest Bruen refers to. 'It's much less clear what it means for the US and our allies', she says, and information is more 'complicated because so much is open-source, and often [mediated]'. The 'big black hole [for the US] is the digital domain, broadly defined'. She suggests that we look to history for guidance, specifically to how America contested the USSR, including in the information space.[26]

The American hybrid experience

[H]ybrid/gray zone warfare is not remotely a new thing, as Clausewitz's 200 year old references to the societal dimension(s) of warfare make clear. However, this aspect was downplayed (and even ignored) particularly on the strategic level in recent decades. Not so anymore.
              – Kelly Greenhill, Associate Professor and International Relations Director,
                                                          Tufts University[27]

The United States has a long history of engaging in what could be anachronistically labelled hybrid warfare, though not in the same way as many other countries. When Washington took over the armies of the rebelling American colonies in 1775, it wanted a conventional force. Yet the success of the revolutionaries was often based on irregular or combined warfare, especially as waged later in the war in the southern colonies by leaders such as Nathaniel Greene and Daniel Morgan.[28]

Through the nineteenth century, the US military's preference for regular warfare coexisted with a talent for irregular warfare, which was used in situations deemed to be of less importance. During America's 'Indian Wars', for example, George Crook used irregular tactics to great effect and was, indicatively, criticized for doing so by his commander Philip Sheridan.[29]

Twentieth-century America engaged in offensive hybrid engagements, but was rarely targeted on home soil (save by criminal cartels). An early example of twentieth-century-American hybrid warfare is the re-creation of the country of Panama. Under Teddy Roosevelt, the United States wanted an independent Panama with a US-controlled canal, and Colombia was unwilling to cede the province. Without crossing the diplomatically challenging threshold of waging open war on Colombia, the US used military and financial assets plus local forces to accomplish the policy goal of Panamanian Independence in 1903.

In the First and Second World Wars, the United States engaged across the full spectrum of warfare, with the capabilities that could be considered hybrid today commanded mostly by the military. 'We were quite strategic', says Rothstein, citing the leadership of Roosevelt and Marshall along with their British allies Churchill and Alanbrooke.[30]

Counter-intuitively, the legacy of the Second World War may have negatively impacted the American military's ability to wage hybrid war today. The overturning of governments, the remaking of the world, the vanquishing of foes with tanks, carrier groups, and heroics – the memory of the Second World War – is a mindset not necessarily suited to the long grind of constant, irritating competition. The American military came to like mass and attrition, which worked for them; irregular or hybrid warfare came to leave some Americans uncomfortable.[31]

A separate challenge emanated from the Cold War. The United States became quite skilled at supporting rebels, undercutting governments and influencing elections, especially in Latin America. Some of these activities were not pretty, however, and perceived as out of line with America's values. At the time they were considered acceptable, though, because they were carried out in the overall context of an ideological conflict in which America was confident she was in the right. Despite many successes during this period, less-than-liberal abuses by, for instance, the CIA and FBI, led to the building of walls between agencies. Whether or not America's Cold War activities constitute hybrid warfare as defined today (an arguable point), these stovepipes left the United States with a reduced capacity to synchronize interagency campaigns – a widely recognized problem that presents yet another stumbling block for America's capability to wage hybrid warfare in the twenty-first century.

The United States, in summary, has a history of deploying non-kinetic tools to promote policy preferences, Alina Polyakova of the Brookings Institution explains. Taking a long view, she says, the United States used a set of tools, including irregular and economic warfare, frequently. 'But we've been critiquing this practice since the Cold War', shifting to a more delineated vision of influence: with kinetic divorced from non-kinetic. 'What's in-between is [now] less easily deployed today [by the

US].'[32] As CSIS' Michael Matlaga and John Schaus write, 'The United States developed decades of experience in countering these types of activities during the Cold War. However, it will have to remember, or re-learn and adapt, if it is to be as successful in the future.'[33]

A frequently cited example of post-Cold War US hybrid action is the engagement with Yugoslavia in the 1990s. 'The US tried to ignore the collapse of Yugoslavia', writes David Phillips of Columbia University. Echoing Rothstein's comments about America only using hybrid approaches when otherwise occupied, Phillips continues:

> [The US] was distracted by other events such as the Soviet Union's demise and the Gulf War. It was only after Srebenica and the realization that forces were needed to extricate peacekeepers that the Clinton administration got more deeply engaged, supporting Bosniac and Croatian forces to reclaim territory. US engagement in Bosnia, which led to the Dayton Peace Agreement, and NATO's Kosovo intervention in 1999 demonstrated the importance of diplomacy backed by a credible threat of force.[34]

After 9/11, the United States continued to see a hard line between war (Afghanistan and Iraq) and peace (elsewhere). Hybrid was not war, nor was it counter insurgency. There were exceptions, however. In the Philippines, where the government faced a challenge from Abu Sayyaf, their American partners were prevented from engaging in a regular approach. The US forces in the country therefore operated irregularly, and successfully, it turned out, especially in comparison to the enormous regular investment in Afghanistan and Iraq.[35]

Some see the Russian invasion of Ukraine in 2014 as a hybrid wake-up call for the US Defense department, though perhaps not for the rest of the government. Great Power contests were back, and NATO could be re-imagined. Some had sensed a shift in international competition long before, but 2014 clarified the challenge and, more or less, gave it a name.

'Bottom line: close observers understood the game was "already afoot" long before 2014', writes Kelly Greenhill of Tufts University,

> and there were lots of examples from which to draw such inferences, including but not limited to Russian-backed cyber attacks in Estonia; (dis)information ops conducted hither and yon by violent non-state actors (as well as certain states); the conduct of the engineered migration pulses into western Europe and beyond, etc.[36]

But Hy Rothstein and others differ with the conclusion that 2014 was an effective wake-up call. They argue that 2014 should have been a 'Sputnik Moment' but that America never 'figured it out' and has not yet been able to alter 'Putin's thinking'.[37] Jakub Kalenský at the Atlantic Council more or less shares this opinion, writing that 'from many public statements it would seem it was [a wake up call], but apparently the reaction of the US government was not strong enough to prevent what happened in [the] 2016 elections'. Kalenský doesn't sense a 2014 Sputnik Moment in Europe, either: 'many governments like to think that Kremlin aggression is just someone else's problem . . . and they do not believe the expert warnings until their own countries get targeted . . . I have seen it with almost every Western European country.'[38]

The interference in the American elections in 2016, being an attack on US soil by a foreign power, sounded a louder clarion call, yet one that the United States and its friends and allies have yet to fully digest.

'I started working on [disinformation] in 2015', writes Kalenský,

since then, by far the most visible event was the meddling into the Presidential elections in 2016 – which was, however, both preceded and followed by massive long-term influence operations aimed at destabilising the US audience, operations that facilitate the shorter-term operations aiming to influence the particular election result . . . I believe that the influence operation is far bigger than just one particular election, and that the operations aimed at destabilisation, subversion, creating and/or amplifying divisions, this is something that is going on for a very long time. I believe that this particular experience with [a] several years-long campaign is pretty important.[39]

The conflict in Syria can be considered another wake-up call, though one that came too late. By the time the US was fully engaged in the conflict, Russia and Iran had already injected themselves subtly (at first) into the fight, leaving the US boxed into a complex fight involving multiple adversarial regional powers.

In the US military today, says Rothstein,

hybrid is more like a training exercise. We have no real insight into why we're doing what we're doing . . . I would like to see the US get serious about the Russian threat and exploit Putin's vulnerabilities . . . put pressure on him . . . The real question[s are] what Russia is doing to undermine liberal democracy, and what are we willing to do to save it.[40]

America's hybrid future

The United States is beginning to recognize how gray zone competitors operate. It has the capability to be a formidable and effective gray zone actor but does not yet have a plan to employ or integrate its capabilities to achieve its objectives.

– 'Competing in the Gray Zone', CSIS[41]

Some in America's Special Operations Forces world recognize that hybrid is already a front, one where our offensive capabilities need to be examined. We already interfere non-kinetically in the affairs of other countries, we just don't always recognize that we are engaging in hybrid warfare. From whose perspective one examines US tactics, against whom they are applied, and when, plays a role in defining the American approach to hybrid warfare.

The US military is, in fact, working on developing clear doctrine for engaging in hybrid warfare. The challenge for defence is that they must prepare for worst case scenarios while also integrating for low-end competition. Worst case scenarios ('big war things') require extremely high-end capability and capacity, though in the case of the US military these big war things are what they have done for a long time. Low-end capability is much more expansive, and requires working with other US agencies. While the military needs to be involved in all aspects (such as early warning), there also needs to remain a line behind which conflicts don't become shooting matches.

Where to draw this line is highly problematic. For instance, if the US Coast Guard floats a cutter through the Taiwan Straight, it may be perceived as so innocuous as to go unremarked. A carrier group, on the other hand, would get attention, but also be highly provocative.

'The main worry of military planners here isn't so much a full-scale amphibious invasion', writes *New York Times* Columnist Nicholas Kristof from Taiwan,

> Rather, they fear the mainland sowing chaos and disrupting the economy as a way of trying to bring Taiwan to heel. Hence the concern about a cyberattack that would take out Taipei's electric grid. Or sabotage of the underwater cables that bring data and internet to Taiwan. Or interference in the South China Sea with tankers carrying oil to Taiwan.[42]

This specific theatre, the Western Pacific, is a hybrid classroom for the US Navy. The Navy is learning to be proactive, but still remain behind the risk threshold: to prevent Chinese faits accomplis without triggering an overreaction.

It's been said that countries feed their armies, but buy their navies. The US Navy has long been slow, based on building and fielding expensive platforms. This requires political and monetary capital. While the post-9/11 focus on counter insurgency was all about land forces, the Navy has awakened to hybrid threats in the South China Sea, along with the Persian Gulf. Giant, floating platforms (those that proved so successful in the Second World War) are now potentially vulnerable to, for example, faster, smaller, cheaper and disposable swarms of craft. These swarms can be deployed much more frequently and prevalently than slow, expensive, platforms. The creation of new islands and the deployment of naval ships disguised as coast guard vessels compounds the confusion. To cope with these new threats requires a massive shift to traditional naval thinking.

A similar revolution in thinking is required to understand America's role in defending itself, friends and allies from hybrid threats in other domains. A nightmare scenario for some smaller countries is that an adversarial neighbour uses hybrid tactics to create a serious crisis that nonetheless remains below the threshold that would trigger a conventional response and bring in allied assistance. Given enough psychological and economic pressure, such a hybrid action could result in a fait accompli on the ground.

'[T]here are various types of very small Russian probing attacks that could leave NATO flummoxed and paralyzed over how to respond', writes Michael O'Hanlon, Senior Fellow at the Brookings Institution. 'These attacks might not reach the threshold . . . to invoke NATO's Article V mutual-defense clause and send military forces in response, yet they could be too serious to ignore.'[43]

America's allies realize this, and at least some have considered the strategy of rapidly escalating conflicts themselves so as to trigger conventional allied aid and, with time, create a case within NATO for an invocation of article 5. That is, the inability to assist allies coping with potentially catastrophic threats that are nonetheless below America's response threshold creates a perverse incentive for US allies to unilaterally escalate conflict. The notion that America's own allies could feel forced to escalate, perhaps drastically, in order to prompt their mighty ally to intervene, should be a great motivation for the US military to think carefully about how to aid our allies in coping with hybrid threats below the threshold calling for conventional force.

'Identifying a hybrid attack/low-intensity conflict is easy'; claims Tufts' Greenhill. 'Defining where it becomes a war AND what and when laws of war come into play is not. This should be deeply concerning.'[44]

Some European scholars and officials cite the US forward presence as an aid, if not a solution, to this problem. Maintaining forces constantly on rotation or training exercises means America has 'skin in the game' even at the early stages of a potential conflict.

'America's commitment to NATO's enhanced forward presence in the Baltics and Poland is essential', says Eitvydas Bajarūnas, Lithuania's Ambassador-at-Large for Hybrid Threats:

> The US presence, the rotation of forces is excellent. [They have a] strange rhetoric problem, but the behaviour is good, including the sanctions. The big challenge to us in the West is to see the game and stay in it, [and the] US is staying in it.[45]

But 'more work is needed', conclude CSIS scholars Matlaga and Schaus,

> to move beyond a clear understanding of the problem into specific actions, operational frameworks, and strategic approaches that could be drawn upon to more consistently and effectively counter gray zone actions directed at the United States. The United States will need to be agile in its responses and proactive measures, both to quickly counter gray zone actions and to limit the predictability that its adversaries have exploited.[46]

Beyond the military, there is the question of better coordination between the various federal entities and between the federal, state and local governments. The local level is where the greatest challenges lie, and also where real resilience can and should be built. Some help in doing so may come from Europe, where some states, being unitary, have had an easier time using their hierarchies to educate and motivate at the regional and local levels of government. Sharing intelligence and trends about and between these local levels of government could potentially help the United States develop resilience at the state and local levels.

'A key component of effective defence now as ever is societal resilience and system redundancy', argues Greenhill, 'the technologies and sources and nature of vulnerabilities have changed; the underlying issue has not.'[47]

Conclusion

Traditional values are more stable and more important for millions of people than this liberal idea, which, in my opinion, is really ceasing to exist.

– Vladimir Putin[48]

In the end, the American public's willingness and ability to stand up for liberal democracy is the last and best line of defence against hybrid threats.

The 'biggest threat to democracy is a poorly educated public', concludes Rothstein, 'education is key'. He believes that in addition to educating the public about history and civics, the US and like-minded countries should 'push back' and 'hold countries accountable' for pushing dangerous notions like 'illiberal democracy'. 'Most liberal democracies will recognise [this] threat to Western Civilisation', he concludes, if we 'lose track of that' then we have lost everything.[49]

Europe should help American leaders make the case that hybrid warfare is a real threat to all of us. Sometimes that gets lost in the United States. The Europeans who feel most acutely threatened by hybrid warfare need to help US leaders clarify to the American people that hybrid is an existential problem for democracy.

Hybrid warfare can potentially allow adversaries to achieve their strategic objectives without firing a shot; if America gives up its constitutional values, the authoritarians win.

Notes

1 This chapter's author interviewed a large number of officials on both sides of the Atlantic. Most of the interviewees insisted on anonymity due to their current positions. Therefore, the majority of the interviews were conducted partially or entirely on-background. (One EU official commented off-record but not on-background, so is directly but anonymously quoted.) Much of the content of this chapter comes either from these anonymous sources or from the author's personal knowledge. The author is, of course, responsible for all of the content in its final form.

2 Alina Polyakova (David M. Rubenstein Fellow, Center on the United States and Europe and Security and Strategy, Brookings Institution), in discussion with the author. June 2019.

3 Polyakova.

4 Polyakova.

5 Taylor Fravel (Arthur and Ruth Sloan Professor of Political Science, MIT University), in correspondence with the author. May 2019.

6 Hy Rothstein (Director of the DoD IO Center for Research, US Naval Postgraduate School), in discussion with the author. June 2019.

7 Joseph F. Dunford, Jr., 'Remarks and Q&A at the Center for Strategic and International Studies' (speech, Washington, DC, 29 March 2016). https://www.jcs.mil/ Media/Speeches/Article/707418/gen-dunfords-remarks-and-qa-at-the-center-for-stra tegic-and-international-studi/.

8 Michael Matlaga and John Schaus, 'Competing in the Gray Zone' (CSIS, 24 October 2018). https://www.csis.org/analysis/competing-gray-zone-0.

9 Andrea Dew (Associate Professor of Strategy and Policy, US Naval War College), in discussion with the author. May 2019.

10 Jakub Kalenský (Senior Fellow, Eurasia Center, Atlantic Council), in correspondence with the author. May 2019.

11 Michael C. McCarthy, Matthew A. Moyer and Brett H. Venable, *Deterring Russia in the Gray Zone* (Carlisle: Strategic Studies Institute, 2019), xv.

12 David L. Phillips (Director, Program on Peace-building and Rights, Institute for the Study of Human Rights, Columbia University), in correspondence with the author. May 2019.

13 Brett Bruen (president, Global Situation Room; former director of Global Engagement, White House), in correspondence with the author. June 2019.

14 Rothstein.

15 Frank G. Hoffman, 'Examining Complex Forms of Conflict: Gray Zone and Hybrid Challenges', *PRISM* 7, no. 4 (8 November 2018). https://cco.ndu.edu/News/Article/16 80696/examining-complex-forms-of-conflict-gray-zone-and-hybrid-challenges/.

16 Frank G. Hoffman, 'The Contemporary Spectrum of Conflict: Protracted, Gray Zone, Ambiguous, and Hybrid Modes of War', in *2016 Index of U.S. Military Strength*, ed. Dakota L. Wood (The Heritage Foundation, 20 June 2015), 25. https://s3.amazonaws .com/ims-2016/PDF/2016_Index_of_US_Military_Strength_ESSAYS_HOFFMAN.pdf.

17 Rothstein.

18 Rothstein.

19 Rothstein.

20 Hoffman, 'The Contemporary Spectrum of Conflict', 25.

21 Rothstein.

22 Rothstein.

23 Polyakova.

24 Kalenský.

25 Bruen.

26 Polyakova.

27 Kelly Greenhill (Associate Professor and International Relations Director, Tufts University; and Research Fellow, Harvard University), in correspondence with the author. June 2019.

28 Rothstein.

29 Rothstein.

30 Rothstein.

31 Rothstein.

32 Polyakova.

33 Matlaga and Schaus, 'Competing in the Gray Zone'.

34 Phillips.

35 Rothstein.

36 Greenhill.

37 Rothstein, in part.

38 Kalenský.

39 Kalenský.

40 Rothstein.

41 Matlaga and Schaus, 'Competing in the Gray Zone'.

42 Nicholas Kristof, 'This Is How a War With China Could Begin', *New York Times*, 4 September 2019, accessed 12 September 2019. https://www.nytimes.com/2019/09 /04/opinion/china-taiwan-war.html.

43 Michael O'Hanlon, 'A Report From NATO's Front Lines', *The National Interest,* 10 June 2019, accessed 20 June 2015. https://nationalinterest.org/feature/report-natos-front-lines-62067.
44 Greenhill.
45 Eitvydas Bajarūnas (Ambassador-at-Large for Hybrid Threats, Ministry of Foreign Affairs of the Republic of Lithuania), in discussion with the author. June 2019.
46 Matlaga and Schaus, 'Competing in the Gray Zone'.
47 Greenhill.
48 RFE/RL, 'Putin Tells FT: "The Liberal Idea Has Become Obsolete"', *Radio Free Europe / Radio Liberty,* 28 June 2019. https://www.rferl.org/a/putin-tells-ft-the-liberal-idea-has-become-obsolete-/30026237.html.
49 Rothstein.

12

China's political warfare in Taiwan

Strategies, methods and global implications

Gulizar Haciyakupoglu and Michael Raska

Introduction

This chapter[1] explores the contours of People's Republic of China's (PRC)[2] hybrid threats and hybrid warfare against Taiwan with an emphasis on political warfare. China's political warfare in Taiwan, which, according to Mark Stokes[3] and Russell Hsiao[4] has been 'the primary target of People's Liberation Army (PLA) political warfare',[5] provides for a case to explore the sophistication and variety in measures employed for political warfare. The political warfare observed in Taiwan has certain aspects that are unique to the context and others that can be pursued in different environments. Taiwan's shared history with PRC before the retreat, the identity question and variation in Taiwanese people's approaches to cross-Straits relations, transpire as concerns that are somehow specific to Taiwan. In addition to these, the size of Taiwan's military against China's, Taiwan's economic benefit from China, 'pro-unification' supporters and parties in Taiwan, Taiwanese media's alleged openness to outside influence and Taiwan's diplomatic position in the global arena emerge as some of the vulnerabilities[6] that an opponent can leverage when waging political warfare.

These concerns may facilitate the penetration of Chinese influence in Taiwan although they, alone or with other measures, do not guarantee full-fledged success. On the other hand, the channels through which Chinese influence is injected in Taiwan can emerge as the channels for political warfare in other countries if and when a country's legal, political, social and economic framework permits. These channels are (1) diplomatic pressure, (2) legal, (3) economic and (4) information domain. NATO Strategic Communications Centre of Excellence's (NATO StratCom COE) report titled 'Hybrid Threats: A Strategic Communications Perspective' proposes these channels as the measures used in Chinese public diplomacy efforts in Taiwan.[7] This chapter abides by the suggested categories and builds on them by expanding each with subcategories and detailed information.

Before moving forward, it must be stated that the political warfare is not a one-way process. Taiwan has its own tools to counter political warfare and spread its influence outside its territories. However, the focus of this chapter is Beijing's political warfare in Taiwan and thus, Taiwan's efforts will not be covered here. It must also be added that China is not the only agent seeking to inject influence and sway opinions on certain political issues in Taiwan. Other countries, some of which are cited in this chapter, allegedly engage in the manipulation of the information domain as well. Here, receiving government's degree of tolerance towards different kinds of external influence plays an important role in the government's definition of the influence as a threat. More importantly, the employment of proxies, such as cyber troops, content farms and co-opted individuals from target population, and galvanization of netizens to act on sentimental issues could hinder the enquiries about the nature and potential orchestrator of attempts. Hence, the threat posed by and the level of CCP's involvement in political warfare against Taiwan emerges as a debate.

Following this Introduction (first section), the chapter is structured as follows: the second section is 'Historical context and changes'; the third section is 'Political warfare through diplomatic, legal, economic and information-based channels' and the fourth section is 'Strategic implications'.

Historical context and changes

The Chinese Civil War resulted in the retreat of Kuomintang (KMT) forces, led by Chiang Kai-shek, to Taiwan, Republic of China (ROC), in 1949. This opened a new chapter in the political warfare between PRC and ROC. From ROC's settlement in Taiwan to the opening up in relations in the cross-Straits, various measures of political warfare were employed to reach, confuse and manipulate the other side of the straits. Megaphones, balloons, floating carriers and radio carried propaganda across the straits.[8] Amid the ongoing political warfare, a number of significant political events influenced the environment in which the political warfare has been conducted.

Beijing improved its international recognition at the expense of Taiwan's with some countries and supranational organizations switching their diplomatic ties from Taipei to Beijing. Among them, in 1971 the United Nations and in 1979 the United States declared a shift from Taipei to Beijing in diplomatic recognition.[9] In 1987 the martial law in Taiwan was lifted.[10] This democratization move was followed by policies that relaxed the interactions across the Straits including the termination of the prohibitions against forming political parties, relaxation of controls over newspapers and loosening of the travel ban to China for visits to relatives.[11] The Democratic Progressive Party (DPP) was established around this period. A few years later, in 1992, the term 1992 consensus was coined after a meeting between Taiwanese and Chinese semi-official representatives who agreed on the 'existence of One China',[12] with China and Taiwan interpreting the term 'One China' differently.[13] In the succeeding years, KMT and DPP demonstrated different approaches to '1992 consensus' in their political discourses. Later in 1996, two weeks before Taiwan's first democratic presidential election, China 'test-fired'[14] missiles towards Taiwan's coast. Lee Teng-hui, whom

'China suspected had pro-independence inclinations',[15] succeeded in the elections despite China's intimidation.[16]

Taiwan's post-martial law liberalization not only impacted the cross-Straits relations but also widened the difference between the political systems of PRC and ROC, and wedded Taiwan to democracy, which, as argued by others, with its openness, can be exploited by authoritarian regimes by way of information operations.[17] The internet and advancements in technology brought about new measures and platforms for political warfare. The new technologies and platforms, among others, allow for easier information and intelligence collection; provide new opportunities for proxy operations; offer alternative channels, such as social media sites, to reach masses with targeted messages; and present cyber operations as an option.

PRC's tactics have also improved and shifted over time. The arguments on changes in PRC's approach claimed an increase in focus on 'narrow groups' or 'individuals' including 'co-opted candidates' and 'proxies' in Taiwan, while firming ties with KMT, investors in China, and enhancing economic relations to appeal to Taiwanese allegedly received more attention previously.[18] Some suggest that the events such as the Sunflower Movement, which voiced concerns about China's economic influence on the island and its potential impact over Taiwan's democracy and DPP's election win, contributed to the shift in China's focus from macro policies to 'narrow groups or even individuals' under Xi Jinping's rule.[19]

The switch from macro to micro targeting and cultivation of ties with candidates, individuals and narrower groups is visible in the allegations voiced in news and scholarly articles. However, cases covered by newspapers and articles also show that the older mechanisms are still alive despite a potential decrease in dependence on these conduits with the emergence of new routes and mechanisms. Akin to this, an article by Project 2049 argues that China's political warfare strategy would 'not change in response to DPP victory itself', but it would be altered in accordance to major swings in 'demographics and political and cultural identity on the island'.[20] The following section details the means used to spread influence and compel Taiwan and Taiwanese to act in line with China's political and military objectives.

Political warfare through diplomatic, legal, economic and information-based channels

The NATO StratCom report on hybrid threats lists diplomacy, economy/finance, legal and information as measures China uses in its public diplomacy efforts in Taiwan. Public diplomacy and political warfare are not synonyms. According to Stokes and Hsiao the main difference between the two lies in the 'target and intend' with public diplomacy aiming to sway the opinions of masses and political warfare encompassing a 'calculated manipulation of opposing side's strategies, defence policies, and broader international norms'.[21] With this differentiation in mind, the measures employed in China's public diplomacy in Taiwan involve diplomacy, economy, legal and information,[22] while the objective of eroding trust in government, influencing strategies, defence policies and international norms expose the political warfare dimension and expand the boundaries of these four measures. Herewith, the venues, agents and measures of China's political warfare in Taiwan will be explored under these four categories with attention to sub-methods that build each category.

Diplomatic pressure

Chinese diplomatic pressure on Taiwan involves the push of companies to avoid referring to Taiwan as a country, luring Taiwan's diplomatic allies to switch sides and hampering Taiwan's participation in international and supranational organizations.

China's pressuring of some companies, including airlines and hotel[23] groups, to avoid referring to Taiwan as a country sparked debates in Taiwan and elsewhere. Some companies, including Qantas, All Nippon Airways and United Airlines, yielded to pressure and changed the way they refer to Taiwan on their websites.[24] Taiwan's profile in the international arena has been dented further with some of its allies switching their recognition from Taipei to Beijing. Burkina Faso and the Dominican Republic are among the countries that shifted their recognition.[25] Taiwan also faces China's roadblock in its participation in supranational and international organization.[26] For instance, Taiwan has not been invited to the World Health Organization's 'decision-making'[27] arm World Health Assembly (WHA), allegedly due to Beijing's 'political pressure'.[28],[29] Between 2009 and 2016, Taiwan attended the WHA as an observer with the 'Chinese Taipei' designation.[30]

These three venues of diplomatic pressure, among others, receive coverage in Taiwanese newspapers and at times become subject of heated political debate amid the political rivalry. Thus, arguably, the diplomatic pressure not only limits Taiwan's manoeuvre space in the international arena but also influences domestic political debates. Impediments to participation in international and supranational organizations on the other hand segue into the legal dimension of political warfare with the problems it begets.

Legal

Taiwan faces difficulties in participating in some international and supranational organizations, allegedly due to China's pressure. This, as also argued by others, restricts Taiwan from having a say on international norms and regulations, and from collaborating with other countries on common concerns. The participation problem and other examples alike emerge as battleground for legal warfare. A core ideal of legal warfare is to fit an act into a legal framework while claiming the opponent's move infringes the law.[31] In this respect, according to Dean Chang (21 May 2012), a number of Chinese laws concerning 'territorial claims over Taiwan' lay the framework of legal warfare and seek to shape opinions of the international community.[32] For instance, the 'anti-secession law', entails an article that allows for the use of 'non-peaceful means' if 'Taiwan independence secessionist forces' – as named by the act – 'cause the fact of Taiwan's secession from China', or 'secession' materializes as a result of an event, or all efforts of 'reunification' fail.[33] Such acts are also employed as discursive warnings. In 2018, the Chinese tabloid *Global Times* argued that by then Premier William Lai could be arrested for his words asserting Taiwan's status as a 'sovereign, independent country' and that he is a 'Taiwan independence worker' under the anti-secession law.[34] Additionally, some interpret 'the 31 measures'[35] China extended to Taiwan as a tool to 'lure Taiwan fully into its economic orbit',[36] attract Taiwanese investment and talent and 'outcompete'[37] Taiwan with the lift of barriers to studying, investing and working in China for Taiwanese.[38] Arguably, these measures, with the diplomatic and economic enticements they encapsulate and the regulatory ease they bring, can be explored in relation to diplomatic, legal as well as economic influence.

Economy

The political warfare of China in Taiwan involves the use of economy as a means to influence policies, decision-making and opinions. Besides, the economic ties between China and Taiwan manifest themselves in Taiwan's political sphere,[39] and the influence of cross-Straits relation on economy find reflection in policies, and feed the political rivalry between DPP, KMT and other parties. Correspondingly, Christopher Walker and Jessica Ludwig (2017) suggest exploring China's business activities in connection to Beijing's influence attempts.[40] There are, among others, two significant, connected passages for China to spread influence by means of economy in Taiwan. First, economic aspects of the cross-straits relations have political repercussions. Second, individuals as well as parties and groups are allegedly pressured or enticed by monetary traits to act and influence in a way aligned with China's policies.

Economic relations between Taiwan and China inform policies, decisions and at times, political choices in Taiwan. The 2014 Sunflower Movement provides for an example. The movement sparked with – among others – concerns about the potential rise of China's economic influence over Taiwan with The Cross-Strait Service Trade Agreement, which sought to reciprocally open some 'service-sector markets' in both countries to one another within the parameters of the Cross-Strait Economic Cooperation framework Agreement (ECFA).[41] The economy continued to be a pressure point after the movement. Jason Li (2019) suggests that China responded to Tsai's election victory in 2016, DPP's 'pro-independence leanings' and Tsai's stance on issues such as the 1992 consensus by 'exploiting' Taiwan's reliance on China's market and constricting Taiwan's economy.[42] Also, while Sunflower Movement scrutinized KMT's cross-Straits economic policies, the potential influence of the cross-straits related economic concerns on DPP's performance in the 2018[43] local elections emerged as a question.

Individuals, parties and groups with financial ties to China form the second channel of influence. Allegations include sponsored trips to China in return for 'assistance in helping select candidates win the elections',[44] sponsoring candidate banquets[45] and channelling funds to political campaigns via the business of Taiwanese operating in China.[46] Also, Taiwan's Ministry of Justice stated that it is inspecting the financial backing behind certain candidates, some of which were allegedly, indirectly financed by China's Taiwan Affairs Office (TAO).[47] Akin to this, the pro-unification Chinese

Unification Promotion Party[48] has been drawing attention with its alleged ties to China and questioned for the source of its funding. The party allegedly spreads its 'pro-unification' support via its strong connections with grassroots organizations such as temples, 'agricultural production and marketing groups' and charities.[49] Also, in 2018, three members of the New Party were charged under the National Security Act for 'espionage' and 'Chinese funding'.[50]

Additionally, some see 'The 31 measures'[51] as another tool to cultivate a larger group of Taiwanese with ties to China. The 31 measures seek to facilitate studying, investing and working in China for Taiwanese. Twelve of the 31 measures concern market access and competition and promise Taiwanese the option to invest in state-owned businesses and take part in public biddings.[52] The remaining ones include measures that aim to attract successful Taiwanese to China to study and establish start-ups and to work in sectors that were hard to enter for Taiwanese before.[53,54] Some argue that the measures grant Taiwanese similar access with Chinese citizens on multiple areas and provide employment prospects for Taiwanese, especially ones working in areas with lack of employment opportunities.[55] Whether and how 31 measures contribute to existing influence efforts is an area to observe.

Information and influence

Chinese influence by way of information is spread through multiple channels in Taiwan, and China's sharp power penetrates into different factions of Taiwanese society and governance with the help of diverse agents. United Front Work Department (UFWD) sits at the centre of various information and influence activities. UFWD undertakings include information gathering, 'co-opt[ing]' and 'control[ing]', 'non-CCP elites', 'promoting "one country, two systems" in Hong Kong, Macao, and Taiwan' and engaging 'pro-China people' from outside China.[56] UFWD is allegedly growing strong under Xi Jinping's leadership with the addition of new divisions and expansion of UFWD directive, especially after the inclusion of Religious Affairs Bureau, State Ethnic Affairs Commission and State Council's Office of Overseas Chinese Affairs under its mandate.[57] The activities of the UFWD allegedly include swaying academic debates on '"sensitive" issues'; acquiring, collaborating with or controlling the narrative in media outside of China; and establishing ties with 'influential' individuals with 'business interests or sympathetic views towards China'.[58] With this, although discussed under this section, UFWD activities stretch into the other aspects discussed earlier.

Within this environment, influence attempts by way of information can be roughly grouped under four, intersecting and interacting categories: activities of the agents of influence, information gathering and espionage; media; disinformation campaigns and cyberattacks. Each will be discussed, respectively.[59]

Agents of Influence, information gathering and espionage

China allegedly seeks to cultivate and deploy agents of influence in Taiwan.[60] For instance, in relation to information gathering and cultivating ties, according to a

Financial Times article, China's TAO allegedly asked the members of the Association of Taiwan Investment Enterprises on the Mainland to join 'study sessions' and 'discussion forums' on Xi Jinping's current policies on Taiwan, citing 'six members in Shanghai and the provinces of Fujian and Jiangsu'.[61] Also, Taiwanese students studying in Guangzhou and Chengdu claimed that the 'local authorities had organized meetings with Chinese student associations to discuss how Taiwan should be ruled after unification'.[62]

Espionage, on the other hand, has constituted a central debate between two sides of the straits with both parties condemning the other of spying. For instance, both China and Taiwan blamed one another of attempting to leverage students as spies. China 'accused' Taiwan of increasing 'efforts to steal intelligence with the aim of "infiltration" and "sabotage"', and claimed that some Chinese students studying in Taiwan have been 'targeted by domestic spies who lure them with money, love and friendship'.[63] As to Taiwan, some of the individuals detained by Taiwan with spying allegations include a PRC student studying in Taiwan,[64] and the bodyguard of the former Taiwanese vice-president Annette Lu.[65] Also, four New Party members were accused of 'provid[ing] intelligence to' CCP in 2017,[66] and there were allegations of a retiree from PLA running a spy network in Taiwan and recruiting individuals including 'Taiwanese military personnel to work for China'.[67]

Media

The media is an essential source for waging political warfare and it is a vital apparatus for China's media/opinion warfare. The media in Taiwan becomes an instrument in China's political warfare with its vulnerabilities that open it to exploitation including 'capital' relations with China (e.g. ownership ties and revenues from advertising), and problems concerning journalistic and industry practices.

Some Taiwanese media entities are enmeshed in a constricting relation with 'Chinese capital, advertising, and circulation market', which results in the censorship and propagation of China lenient content especially in private media companies.[68] Taiwanese Media's capital relation with China is embodied in various, public examples. For instance, the Want Want Group, which owns various media outlets,[69] profits from its businesses operating in China.[70] The group's chairman has been accused of accommodating biased, pro-Beijing reporting.[71] Also, a Reuters article, upon interviewing 'ten reporters and newsroom managers' and analysing 'internal documents', suggested that 'at least five Taiwan media groups' received payment from 'mainland authorities' to give them 'coverage in various publications and on a television channel'.[72]

Poor journalistic practices exacerbate the problem,[73] and as some argue, the twenty-four-hour news cycle and pressure to produce push verification to the background. For instance, the National Communications Commission (NCC) 'fine[d]' CtiTV News for 'failing to fact-check'.[74] The media outlet was also scrutinized for the high amount of coverage it allocated to Han Kuo-yu on certain days in February 2019.[75] At times, the lack of accuracy checks on the information in circulation results in misleading information travelling from one platform to the other without questioning. This becomes especially problematic against the allegations of some Taiwanese journalists making 'news' out of information on social media platforms, as argued by the Reuters Institute and Oxford University 2018 Digital News Report[76] and others.[77] The example is given in the following section.

Before moving forward, it is essential to state that the focus on China does not mean that the domestic political actors do not have influence over Taiwanese media. For instance, according to the 2019 Freedom in the World Report many Taiwanese news outlets 'display strong party affiliation in their coverage'.[78] Despite the interaction and intersections between the domestic and external influence over media, this article elaborates on China's influence over Taiwanese media as the topic of this study concerns China's political warfare in Taiwan.

Disinformation campaigns and information manipulation in cyberspace

Disinformation campaigns and other attempts at online information manipulation may help sway opinions and decision-making, and with that, pollute the information domain in Taiwan. While there is a rough internal and cross-straits split and some experts explore the related issues with respect to these two dimensions, a clear-cut separation between internal and external agents and dynamics is rather troublesome for – primarily – three reasons. First, proxies in Taiwan are allegedly recruited or used for the benefit of external agents. Second, 'pro-unification' supporters in Taiwan hold a particular view on cross-strait relations and some may be prone to pass information confirming their views on cross-straits issues and at times propagate their view in online and offline spaces. The second point is particularly important as in Taiwan, where freedom of speech and democracy are upheld, pro-unification supporters have the freedom to voice their opinions, and they are a part of the political debate. The freedom of expression they enjoy demonstrates the good functioning of democracy in this regard. Third, some of the political debates segue into issues concerning cross-straits relations and blur the boundaries between domestic and external political issues. More importantly, challenges of attributing an incident to the actual perpetrator of the act, especially when proxies are leveraged, leave room for a debate on the main orchestrator of an act in some cases. With this in mind, some of the issues that invite manipulation, channels leveraged in disinformation campaigns and agents involved require a closer look.

There are a wide variety of issues that have been tainted by disinformation, such as military affairs, policies and acts of politicians, including the steps taken by President Tsai. Among them, military and defence-related information contribute to the construction of an opinion on the power play between Taiwan and China amid the risk of China's military intervention in Taiwan. The narratives on China's military spending, capacity of China and Taiwan's forces, and military drill of both sides, regardless of their accuracy, potentially kindle or subside fears. More importantly, in some occasions, real or manipulated cases of kinetic acts are coupled with disinformation. The fake photo showing 'Chinese bombers near close to Taiwan's Jade Mountain' is an example.[79] Smear campaigns and attacks on military, political and other public figures compose another line of disinformation campaign. For instance, some media outlets operating in China and Hong Kong have 'misquoted' or 'obscured' the statements of Taiwanese officials including 'retired former generals, high-level defence officials, lawmakers', and 'entertainers' allegedly to stain their reputation or create the impression that they 'support a particular political position held by the CCP'.[80]

The use of disinformation during the 2018 local election period also emerged as a debate, with division on – among others – the source and influence of disinformation in the run-up to the election. For instance, various government authorities accused China of leveraging disinformation to sway public opinion in Taiwan before the elections.[81] On the other hand, after the elections, some KMT lawmakers argued that the DPP is pointing at the 'fake news' as an excuse for its poor performance in the election and blamed President Tsai's administration for suppressing 'freedom of speech and the press in the name of curbing the spread of false news reports'.[82] During the election period there was disinformation targeted at the Kaohsiung candidate Chen Chi-mai, while some claimed that his opponent who later won the race, Han Kuo-yu, was supported by China.[83] With regard to the use of disinformation during the elections in general, the Criminal Investigation Bureau shared that it received sixty-four claims of disinformation and passed forty of them to prosecutors.[84]

Chinese agents allegedly leverage multiple channels to penetrate disinformation in Taiwan. Michael J. Cole identifies some of the channels used by China in disseminating disinformation in Taiwan as 'state-run media (e.g., Global Times, China Review News); government-linked Weibo accounts; Internet platforms known as "content farms" or "content mills" (e.g., COCO01.net); media controlled by or associated with the PLA-linked 311 Base (Psychological Operations, and Legal Warfare Base, or 61716 Unit) in Fuzhou, Fujian Province; Facebook groups'; and 'online forums like PTT Gossiping (批踢踢八卦板)'.[85] Wikipedia has also been a battleground where entries on Taiwan were edited and reversed multiple time.[86] Disinformation is not limited to one of these sites; it occasionally travels from one platform to the other amplifying the visibility and arguably trustworthiness of the information. Official Chinese media outlets such as the China Review News and *Global Times* – allegedly – engage in propaganda or disinformation,[87] and some information promoted by such sources find their ways to Taiwanese newspapers and TV. The Reuters Institute and Oxford University 2018 Digital News Report argued that the Taiwanese media published stories originating from PLA run social media sites on PLA aircraft and ships 'patrol[ing]' Taiwan.[88] This circles back to the discussion on poor journalistic practices.

The content farms, cyber troops and bots are central to the debates concerning information manipulation in Taiwan. COCO01.net,[89] Qiqi Kan Xinwen (琦琦看新)[90] and COCO02.net[91] are some of the content farms labelled as conveyors of disinformation. The Common Wealth magazine claimed that 'a group of pro-blue fan pages' have based their content on 'content farms' such as 'mission-tw.com', 'nooho.net' and 'taidushashi'.[92] This is problematic given the possible followership of content farms. While the orchestrators behind these content farms could be hard to pinpoint, they are scrutinized for housing misleading content.

Some of these content farms also have Facebook pages. With regard to Facebook pages, Paul Huang, in an article in *Foreign Policy*, casted doubt on the authenticity of 'Han Kuo-yu Fans For Victory! Holding Up a Blue Sky' fan page, which was established a day after Han Kuo-yu announced his candidacy for the local elections.[93] Huang's search into the admins of the fan page revealed that there were three LinkedIn profiles with the same name three of the six admins of the fan page.[94] While all claimed to be Peking University graduates and Tencent employees, two profiles stated that they 'worked in public relations for many foreign companies'.[95] A further look into the phrase 'worked in public relations for many foreign companies' led Huang to 249 LinkedIn profiles with similar characteristics including 'mugshot-style photos cropped from decades-old graduation pictures and claims of being Tencent employees and Peking University graduates', suggesting a link between them.[96]

The employment of cyber troops and bots to inject disinformation in different platforms, cheerlead a side of a debate or counter arguments against the view they support is another important dimension of the problem. According to Monaco (2017), the use of manual propaganda is more prominent, although bots activity is observed occasionally, at times in domestic campaigning efforts.[97] For instance, in Sia et al.'s inquiry into the Diba[98] case where Diba members made a call to flood President Tsai's Facebook page with comments, they did not encounter fully automated accounts while they found 'evidence of heavy coordination for mainland accounts' and suggested that automation could have been coupled with 'human intervention'.[99] According to Monaco (2017), while there was no clear indication of China's 50-cent party cyber troop's engagement in the incident, findings such as the use of narratives aimed at 'distracting or stifling discussion, rather than arguing' and 'little evidence of automation' conformed to King et al.'s research exploring 50-cent army.[100]

According to Monaco (2017), bot use remains limited.[101] One example offered by Monaco is the use of bots in the domestic political rivalry of 2014 Taipei mayoral race. While the independent candidate, Ko Wen-je's campaign allegedly involved the use of crawler bots for information gathering and targeted messaging built on the information collected, his opponent KMT candidate Sean Lien's campaign allegedly benefited from inauthentic accounts to spread information favouring Lien, countering Ko Wen-je.[102] On the other hand, Major General of Taiwanese military's cybersecurity command unit Ma Ying-han argued that the 50-cent party is gradually 'replaced by artificially intelligent editing robots'.[103] Whether the use of bots will increase in the future remains a question. As to inauthentic accounts, some recently argued that there are PTT (bulletin board) and Facebook accounts available for purchase.[104] As purchased accounts would come with history, their propaganda may draw more attention and incite trust then a fake account with a constructed or no history.

The use of proxies and multiplicity of disinformation agents and channels complicate attribution and make it harder to judge whether some attempts are coordinated by the Chinese government or carried by galvanized citizens. Further complicating the problem, Beijing's immersion into Taiwanese domestic politics beclouds the separation between Chinese agents, and politically motivated domestic actors, such as 'pan-blue forces'.[105] According to Michael J. Cole, there has been cases where

'Chinese disinformation efforts have overlapped with – and in some cases appear to have co-opted – traditional blocking action by opposition legislators and civic groups opposed to reforms'.[106] The disinformation on pension reform and burning of incense are two examples. Furthermore, the use of information push and manipulation tactics for domestic policy by local agents and politicization of the debate on disinformation pollute the information domain and arguably damage trust in politics and politicians further.

Information manipulation tactics also influence the domestic political rivalry. This creates a fault line that can be exploited by external agents, who may amplify disinformation or biased information circulated by or on local political actors or their supporters. Online groups backing different political camps could have various motivations and come in different forms including online citizens voluntarily supporting political personalities they follow; 'political public relations' or 'marketing companies' motivated by monetary benefits or 'trading of favours'; and 'party workers and advisors' of different political camps.[107] These groups could have different aims and some, such as citizens supporting a political group, could unknowingly contribute to the circulation of misleading information. 'The Global Disinformation Order: 2019 Global Inventory of Organised Social Media Manipulation', by Samantha Bradshaw and Philip N. Howard, argues that there are politicians and political parties in Taiwan that engage in 'social media manipulation'.[108]

Some government divisions were also embroiled in discussions about 'cyber armies'. For instance, KMT Legislator Arthur Chen called on Control Yuan and the Ministry of Justice to 'investigate the Council of Agriculture (COA)' on its 'cyber army', for which it allegedly budgeted to hire 'online workers for policy promotion', but according to Chen's claim 'funded Facebook groups to attack its opponents' instead.[109] COA minister Chen Chi-chung countered the allegations asserting that the council took initiatives to counter disinformation in a fast manner amid the surge in disinformation about farmers and agriculture industry.[110] Amid the political rivalry and blurring boundaries of political communication, as others also suggest, the issue of disinformation campaigns become politicized and domestic debates on disinformation, coupled with the external threat, contribute to the emergence of an information environment prone to information pollution.

This section has focused on allegations of China's manipulation by way disinformation and local political debates on disinformation that interact with or aid China's alleged influence objectives. Here it is essential to note that attribution of the activities of content farms, cyber troops and other intermediaries could be challenging and motivations of these groups likely vary. Nonetheless, regardless of the main orchestrators and aims, these intermediaries often pollute the information environment with manipulative, biased or false information. Also, it is important to state that China is not the only agent accused of injecting influence in Taiwan. For instance, Ketty Chen and Michael J. Cole argue that some conservative churches and institutions in the United States aided the efforts of 'anti-LGBT movement' in Taiwan against the same-sex marriage referendum.[111] Nevertheless, as this article concern's China's political warfare in Taiwan, this section only explored information manipulation attempts in relation to China's political warfare.

Cyberattacks

Taiwan is not foreign to cyberattacks. Targets allegedly include government bodies; NGOs; educational institutions; technology, finance and manufacturing companies; hospitals and others.[112] While attribution is getting harder with the sophistication of techniques, President Tsai argued that North Korea, Russia and China are using Taiwan as a 'test-bed' to advance their 'cyber-hacking' techniques before deploying them in other foreign countries.[113] Majority of the attacks potentially 'come from groups supported by China' according to Howard Jyan, director of Executive Yuan's Cybersecurity department, who lists 'matching patterns', 'sophistication' and other factors as indicators.[114] Also, a FireEye report on 'Cyber Threat Activity Targeting Elections' said it 'suspected Chinese threat actors target Taiwanese government entities with election-themed lures, utilizing TAIDOOR malware'[115] with reference to 2018.

Future assaults could be harder to detect and cause more damage. For instance, there are signs of advancement in techniques with the hackers' using of 'online platforms such as search engines to break into systems'.[116] Hackers allegedly hide behind platforms such as Google and blogs and escape from investigators' attention by carrying their activities behind the scenes of a running platform.[117] Also, attackers allegedly navigate their hacks through other countries, which make it harder to pin the actual location of the hacker.[118]

Strategic implications

In the twenty-first century, China continues to pursue the development, deployment and exercising of political warfare as a means to create advantages and influence events or strategic choices of not only Taiwan but also on the global stage.[119] The resurgence of great power rivalries, particularly notable in East Asia, suggests that while wars and conflicts aren't inevitable, neither are they inconceivable. In potential military confrontations, however, between adversaries armed with substantial conventional arsenals and stand-off precision strike systems, there are considerable escalatory risks. Accordingly, China, Russia and the United States are engaging in competitive strategies to avoid large-scale wars of attrition, and instead rely on 'peacetime' non-military diplomatic, information and economic actions coupled with paramilitary operations to gain influence and territory without having to escalate to a major conflict.[120]

These 'indirect' actions include the use of information operations and political warfare, cyberattacks, electronic warfare as well as paramilitary operations in disputed areas. The progressive complexity of cyber and information operations is reflected in cross-domain strategic interactions – between cyber, physical and cognitive information domains, civil and military spheres, and involves both state and non-state actors.[121] These include confrontations in and out of cyber space, cyberattacks on physical systems and processes controlling critical information infrastructure, information operations and various forms of cyber espionage. Accordingly, nearly all great powers are developing advanced cyber capabilities – whether defensive, offensive or intelligence-driven, which are increasingly used as instruments of warfare – as a key enabler and force-multiplier of 'kinetic' operations – enabling actions, capabilities and effects of land, sea, air, space and intelligence operations in all domains.[122]

The resulting progressive complexity in strategic interactions and interdependencies between cyber, information, cognitive and physical domains present new challenges on traditional conceptions of deterrence and defence. In particular, the convergence of both military and non-military instruments of warfare through cyber and information means brought by emerging technologies are often viewed in the context of two interrelated strategic challenges: (1) 'cross-domain deterrence and compellence' (CDD&C) and (2) asymmetric Anti-Access/Area-Denial challenges – with both having significant impact on the character of warfare, particularly in East Asia. CDD&C refers to the act of deterring an action in one domain with a threat in another domain, where the domains are defined as land, under the land, at sea, under the sea, in the air, in space and in cyberspace, and may often use economic sanctions and other diplomatic, political and informational tools. In this context, CDD&C may leverage on both deterrence – dissuading an actor from taking an action before they act; and coercive diplomacy – persuading an actor to stop a particular course of action after they initiated action. In other words, cross-domain coercion uses threats of force in multiple domains to influence an opponent's strategic choices.[123]

The concept of CDD&C is not new and has long existed in the history of warfare. For example, with the advent of air power in the early twentieth century, the concept of 'counter-value pre-emptive strikes' was seen as an attempt to gain an offensive advantage – that is, the case of Japanese attack on Pearl Harbor. There are many other historical examples of CDD&C strategies. For example, NATO relied on the threat of nuclear use to deter superior conventional Soviet forces. Soviet advances in space and ballistic missile technology threatened the credibility of US/NATO nuclear forces by providing Soviets with means to threaten the US homeland in response to US/NATO nuclear threats. The United States used actions in multiple domains – a naval blockade, threat of an air campaign, and changes in nuclear posture – to compel the removal of Soviet missiles from Cuba while deterring an escalatory response through local conventional naval superiority and global strategic nuclear retaliatory capabilities.[124] Today, however, China relies on varying CDD&C strategies to project power and influence in areas vital to their strategic interests such as Taiwan by adopting measures that would be effective with minimum probability of proving retaliatory escalation. The use of cyber means as political instruments of warfare is increasingly reflected in Taiwan as well as the ongoing territorial disputes over the South China Sea.[125]

Consequently, when contemplating how China's political warfare may further affect security and defence trajectories, US allies and strategic partners in East Asia, including Japan, South Korea, Taiwan and Singapore, will have to plan for China's increasing use of its 'non-kinetic toolkits': What types of challenges does this present for them? How will they operate in a contested environment characterized by the diffusion of sophisticated longer-range adversary capabilities and methods such as ballistic missiles, submarines, weapons of mass destruction and offensive space, cyberspace and information warfare assets? At the same time, however, the character of future conflicts in the regional 'grey zones' may also likely reflect low-level type intensity conflicts in 'peripheral campaigns', rather than high-end missions – given the considerable escalatory risks. However, in a context where the battle space is crowded with both legally constituted combatants and non-combatants, this will present new challenges. Consequently, military-technological advantages will not be effective without corresponding strategic, organizational and operational adaptability – from identifying new techniques, tactics and procedures and ways and means to counter them.

Ultimately, the effectiveness of China's political warfare must be viewed in a relative context – through the lens of *competitive strategies* reflected in the efforts to develop effective counter-measures and responses. A key requirement will be the capacity of the select states and their militaries to educate both the officer corps and the rank-and-file on the changing character of war, what the laws of armed conflict permit military personnel to do. Under the conditions of strategic ambiguity, regional militaries will therefore have to redefine their 'theories of victory'. Ultimately, the next-wave of China's political warfare will increasingly aim to shape regional as well as global strategic choices, including defence planning, management and political priorities, propelling the need for effective strategic and operational counter-responses to prepare for, fight, win and deter new types of conflicts.

Notes

1 Please note that this chapter was written after 2018, before 2020 elections in Taiwan.
2 This study focuses on Chinese Communist Party's (CCP) attempts to inject influence in Taiwan. By referring to China, it does not intend to refer to China or Chinese citizens as a whole.
3 Executive Director of the Project 2049.
4 Executive Director of the Global Taiwan Institute.
5 Mark Stokes and Russell Hsiao, 'The People's Liberation Army General Political Department: Political Warfare with Chinese Characteristics', *Project 2049* (14 October 2013): 2. Retrieved From: https://project2049.net/2013/10/14/the-people s-liberation-army-general-political-department-political-warfare-with-chinese-ch aracteristics/.
6 'Chinese Public Diplomacy in Taiwan', in *Hybrid Threats: A Strategic Communications Perspective*, eds Sean Aday, Māris Andžāns, Una Bērziņa-Čerenkova, Francesca Granelli, John-Paul Gravelines, Mils Hills, Miranda Holmstrom, Adam Klus, Irene Martinez-Sanchez, Mariita Mattiisen, Holger Molder, Yeganeh Morakabati, James Pamment, Aurel Sari, Vladimir Sazonov, Gregory Simons and Jonathan Terra (NATO Strategic Communications Centre of Excellence (NATO StratCom COE), 8 April 2019), 67. Retrieved From: https://www.stratcomcoe.org/hybrid-threats-strategic-co mmunications-perspective.
7 'Chinese Public Diplomacy in Taiwan' (NATO Strategic Communications Centre of Excellence (NATO StratCom COE), 8 April 2019), 67.
8 Russell Hsiao, 'CCP Propaganda against Taiwan Enters the Social Age', *China Brief* 18, issue 7 (24 April 2018). Retrieved From: https://jamestown.org/program/ccp-p ropaganda-against-taiwan-enters-the-social-age/.
9 Sigrid Winkler, 'Taiwan's UN Dilemma: To Be or Not To Be', Brookings, 20 June 2012. https://www.brookings.edu/opinions/taiwans-un-dilemma-to-be-or-not-to-be/.

'Taiwan Fights for Allies and Identity Amid Chinese Pressure', *The Straits Times*, 22 August 2018. https://www.straitstimes.com/asia/east-asia/with-friends-like-these -taiwans-battle-for-allies-and-identity.

10 Chou Hui-ching, 'Lifting Martial Law and Opening-up Taiwan', *The CommonWealth Magazine*, 24 December 2018. https://medium.com/commonwealth-magazine/lift ing-martial-law-and-opening-up-taiwan-a0965ccca511. See Also 'Taiwan Country Profile', *BBC*, 1 February 2019. https://www.bbc.com/news/world-asia-16164639.

11 Hui-ching, 'Lifting Martial Law and Opening-up Taiwan'. See Also 'Taiwan Country Profile', *BBC*.

12 'Chinese Public Diplomacy in Taiwan' (NATO Strategic Communications Centre of Excellence (NATO StratCom COE), 8 April 2019), 66.

13 See JM Norton, '"One China," 5 Interpretations', *The Diplomat*, 27 July 2016. https:// thediplomat.com/2016/07/one-china-5-interpretations/.

14 'Nations Condemn Chinese Missile Tests', *CNN*, 8 March 1996. http://edition.cnn.c om/WORLD/9603/china_taiwan/08/.

15 Michael J. Cole, 'The Third Taiwan Straits Crisis: The Forgotten Showdown Between China and America', *The National Interest*, 10 March 2017. https://nationalinterest.org /feature/the-third-taiwan-strait-crisis-the-forgotten-showdown-19742.

16 'Nations Condemn Chinese Missile Tests', *CNN*. See Also Cole, 'The Third Taiwan Straits Crisis'. See Also Chris Horton, 'Specter of Meddling Looms Over Taiwan's Elections', *The New York Times*, 22 November 2018. https://www.nytimes.com/2018/1 1/22/world/asia/taiwan-elections-meddling.html.

17 Michael J. Cole, 'The Battle between Taiwan's Democratic Ideals and China's Subversive Proxies: Where Do We Draw the Line', *Taiwan Sentinel* 3 April 2019. https://sentinel.tw/battle-taiwans-democracy-versus-ufw/. See Also Hsiao, 'CCP Propaganda against Taiwan Enters the Social Age'.

18 Michael J. Cole, 'Chinese Interference in Taiwan's Electoral Mechanisms: Means and Aims', *Global Taiwan Brief* 3, issue 24 (12 December 2018). http://globaltaiwan.org/2 018/12/vol-3-issue-24/. See also Kathrin Hille, 'China's Sharp Power Play in Taiwan', *Financial Times*, 21 November 2018. https://www.ft.com/content/5c272b90-ec12 -11e8-89c8-d36339d835c0.

19 Hille, 'China's Sharp Power' Play in Taiwan'.

20 Alison Bartel, 'Chinese Political Warfare after Taiwan's Elections: Tsai's Victory', *Project 2049 Institute*, 9 February 2016. https://project2049.net/2016/02/09/chinese -political-warfare-after-taiwans-elections-tsais-victory/.

21 Stokes and Hsiao, 'The People's Liberation Army General Political Department: Political Warfare with Chinese Characteristics'.

22 'Chinese Public Diplomacy in Taiwan' (NATO Strategic Communications Centre of Excellence (NATO StratCom COE), 8 April 2019), 67.

23 'Taiwan Hotel Axes Marriott Contract over China Naming Row', *The Straits Times*, 16 August 2018. https://www.straitstimes.com/asia/east-asia/taiwan-hotel-axes-mar riott-contract-over-china-naming-row.

24 Sui-Lee Wee, 'Giving in to China, US Airlines Drop Taiwan (in Name at Least)', *The New York Times*, 25 July 2018. https://www.nytimes.com/2018/07/25/business/t aiwan-american-airlines-china.html. See Also Samantha Hoffman, 'Grasping Power with Both Hands: Social Credit, the Mass Line, and Party Control', *The Jamestown Foundation China Brief* 18, Issue 16 (10 October 2018). https://jamestown.org/pro gram/grasping-power-with-both-hands-social-credit-the-mass-line-and-party-c ontrol/. See Also Josh Rogin, 'China Takes Its Political Censorship Global: Will

America Resist?', *The Washington Post*, 27 July 2018. https://www.washingtonpost
.com/opinions/global-opinions/china-takes-its-political-censorship-global/2018/07
/26/898d40dc-90f6-11e8-bcd5-9d911c784c38_story.html. See Also 'Beijing's Demand
to Refer to "China Taiwan" Still being Defied by US Airlines', Bloomberg in South
China Morning Post, 26 June 2018. https://www.scmp.com/news/china/diplomacy
-defence/article/2152459/beijings-demand-refer-china-taiwan-still-being-defied.

25 'China Accused of "dollar diplomacy" as Taiwan Loses Second Ally in a Month', *The
Guardian*, 24 May 2018. https://www.theguardian.com/world/2018/may/24/taiwan
-criticises-china-after-burkina-faso-ends-diplomatic-relations.

26 'MOFA Condemns China for Blocking Taiwan's WHA Participation', *Taiwan
Representative Office in Singapore*, 7 May 2019. https://www.roc-taiwan.org/sg_en/
post/9593.html. See Also Jacques deLisle, 'Taiwan in the World Health Assembly: A
Victory with Limits', *Brookings*, 13 May 2009. https://www.brookings.edu/opinions/
taiwan-in-the-world-health-assembly-a-victory-with-limits/.

27 World Health Organization, World health Assembly. http://www9.who.int/media
centre/events/governance/wha/en/.

28 'Taiwan Slams WHO after being Left Out of Major International Meet Due to
Pressure from China', *The Straits Times*, 8 May 2018. https://www.straitstimes.com/a
sia/east-asia/taiwan-slams-who-after-being-left-out-from-major-international-mee
t-due-to-pressure. See also 'Taiwan Accuses World Health Organisation of Bowing
to Beijing over Invitation to Top Health Meeting', *South China Morning Post*, 8 May
2018. https://www.scmp.com/news/china/policies-politics/article/2145129/taiw
an-accuses-world-health-organisation-bowing-beijing. See also, Lee I-chia, 'More
Countries Irked by Chinese Bullying at WHO', *Taipei Times*, 8 April 2019. http://www
.taipeitimes.com/News/taiwan/archives/2019/04/08/2003713011.

29 The Covid-19 broke out during the review process of this article. Taiwan raised
concerns about its 'exclusion from' the WHO amid the spread of the novel
Coronavirus (2019-nCoV). See Huileng Tan, 'Taipei Lashes Out at China for
Blocking Taiwan's Access to the World Health Organization', *CNBC*, 6 February 2020.
https://www.cnbc.com/2020/02/06/coronavirus-taiwan-lashes-out-at-china-for-block
ing-who-access.html. See also 'Coronavirus: Taiwan Calls China "vile" for Restricting
Island's Access to WHO on Wuhan Virus', *The Straits Times*, 4 February 2020. https:/
/www.straitstimes.com/asia/east-asia/coronavirus-taiwan-calls-china-vile-for-restri
cting-islands-access-to-who-on-wuhan.

30 'US Senators Pass Bill on Taiwan's WHA Efforts', *Taiwan Republic of China Taipei
Economic and Cultural Office in Miami*, 25 May 2019. https://www.roc-taiwan.org
/usmia_en/post/5109.html. See also 'US Strongly Backs Taiwan's WHA Bid', *Taipei
Times*, 11 May 2017. http://www.taipeitimes.com/News/taiwan/archives/2017/05/11
/2003670360.

31 Dean Cheng, 'Winning Without Fighting: Chinese Legal Warfare', *The Heritage
Foundation*, 21 May 2012. https://www.heritage.org/asia/report/winning-without-fi
ghting-chinese-legal-warfare.

32 Cheng, 'Winning Without Fighting: Chinese Legal Warfare'.

33 'Anti-Secession Law (Full text)(03/15/05)', *Embassy of the People's Republic of China
in the United States of America*, 15 March 2005. http://www.china-embassy.org/eng/zt
/999999999/t187406.htm.

34 Jeanny Kao, Ben Blanchard and Michael Perry, 'Taiwan, China Spar over Taiwan
Premier's Independence Remarks', *Reuters*, 3 April 2018. https://www.reuters.com
/article/us-taiwan-china/taiwan-china-spar-over-taiwan-premiers-independence-

remarks-idUSKCN1HA09R. See Also Simon Tisdall, 'Will China Turn Taiwan into the Next Crimea?', *The Guardian*, 3 April 2018. https://www.theguardian.com/world /2018/apr/03/how-safe-is-taiwan-from-becoming-the-next-crimea-us-china.

35 Twelve of the 31 measures concern market access and competition and promise Taiwanese the option to invest in state-owned businesses and take part in public biddings. The remaining nineteen on the other hand aim to attract successful Taiwanese to China to study and establish start-ups and to work in sectors that were hard to enter for Taiwanese before. See Gunter Schubert, 'China's 31 Preferential Policies for Taiwan', *Taiwan Sentinel*, 23 March 2018. https://sentinel.tw/china-31pp -taiwan-no-threat/. See Also 'Chinese Public Diplomacy in Taiwan', (NATO Strategic Communications Centre of Excellence (NATO StratCom COE), 8 April 2019).

36 Schubert, 'China's 31 Preferential Policies for Taiwan'.

37 Jason Li, 'China's Surreptitious Economic Influence on Taiwan's Elections', *The Diplomat*, 12 April 2019. https://thediplomat.com/2019/04/chinas-surreptitious-ec onomic-influence-on-taiwans-elections/.

38 During the review process of this chapter, in November 2019, China introduced additional '26 measures'. This move came months before 2020 elections. The additional measures include provisions such as providing Taiwanese "Chinese consular protection abroad." Arguably, the '31 measures' and the additional '26 measures' with the diplomatic and economic enticements they encapsulate and the regulatory ease they bring can be explored in relation to diplomatic, legal as well as economic influence. See Sara Zheng, 'Beijing Extends Sweeteners for Taiwanese Weeks before Taipei Election', *South China Morning Post*, 4 November 2019. https:/ /www.scmp.com/news/china/politics/article/3036194/beijing-extends-sweeteners-t aiwanese-weeks-taipei-election.

39 Li, 'China's Surreptitious Economic Influence on Taiwan's Elections'.

40 Christopher Walker and Jessica Ludwig, 'From "Soft Power" to "Sharp Power": Rising Authoritarian Influence in the Democratic World', in *Sharp Power: Rising Authoritarian Influence*, National Endowment for Democracy (2017): 18. https://www.ned.org/wp-co ntent/uploads/2017/12/Sharp-Power-Rising-Authoritarian-Influence-Full-Report.pdf.

41 The Cross-Strait Service Trade Agreement sought to reciprocally open some 'service-sector markets' in both countries to one another within the parameters of the Cross-Strait Economic Cooperation framework Agreement (ECFA). See JoAnn Fan, 'The Economics of the Cross-Strait Services Agreement', *Brookings*, 18 April 2014. https:// www.brookings.edu/opinions/the-economics-of-the-cross-strait-services-agreement/. Fan, 'The Economics of the Cross-Strait Services Agreement'. See Also Ming-sho Ho, 'The Activist Legacy of Taiwan's Sunflower Movement', *Carnegie Endowment for International Peace*, 2 August 2018. https://carnegieendowment.org/2018/08/02/acti vist-legacy-of-taiwan-s-sunflower-movement-pub-76966.

42 Li, 'China's Surreptitious Economic Influence on Taiwan's Elections'.

43 Please note that this article was written after the 2018 local elections and before the 2020 elections.

44 Michael J. Cole, 'Chinese Interference in Taiwan's Elections is Part of a Two-Pronged Attack on Taiwan's Democracy', *Taiwan Sentinel*, 24 October 2018. https://sentinel .tw/chinese-interference-in-taiwans-elections-is-part-of-a-two-pronged-attack-on -democracy/.

45 Jason Pan, 'Elections: China Is Meddling in Elections, Officials Say', *Taipei Times*, 25 October 2018. http://www.taipeitimes.com/News/taiwan/archives/2018/10/25/2 003702996.

46 Horton, 'Specter of Meddling Looms Over Taiwan's Elections'. See Also Aaron Tu, Lin Ching-chuan and William Hetherington, 'PRC Funding of Campaigns Probed', *Taipei Times*, http://www.taipeitimes.com/News/front/archives/2018/10/23/2003702 864. See Also Cole, 'Chinese Interference in Taiwan's Elections is Part of a Two-Pronged Attack on Taiwan's Democracy'.

47 Cole, 'Chinese Interference in Taiwan's Elections is Part of a Two-Pronged Attack on Taiwan's Democracy'. See Also Tu, Ching-chuan and Hetherington, 'PRC Funding of Campaigns Probed'.

48 Unionist Party or China Unity Promotion Party in other sources.

49 'United Front Target Taiwan's Grass Roots: Gangs, Temples, Business', *The CommonWealth Magazine*, 22 August 2018. https://english.cw.com.tw/article/article .action?id=2083.

50 Jason Pan, 'New Party's Wang, others Charged with Espionage', *Taipei Times*, 14 June 2018. http://www.taipeitimes.com/News/front/archives/2018/06/14/2003694843. See also Russell Hsiao, 'CCP Influence Operations and Taiwan's 2020 Elections', *The Diplomat*, December 2019. https://magazine.thediplomat.com/#/issues/ -LulURInylDibWqHgwOj.

51 '31 Measures come under the Legal section in Chinese Public Diplomacy in Taiwan' (NATO Strategic Communications Centre of Excellence (NATO StratCom COE), 8 April 2019). However, it is economic dimension is as, if not more, important.

52 Schubert, 'China's 31 Preferential Policies for Taiwan'.

53 Schubert, 'China's 31 Preferential Policies for Taiwan'.

54 The 26 additional measures expand on the 'preferential economic measures' and include provisions targeting businesses as well as individuals. See Russell Hsiao, 'Fortnightly Review: China Amplifies "Soft-Hand" Strategy with Additional 26 Preferential Economic Measures as Taiwan Elections Loom', *Global Taiwan Brief* 4, Issue 22. http://globaltaiwan.org/2019/11/vol-4-issue-22/.

55 Kristin Huang, 'Taiwanese given Equal Status on China's Mainland, but Is Beijing just Trying to Buy their Support?', *South China Morning Post*, 1 March 2018. https://ww w.scmp.com/news/china/policies-politics/article/2135291/taiwanese-given-equal-st atus-chinas-mainland-beijing.

56 Charlotte Gao, 'The 19th Party Congress: A Rare Glimpse of the United Front Work Department', *The Diplomat*, 24 October 2017. https://thediplomat.com/2017/10/the -19th-party-congress-a-rare-glimpse-of-the-united-front-work-department/.

57 Geopolitical Monitor, 'A Brief History of China's United Front – Analysis', *Eurasia Review*, 28 March 2019. https://www.eurasiareview.com/28032019-a-brief-history-of -chinas-united-front-analysis/.

58 Geopolitical Monitor, 'A Brief History of China's United Front – Analysis'.

59 Please note that some examples delivered in this section include allegations covered in newspapers. As the chapter also seeks to survey local political debates on disinformation, accounts covered on newspapers are a part of the discussion. Nonetheless, examples including papers are delivered as allegations as newspaper coverages could also be questioned as per the section on journalism.

60 Here it must be stated for certain allegations it is rather difficult to make a conclusive judgement, as there is no criteria to judge accepted and rejected threshold of influence. It is also not possible to measure the intent, especially when claimed attempts to recruit agents of influence fit the legal framework and usual proceeding of exchanges.

61 Kathrin Hille, 'China Lures Taiwanese into "brainstorming" Talks on Island's Future', *Financial Times*, 6 February 2019. https://www.ft.com/content/4eb88028-263f-11e9 -8ce6-5db4543da632.

62 Hille, 'China Lures Taiwanese into "brainstorming" Talks on Island's Future'.

63 'China Tells Taiwan to Stop Spying as TV Show Details Honey Traps', *The Guardian*, 16 September 2018. https://www.theguardian.com/world/2018/sep/16/china-tells-ta iwan-to-stop-spying-as-tv-show-details-honey-traps.

64 'Taiwan Detains Chinese Student in Unusual Suspected Spying Case', *Reuters*, 10 March 2017. https://www.reuters.com/article/us-taiwan-china-students/taiwan-d etains-chinese-student-in-unusual-suspected-spying-case-idUSKBN16H13T.

65 Michael Bristow, 'China Accused by Taiwan of Stepping Up Spy Operations', *BBC*, 18 March 2017. http://www.bbc.com/news/world-asia-39307866.

66 Sean Lin, 'New Party Decries Arrest of Members', *Taipei Times*, 20 December 2017. http://www.taipeitimes.com/News/taiwan/archives/2017/12/20/2003684307.

67 Jason Pan, 'Chinese Spy Ring Leader Gets Four-Year Prison Term', *Taipei Times*, 20 September 2015. http://www.taipeitimes.com/News/front/archives/2015/09/02/20 03626732.

68 Huang Jaw-Nian, 'The China Factor in Taiwan's Media: Outsourcing Chinese Censorship Abroad', *China Perspectives* 3 (2017): 27, 35. http://journals.openedition .org/chinaperspectives/7388.
    According to Huang Jaw-Nian (2017) China took three steps targeting international, sectoral and corporate levels to '"outsource[d]" its censorship' to Taiwanese private media firms. First, with regard to the international level, China sought to render Taiwan economically reliant on China to target its 'hegemonic and unification propaganda' at Taiwan. Second, with regard to the sectoral level, the Chinese government had the prospect to 'co-opt Taiwanese media capitalists as its local collaborators in Taiwan' amid Taiwan's growing 'economic dependence on China'. Third, with regard to the corporate level, the Chinese government together with the help of Taiwanese media capitalists influenced Taiwanese media companies to shape their corporate and market frameworks in accordance to 'Beijing's mass communication policies' and with that integrated self-censorship in Taiwanese media on issues that are sensitive to China. See Jaw-Nian, 'The China Factor in Taiwan's Media'.

69 Russell Flannery, 'Billionaire's Media Push Tests the Toughness of a Taiwan "Strawberry"', *Forbes*, 6 August 2014. https://www.forbes.com/sites/russellflannery/ 2014/08/06/billionaires-media-push-tests-the-toughness-of-a-taiwan-strawberry/. See Also Wang, 'China Times Group Is Sold to Want Want', *Taipei Times*, 5 November 2008. http://www.taipeitimes.com/News/biz/archives/2008/11/05/2003427822.

70 Wang, 'China Times Group Is Sold to Want Want'.

71 Andrew Higgins, 'Tycoon Prods Taiwan Closer to China', *The Washington Post*, 21 January 2012. https://www.washingtonpost.com/world/asia_pacific/tycoon-prods -taiwan-closer-to-china/2012/01/20/gIQAhswmFQ_story.html.

72 Yimou Lee and I-hwa Cheng, 'Paid "news": China using Taiwan Media to Win Hearts and Minds on Island – Sources', *Reuters*, 9 August 2019. https://www.reuters.com/a rticle/us-taiwan-china-media-insight/paid-news-china-using-taiwan-media-to-win -hearts-and-minds-on-island-sources-idUSKCN1UZ0I4.

73 Michael J. Cole, 'The Impact of China's Disinformation Operations against Taiwan', *The Prospect Foundation*, 10 March 2018. https://www.pf.org.tw/article-pfch-2049-

6365?fbclid=IwAR2OaNLFoSGpuaeqQneeQLrEDyk43id89j8Ry7IWO7kUPn5fVPx
m_DzO7FA.

74 Shelley Shan, 'NCC Fines CtiTV NT$1m for Failing to Fact-Check', *Taipei Times*,
28 March 2019. http://www.taipeitimes.com/News/front/archives/2019/03/28/20
03712314/1.

75 Shan, 'NCC Fines CtiTV NT$1m for Failing to Fact-Check'.

76 Lihyun Lin, 'Taiwan', *Reuters Institute and Oxford University 2018 Digital News
Report*. http://www.digitalnewsreport.org/survey/2018/taiwan-2018/.

77 Cole, 'The Impact of China's Disinformation Operations against Taiwan'.

78 'Taiwan', *Freedom in the World 2019*. https://freedomhouse.org/report/freedom-world
/2019/taiwan.

79 Hsiao, 'CCP Propaganda against Taiwan Enters the Social Age'.

80 Hsiao, 'CCP Propaganda against Taiwan Enters the Social Age'.

81 Pratik Jakhar, 'Analysis: Fake News' Fears Grip Taiwan Ahead of Local Polls', *BBC
Monitoring*, 21 November 2018. https://monitoring.bbc.co.uk/product/c200fqlq. See
Also Chien Li-chung, Chung Li-hua and Jonathan Chin, 'China using Fake News to
Divide Taiwan', *Taipei Times*, 16 September 2018. http://www.taipeitimes.com/News/
front/archives/2018/09/16/2003700513.

82 Shelley Shan, 'Tsai Government Stifling Freedom of Speech: KMT', *Taipei Times*,
10 April 2019. http://www.taipeitimes.com/News/taiwan/archives/2019/04/10/2
003713133.

83 Horton, 'Specter of Meddling Loom's Over Taiwan's Elections'.

84 Pan, 'Elections: China Is Meddling in Elections, Officials Say'.

85 Cole, 'The Impact of China's Disinformation Operations against Taiwan'.

86 Carl Miller, 'China and Taiwan Clash over Wikipedia Edits', *BBC*, 5 October 2019.
https://www.bbc.com/news/technology-49921173.

87 Cole, 'The Impact of China's Disinformation Operations against Taiwan'.

88 Lin, 'Taiwan'.

89 Cole, 'The Impact of China's Disinformation Operations against Taiwan'.

90 Li-chung, Li-hua and Chin, 'China using Fake News to Divide Taiwan'.

91 Li-chung, Li-hua and Chin, 'China using Fake News to Divide Taiwan'.

92 Rebecca Lin and Felice Wu, 'Taiwan's Online "Opinion War" Arrived', *The Common
Wealth*, 27 April 2019. https://english.cw.com.tw/article/article.action?id=2375.

93 Paul Huang, 'Chinese Cyber-Operatives Boosted Taiwan's Insurgent Candidate',
Foreign Policy, 26 June 2019. https://foreignpolicy.com/2019/06/26/chinese-cyber
-operatives-boosted-taiwans-insurgent-candidate/.

94 Huang, 'Chinese Cyber-Operatives Boosted Taiwan's Insurgent Candidate'.

95 Huang, 'Chinese Cyber-Operatives Boosted Taiwan's Insurgent Candidate'.

96 Huang, 'Chinese Cyber-Operatives Boosted Taiwan's Insurgent Candidate'.

97 According to Monaco and Google Jigsaw (2017), the use of manual propaganda
is more prominent, although bots activity was observed in domestic campaigning
efforts.

98 Diba is a Reddit-like online platform.

99 As cited in Nicholas J. Monaco and Google Jigsaw, 'Computational Propaganda in
Taiwan: Where Digital Democracy Meets Automated Autocracy', Computational
Propaganda Research Project, Working Paper No. 2017.2 (2017): 23. http://blogs.oii
.ox.ac.uk/politicalbots/wp-content/uploads/sites/89/2017/06/Comprop-Taiwan-2.pdf.

100 Monaco and Jigsaw, 'Computational Propaganda in Taiwan', 25.

101 Monaco (2017), the use of manual propaganda is more prominent, although bots activity is observed occasionally in domestic campaigning efforts.
102 Monaco and Jigsaw, 'Computational Propaganda in Taiwan', 10, 11, 12.
103 Ma ying-han as cited in Nick Aspinwall, 'Taiwan Gathers to Repel China's "Hard Power in Soft Power Glove"', *The News Lens*, 10 October 2018. https://international .thenewslens.com/article/105793.
104 As reported by Jessica Drun, 'Taiwan's Social Media Landscape: Ripe for Election Interference?', *Center for Advanced China Research*, 14 November 2018. https://www .ccpwatch.org/single-post/2018/11/13/Taiwans-Social-Media-Landscape-Ripe-for-El ection-Interference.
105 Michael J. Cole, 'Will China's Disinformation War Destabilize Taiwan?', *The National Interest*, 30 July 2017. https://nationalinterest.org/feature/will-chinas-disinformation -war-destabilize-taiwan-21708.
106 Cole, 'Will China's Disinformation War Destabilize Taiwan?'.
107 Lin and Wu, 'Taiwan's Online "Opinion War" Arrived'.
108 Samantha Bradshaw and Philip N. Howard, 'The Global Disinformation Order: 2019 Global Inventory of Organised Social Media Manipulaiton', University of Oxford Computational Propaganda Research Project, 10. https://comprop.oii.ox.ac .uk/wp-content/uploads/sites/93/2019/09/CyberTroop-Report19.pdf.
109 Chen Yun, 'KMT Legislator Calls for Probe into COA's "cyberarmy"', *Taipei Times*, 17 March 2019. http://www.taipeitimes.com/News/taiwan/archives/2019/03/17/2 003711666.
110 Yun, 'KMT Legislator Calls for Probe into COA's "cyberarmy"'.
111 Ketty Chen as cited in Daniel Flitton, 'The Role of US Christian Conservatives in Taiwan's LGBT Referendum Defeats', *The News Lens*, 14 December 2018. https:// international.thenewslens.com/article/110165. See Also Michael J. Cole, 'As Taipei Celebrates Diversity, Anti-LGBT Group Warns of "Nefarious" Western Influence', *Taiwan Sentinel*, 28 October 2018. https://sentinel.tw/as-taipei-celebrates-diversity -anti-lgbt-group-warns-of-nefarious-western-influence/.
112 'Taiwan Braces for Chinese Cyber Attacks Ahead of Elections', *The Straits Times*, 20 September 2018. https://www.straitstimes.com/asia/east-asia/china-ramps-up -cyberattacks-on-taiwan-ahead-of-elections. See Also 'Taiwan Braced for Wave of Cyberattacks form Mainland China Ahead of Local Elections', *South China Morning Post*, 20 September 2018. https://www.scmp.com/news/china/politics/article/2164950 /taiwan-braced-wave-cyberattacks-mainland-china-ahead-local.
113 'Taiwan Braces for Chinese Cyber Attacks Ahead of Elections', *The Straits Times*.
114 'Taiwan Braces for Chinese Cyber Attacks Ahead of Elections', *The Straits Times*. See Also 'Taiwan Braced for Wave of Cyberattacks form Mainland China Ahead of Local Elections', *South China Morning Post*.
115 FireEye, 'Cyber Threat Activity Targeting Elections', 6. https://www.fireeye.com/c ontent/dam/fireeye-www/products/pdfs/pf/gov/eb-cyber-threat-activity.pdf.
116 'Chinese Cyberattacks on Taiwan Government Becoming Harder to Detect – Source', *Channel News Asia*, 15 June 2018. https://www.channelnewsasia.com/news/world/ chinese-cyberattacks-on-taiwan-government-becoming-harder-to-detect---source- 10436212.
117 'Chinese Cyberattacks on Taiwan Government Becoming Harder to Detect – Source', *Channel News Asia*.
118 'Chinese Cyberattacks on Taiwan Government Becoming Harder to Detect – Source', *Channel News Asia*.

119 Thomas Mahnken, 'Thinking about Competitive Strategies', in *Competitive Strategies for the 21st Century*, ed. Thomas Mahnken (Stanford: Stanford University Press, 2012).

120 Mark Gunznger, Bryan Clark, David Johnson and Jesse Sloman, *Force Planning for the Era of Great Power Competition* (Washington, DC: Center for Strategic and Budgetary Assessments, 2017).

121 US Joint Staff, *Joint Force Development, Cross-Domain Synergy in Joint Operations: A Planner's Guide* (Washington, DC: US Department of Defense, 2016). Available at: http://www.dtic.mil/doctrine/concepts/joint_concepts/cross_domain_planning_guide.pdf.

122 US Department of Defense, 'The DoD Cyber Strategy', 2015, 13–15. Available at: http://www.defense.gov/Portals/1/features/2015/0415_cyberstrategy/Final_2015_DoD_CYBER_STRATEGY_for_web.pdf.

123 Mallory King, 'New Challenges in Cross-Domain Deterrence', *RAND Perspective*, no 259. Available at: https://www.rand.org/content/dam/rand/pubs/perspectives/PE200/PE259/RAND_PE259.pdf.

124 Lawrence Livermore National Laboratory, 'Cross-Domain Deterrence Seminar', 18–19 November 2014. Available at: https://cgsr.llnl.gov/content/assets/docs/SummaryNotes.pdf.

125 In July 2015, for example, as the Permanent Court of Arbitration in the Hague conducted a hearing on the South China Sea Arbitration brought by the Philippines against China, the Court's website went offline. The site was also infected with malware, leaving visitors interested in the case at risk of data theft. Based on the analysis of the software and infrastructure used, the attack's origin was attributed to China. The incident follows a pattern of spiking cyber activities relative to the rising tensions in the South China Sea. This is evident, for example, in the cyberattacks on Vietnamese targets as China moved an exploration oil rig into contested waters in mid-2014. On 29 July 2016, a major cyber-attack targeted Vietnam's two largest airports and Vietnam Airlines – the flight screens at the airports showed messages critical of Vietnam's claims to the South China Sea, and the airport's sound system broadcasted anti-Vietnamese and Philippines slogans. A Chinese patriotic hacktivist group 1937cn claimed responsibility for the attack.

13

Hybrid warfare in the Baltics

Dorthe Bach Nyemann

Introduction

Scholars interested in hybrid threats and hybrid warfare currently debate which strategies best apply in countering these challenges – at the national as well as international level. One key question is whether it is possible to deter actors from pursuing hybrid warfare operations.[1] There are numerous difficulties with hindering deniable or covert actions which are often taking place below the threshold of an armed attack, whereas there are potentially high strategic gains for the adversary who only faces low expenses and low risks – politically as well as militarily – compared to conventional confrontations.[2]

Taking a closer look at Russian goals and actions in the Baltic States after 2014, the aim of this case study is to show that actions amounting to hybrid threats do occur in the Baltic States. However, the case study has not been able to find evidence of coordinated and synchronized attacks across a broad spectrum of societal functions that would amount to hybrid operations or hybrid warfare. Furthermore, the case study aims to render probable that this – the lack of evidence of hybrid operations in the Baltic States – can at least be partly explained by initiatives taken by the Baltic States themselves in conjunction with initiatives from NATO and the EU to successfully deter Russia from taking further steps. The argument goes that so far, these responses have deterred Russia from pursuing more significant influence in the region. Instead, the case study detects a broad Russian institutional framework for possible future operations in the Baltic States. The institutional framework is 'ready to use' if better conditions for Russian activities should appear down the line.

The chapter is divided into five sections. The first section consists of a short presentation of the conceptualization of hybrid warfare utilized in this chapter, and how we may positively identify a hybrid operation. In the second section, the strategic value of the Baltic States to Russia is discussed in order to evaluate whether it is reasonable to expect hybrid operations or other types of Russian actions in the area. In the third section the chapter goes through an overall assessment of the levers of power which Russia has used in order to influence and ultimately change political priorities in the Baltic States. Can this be identified as a hybrid operation or is it something else? The fourth section presents a case of successful hybrid deterrence in the Baltics, by going through a range of arguments as to why the case study does not find an ongoing hybrid operation in the region. This is done by presenting illustrative examples of actions taken by the Baltic States from 2007. In addition, the study presents measures by NATO and the EU and the negative consequences that these have had for Russia. Finally, the chapter discusses the extent to which these initiatives can explain the lack of hybrid warfare in the Baltic States.

Before proceeding, it is necessary to address some methodical issues. First, hybrid warfare and hybrid threats are characterized as ambiguous, covert, low-level actions, making it difficult to attribute them to an actor and consequently making it hard to realize connections between different incidents and a broader picture of a coordinated synchronized attack.[3] Moreover, hybrid warfare can scale up and down in intensity, preventing clear distinctions between legitimate influence and illegal interference.[4] Without access to classified material in the three countries, relying on official documents and published reports, it is impossible to draw absolute conclusions as to whether hybrid warfare is taking place in the Baltic States.

A second problem arises when trying to make the case of successful deterrence. It is not possible to prove why we do *not* see an operation. There could be many reasons for this, not at all connected to the initiatives or responses taken by the individual states or internationally. These factors must be taken into account when we discuss why Russia is not pursuing a higher level of interference in the Baltic States.

Given the many elements that can and do play a part in an analysis of hybrid warfare, this case study will only be able to provide illustrative examples of Russian activities in and countermeasures by the three countries. Referring to other works that provide greater depth on separate issues, the aim is to give an overall picture of the Russian engagement in the Baltic States. Choosing this approach, however, does open up for a relevant critique of missing pieces to the puzzle or lack of documentation.

Identifying hybrid warfare in the Baltic States

Hybrid warfare and hybrid threats are contested concepts and currently an arena for much scholarly debate.[5] In order to make these concepts useful tools for an analysis of the current situation in the Baltic States – which is the purpose of this chapter in particular – a short presentation of variables and distinctions is necessary.

This case study makes a distinction between *hybrid threats* and *hybrid actions* on the one hand and *hybrid warfare* and *hybrid operations* on the other hand. Hybrid threats are deniable or covert actions by an aggressor in a target state involving instruments of power such as cyberattacks (not amounting to an armed attack), information operations, economic pressure or other unfriendly activities often performed by third-party malign non-state actors.[6] These tactics are tailored to specific vulnerabilities in the societal functions of the target state. The purpose is to affect the perceptions of citizens in the targeted state and to create effects in the whole society, including the private sector and civil society, without triggering decisive responses, including armed responses.[7]

These tactics amount to hybrid warfare *if* the hybrid actions are *coordinated* and *synchronized,* thus enhancing their effect, *and if* they are combined with the threat or use of military means – conventional or irregular – signifying a hybrid operation.[8] Given the deniable, covert and ambiguous character of hybrid actions, the problem of realizing whether a state is facing a hybrid warfare scenario is complicated. Ideally, states must react to hybrid threats *before* the situation evolves to a case of hybrid warfare.[9]

The current strategic value of the Baltic States for Russia

Since 1991, Russia has sought to persuade the Baltic governments to make political choices favourable to Russia, directed not least at the large numbers of Russian minorities living in the area.[10] The Baltic States, in turn, have acted utterly different on a range of policy matters of importance to Russia. After many years of negotiation and adaption to Western standards and procedures, they all became members of both NATO and the EU in 2004, which constituted *the low point* in Russia's relations with these former members of the Soviet Union. In the aftermath, Russia's ability to use military and economic pressures as tools for influence in the Baltic States became significantly delimited.

After 2004, Russia has sought to employ a variety of other means and methods to 'stay' influential in the region. The first demonstration of these means and methods took place in Estonia in 2007. At that time, the Estonian government decided to relocate a monument of Soviet troops from central Tallinn to a nearby military cemetery. The monument depicted a Soviet soldier who died while fighting to take Tallinn back from Nazi occupation in the Second World War. In the years prior to 2007, the statue had become a focal point of tension between different groups in Estonia.[11] For the local Russian minority, it had come to represent the 'liberator' from fascism while for the Estonians, it represented the 'oppressor' and reflected the many years as a part of the USSR. As is well known, the relocation of the monument caused the infamous widespread and severe cyberattacks on Estonian society.[12]

However, other related actions were simultaneously taking place, coordinated towards the same political aim, that is, getting Estonia to abide by Russian interests, respecting the Russian interpretation of history and securing the preservation of Russian cultural heritage. Simultaneously with the cyberattacks, organized riots took place in Estonia and at the Estonian Embassy in Moscow, culminating with an attack on the Estonian ambassador to Russia at a press conference. The riots were accompanied by looting and destruction, and more than 200 people were arrested.[13] Russian one-eyed media reports on police violence towards Russian minority demonstrators and the absence of reports on the violent actions of demonstrators fuelled an array of angry statements from Russia, including a statement by a member of the Russian parliament that this event should be a cause for war.[14] Although no Russian sanctions were announced, many Estonian companies lost trade revenue. This might be due to a patriotic reaction by Russian business owners, however, a ban on heavy commercial truck traffic at a border bridge in Narva did involve a government decision.[15] In an analysis from 2008, Rain Ottis labels Russia's efforts in Estonia as information warfare.[16]

In hindsight, the actions in 2007 – coordinated and synchronized with escalatory effects across Estonia's societal functions, including deniable and ambiguous violent actions by non-state actors – appear to be a hybrid operation, albeit not a very successful one. Estonia neither changed its political practices, nor its decisions or priorities. On the contrary, the connections to the West and the commitment between NATO and Estonia grew even stronger after 2007 and came to include many more policy areas and interdependencies than before. Specifically, cyber-security and cyber defence have become part of the NATO agenda through continuous Estonian legwork. The Russian actions helped the Baltic States to re-establish NATO as a collective defence alliance and not just a toolbox for military expeditions outside of the Alliance as had become the case since the early 1990s.

What are Russia's strategic objectives in the Baltic States today? In Russia, there is still a widespread nostalgia for the imperial past, and for various reasons, many in Moscow consider the Baltic States as residing within Russia's 'natural' sphere of influence and refuse to acknowledge them as sovereign and independent.[17] A large number of ethnic Russians remain in Estonia (more than a quarter of the population) and Latvia (where 40 per cent speak Russian as their first language, and around 25 per cent are ethnic Russians). A smaller but still substantial number of ethnic Russians remain in Lithuania (4.5 per cent in 2018).[18] To Russia, this justifies pursuing Russian influence, interest and in some instances even intervention in these countries.

Russia's political, economic, military and even geopolitical interests in the Baltic States are, however, quite limited. The region does not even house a valuable transit route for energy transportation. As a consequence, Russia's foreign policy pays insignificant attention to the Baltic States. In the perception of the Baltic States, Russia is *the* main threat – but the interest is not reciprocated by Russia.[19] Russia might have an interest in splitting the NATO Alliance and EU cooperation, if possible, and weakening the Baltic States could be a stepping stone in such a strategy. If tested, however, this gamble would risk weakening Russia and even further consolidating NATO and EU cooperation as was the case with Estonia in 2007.[20]

Against this backdrop, how valuable is it for Russia to maintain its influence in the Baltic States, and can Russia realistically expect to expand its influence and power in these countries? Russia's policies have turned out to be less assertive here than in other regions, such as the south Caucasus or the Balkans. Russia seems to be driven by pragmatism towards the Baltic States.[21] An indirect approach to evaluating the importance of the Baltic States to Russia is to examine the domestic efforts of the Russian leadership to influence Russian citizens' perceptions of the Baltic States. In Russian TV coverage between 2014 and 2018, negative coverage of Europe is concentrated around countries like France (17 per cent), Germany (12 per cent), the UK (10 per cent) and the EU (9 per cent), whereas the Baltic States get less than 1 per cent of the attention.[22]

Thus, if TV coverage is interpreted as part of preparing the Russian public for potential conflict, as some analysts suggest,[23] the Baltic States are currently not a high-value target for Russia. This is a crucial point to keep in mind when seeking to evaluate the success of countermeasures against Russian hybrid threats in the Baltic States. In all likelihood, Russia could and would engage much more in hybrid actions, even amounting to hybrid warfare, if on the one hand such an operation stood a chance of being successful, and if the Baltic States constituted a vital national interest to Russia on the other.

Russian advancement in the use of levers of power

An assessment of Russia's capabilities as a hybrid warfare actor in the Baltic States requires a comprehensive review of Russia's use of its levers of power against the societal functions of these states, from the military and the informational to the social, the political and the economic sphere.[24] Putting the puzzle together piece by piece provides us with an overall picture of Russia's practices in the Baltic States, where a wide range of levers are available and perfected through extensive experience and training. Capabilities of influence in different spheres can be institutionalized through the establishment of organizations, ongoing practices, shared understanding within specific groups and flows of resources to maintain all of the above. Identifying an institutional framework of influence within the different spheres will provide an understanding of Russia's current position and also of the level of preparedness for future actions in the area.

Military

The rise of hybrid warfare can be traced to the success of traditional military deterrence from the West. Since becoming members of the NATO Alliance, the Baltic States enjoy the comfort of the security umbrella in article 5 of the NATO treaty, including the credibility of the whole Alliance.[25] Even though the Baltic States are part of NATO, their geography still makes them vulnerable targets, and Russia's development of conventional military capability has made the Baltic States question if security guarantees under article 5 are a sufficient deterrent against Russian aggression. Since 2008, Russia has launched massive military reforms and improved the quality of its forces as well as its confidence regarding military performance. Russia is displaying its military on the borders of neighbouring countries, in airspace and in the maritime zones. In 2014, the overall number of intercepts made by the NATO Baltic Air Policing mission was more than 130.[26]

Russia regularly organizes exercises close to the Baltic borders, intimidating its neighbours and instilling fears that these exercises hide preparations for real attacks. Russia is overwhelmingly stronger than the forces in the Baltic area and has regional conventional superiority.[27] Among the greatest concerns is the introduction of advanced weapon systems – Iskander-M ballistic missiles and the S-400 long-range air defence system – which would severely delay NATO reinforcements to the region.[28] However, the most prominent risk is that military superiority combined with actions in other spheres using non-military means could substantially weaken the Baltic States' internal legitimacy and coherence. In an internal crisis, Russia could use its military strength and presence to put pressure on the Baltic States, staying below the threshold of article 5 of the NATO treaty, but still applying irregular military force in a manner similar to the scenario in Ukraine. This could include applying previously placed equipment, using perfidy at sea and on land, engaging in cyberattacks and information operations with assistance from local malign non-state actors combined with other covert actions to achieve a 'frozen conflict' situation prior to NATO deployment. In order to be successful, such an operation will rely on Russia activating strong levers of power in the non-military spheres in the Baltic States.

Information

Russia has established an international institutional framework of disinformation through social media, including interception tools to engage in personalized harassments and direct messaging on civilian mobile devices on a massive scale.[29] Russia has practised these abilities in Ukraine and Syria and through election meddling all over Europe and in the United States.[30] Russia has even targeted NATO personnel in the 'Enhanced Forward Presence' mission in the Baltic States.[31] The targeting of foreign military personnel has been widely practised by Russia in Eastern Ukraine, with tactical level messages trying to demoralize the soldiers and stressing the trust between various levels of command or by targeting families and relatives remote from the battlefield by means of disturbing messages.[32]

Despite evidence of effective use of social media targeting both individuals and large groups internationally, there is little evidence that suggests that Russia pursues influence through systematic election meddling or systematic individual or group targeting using social media in the Baltic States. One of Latvia's security agencies, 'The Constitution Protection Bureau', concluded in its annual report from 2018 that close media monitoring and an intensified analysis of Russian propaganda initiatives showed *no* attempts to influence the outcome of the 2018 election in Latvia. There were indications of high levels of information gathering on the election by Russia, but this was mostly done using open-source material.[33] The Digital Forensic Research Lab has investigated online campaigns for a boycott of the 2019 EU Parliament Election, also in Latvia. What they found was just a small group of accounts belonging to local Latvians trying to target Latvian Facebook users. Even when these groups themselves translated their messages into Russian, there is no evidence of amplified likes or shares from outside the small community or any other Russian meddling.

Over an extended period, Russia has used mass media to influence the Baltic public,[34] overtly through Russia Today, Sputnik and other media with a direct connection to the Russian regime and covertly with money and instructions to private media on what stories to bring, even artificially boosting audience numbers in specific headlines. One example is the media Baltnews, officially an independent media website present in all three countries, but financed by media companies in the Netherlands and Serbia linked to Russia. The flow of finances and the daily instructions by skype sessions on headlines and themes have been uncovered, but these media and a range of others continue their state-sponsored propaganda.[35]

The tailored messages for the public in the Baltic States have three overall themes:[36]

1) Anti-Americanism, the decay and instability of all Western institutions (specifically EU and NATO), values and societies.

2) Human rights problems, for all residents not belonging to the Baltic majority – Russian speakers, ethnic Russians, Poles and other minorities.
3) Anti-fascism, claiming that the fascist history of the Baltic States with their support of the Nazi regime is still part of the modern states' practices.

These themes are similar to what Russia presents with relevant local angles to the public in Ukraine and to their home audience through Russian media.[37]

Naturally, the question this brings up is which effect, if any, it has had on the Baltic public? Taking Estonia as an example, 71 per cent of non-Estonians do rate Russian TV channels as a very important or quite important source of information. However, most viewers are also exposed to other media and therefore learn about opposite media perspectives. Surveys show that only 29 per cent of the non-Estonians believe that NATO constitutes the main security guarantee for Estonia compared to 70 per cent of ethnic Estonians, and 46 per cent of non-Estonians see good relations with Russia as critical for security, while only 15 per cent of ethnic Estonians agree.[38] However, it is doubtful that this proves any aspiration for more Russian influence or even critical or less patriotic views on Estonia. One must be cautious in evaluating differences of opinion as a measurement of a lack of support for the state or the government's legitimacy. Asked if willing to participate in defence activities according to skill and ability, 64 per cent of ethnic Estonians answered yes, while this was true for 46 per cent of the Russian-speaking respondents. Moreover, 73 per cent of non-Estonian respondents compared to 83 per cent of ethnic Estonian respondents believed armed resistance was necessary in case of a foreign military attack on Estonia.[39]

Another well-researched case for societal destabilization through information is Latvia. The Defence Academy of Latvia has published a study on the possibility of societal destabilization in Latvia from 2016 which shows that one-fifth of the public mostly relies on Russian media for information and that the level of trust in the government and parliament overall is low. In 2015, only 17 per cent of the entire population tended to trust the national parliament.[40] The negative Russian narratives explained earlier have gained a high level of acceptance in views held by groups with low incomes, low to medium level education and in areas with high numbers of Russian-speaking residents. For example, 55 per cent of the Russian-speaking residents believe that restoration of fascism is taking place in Latvia.[41] As disturbing as this may be, the study also highlights that the Russian-speaking residents consume both Latvian and Russian media news, and that the trust in Russian media is almost four times lower than in Latvian media. Even though some of the negative narratives have been adapted by the large groups of Russian-speaking Latvians, 91 per cent of the public in Latvia identifies itself as Latvian, 54 per cent as European and only 12.7 per cent as Russian.[42] Even accepting rivalling identifications, the vast majority of Latvians clearly lean towards Western identification.

Overall, Russia does seem to have some success in using media to enhance the Russian narrative and to underpin the divide, social as well as ethnic, in the Baltic States. The means seem mostly to be 'old fashioned' public diplomacy, influencing the public by their free choice of information and media.

Social

The institutional framework of influence is underpinned by more than just providing and shaping information. Russia has taken a range of other initiatives to try to influence perceptions of Russia and mobilize groups in the Baltic States. Most Russian speakers in the Baltic States can be categorized as 'imperial' communities of minorities that never left their homes, but found themselves without citizenship after the independence of the Baltic States. They suddenly became subject to a naturalization process, including language tests. These policies reinforced perceptions of injustice and non-inclusion among the ethnic Russian communities in the Baltic States, already in the early 1990s. These feelings were fuelled by problems of inequality in the labour market and reinforced by (voluntary) community segregation. Even though much has been done to ensure a more inclusive integration in later years – the Baltic States made themselves vulnerable to Russian influence policies in the social sphere by their own doing in the early stages of independence.[43]

One example of Russian influence in the social sphere is the institutionalization of its compatriot policy, which among other things includes substantial and often covert funding of local NGOs with close connections to Kremlin.[44] To Russia, compatriots include former Russian citizens living abroad, former citizens of the USSR, descendants of compatriots and foreign citizens who admire Russian culture and language.[45] The compatriot policy is executed through centres around the world which promote Russian culture, language and interest coordinated by, for example, the Rossotrudnichestvo agency under the Ministry of Foreign Affairs.

The 'Russki Mir' initiative from 2007 is represented in all three countries.[46] The Russian compatriot policy is more than a promotion of culture and language. It includes 'fighting the falsification of history' and protecting the rights of compatriots.[47] In this way, it also becomes a valuable tool in promoting negative narratives on the Baltic States and a tool to maintain close contact with Russian minorities. Though the compatriot policy, Russia already has – internationally and locally – the institutional framework to support and inflame protest movements with finances, narratives and organization. The compatriot policy is widely subsidized in the Baltic States by funds from Kremlin to different subgroups of NGOs that are supporting Russian interests.[48] It is one thing to inform and another thing to mobilize social groups. A survey conducted in Latgale, an eastern region of Latvia, described by Russia as the most discriminated against area in Latvia, found no separatist tendencies by the responders. In fact, 78 per cent of those speaking the Latgalian dialect said that they would support Latvia if Russia started activities directed against the state. Moreover, the influence of Russia's public diplomacy appeared to be very low. Seventy-six per cent had not heard of the organization 'Rossotrudnichestvo', and only 6 per cent had positive attitudes towards the organization.[49] Besides, attitudes do not always lead to actions. People in Latvian society are generally neither socially or politically active, and participation in NGOs, political parties or even interest groups is meagre. Russia will find that it is tough to mobilize dissatisfied citizens in Latvia, where the most dissatisfied group tends to share the opinion that they cannot influence social or political structures regardless.[50]

Political

Direct political influence on parties and politics has been dealt with somewhat differently in the three Baltic States. Even though the NGOs supporting Russian views and interests in the Baltic States may not be very visible or widely supported by the public, it does not mean that Russia is without influence at the political level. An article dating back to 2015 on how Russia funds NGOs in the Baltics, edited by Sanita Jemberga with input from a large research group from different media in all three countries, tries to give an overview of the connection between Russian funding and its influence in political organizations.[51] According to the article, Russia supports more than forty organizations in the Baltic States, which are receiving millions of Euros each year. Around 68 per cent of the recipients are somehow connected to pro-Kremlin political parties. Taking a closer look at the organizations, it is obvious that Russia supports these groups and individuals, involving systematic support of the narratives also promoted by Russian media. In Estonia, the three organizations 'Legal Information Centre for Human Rights', 'Estonia without Nazism' and 'the Integration Media Group' all underpin the Russian narrative. Two of the organizations are headed by Andrei Zarenkov. Zarenkov has attempted to be elected to the national parliament and also to local councils, without any luck.[52] In Estonia, influencing the political level directly though political parties has proven hard. No ethnic Russian parties have been represented in the Riigikogu since 2012. The majority of non-Estonians vote for the Centre Party, which is not an ethnicity-based party.[53] Also, in Estonia, there are no organized groups of any kind who advocate separatism for the Russian-speaking population.[54] In Lithuania, the picture is similar. The funded NGOs are 'Centre for Human Rights' and 'Centre for Defence and Research of the Fundamental Rights', both connected to the movement 'Lithuania without Nazism'. Their statements tend to match views from the Russian foreign ministry, and they also try to promote influence in Lithuanian parties.[55]

Focusing on Latvia, the Constitution Protection Bureau finds that all types of parties and media are exposed to Russian propaganda, but that the parties 'Latvia Union of Russians' and the 'Harmony Party' are mostly exposed. The efforts by Russia to influence the political debate in Latvia include tailored statistics, public opinion polls, pseudo-expert viewpoints and more.[56] As in the other Baltic countries, anti-fascist events are used to bring veterans and right-wing supporters together in marches as well as in roundtable discussions. The core participants are supported by NGOs financed by Russia and closely connected to the party 'Russian Union'. The group appears insignificant with respect to political influence with few members, and it is well known to Latvian security services.[57]

In conclusion, even if there is presently no sign of systematic election meddling by Russia in the Baltic States, this case study demonstrates that there are indications of a well-established institutional framework for long-term political influence.

Economics

Since 1991, the Baltic States' dependence on Russian trade and energy has diminished substantially. In 2015, Estonia had less than 10 per cent of its foreign trade with Russia, and only 10 per cent of its energy resources came from there.[58] The lack of economic dependencies has diminished the Russian lever of power in the economic sphere and also the possibilities of using energy as a tool for economic and political pressure. This helps explain the limited focus on Russia's use of its economic influence and covert economic activities in the Baltic States by the countries' national intelligence agencies. In the national threat assessment from Lithuania 2018, an increase in foreign companies seeking to operate in the financial sector has, however, been noticed. The possibility of third-country companies operating in strategic sectors under cover of an EU registered company has also caught the attention of the Lithuanian authorities in the 'National Threat Assessment 2019'.[59] The Estonian Foreign Intelligence Service raises the same sort of concerns, but mentions no details.[60] These aspects of hybrid threats do not get any attention in the Latvian assessment from 2019.[61] More attention should be paid to covert economic activities and to organized economic crime in the Baltic States in future research. This will help us understand how this lever of power can underpin the social, political and informational levers of power as hybrid threats or even in coordinated efforts amounting to hybrid warfare. We should expect a lot more activity within covert economic activities than this case study has been able to present.

Adding cyber to Russian levers of power

The institutionalized framework for influence in the social sphere applying information operations is assumed to be supplemented by substantial espionage activities, including hacking into the critical infrastructure of the Baltic States, thus providing Russia with knowledge on how these states function and how their vulnerabilities are best addressed. Moreover, there is evidence showing specific Russian interest in cyber activities related to the membership of NATO and the EU in all three states' threat assessments. The state organized cyber espionage is supplemented by cybercrime activities and the involvement of patriotic hackers – third-party actors supporting Russian interest as well as their own financial gains.[62] In 2018, repeated Russian attempts to spy through cyber means in the Lithuanian energy sector were observed. The penetration is ongoing in state institutions, in private companies and with private citizens.[63] The capabilities that Russia now possesses in the cyber domain can be activated in a hybrid warfare situation, making Russia able to deeply affect the Baltic societies, provided the conditions are more fruitful than today. The partly unknown level of cyber capabilities that Russia possesses implies a worrisome continuum from peaceful influence policies to hybrid threats, encompassing grey zone interference strategies with the possibility of engaging in hybrid warfare.

Russian use of levers of power in the Baltic States

Russian foreign policy is often more tactical than strategic, relying on opportunities that come up.[64] This makes it less predictable and lowers the possibility of coordinated synchronized actions on the one hand, while enhancing sudden creative escalations on the other hand. The analysis of Russian levers of power in the Baltic States shows a range of different actions taken by Russia, characterized as hybrid threats. Russia seeks to uphold its influence in the region by a variety of non-military means and by maintaining military balance towards the NATO Alliance. Russia is maintaining an institutional framework of influence in the social, informational and political spheres and may be more involved in economic activities than apparent at first sight. There is also a high presence in the cyber domain of critical infrastructure as well as espionage on the vital state institutions. At the same time, Russia's actions appear to be at a low level. The use of social media is unsystematic and sporadic. The social, organizational and political mobilization of Russian speakers has been characterized by sporadic activities involving few groups and individuals, and obvious opportunities for election meddling have not been used. Russia may judge its possibilities for success in the Baltic States as too low to put in the effort, not least because of the initiatives taken by the states themselves in conjunction with NATO and the EU. In conclusion, the Russian institutional framework for influence is well established, but presently not heavily maintained or coordinated.

Can actions taken by states and international partners explain Russia's lack of success in the Baltic States?

A more aware public with a wide range of information

It is often seen as *the* critical vulnerability of the Baltic States that they have a large minority of ethnic Russians and Russian-speaking citizens. In 2019, the Digital Forensic Research Lab measured the influence of adverse reporting on NATO deployment in the Baltic States, following the coverage by Sputnik in both the local languages and in Russian on three topics related to NATO deployment. The Lab found more negative framing of the NATO deployment by Sputnik than what was released by local public media in all three countries. The good news they discovered was that in 2019, Sputnik and other Russian state-sponsored media have low levels of views in all three countries compared to other media. If compared to the use of the private web portal Delfi, the largest web portal in the Baltic States which has news in both local languages and Russian, Delfi has substantially more views and a significant reach.[65] Delfi has no clear sympathies or political interests and has gained popularity in recent years. In 2015, Estonia established channel EVT + a Russian language channel to provide the public with information, not produced in Russia.[66] The education in digital vulnerabilities has also taken many shapes and forms in the three countries, making the public conscious of cybercrime, hacking and misinformation. One example is the Estonian site Propastop.org, a volunteer site that investigates Russian misinformation and broadcasts its findings to the public in four different languages, including Russian. One successful example of news checking in Latvia is the 'Lie Detector' section of the Latvian news portal lsm.lv, which checks whether Latvian politicians and officials are telling the truth. Another is the Latvian media expert Mārtiņš Kaprāns who regularly reveals Russian disinformation about Latvia, the Baltic States and NATO on the website of the Centre for European Policy Analysis (CEPA, www.cepa.org).

Local initiatives to exclude Russia from taking advantage of vulnerabilities and supporting the institutional framework of influence

Since resilience measures can take numerous shapes and forms and initiatives have been ongoing in the Baltic States, this section will only scratch the surface in order to illustrate the variety of local initiatives that are taking place in the different spheres.

Using an example from industrial policy, in March 2018 the Law of the Protection of Objects of Importance to Ensuring National Security came into force in Lithuania. The law provides a national authority with a mandate to decide if an investor does not conform to the national security interest of Lithuania. The regulation was made in order to prevent Russian entities from entering under the cover of an EU-based company and thus operating with fewer restrictions under EU law. This came about after the discovery of the concealed collection of data through the AFK Sistema controlled Kronshtadt Group by Russia. The company had won a bid to establish digital cartographic data centres in Lithuania and collected data useable for battlefield simulators, UAVs and software to the Russian military.[67] This illustrates how industrial screening, EU regulation and local law and economics as well as military concerns have to be aligned to enhance resilience and to prevent coordinated hybrid activities. The example also points to the difficulties of both identifying and launching coordinated initiatives against hybrid threats.

Already in 2015, Estonia got rid of legal loopholes and enabled swift reactions in case of a covert military operation conducted by non-state actors. Any armed personnel without insignia are now by law considered terrorists and can be engaged. The Estonian forces do not use any military equipment from Russia. This makes an 'insurgent's weapons arsenal' from Russia easy to pinpoint and react to. Moreover, whole-of-government exercises test scenarios, including mass riots, cyberattacks, disruption of critical infrastructure and the combination of civilian and military efforts.[68] Such initiatives underpin awareness in the broader public. The Baltic States have also focused on less measurable initiatives seeking to become less vulnerable and more robust by continually improving welfare and security for all societal groups.

Mobilization of the public

Regarding traditional military deterrence of Russia, the Baltic States could do much more than what is done today. Only 22,000 citizens are under arms in the three countries. This is a low number compared to countries like Finland or Israel, even adding the 30,000 reservists who are not equipped or trained according to the same standards.[69] The military priorities do not support the official perceptions of an aggressive neighbour to the East with malign intentions. Since 2014, the Baltic States have, however, all expanded their defence spending from around 1 per cent of GDP to over 2 per cent in 2019. This can be explained by Russian actions, but the pressure from the US Trump administration is a more likely reason for this rapid change.

When it comes to mobilizing the public to protect the state from foreign interference, the picture is somewhat different. There is a growing home guard of volunteers in the Baltic States. In Estonia, there is even a cyber defence league of volunteers, consisting of IT specialists, engineers and lawyers among other professionals with multidisciplinary skills, who engage in frequent tabletop exercises and large-scale cyber events to prepare for coming cyberattacks.[70] This commitment builds societal competence by gaining practical insights on strategic, operational and tactical skills and tools. Moreover, Estonia has held mobilization exercises with 20,000–30,000 persons and has prepared for partisan groups to step in after a possible invasion.[71]

NATO and EU initiatives to deter Russian activities in the Baltic States

At the NATO summit in Warsaw in September 2014, the Alliance decided on a vast number of initiatives aimed at increasing traditional military deterrence against Moscow. Most notable were the so-called Enhanced Forward Presence in the Baltic States and Poland, an upgraded NATO Response Force, Graduated Response Plans and a modernized command structure.[72] As stated by Martin Zapfe, 'The main function of NATO's EFP is to help deter a conventional Russian attack by providing a tripwire, the engagement of which would all but guarantee that the Alliance as a whole would respond in some way.'[73] In other words, these initiatives by NATO were tailored with conventional scenarios in mind. The modernization of the NATO command structure included the establishment of Multinational Division North East and of Multinational Division North, division-level headquarters with division-level formations comprised of two to four brigades with various support units. The Baltic States have never previously had this capacity due to their modest size. The improved organization enables activities with the Multi-National Corps Northeast based in Szczecin, Poland, and ensures closer cooperation and coordination with the rest of the Alliance. The NATO initiatives focus on traditional deterrence, but have additionally provided joint comprehensive situational awareness across the Baltic States and Poland that can detect actions across state borders and establish broader contact from NATO to the relevant state agencies and back. This goes on continually from peacetime through crisis and to conflict. The existing solutions in the Baltic States will, however, likely fail in case of a Russian invasion if not further strengthened with both local mobilization and with a Baltic corps headquarters with NATO-trained, Baltic commanders and staff, as concluded in a recent study.[74]

The fear of Russian aggression against the Baltic States has been very productive in improving cooperation between the EU and NATO. One example is the 'military mobility' initiative, which addresses the use of roads, bridges and other means of transportation for military deployment. The EU initiative includes the reduction of legal and bureaucratic constraints on military logistics across borders. Military mobility became a relevant topic for EU-NATO cooperation as a result of an analysis initiated by the Estonian Presidency in 2017. The analysis showed a range of insufficiencies in the Baltic States and the North Sea-Baltic Corridor regarding the transportation of military vehicles and equipment. The ensuing resolution is explicitly targeting hybrid threats to transportation and related critical infrastructure. It brings together military and civilian actors at all levels, including NATO and NATO partners, to establish common standards, transportation regulations, movement permissions and more.[75] Military mobility cooperation is just one example of a range of initiatives which have gained momentum, funding, legitimacy and speed of implementation due to the threat of hybrid warfare in the Baltic States. The agenda of hybrid threats has paved the way for the construction of a platform for EU security and defence policies that do not duplicate or compete with NATO, but supplement harder military engagements with softer approaches.

Other initiatives from the EU which aim at countering hybrid threats in general and the Russian threat more explicitly are 'The Hybrid Fusion Cell', an entity placed inside the European External Action Service (EEAS) from 2015, an action plan against disinformation from 2018[76] and further strengthened in 2019 ahead of the European Parliament elections, a Computer Emergency Response Team and a Social Media Assurance Service. A more offensive measure is the new sanctions regime on cyber from May 2019. Moreover, the Commission has launched a sanctions regime against the use of chemical weapons. Both regimes try to surpass the problem of deniability and attribution to states which is one of the fundamental challenges of hybrid threats. The new sanction regimes target individuals directly instead of pursuing state responsibility. Other initiatives address the protection of critical infrastructure and try to improve a whole-of-government approach to hybrid threats.[77] It would not be wrong to suggest that the hybrid threats debate has helped the EU to enhance cooperation on security issues and to take the debate on European defence and strategic autonomy to a whole new level than previously achievable.

Are the Baltic States a good case for the possibilities of deterring hybrid warfare?

This case study has pieced together three elements relevant to a possible Russian hybrid operation in the Baltic States, by looking at Russian priorities and aims, Russian capability to act as a hybrid actor and Russian opportunities for success if approaching a hybrid warfare strategy towards the Baltic States.

First of all, the case study asked whether Russia is willing to invest the risk and necessary resources in order to make decisive changes in the Baltic States by coordinated and synchronized activities across a broad spectrum of societal functions, including the threat of or use of force? The study finds that the Baltic States do not have a very high priority in Russian foreign policy. Although destabilizing the Baltic States could bring severe problems to both the EU and NATO, the risk of the opposite, that is, the consolidation of these organizations in times of crisis, is very high. There is no indication that Russia will use hybrid warfare in the Baltic States as a means to that end, however, continuous low-scale hybrid threats must be expected. The fact that the

Baltic States are not of high priority to Russia's core interest provides a vital explanation for the lack of hybrid warfare in those states.

By unpacking Russian influence and actions in the Baltic States, the case study shows that Russia does have substantial capabilities as a hybrid actor. The analyses of Russian levers of power uncover a well-established institutional framework for influence in all societal functions. There is a close connection and coordination between activities in the informational, social and political spheres, where organizations, media and dedicated individuals play a role by continuously reclaiming and framing negative narratives about the leadership in the Baltic States, underpinning a discourse of the systematic discrimination, segregation and unjust treatment of Russian speakers and other minorities.

The use of mass media, social media and NGOs' political messaging are all well attuned, closely monitored and financed by Russia, openly and covertly. Russian information operations are an advanced, professionalized and internationally institutionalized practice. Russia has had some success in claiming deniability and using third-party actors, even locals, as the primary practitioners, and as a result of this creating some ambiguity as to how to react to different activities in the informational, social and political spheres. Russia does also possess cyber capabilities that can be applied in conjunction with other instruments of influence, however, this has not been practised so far. It has not been possible to find much evidence of economic pressures or cyber-related activities by Russia in the Baltic States. This may be due to lack of research – not lack of actions. On occasion, Russia shows its military muscle in the Baltic States, but not in conjunction with other activities or as part of a coherent operation. Even though Russia does seem to have a range of capabilities to engage in hybrid warfare activities in the Baltic States, the activities found in this case study appear scattered, not systematically applied and not well coordinated. The institutional framework is present, but an active continuous 'shaping of the battlefield' is at worst low-key and unambitious.

The presence of hybrid threats, but lack of hybrid warfare in the Baltic States leads to considerations regarding Russian opportunities in the area. Russia faces numerous obstacles vis-à-vis the Baltic States, most importantly, traditional military deterrence by NATO. Russia realizes, as does NATO, that the entire credibility of NATO is at stake if NATO does not protect the Baltic States. Recent initiatives by NATO have signalled to Russia that NATO is held accountable by the Baltic States. Looking below the threshold of an armed attack where we expect to find a range of activities in a hybrid warfare scenario, the EU and the individual states have taken many different initiatives to counter Russian activities since 2007 and even more so after 2014. The societal resilience in the Baltic States, the mobilization of the public, the legal preparedness for crises and conflicts, initiatives to diversify the media landscape also for a Russian-speaking public – all of this has amplified a deterrence by denial strategy in the Baltic States. Despite Russia's success in convincing large groups in the Baltic societies of injustice and minority discrimination and even growing fascism, there are no signs of political or violent mobilization against the Baltic governments or state institutions. Moreover, the large groups of Russian-speaking minorities seem to identify significantly more with Western values and the EU than the Russian alternative. Russian opportunities for successfully undermining, destabilizing or delegitimizing the Baltic States, their EU commitment or the NATO memberships are meagre. If Russian actions lead to worse counteractions and towards unity within the West, the appeal of hybrid strategies is undermined.[78]

In conclusion, this case study shows that having the capability to engage in hybrid warfare activities is not sufficient. Hybrid warfare is a low-cost strategy with potentially high gains. However, the combination of traditional military deterrence and a broad deterrence by denial below the threshold of an armed attack in conjunction with international support has decreased the Russian appetite for further engagement in the Baltic States. Combined with the low priority of the Baltic States in Russian foreign policy, this explains the lack of hybrid warfare and the low intensity of hybrid threats. On the other hand, we must expect Russia to continue to improve and maintain a broad institutional framework for influence in the Baltic States across the societal functions. The development of countermeasures is, therefore, a process that has to continue.

Notes

1 Michael Rühle, 'Deterring Hybrid Threats: The Need for a More Rational Debate', *NDC Policy Brief*, No. 15 (July 2019); Heine Sørensen and Dorthe Bach Nyemann, *Going Beyond Resilience – A Revitalized Approach to Countering Hybrid Threats* (Hybrid CoE, 2018); Andrew Radin, *Hybrid Warfare in the Baltics – Threats and Potential Responses* (RAND Corporation, 2017); Sean Monaghan, Patrick Cullen and Njord Wegge, *MCDC Countering Hybrid Warfare Project: Countering Hybrid Warfare* (MCDC, March 2019).

2 Heine Sørensen and Dorthe Bach Nyemann, *Deterrence by Punishment as a Way of Countering Hybrid Threats: Why We Need to Go beyond Resilience in the Gray Zone* (MCDC, 2019).

3 Patrick Cullen and Erik Reichborn-Kjennerud, *MCDC Countering Hybrid Warfare Project: Understanding Hybrid Warfare* (MCDC, 2017).

4 Charles Parton, 'China – UK Relations – Where to Draw the Border Between Influence and Interference?', *RUSI Occasional Paper* (Royal United Services Institute, February 2019), 3.

5 Erik Reichborn-Kjennerud and Patrick Cullen, 'What Is Hybrid Warfare?', *NUPI Policy Brief*, No. 1 (NUPI 2016); Cullen and Reichborn, *Understanding Hybrid Warfare*; Radin, *Hybrid Warfare in the Baltics*; Rühle, 'Deterring Hybrid Threats'; Sørensen and Nyemann, *Deterrence by Punishment*.

6 Radin, *Hybrid Warfare in the Baltics*, 5.

7 Sean Monaghan, 'Countering Hybrid Warfare: So What for the Joint Force?', *PRISM, National Defense University Press* 8, no. 2 (October 2019): 4.

8 Sørensen and Nyemann, *Deterrence by Punishment*, 3.

9 Monaghan et al., *Countering Hybrid Warfare*, 17–18.

10 Alexander Sergunin, *The Baltic Sea Region after the Ukraine Crises and Trump – A Russian Perspective* (DIIS, 2019), 10; Henrik Praks, 'Hybrid or Not: Deterring and Defeating Russia´s Ways of Warfare in the Baltics – the Case of Estonia', *Research Paper*, No. 124 (Rome: NATO Defense College, December 2015), 3.

11　Rain Ottis, 'Analysis of the 2007 Cyber Attacks against Estonia from the Information Warfare Perspective', in *Proceedings of the 7th European Conference on Information Warfare and Security, Plymouth* (Reading: Academic Publishing Limited, 2008), 163–8.

12　Anna Tiido, *Russians in Europe: Nobody´s Tool – The Examples of Finland, Germany and Estonia* (Tallinn: International Centre for Defence and Security, September 2019), 11.

13　Tiido, *Russians in Europe,* 11.

14　Ottis, 'Analysis of the 2007 Cyber Attacks', 2.

15　Tiido, *Russians in Europe*, 11.

16　Ottis, 'Analysis of the 2007 Cyber Attacks'.

17　Elias Götz, 'Putin, the State, and War: The Causes of Russia's Near Abroad Assertion Revisited', *International Studies Review* 19, no. 2 (2017): 242–6.

18　Tiido, *Russians in Europe*, 2.

19　Toms Rostoks and Nora Vanaga, *Creating an Effective Deterrent against Russia in Europe: Military and Non-Military Aspects of Deterrence* (Riga: Friedrich Ebert Stiftung, November 2018), 4–5; Bergmane, Una, 'Fading Russian Influence in the Baltic States', *Orbis* 64, no. 3 (2020): 479–488.

20　Praks, 'Hybrid or Not', 2; Rostoks and Vanaga, *Creating an Effective Deterrent*, 6.

21　Sergunin, *The Baltic Sea Region after the Ukraine Crises*, 44.

22　Natalia Popvych, Oleksiy Makukhin, Liubov Tsybulska and Ruslan Kavatsiuk, *Image of European Countries on Russian TV* (Estonian Center of Eastern Partnership and Ukraine Crisis Media Center, May 2018), 22, 28.

23　Popvych et al., *Image of European Countries*, 35.

24　Monaghan et al., *Countering Hybrid Warfare,* 13–15.

25　Monaghan et al., *Countering Hybrid Warfare*, 40.

26　Praks, 'Hybrid or Not', 6.

27　Radin, *Hybrid Warfare in the Baltics*, 29.

28　Praks, 'Hybrid or Not', 6–7.

29　Kier Giles, 'Time to Shed More Light on Russian Harassment of NATO Forces' Families', *Chatham House*, 14 August 2019.

30　Lucan Ahmad Way and Adam Casey, 'Is Russia a Threat to Western Democracy? Russian Intervention in Foreign Elections, 1991-2017' (Draft Memo for Global Populisms as a Threat to Democracy, 3 November 2017).

31　Rostoks and Vanaga, *Creating an Effective Deterrent*, 10.

32　Aaron F. Brantly, Nerea Cal and Delvin P. Winkelstein, *Defending the Borderland – Ukrainian Military Experience with IO, Cyber and EW* (Army Cyber Institute at West Point, 2017), 36.

33　Constitution Protection Bureau of the Republic of Latvia, *Annual Report 2018* (2019), 26–30.

34　Tiido, *Russians in Europe*; Holger Roonemaa and Inge Springe, 'Fake News, Money from Russia – Moscow´s Mouthpieces', *RE:Baltica*, 29 August 2018.

35　Roonemaa and Springe, 'Fake News, Money from Russia'.

36　Roonemaa and Springe, 'Fake News, Money from Russia'.

37　Popvych et al., *Image of European Countries*.

38　Tiido, *Russians in Europe*, 12.

39　Juhan Kiviränk, *Public Opinion and National Defence: Report to the Ministry of Defence* (Tallinn: Turu-uuringute AS, March 2019), 6.

40　Leva Berzina, *The Possibility of Societal Destabilization in Latvia: Potential National Security Threats* (National Defence Academy of Latvia – Center for Security and Strategic Research, 2016), 5, 17.

41 Berzina, *The Possibility of Societal Destabilization*, 9.
42 Berzina, *The Possibility of Societal Destabilization*, 26.
43 Tiido, *Russians in Europe*, 11.
44 Gudrun Persson, 'Russian Influence and Soft Power in the Baltic States: The View from Moscow', in *Tools of Destabilization: Russian Soft Power and Non-Military Influence in the Baltic States*, ed. Mike Winnerstig (Stockholm: Swedish Defence Research Agency, 2014).
45 Heather A. Conley and Theodore P. Gerber, *Russian Soft Power in the 21st Century – An Examination of Russian Compatriot Policy in Estonia* (CSIS, 2011), 12.
46 Persson, 'Russian Influence', 23–4.
47 Conley and Gerber, *Russian Soft Power*, 13–14.
48 Persson, 'Russian Influence'.
49 Berzina, *The Possibility of Societal Destabilization*, 12–13.
50 Berzina, *The Possibility of Societal Destabilization*, 14.
51 Santia Jemberga, 'Kremlin's Millions: How Russia Funds NGOs in Baltics', *RE:Baltica*, 4 September 2015.
52 Jemberga, 'Kremlin's Millions', 5.
53 Tiido, *Russians in Europe*, 13.
54 Praks, 'Hybrid or Not', 4.
55 Jemberga, 'Kremlin's Millions', 7.
56 Constitution Protection Bureau of the Republic of Latvia, *Annual Report 2018*, 31–4.
57 Jemberga, 'Kremlin's Millions', 10.
58 Praks, 'Hybrid or Not', 3.
59 State Security Department of the Republic of Latvia, *National Threat Assessment 2019* (2019), 51–2.
60 Estonian Foreign Intelligence Service, *International Security and Estonia* (2019), 3.
61 Constitution Protection Bureau of the Republic of Latvia, *Annual Report 2018*.
62 Estonian Foreign Intelligence Service, *International Security and Estonia*, 48–53; Constitution Protection Bureau of the Republic of Latvia, *Annual Report 2018*, 37–9.
63 State Security Department of the Republic of Lithuania, *National Threat Assessment 2019*, 34–6.
64 Andrei Soldatov and Irina Borogan, 'Russia's Approach to Cyber: The Best Defence Is a Good Offence', in *Hacks, Leaks and Disruptions: Russian Cyber Strategies*, eds Nicu Popescu and Stanislav Secrieru (Chaillot Papers no. 148, October 2018), 20.
65 Nika Aleksejeva, '#BalticBrief: Sputnik Takes Aim at a Russian-Speaking Audience', *Digital Forensic Research Lab*, 5 April 2019, 8.
66 Praks, 'Hybrid or Not', 8.
67 State Security Department of the Republic of Lithuania, *National Threat Assessment 2019*, 49–53.
68 Praks, 'Hybrid or Not', 9.
69 Richard D. Hooker, *How to Defend the Baltic States* (Washington, DC: Jamestown Foundation, October 2019), 14.
70 Andrus Padar, 'Talk on Civil Military Cooperation in Cyber Defence' (Hybrid Threats against Critical Infrastructure, The citadel in Copenhagen: Danish Home Guard, 2019).
71 Padar, 'Civil Military Cooperation'.
72 Jens Ringsmose and Sten Rynning, 'Now for the Hard Part: NATO's Strategic Adaption to Russia', *Survival* 59, no. 3 (July 2017): 129–46.

73 Martin Zapfe, 'Deterrence from the Ground Up: Understanding NATO's Enhanced
    Forward Presence', *Survival* 59, no. 3 (July 2017): 150.
74 Hooker, *How to Defend the Baltic States*, 17.
75 European Parliament, *European Parliament Resolution of 11 December 2018 on
    Military Mobility*, P8_TA(2018)0498 § (2018), para. Z,1,10.
76 European Parliament, *European Parliament Resolution of 23 November 2016 on EU
    Strategic Communication to Counteract Anti-EU Propaganda by Third Parties* (2016).
77 Council of the European Union, 'Cyber-Attacks: Council Is Now Able to Impose
    Sanctions', *Press Release*, 17 May 2019; European Commission, 'A Europe That
    Protects: Good Progress on Tackling Hybrid Threats', *Press Release*, 29 May 2019.
78 Sergunin, *The Baltic Sea Region after the Ukraine Crises*, 44.

14

De-hybridization and conflict narration

Ukraine's defence against Russian hybrid warfare

Niklas Nilsson

Introduction

Although Russia's actions in Ukraine have rightfully raised questions regarding the vulnerabilities to hybrid warfare in Western societies and their defensive capabilities, very little has been written on Ukraine's responses and the particular forms they have taken. Indeed, if Russia's aggression is the defining example of contemporary hybrid warfare, then Ukraine's response amounts to an inherently interesting case of hybrid warfare defence. This chapter focuses on two key components of Ukraine's defensive actions.

These include, first, Ukraine's military response to the war in Donbas. The fighting has gone through several phases, with escalating and increasingly overt Russian military involvement before stagnating into a positional war fought from trenches through artillery and snipers. The chapter argues that Ukraine's military response served to de-hybridize military violence in the conflict, by denying Russia the ability to conceal its aggression as a local insurgency and providing the fighting with features reminiscent of a classic interstate war for territory. This is the result of an extensive build-up of Ukraine's military based on the principle of mass. Ukraine's new army is clearly designed to fight over extended periods across vast ranges of territory, at high intensity against a peer adversary, and is deployed along the full stretch of the Donetsk and Luhansk frontlines. Second, Ukraine has made a comprehensive effort to take control of the conflict narrative, addressing the fundamental vulnerability implied in Russia's depiction of the conflict as a civil war, an internal Ukrainian affair. In this regard, Ukraine has exposed Russia's direct involvement in the fighting in Donbas. It has sought to boost confidence in its armed forces, both domestically and internationally, and it has embarked on a soft-power campaign to improve living standards locally in Ukraine-controlled territory adjacent to the frontlines.

Russia's operations in 2014 to sever Crimea and parts of Donbas from Ukraine indeed served as a wake-up call for Western policymakers, prompting rethinking of military doctrine to a renewed focus on territorial defence.[1] The Russian modus in Ukraine also increased awareness across Europe of the need for wider societal preparedness to counter a wide range of non-kinetic threats. Indeed, aside from its overt conventional military involvement in Ukraine, Russia employed a range of covert and unconventional methods to prepare the ground for land grabs, assure deniability of its operations, delay the reaction of Ukrainian authorities and influence perceptions of the conflict, in Ukraine as well as internationally. Russia's strategy in Ukraine has thus comprised an integrated campaign, featuring a sophisticated combination of military and non-military tools, corresponding to the notion of hybrid warfare introduced in this volume.[2]

The various methods that Russia has employed against Ukraine have gained considerable political and scholarly attention across Western Europe and the United States, and hybrid warfare is only one among several concepts utilized to describe them. Indeed, the conflict in Ukraine has given rise to a new genre in the security literature, revisiting Soviet military studies and utilizing a range of different but overlapping concepts in attempts to describe Russia's 'new' way of war as, for example, non-linear warfare, full-spectrum conflict, hybrid warfare, new-generation warfare and political warfare.[3] The renewed security debate since 2014 reflects confusion regarding Russian intentions, strategy and tactics as well as proper descriptions of the complex current security environment. Arguably, it also constitutes a dazed reaction in the West to the end of a period of relative stability in relations with Russia, rather than any distinctive novelty in Russia's strategy for projecting power and influence abroad. Indeed, Russia's operations in Ukraine had antecedents in the 2008 war in Georgia, the 2007 cyber- and information operations in Estonia, the counterinsurgency wars in Chechnya, Russia's support for the separatist regions of Abkhazia, South Ossetia and Transnistria, as well as in Soviet-era 'active measures'. Neither are the observed features of hybrid warfare, the strategic combination of a wide range of means, including, for example, military and economic power, subversion and information operations towards a unified purpose, a distinctively Russian invention – rather they are likely as old as human conflict.[4] Yet despite the vast amount of analysis on Russia's modus in Ukraine produced since 2014, and the growing body of work on vulnerabilities and ways to address these in Western societies, the responses crafted by Ukraine itself, despite being the country most immediately affected by Russian hybrid warfare, remains a neglected topic. The chapter seeks to address this omission.

The chapter begins with a brief overview of Russia's operations in Crimea and Donbas, exploiting Ukraine's serious vulnerabilities at the outset of the conflict through a series of tailor-made actions to prevent a comprehensive military response. It then proceeds to discuss Ukraine's responses including the country's conventional military build-up, its exposure of Russia's military involvement, and its creation of a strategic information campaign promoting Ukraine's own narrative of the conflict. The chapter concludes that the motives and modus of Russia's aggression has prompted Ukraine to devise a two-pronged response combining military and non-military tools, and therefore amounting to a strategy for hybrid warfare defence. The result is arguably more understandable and manageable for Ukraine's government and society, as well as the country's international partners than an obscure hybrid conflict: an interstate war where an external aggressor occupies Ukrainian territory and where Ukraine sees itself forced to respond in kind.

Russia's operations in Crimea and eastern Ukraine

Russia's operation to annex Crimea was set in motion as Ukraine's Maidan Revolution, ongoing since fall 2013, resulted in clashes between demonstrators and authorities, forcing President Viktor Yanukovych to leave the country on 22 February 2014. The quick and effective operation to annex Crimea drew on the highly specific operational environment in the peninsula, where Russia enjoyed considerable advantages. These included the element of surprise, a strong pre-existing military and intelligence presence due to the basing of its Black Sea Fleet in Sevastopol, including a Naval Infantry brigade,[5] as well the large Russian-speaking and pro-Russian population of the peninsula. This latter fact stemmed both from the historical affiliation of Russian-speaking Crimeans with Russia, and from an ambitious information operation intended to project fears that Ukraine's new government was dominated by 'fascists', posing a threat to Russians and Russian speakers in the country.[6]

From 22 February, Russia transferred Spetznaz detachments and special forces operators to Crimea carrying no insignia, the infamous 'little green men' or 'polite people'. These forces moved quickly to take control of the Crimean Parliament and other local government buildings, as well as Simferopol airport and other key locations on the peninsula.[7] Simultaneously, marine infantry units moved to besiege Ukrainian military bases, preventing any effective response from locally based government troops and facilitating the subsequent build-up of conventional forces. In Kyiv, the obscurity of the scenario playing out on the ground stymied efficient decision-making and prevented timely actions to thwart the Russian takeover of Crimea.[8] Ukrainian decision makers were acutely aware of the 2008 scenario in Georgia as a caution that Russia could utilize any rash action to motivate a military intervention to 'protect' Russian speakers and Russian citizens.[9]

After Russian forces established control of Crimea, a new, pro-Russian government was installed, which declared secession from Ukraine on 16 March after orchestrating a referendum on Crimea's status. It then requested to become part of the Russian Federation. Russia complied on 18 March, marking the formal annexation of Crimea. Vladimir Putin acknowledged and took credit for the decision to launch the operation in March 2015.[10] The operation was effectively decided, executed and concluded before the new Ukrainian government or its partners in the West could acquire a picture of the situation on the ground, let alone mount anything in the way of a response. It thus achieved a clear outcome, as Russia views the annexation of the peninsula as an accomplished and non-negotiable fact.

The subsequent operation in eastern Ukraine was completely different, in terms of its execution and aims. Indeed, although it is difficult to assess with certainty Moscow's actual planning and motives, the available evidence suggests that Russia never aimed to annex Donetsk and Luhansk.[11] Instead, Russia's strategy regarding these territories has seemingly been to establish inherently unstable entities within Ukraine outside the control of the central government, intended as levers in interactions with Kyiv and as internal breaks on foreign policy decision-making contrary to Moscow's interests. It therefore remains essential, from Moscow's perspective, that contrary to Crimea, the future of Donbas and Luhansk remains open to negotiation – the two 'Republics' are arguably more useful to Russia as future parts of Ukraine than as separate entities or as parts of the Russian Federation.[12] There are clear precedents for this strategy in Moldova's Transnistria, Georgia's Abkhazia and South Ossetia before 2008 and Russia's approaches to the Nagorno-Karabakh conflict between Azerbaijan and Armenia.

The drawn-out conflict in eastern Ukraine has gone through several phases. Initially, Russia sought to fuel a movement for the creation of 'Novorossiya', a construct engineered by Putin advisor Vladislav Surkov and intended to establish a confederation of 'people's republics', aside from Donetsk and Luhansk also encompassing large parts of southern and eastern Ukraine, including Kharkiv, Kherson, Dnipropetrovsk, Mykolaiv, Odesa and Zaporizhia.[13] Aside from several Russian frontal figures of the Novorossiya movement, such as Denis Pushilin, Igor Girgin, aka Strelkov and Igor Bezler, the movement was in many cases locally led and organized by Ukrainians, including businessmen and activists, whose activities were nevertheless coordinated and funded from Russia. Surkov personally oversaw this project, as has been revealed by tranches of leaked emails that detail communications between him and agents responsible for activities in Ukraine, focusing on mobilizing political support in cities and regions that would prospectively be subverted within the project.[14]

Local campaigns for Novorossiya featured anti-government protesters paid to demonstrate, media outlets and journalists paid to provide news coverage, local commissions and conferences advocating constitutional reform and federalization, and social media campaigns (often featuring non-existing individuals), all to create the impression of a wide movement with broad popular support – and all at Russia's expense. The Novorossiya project also included planned provocations, violent actions and sabotage, particularly in Kharkiv and Odesa, in order to destabilize the targeted regions in question. Ukraine's Security Service SBU also averted an attempt to foment a separatist movement in Besarabia under the proclamation of a 'People's Council' that would advocate secession from Ukraine, while local activist groups would conduct sabotage against vital infrastructure, according to a plan drawn up by the Transnistrian KGB operative Dmitry Soin.[15] The project nevertheless failed to gain traction, as the movement did not gain a substantial following beyond the Donetsk and Luhansk People's Republics (DNR and LNR) and was met by a successful mobilization of Ukrainians opposed to it. The leaders of DNR and LNR announced the abandonment of Novorossiya in May 2015.[16]

In the course of spring 2014, political activity and occasional clashes between activists took place in several locations across southern and eastern Ukraine, the events in Odessa in May being the most tragic as forty-two pro-Russian activists were killed in a fire.[17] Nevertheless, it was becoming clear that the effort to foment support for a larger secessionist movement was failing, and met increasing resistance from Ukrainian authorities and citizens. However, separatist groupings and pro-Russian activists, spearheaded by Russian special forces,[18] succeeded in capturing local administration buildings and establishing control over the cities of Donetsk, Luhansk, Kramatorsk, Slovyansk and Krasny Liman, proclaiming the DNR and LNR.[19] Ukraine launched what was designated an Anti-Terrorist Operation (ATO) to defeat separatist militias, aided by several volunteer units.[20] From the outset, Russia sought to achieve its objectives in eastern Ukraine without having to intervene overtly in the conflict, limiting its involvement to detachments of special forces and security contractors operating under fake identities[21] while backing the separatist forces politically and economically, along with instructors and equipment.[22]

In April and May 2014, Ukrainian forces managed to mount sufficient pressure on the separatist militias in cities under their control to force a more substantial Russian intervention. The first battle of Donetsk airport, which featured volunteers from Russia along with separatist fighters, marked the beginning of steady reinforcements and a shift towards more conventional tactics. From June, Russia steadily resupplied the separatist side with manpower and heavy equipment, including armour and air defence systems. However, the Ukrainian side continued to gain ground over the summer and in August threatened to drive a wedge between the two separatist territories. As the separatist side faced the threat of defeat, Russia sent in an estimated 3,500–6,000 mechanized troops organized in battalion tactical groups,[23] with heavy artillery support from across the border,[24] rolling back the Ukrainian advances and inflicting several crushing defeats on Ukrainian forces, most prominently at Ilovaisk. After the signing of the Minsk Protocol in September 2014, Russia undertook a more concerted effort to train and equip the separatists, mounting a new offensive in January 2015. Ukraine signed the Minsk II agreement after the defeat of Ukrainian forces at Debaltseve.[25] Russia's involvement in the fighting peaked at 10,000 troops by the end of 2014, after which a similar number of Russian troops remained in rotation in the two territories.[26]

Thus, by early 2015, Ukraine's mobilization and Russia's heavy reinforcement of the separatist side had effectively transformed the initial fighting between separatist proxy forces and weak, underequipped Ukrainian forces into a standoff between two much more formidable forces. Although fighting has continued after the signing of Minsk II, this has primarily featured static trench warfare along the by now heavily fortified Donetsk and Luhansk frontlines, with few territorial gains on either side. In a very different type of operation comparing to Crimea, Russia was required to improvise and gradually commit increasing numbers of conventional units and combined arms to attain its objectives. In the course of 2014 and 2015, the conflict thus transitioned from an insurgency fought by local Russian proxies, via mechanized manoeuvre warfare, which aside from Russia's continued denial of its involvement attained highly conventional features, into positional, low-intensity fighting.

Ukraine's responses

De-hybridizing military violence

During Russia's annexation of Crimea and at the outset of the war in the East, Ukraine was extremely ill prepared for fighting a war, in terms of both the unconventional and conventional means that Russia deployed in the conflict. Ukraine had inherited a Soviet-style army that, while sizeable on paper, was overall severely underfunded, underequipped and undertrained. Ukraine took some steps towards reforming and modernizing its armed forces in the aftermath of the 2004 Orange revolution, with the aim of transforming them into a smaller, professionalized and well-equipped force spearheaded by Joint Rapid Reaction forces deployable to international peacekeeping missions. These reforms were nevertheless stymied by a lack of funding along with the bitter political infighting of the post-revolutionary period.[27]

Since the breakdown of the USSR in 1991, Ukraine and Russia have on occasion clashed over the ownership and use of territory; the most prominent dispute emerged over Tuzla Island in the Kerch strait in 2003.[28] Crimea, and particularly Sevastopol, was considered a potential flashpoint long before 2014.[29] Following the 2004 Orange revolution, the Ukrainian and Russian sides disputed the pricing and transit of natural gas – with broad international implications since Ukraine is a key transit country for Russia's westward gas exports.[30] However, despite these latent tensions, and especially under Yanukovych, it appears that the prospect of a future territorial war with Russia was an impermissible idea in strategic and doctrinal thinking in Ukraine, implying that no force deployment or exercises were conducted in accordance with such a scenario.[31] Indeed, Ukraine's most important military commands and units remained based in the Western part of the country, a largely untouched remnant of the Soviet military districts; prior to 2013, no command had de facto operational responsibility for defending the East.[32] Moreover, the penetration of Russian intelligence services into Ukraine's armed forces, intelligence agencies and political institutions became particularly intense during this period, as an effect of the client-patron relationship between the Yanukovych government and Moscow and the deeply entrenched corruption in Ukraine's politics and state bodies.[33] Thus, as Russia set its operations in Crimea and eastern Ukraine into motion in 2014, it was able to outmanoeuvre decision makers in Kyiv as well as Ukraine's armed forces. Russia also sought to exploit linguistic divisions in Ukrainian society, particularly through identity-focused information operations painting the picture of a right-wing onslaught of nationalistic Ukrainian speakers against Russian speakers and ethnic Russians.[34]

At the time of the annexation of Crimea, Ukraine was capable of fielding a modest 6,000 soldiers from an army that, on paper, comprised 130,000 servicemen to carry out the ATO against separatist forces.[35] Instead, Ukraine had to rely on over fifty volunteer units to carry out much of the fighting, particularly in the summer of 2014. These militias were highly heterogeneous in their political and ideological motivations as well as in terms of their sources of funding, spawned from political groups as well as local civic initiatives and foreign fighters, including Chechens and Georgians, joining the Ukrainian side. Several of these battalions, such as Azov, Ukrainian Volunteer Corps (DUK)[36] and Aidar, included sizeable elements of nationalistic right-wing activists among their members. Yet others, such as Donbas and Dnipro-2, stemmed from local volunteer initiatives.[37] Many of these volunteer forces acquired funding from private individuals (most prominently Ukrainian oligarchs such as Ihor Kolomoisky). Yet others afforded their activities and equipment through crowdfunding (one example of the significant role of Ukrainian civil society in responding to Russia's aggression against the country) or from Ukrainians and other sympathizers abroad.[38]

In the summer of 2014, these forces were only weakly coordinated with Ukraine's military command and displayed great heterogeneity in professionalism, discipline and fighting skill. Nevertheless, several of these volunteer groups made substantial and sometimes decisive contributions to the fighting – for example, members of DUK were among the famous 'cyborgs' defending Donetsk airport.[39] Azov has become regarded as the most effective among the volunteer battalions, playing a crucial role in the June 2014 counteroffensive to recapture Mariupol and the June 2015 battle of Marinka, among others.[40] The raising and funding of the volunteer battalions can be considered a response in kind to the undeclared proxy warfare that Russia deployed in eastern Ukraine – a response that proved necessary in light of the vastly degraded capacity of the country's regular forces.

Indeed, Ukraine's experiences from the war in Donbas suggest that attempts to emulate the US military, in terms of building smaller but more capable forces supported by the latest military technology may not be a sustainable path forward for smaller forces with scarce resources such as those of Ukraine. A key problem during the 2014 fighting was the army's lack of manpower, reserves and equipment stockpile – translating into a very low tolerance for attrition. From 2014 onwards, Ukraine has sought to address the problem of military weakness by, as Sanders puts it, 'embracing a return to mass and positional warfare'.[41] In response, and by using Russia's aggression against the country as a rallying point, the Ukrainian government has undertaken, at least on paper, a highly ambitious reform programme of its armed forces. Defence funding was increased to 3 per cent of GDP. By reintroducing conscription, the manpower of the armed forces grew to 250,000, with an additional operational reserve of 130,000.[42] To this can be added forces in the National Guard, created out of the reformed interior troops, and the Territorial Defence Forces. Moreover, in order to exert control of armed formations under its command, most of the volunteer battalions were subordinated to the National Guard or other parts of the Interior Ministry. They thereby acquired a formal role in Ukraine's force structure (although some of these groups nevertheless retain a high degree of de facto autonomy from the state through their political and business connections, funding streams and public relations operations).[43]

Although Ukraine's military reform has been fraught with setbacks, including in terms of funding, resistance to change in parts of the military organization, corruption and institutional infighting,[44] Ukraine can display a military in 2020 is radically different from 2014, in terms of manpower, command, training and equipment. These changes are also reflected in the comparatively static nature that the fighting in Donbas has displayed since 2015 and the signing of Minsk II. Ukraine's military build-up and deployments to the frontline implies that any offensive from the separatist or Russian side would be very costly. In the assessment of Ukraine's Military Intelligence Service (HUR), Russia is 'comfortable' with the current situation and will aim to retain the status quo in the occupied territories for an indefinite time, while using other, non-kinetic means, to influence Ukraine.[45] Likewise, although a Ukrainian offensive to retake the DNR and LNR territories could be feasible given the separatist and regular Russian forces currently deployed to the regions, Russia's ability to mount a heavy counteroffensive from Russian territory poses a significant deterrent against any such initiative. As put by Ukraine's Joint Forces Commander, 'there is no military solution to this conflict'.[46] Instead, the frontline around DNR and LNR has stagnated into a largely positional war, where units are deployed head-to-head, brigade for brigade in a vast system of trenches, often separated by only a few hundred metres of no man's land.

In 2018, Ukraine introduced a law transforming the ATO into a Joint Forces Operation (JFO), recognizing Russia's 'armed aggression' against Ukraine, designating

Donetsk and Luhansk as 'temporarily occupied territories' and transferring command from the non-military Security Service SBU (previously commanding the ATO) to Ukraine's general staff. Aside from placing the operation unequivocally under military command and thus signalling a coherent military approach to stabilizing and eventually liberating the occupied territories, the introduction of the JFO recognized that Ukraine is primarily fighting Russian and Russian-supported forces in the East, rather than local separatists.[47] Ukrainian forces regularly make small advances in order to recapture territory allotted to them by the Minsk II agreement, and artillery and sniper fire occur regularly along the confrontation line, inflicting a steady stream of casualties on both sides. However, high-intensity fighting has been largely absent since 2015 (the most prominent exception being the 2017 battle for Avdiivka) mirroring the limited willingness or capacity on either side to fundamentally alter realities on the ground.

Thus, Ukraine's ability to draw on the experience of the invasion of Crimea by responding with conventional military force to Russia's attempt at covertly infiltrating Donbas was instrumental in transforming and clarifying perceptions of the conflict, domestically and internationally. Ukraine's response served to de-hybridize military violence in Donbas, by exposing and engaging an initially ambiguous opponent covering behind ostensibly domestic insurgents. This transformation has served to call out Russia's agency, making it clear that Ukraine is responding to external aggression, not fighting a local insurgency as Moscow claims. The approach has had the added benefit, from Ukraine's perspective, of largely containing military violence in Donbas to the physical frontlines along the DNR and LNR. These clarified features of the fighting have been important in the Ukrainian government's effort to uphold and unify domestic backing for the war effort, and in mobilizing international support for the country.

Exposing Russian involvement

A key objective of Ukraine's defensive posture in the East has been to expose Russian involvement in the conflict. From the outset, Moscow denied any involvement of the Russian military in eastern Ukraine. In 2015, President Putin admitted that Russian military intelligence operatives were indeed present in Ukraine, but no regular troops.[48] Instead, Moscow has claimed, first, that the forces fighting on behalf of the separatist side in DNR and LNR consist exclusively of local militias. When confronted with incontrovertible evidence that Russian servicemen had indeed been killed or taken prisoner during the fighting, Moscow conceded that they had 'volunteered' in the conflict, taking a leave of absence from their postings in the Russian armed forces. Moreover, Russia has denied supplying the separatist forces with equipment, fuel and funding, arguing that all lethal material observed in use by the separatists has been captured from the Ukrainian army, recovered from old weapons caches or supplied by foreign sympathizers other than Russia.[49]

In reality, the troops fighting on behalf of the DNR and LNR are a complex mix of local separatist militias, along with regular Russian forces and international volunteers and mercenaries. These forces are since 2016, respectively, formed into the DNR 1 and

LNR 2 Army Corps in the two 'republics'. The formation of this heterogeneous group of fighters into Army Corps, along with the assassinations of several overly independent-minded and power seeking militia commanders, reflects the subordination of these forces to the operational command of the Eighth Army headquartered in Novocherkassk. Although it may be difficult to exercise absolute control over these forces due to discipline problems, all higher command positions are today manned by Russian officers and the two Army Corps are fully dependent on air defences, communications, logistics, supplies and training controlled by the Eighth Army and supplied to DNR and LNR via Rostov-na-Donu.[50] Ukraine's HUR describes the setup as an intricate system of cover legends and covert logistical support for regular servicemen in Ukraine, supported by a sizeable deterrent force along the border while local separatists and mercenaries function as 'cannon fodder' at the front.[51]

In 2019, Ukraine's armed forces estimated the total number of separatist and Russian regular forces in the DNR and LNR to 37,000.[52] In addition, Russia deploys large forces in close proximity of Ukraine's border, which have during exercises comprised up to 75,000 servicemen and could quickly enter the fighting in eastern Ukraine, for example, in case of a Ukrainian offensive to retake the two regions.[53] Other forces fighting on behalf of DNR and LNR include various militias from the Russian Federation, including the (initially) largely Chechen manned Vostok battalion, foreign mercenaries, as well as the Wagner group, the Russian private security contractor firm that has made headlines for its activities in Syria.[54]

Russia's insistence on denying its direct military involvement in the conflict in eastern Ukraine, despite overwhelming evidence to the contrary, served to obfuscate realities on the ground at the outset of the conflict, delaying reactions from Kyiv as well as its Western partners in response to the unfolding war. Today, the reality of a strong Russian military presence on the ground in these territories is widely understood in Europe and the US, however, the denial of direct involvement still serves a dual purpose from Russia's perspective. First, it relieves Moscow of accepting partisanship in the conflict and any stated responsibility for a long-term military and economic commitment to the separatist projects in eastern Ukraine. Second, and most important, it allows Moscow to depict the conflict in eastern Ukraine as a civil war between the central government and the Russian-speaking population of the East.

Aside from the domestic political benefits of this narrative in Russia, Moscow's insistence on the war being an internal Ukrainian affair allows it to pose as a potential mediator in its pursuit of a solution to the conflict that involves constitutional reform and federalization – as stipulated in the Minsk II agreement. This would imply a 'special status' for the two regions, implying a high degree of autonomy along with influence and veto powers over the central government.[55] By extension, this would provide Russia with a permanent tool for exercising influence over the Ukrainian government, including the country's foreign policy decision-making and relations with NATO and the EU.[56] Indeed, as the leaked email correspondence of Putin advisor Surkov reveals, a federalization of Ukraine has constituted one of Russia's main objectives ever since the launch of the Novorossiya project.[57]

For the same reasons, the Ukrainian side perceives it as crucial to expose direct Russian involvement.[58] Evidence to support this claim is plentiful.[59] Aside from

Russian servicemen and intelligence operatives captured in Ukraine, evidence includes a plethora of Russian military equipment from recovered rations and personal documents, latest-issue uniforms and firearms, to footage and sightings of state-of-the-art armour, anti-air and artillery systems. One central feature of this information warfare has been the practice of Ukraine's intelligence agencies, most prominently the Security Service (SBU), to rapidly disseminate incriminating evidence through their own webpages and in social media. The perhaps most important example included intercepts of telephone conversations between separatist commanders in immediate connection with the downing of Malaysia Airlines Flight 17 on 17 July 2014; in itself pivotal in drawing Western attention to the war.[60] Moreover, NGOs such as Bellingcat, InformNapalm and Forensic Architecture have played an important role in these revelations, including Russia's transfer into Ukraine of the Buk-1 air defence system responsible for downing flight MH17, as well as the considerable involvement of T72B3 tanks in the battle of Ilovaisk. T72B3 is a new iteration of the T72 that had not begun export at the time and was in use only by Russia's armed forces.[61]

Evidence of Russian involvement is a standard talking point in briefings provided by the Ukrainian military to foreign visitors, detailing observations and footage of Russian military equipment deployed in DNR and LNR, controverting Russian denials of any such transfers of equipment. These include the Orlan-10 UAV, Torn-MDM signal intelligence stations, Repelent-1 anti-drone complexes, Kasta-2E2 radars, Krasnopol laser-guided grenades, and Kornet antitank missiles, all representing modern Russian equipment that can hardly have been captured from Ukrainian forces.[62] Another notable new weapons system spotted in Donbas is the Tornado-S (9A52-4) MLRS, which was specifically and probably accidentally mentioned in the Minsk II agreement – it was at the time in use only by the Russian armed forces and the mention thus constituted an indirect confirmation of Russia's direct military involvement.[63]

Moreover, several pieces of advanced Russian electronic warfare equipment have been observed in the DNR and LNR, including IL269 Krashukha-2, R-934BM, R-378BM and R-330ZH, RB-341V 'Leer-3', and RB-636 'Svet-KU'.[64] Aside from providing evidence of Russian deployment and/or transfers of advanced equipment to the separatist side, and of trained personnel to operate it, this also indicates that that Russia's arms industry is utilizing Donbas as a testing ground.

It may seem odd that representatives of Ukraine's armed forces go to such lengths to detail evidence of the Russian military presence in DNR and LNR. After all, the fact of Russia's involvement has been recognized by Ukraine's international partners at least since the summer of 2014 and is since the same year monitored by the OSCE Special Monitoring Mission to Ukraine (SMM).[65] However, Ukraine's effort in this regard signifies uncertainty as to whether this point has really landed internationally. Since international organizations such as the UN and OSCE through their composition will take positions that reflect compromise between the involved actors, and since the diplomatic missions of several countries operate on a similar basis, Ukrainian authorities perceive it as necessary to constantly repeat and reinforce Ukraine's own conflict narrative, in competition with that presented by Russia. Moreover, since the Minsk agreements stipulate the withdrawal of military equipment to a set distance from the frontline, it becomes particularly important for Ukrainian authorities to highlight that violations in this regard are committed by Russia, not the separatists.[66]

From Ukraine's perspective, exposing Russian involvement is a key part of presenting the conflict as an interstate war, triggered by Russia's subversion of Ukrainians and subsequent invasion of Ukraine. Domestically, an understanding of the conflict as a civil war waged by Kyiv against its citizens would have had detrimental consequences and could potentially have pitted Ukrainian citizens against each other far beyond Donetsk and Luhansk – which was indeed what Russia sought to achieve in the spring of 2014. Yet first Ukraine's civil society and then national authorities proved capable of mobilizing and rallying the population at large in the face of an external threat – seemingly to a far greater extent than Russian intelligence services had estimated at the outset of the conflict.[67]

Moreover, the international support for Ukraine's territorial integrity hinges on its victimhood to Russian aggression, which also puts the conflict in a very different international-legal perspective. This has not only raised sympathies for Ukraine, but also obliged the international community to devise a response, through the sanctions regime against Russia. Ukraine's efforts to highlight Russia's military presence in the country thus serve to keep the issue on the international political agenda and to motivate continuity in the sanctions regime.

Informational defences and the military's image

Although the actual fighting in and around the DNR and LNR has over time consolidated into positional land warfare, the war has also demanded a considerable informational effort on the part of Ukraine's armed forces. Indeed, whereas military activity on both sides has gradually stagnated along a relatively stable frontline, the competing strategic narratives remain crucial to perceptions of the war, as well as potential paths forward in negotiations. For both Russia and Ukraine, this informational aspect of the war effort has domestic as well as international dimensions.

From the very beginning of Russia's operations in Crimea and Donbas, information operations functioned as an important enabler of these operations. From the deployment of 'little green men' in Crimea to the mobilization of ostensibly domestic separatist fighters in Donbas, Russia promoted the narrative of an imminent threat to Russians and Russian speakers in Ukraine, posed by the ascent of a 'fascist junta' in Kyiv, through Russian state media, social media and agents of influence.[68] In order to sustain these claims, several examples have emerged of fabricated war crimes allegedly committed by Ukrainian forces.[69] Although this should not obscure the existence of evidence that both sides in this conflict have indeed committed real war crimes,[70] Russia engaged in a strategy of scaremongering in order to fuel polarization in Ukrainian society, locally in Crimea and Donbas, as well as in Ukraine at large. Regarding Ukraine's military and war effort, Russian information campaigns have made a point of underscoring the weakness and incompetence of Ukraine's armed forces, seeking to demoralize troops as well as Ukrainian society by reinforcing the sense that resistance is ultimately futile and that the country is defenceless. Russia has also sought to depict Ukraine as strategically isolated – portraying NATO and the EU as responsible for the conflict by interfering in Ukraine and actively provoking Russia, but simultaneously as disinterested in Ukraine per se.[71]

In its response to Russia's comprehensive information operations, Ukraine has attempted, in large part successfully, to delimit Russia's information channels in the country. The effort has included banning the popular Russian social networks VKontakte and Odnoklassniki, the Yandex search engine and the Mail.ru email service.[72] Ukrainian cable providers were also ordered to stop the broadcasting of major Russian state-controlled TV channels, including Rossiya 1, Channel One, NTV and Rossiya 24, which have functioned as megaphones of Russian state propaganda.[73]

Ukraine and its reforming military has also made a considerable effort to promote its own, competing narrative, ranging from the highly localized setting of the conflict zones around DNR and LNR, via national political mobilization in Ukraine, to the international political arena. In Donbas, local administrations are implementing what they describe as a soft-power campaign, assisted by the central government. Indirectly, this campaign also benefits from humanitarian and post-conflict reconstruction projects supported by foreign donors such as UNDP, EIB and USAID, which are allowed to operate only on Ukrainian-controlled territory. Various projects focus on reconstructing infrastructure schools, houses, water and gas supply in order to demonstrate to inhabitants of DNR and LNR that life is essentially better on the Ukrainian-controlled side of the frontline.[74] Although Ukraine imposed an economic blockade on DNR and LNR in 2017, residents of these regions can still cross the demarcation line, which large numbers of people do in order to collect pensions, acquire documents such as passports, work, trade or visit relatives.[75]

Ukraine's military has innovatively deployed Civil-Military Cooperation (CIMIC) – a concept otherwise developed for expeditionary missions and international peacekeeping missions – to its own domestic context, a unique experience in the effort of winning the 'hearts and minds' of Ukraine's own population in Donbas. In Ukraine's domestic context, CIMIC has included reconstruction of infrastructure for civilian use as well as the provision of information on the activities of Ukraine's military and domestic and foreign policy, including the activities of NATO and the EU in Ukraine. In a region whose population has traditionally been Russia-oriented and suffered from isolation and neglect from the central authorities in Kyiv, this effort is, according to representatives of the Ukrainian military, making a substantial difference in influencing local opinion about the conflict.[76] The effort also includes Ukrainian radio broadcasting aimed at the occupied territories, seeking to provide at least some informational counterweight to the overwhelming Russian media supremacy in these regions.[77]

Aside from its vastly improved fighting capability, Ukraine's reformed military has also acquired an important symbolic role in contravening the Russian narrative described earlier. Indeed, Ukraine's Ministry of Defence has invested in demonstrating competence and heroism in the face of Russian claims to the contrary. One example is the campaign 'Army Rebirth' in cooperation with Stratcom Ukraine, highlighting the positive achievements of Ukraine's armed forces.[78] Another is the elevation of the 'cyborgs' defending Donetsk airport, not least through providing government funding for the locally produced film 'Cyborgs: Heroes never Die'.[79] The Ukrainian military's strategic communication also involves publicizing its participation in international exercises, particularly with NATO, which serve the triple purpose of learning and developing as a force, showing an interoperable commitment to NATO, and demonstrating to the Ukrainian public that the country is not internationally isolated but enjoys support from important partners in the West. The presence of international trainers from NATO and EU countries in Ukraine similarly provides both a transfer of knowledge and a symbol of support.[80] Moreover, the US decision in 2018, after a long delay, to sell Ukraine Javelin antitank missiles improved the defensive capabilities of the Ukrainian army but even more importantly constituted a symbolic gesture of support beyond words, sanctions against Russia and provisions of non-lethal equipment. The purchase of a second batch of Javelins was agreed in 2019.[81]

The general message of Ukraine's information campaign is addressed to both the Ukrainian public and international partners. Domestically, it signals that the country is neither defenceless nor abandoned and that it is indeed possible to resist and repel Russian aggression. To partners in the West, that the country is capable of safeguarding its territorial integrity and that efforts to support it are not wasted.

Finally, Ukraine's narrative concerning the conflict is fundamentally underpinned by the notion that the country constitutes the frontline in an all-encompassing Russian aggression against the West – a civilizational conflict that threatens the values of the Western security community as much as the Ukrainian state. Therefore, according to this narrative, the stakes in the conflict and its outcomes for NATO and the EU are considerable and should motivate sustained attention and significant efforts to support Ukraine's territorial integrity. Giving up Ukraine would encourage further Russian aggression and the next victim may well be a member state in these organizations.[82]

Conclusion

The conflict between Russia and Ukraine is far from settled, yet the military dimension of the war in Donbas has settled into a mostly static frontline. Neither side will likely continue to pursue a military solution at this stage or to seek any significant alteration of realities on the ground. The conflict's future, as well as that of Ukraine, will be decided through diplomatic wrestling between Ukraine, Russia and the West over the implementation of the Minsk agreement. At the time of this writing, the most recent summit within the Normandy format in December 2019 saw some progress towards a cease-fire agreement and exchanges of prisoners, although positions remain locked regarding the fateful question of the future status of the separatist territories within Ukraine.[83]

However, the military standoff in itself says something important about defending against the type of hybrid warfare that Russia has deployed in Ukraine. Judging from the sequence of events, Russia did not initially intend to fight the war through a display of conventional military force. It was gradually compelled to do so by Ukraine's military response. Moreover, Russia's ambition at the outset of the operation, as suggested by the far-reaching aims of the Novorossiya project, indicates that Ukraine averted the loss of control over far larger areas than those currently constituting the DNR and LNR. Although Russia has reason to be content with the outcome achieved – the two separatist regions arguably constitute considerable and sufficient leverage on Kyiv – the situation could have been much worse in Ukraine's perspective.

It is not possible to ascertain Ukraine's intentionality regarding this effect – indeed, Ukrainian authorities likely took decisions on the response in light of the immediate conflict dynamics and the resources available, with unforeseeable long-term consequences. Nevertheless, in the course of the fighting in Donbas, Ukraine's conventional response did deny Russia the option of masking its aggression as a local insurgency, thus serving to de-hybridize the military violence. Ukraine forced Russia's hand in having to escalate its deployment of regular forces to the war, making all attempts at denying its involvement utterly unconvincing. This was combined with an effort to take control of the conflict narrative, by publicizing evidence of Russia's involvement, restricting Russia's information channels and systematically communicating Ukraine's own perspective of the unfolding events. Combined, these responses amount to a strategy for hybrid warfare defence that enabled Ukraine to deflect the imagery of a civil conflict, instead demonstrating that this is fundamentally a defensive war against an external aggressor. Despite the destruction and tragedy brought about by the fighting, this has made a substantial difference for Ukraine's internal cohesion as well as for the sustained support offered to the country from the West. The ensuing character of the fighting has arguably been more understandable and perhaps manageable to both Ukraine and the West. Trenches, tanks, standard-issue uniforms and drones are simply more graspable images of war than little green men, obscure separatist movements and information operations.

Indeed, the exposure of Russia's hybrid strategy and subversive tactics in the initiation of the war has resonated heavily in the West, effectively ending the strategic pause in much of Western Europe during the period of détente following the end of the Cold War, with implications for security strategies, doctrines and national defence budgets. While Russia's modus in Ukraine in 2014 had clear similarities with its preparations for war with Georgia in 2008, the war in Ukraine reverberated much more strongly with Western governments due to the country's size, geographical location, and presence on the mental maps of Western decision makers.[84] Of course, another factor is the considerably improved efficiency demonstrated by Russia's armed forces, compared to 2008. Moreover, and in direct relation to Ukraine's ability to devise a response, the war in Donbas has extended over a long period of several years. In sharp contrast to the scenarios in Georgia and Crimea, this has provided ample time for Ukraine's international partners to fathom developments and react to them.

Whereas the war in Ukraine has been a catalyst for the security debate in NATO and the EU, this debate has to a large extent focused on the subversive and non-kinetic components of what is essentially a strategy aiming to amplify the application of traditional material means of statecraft, primarily military and economic power. An essential component of this strategy is the use of conventional military force, or the threat thereof. Indeed, the evolution of Russia's operation in eastern Ukraine demonstrates that while relying on proxy forces and political subversion can go a long way towards destabilizing an adversary, these approaches alone have clear limits in the pursuit of strategic objectives. In this light, the case of Ukraine demonstrates the potential of asymmetry – otherwise usually denoting the means by which a weaker party can defeat a stronger adversary by deploying unconventional means aimed at particular weaknesses. Yet in Ukraine, the reverse is true: Ukraine, as a weaker party, responded conventionally to a much stronger opponent deploying unconventional means for the sake of obscuring its actions and intentions.

Notes

1   Niklas Granholm, Johannes Malminen and Gudrun Persson, *A Rude Awakening: Ramifications of Russian Aggression Towards Ukraine* (Stockholm: Swedish Defence Research Agency, 2014).
2   Niklas Nilsson, Mikael Weissmann, Björn Palmertz and Henrik Häggström, *Introduction*, 2020, this volume.
3   Jānis Bērziņš, *Russia's New Generation Warfare in Ukraine: Implications for Latvian Defense Policy* (National Defence Academy of Latvia, 2014); Mark Galeotti, *Russian Political Warfare: Moving Beyond the Hybrid* (London and New York: Routledge, 2019); Mark Galeotti, 'Hybrid, Ambiguous, and Non-linear? How New Is Russia's "new way of war?"', *Small Wars & Insurgencies* 27, no. 2 (2016). https://doi.org/10.1 080/09592318.2015.1129170; Timothy Thomas, 'The Evolution of Russian Military Thought: Integrating Hybrid, New-Generation, and New-Type Thinking', *The Journal of Slavic Military Studies* 29, no. 4 (2016). https://doi.org/10.1080/13518046.2016 .1232541; Oscar Jonsson and Robert Seely, 'Russian Full-Spectrum Conflict: An Appraisal After Ukraine', *The Journal of Slavic Military Studies* 28, no. 1 (2015). https:// doi.org/10.1080/13518046.2015.998118 .
4   Williamson Murray and Peter R. Mansoor, *Hybrid Warfare: Fighting Complex Opponents from the Ancient World to the Present* (New York: Cambridge University Press, 2012).
5   Michael Kofman, Katya Migacheva, Brian Nichiporuk, Andrew Radin, Olesya Tkacheva, and Jenny Oberholtzer, *Lessons from Russia's Operations in Crimea and Eastern Ukraine* (Santa Monica: Rand Corporation, 2017), 6.
6   Jolanta Darczewska, *The Anatomy of Russian Information Warfare: The Crimean Operation, A Case Study* (Warsaw: Centre for Eastern Studies, 2014); Bettina Renz, 'Russia and "hybrid warfare"', *Contemporary Politics* 22, no. 3 (2016). https://doi.org /10.1080/13569775.2016.1201316 , 287–90; Nicu Popescu, 'Hybrid Tactics: Neither New nor only Russian' (European Union Institute for Security Studies, 2015).
7   An inheritance of the USSR's system of regional autonomies, Crimea enjoyed the status of an Autonomous Republic within Ukraine, with considerable self-government and its own Parliament in Simferopol.
8   Kofman et al., *Lessons from Russia's Operations in Crimea and Eastern Ukraine*, 8–16, 19, 23–4.
9   Roy Allison, 'Russian Deniable Intervention in Ukraine: How and Why Russia Broke the Rules', *International Affairs* 90, no. 6 (2014): 1261.
10 BBC, 'Putin Reveals Secrets of Russia's Crimea Takeover Plot', 9 March 2015.
11 Kofman et al., *Lessons from Russia's Operations in Crimea and Eastern Ukraine*, 75.
12 Tatiana Stanovaya, 'What the West Gets Wrong About Russia's Intentions in Ukraine', *Foreign Policy*, 6 December 2019.

13 Adam Taylor, "'Novorossiya," the Latest Historical Concept to Worry about in Ukraine', *The Washington Post*, 18 April 2014.

14 Aliya Shandra and Robert Seely, *The Surkov Leaks: The Inner Workings of Russia's Hybrid War in Ukraine* (London: Royal United Services Institute, 2019), 25–35.

15 Shandra and Seely, *The Surkov Leaks*; UNIAN, 'Ukrainian MP was in 2015 Set to Take Lead of "Bessarabian People's Republic" – SBU Chief', 9 October 2018.

16 Andrei Kolesnikov, 'Why the Kremlin Is Shutting Down the Novorossiya Project' (Carnegie Moscow Center, 2015).

17 BBC, 'How did Odessa's Fire Happen?', 6 May 2014.

18 James Miller et al., *An Invasion by Another Name: The Kremlin's Dirty War in Ukraine* (Institute of Modern Russia; The Interpreter, 2015).

19 Kofman et al., *Lessons from Russia's Operations in Crimea and Eastern Ukraine*, 38–40.

20 Margerete Klein, 'Ukraine's Volunteer Battalions – Advantages and Challenges', *RUFS Briefing no. 27* (Swedish Defence Research Agency, 2015).

21 Miller et al., *An Invasion by Another Name*.

22 Mark Galeotti, *Armies of Russia's War in Ukraine* (Oxford and New York: Osprey Publishing, 2019), 17.

23 Kofman et al., *Lessons from Russia's Operations in Crimea and Eastern Ukraine*, 43–5.

24 Bellingcat, 'Russia Ante Portas: Updated Satellite Imagery Shows Border Crossings and Artillery Sites', 15 June 2015.

25 Kofman et al., *Lessons from Russia's Operations in Crimea and Eastern Ukraine*, 43–5.

26 Galeotti, *Armies of Russia's War in Ukraine*, 34.

27 Deborah Sanders, "'The War We Want; The War That We Get": Ukraine's Military Reform and the Conflict in the East', *The Journal of Slavic Military Studies* 30, no. 1 (2017): 33–6. https://doi.org/10.1080/13518046.2017.1271652 .

28 Sophie Lambroschinski, 'Russia/Ukraine: Prime Ministers Meet Today over Tuzla Dam Dispute', *Radio Free Europe/Radio Liberty*, 24 October 2003.

29 Ashkold Krushelnycky, 'Fears that Crimea Could be Next Flashpoint for Conflict with Russia', *Radio Free Europe/Radio Liberty*, 24 August 2008.

30 Tom Parfitt, 'Russia Turns off Supplies to Ukraine in Payment Row, and EU Feels the Chill', *The Guardian*, 2 January 2006.

31 Author's interview, Oleksyi Melnyk, Razumkov Centre, Kyiv, 30 May 2019.

32 Andrzej Wilk, *The Best Army Ukraine Has Ever Had: Changes in Ukraine's Armed Forces since the Russian Aggression* (Warsaw: Centre for Eastern Studies, 2017), 14–15.

33 Taras Kuzio, 'Russianization of Ukrainian National Security Policy under Viktor Yanukovych', *The Journal of Slavic Military Studies* 25, no. 4 (2012): 14–15. https://doi.org/10.1080/13518046.2012.730372; Isabelle Facon, *Reforming Ukrainian Defense: No Shortage of Challenges* (Paris: Institut francais des relations internationales, 2017), 14–15.

34 Scott E. McIntosh, 'Kyiv, International Institutions, and the Russian People: Three Aspects of Russia's Current Information Campaign in Ukraine', *The Journal of Slavic Military Studies* 28, no. 2 (2015). https://doi.org/10.1080/13518046.2015.1030263; Darczewska, *The Anatomy of Russian Information Warfare*.

35 Sanders, "'The War We Want; The War That We Get"', 37.

36 DUK is a volunteer battalion formed by the Pravy Sector political movement.

37 Galeotti, *Armies of Russia's War in Ukraine*, 55–6.

38 Kimberly Marten and Olga Oliker, 'Ukraine's Volunteer Militias May have Saved the Country, But Now They Threaten It', *War on the Rocks*, 14 September 2017.

39 Amos C. Fox, *Cyborgs at Little Stalingrad: A Brief History of the Battle of the Donetsk Airport, Land Warfare Paper 125* (Arlington: The Institute of Land Warfare, 2019).

40 BBC, 'Ukraine Crisis: Kiev Forces Win Back Mariupol', 13 June 2014, 42; Sanders, 'The War We Want; The War That We Get', 42.

41 Sanders, 'The War We Want; The War That We Get', 48.

42 Stepan Poltorak, 'Reforming Ukraine's Armed Forces while Facing Russia's Aggression: The Triple Five Strategy', *RUSI Newsbrief* 37, no. 4 (2017): 3.

43 Marten and Oliker, 'Ukraine's Volunteer Militias'; Teemu Saressalo and Aki-Mauri Huhtinen, 'The Information Blitzkrieg — "Hybrid" Operations Azov Style', *The Journal of Slavic Military Studies* 31, no. 4 (2018). https://doi.org/10.1080/13518046.20 18.1521358; Facon, *Reforming Ukrainian Defense*, 26–7.

44 Adriana Lins De Albuquerque and Jakob Hedenskog, *Ukraine: A Defence Sector Reform Assessment* (Stockholm: Swedish Defence Research Agency, 2015); Facon, *Reforming Ukrainian Defense*, 22ff.

45 Author's Interview, representatives of Ukraine's Military Intelligence Service (HUR), Kyiv, 29 May 2019.

46 Author's Interview, Major General Bohdan Bondar, Joint Forces Commander, Kramatorsk, 28 May 2019.

47 Vera Zimmerman, 'What does Ukraine's New Military Approach Toward the Donbas Mean?', *UkraineAlert* (Atlantic Council, 2018).

48 Shaun Walker, 'Putin Admits Russian Military Presence in Ukraine for First Time', *The Guardian*, 17 December 2015.

49 UNIAN, 'Putin Claims Militants in Donbas get Military Hardware from Countries "Sympathizing with Them"', 19 December 2019.

50 Galeotti, *Armies of Russia's War in Ukraine*, 20–41.

51 Author's Interview, representatives of HUR.

52 Author's Interview, Major General Bohdan Bondar.

53 Galeotti, *Armies of Russia's War in Ukraine*, 34–5.

54 Alec Luhn, 'Volunteers or Paid Fighters? The Vostok Battalion Looms Large in War with Kiev', *The Guardian*, 6 June 2014; Nathaniel Reynolds, *Putin's Not-So-Secret Mercenaries: Patronage, Geopolitics, and the Wagner Group* (Carnegie Endowment for International Peace, 2019); Ivan Nechepurenko, Neil MacFarquhar and Thomas Gibbons-Neff, 'Dozens of Russians Are Believed Killed in U.S-Backed Syria Attack', *The New York Times*, 13 February 2018.

55 Dana Dascalu, 'Frozen Conflicts and Federalization: Russian Policy in Transnistria and Donbass', *Journal of International Affairs* (Columbia /SIPA, 2019).

56 Author's interview, Oleksyi Melnyk.

57 Shandra and Seely, *The Surkov Leaks*.

58 Author's interview, Oleksyi Melnyk.

59 See, e.g. Adam Cech and Jakub Janda, *Caught in the Act: Proof of Russian Military Intervention in Ukraine* (Wilfrid Martens Center for European Studies, 2015).

60 James Miller and Michael Weiss, 'How We Know Russia Shot Down MH17', *Daily Beast*, 12 July 2017.

61 Bellingcat, 'MH17 – The Open Source Evidence', 8 October 2015; Forensic Architecture, 'The Battle of Ilovaisk: Mapping Russian Military Presence in Eastern Ukraine August-September 2014', 19 August 2019.

62 Briefings given to Author by representatives of Ukraine's Joint Forces.

63 Andras Racz and Sinikukka Saari, 'The New Minsk Ceasefire: A Breakthrough or Just a Mirage in the Ukrainian Conflict Settlement?', *FIIA Comment 5* (The Finnish Institute of International Affairs, 2015).

64 Briefings given to Author by representatives of Ukraine's Joint Forces.

65 Johan Engvall, *OSCE and Military Confidence-Building in Conflicts: Lessons from Georgia and Ukraine* (Stockholm: Swedish Defence Research Agency, 2019).

66 Interview, representatives of HUR.

67 Kofman et al., *Lessons from Russia's Operations in Crimea and Eastern Ukraine*, 63–4.

68 Margarita Jaitner, 'Russian Information Warfare: Lessons from Ukraine', in *Cyber War in Perspective: Russian Aggression against Ukraine*, ed. Kenneth Geers (Tallinn: NATO Cooperative Cyber Defence Center of Excellence, 2015); Sam Sokol, 'Russian Disinformation Distorted Reality in Ukraine: Americans Should Take Note', *Foreign Policy*, 2 August 2019.

69 Arcady Ostrovsky, 'The Crucifixion of a 3-Year Old, the U.S. Helped Kiev Shoot Down Flight 17, and Other Tales the Kremlin Media Tell', *StopFake*, 31 July 2014.

70 Amnesty International, 'Ukraine: Mounting Evidence of War Crimes and Russian Involvement', 7 September 2014.

71 Vladimir Sazonov, Kristiina Müür and Holger Mölder, eds, *Russian Information Campaign against the Ukrainian State and Defence Forces* (Tartu: NATO Strategic Communications Centre of Excellence, 2016).

72 Alec Luhn, 'Ukraine Blocks Popular Social Networks as Part of Sanctions on Russia', *The Guardian*, 16 May 2017.

73 Stephen Ennis, 'Ukraine Hits Back at Russian TV Onslaught', *BBC*, 12 March 2014.

74 Author's observations and interviews with representatives of the Civil-Military administration, Kramatorsk, 28 May 2019.

75 Thomas de Waal, *Uncertain Ground: Engaging with Europe's De Facto States and Breakaway Territories* (Washington, DC: Carnegie Endowment for International Peace, 2018), 64–8.

76 Author's interview, Col. Ruslan Miroshnichenko, Deputy Chief of Staff of JFO HQ, Head of Army CIMIC, Kramatorsk, 28 May 2019.

77 Author's Interview: Colonel, Ukraine's Armed Forces, Kyiv, 30 May 2019.

78 'Army Rebirth: Story of Ukrainian Army's Revival by the Ones Who Made It Possible', *Stratcom Ukraine*, accessed 3 March 2020.

79 AFP, '"Cyborgs" War Drama Replays Real-life Ukraine Battle', 12 February 2018.

80 Author's Interview: Colonel, Ukraine's Armed Forces.

81 RadioFreeEurope/RadioLiberty, 'Ukraine Says It has New Contracts For Second Batch of U.S. Javelin Missiles', 27 December 2019.

82 Valeria Lazarenko, 'Conflict in Ukraine: Multiplicity of Narratives about the War and Displacement', *European Politics and Society* 20, no. 5 (2018). https://doi.org/10.1080/23745118.2018.1552108 .

83 Katya Gorchinskaya, 'The Normandy Summit Ended With No Breakthroughs: What Has It Achieved?', *Forbes*, 10 December 2019.

84 Niklas Nilsson, *Russian Hybrid Tactics in Georgia* (Washington, DC and Stockholm: Central Asia-Caucasus Institute & Silk Road Studies Program, 2018).

15

Iran's hybrid warfare capabilities

Rouzbeh Parsi

What is hybrid warfare?

There seems to be a certain allure in ignoring historic precedents when discussing developments in warfare. To be fair the art of war has in some ways changed quite significantly in the last 200 years. Technological advances such as the machine gun, aircraft and missile technology have transformed the battlefield into a battle space, adding a dimension as it were. These technological innovations have also affected classic constraints of time and space (logistics and geographical distance). In more recent times cyberwarfare has added yet another layer to how and 'where' war can be waged. But war is not a matter of 'mere' technology, it is an extension of the societies that fight them, and modern mass society has both generated mass conscription armies (French Revolution and the Napoleonic Wars) and increasingly more specialized warfare requiring highly trained soldiers, matching expert-heavy modern civilian life.

In his article Mikael Weissmann[1] argues back and forth as to whether hybrid warfare is something new or just good old warfare in a new shape. His ambivalence is indicative of the difficulty in pinpointing a qualitatively new element that can be said to distinguish contemporary warfare from what preceded it. In essence most of the individual definitional elements of warfare have not changed much since the twentieth century; it is rather their combination that, today, results in a somewhat different beast, a synergy effect of sorts. This synergy is also intimately connected to the dynamics of the conflict, involving variables such as whether the driving actors are directly or indirectly involved, how they view their own actions and perceive those of the suspected enemy.[2]

Thus, to a certain extent the discussion about hybrid warfare[3] is actually about how well warfare, in a historical perspective, is understood. What is it that supposedly sets hybrid warfare apart? Irregular forces have always been part of war, independent/ unified command is an ebb and flow determined by the nature of the entities waging the war, when is there peace and how does war break out? Even the rules of war, when codified, define what is legitimate war and who is to fight it and hence the excluded forms of warfare are by definition irregular war and warfare. States were never wholly unified and are most certainly not rational actors. The notion that the modern nation state encompasses such traits is more Weberian ideal type than actual practice and historical experience.[4]

Threat perception and rational behaviour

While Iran is considered a revolutionary state, it has in many ways become a status quo power more intent on safeguarding its own survival than exporting the revolution. This is not surprising, as the revolution now has turned forty, and while the state still insists on the revolutionary framing and rhetoric, Iranian society has in many ways moved on. While Iran in Western narratives often is portrayed as the belligerent power trying to upend the international order,[5] Tehran views itself as being under siege and believes that it is being deprived of its rightfully prominent position in the region. Be that as it may, it is clear that Iran is actually more in the cross hairs of the United States and its regional allies now than it was during the hot phase of the revolution and the war against Iraq. Today the United States has a much stronger military presence in the Persian Gulf and other countries neighbouring Iran. In addition, there is a history of secessionist groups in Iran, such as the Baluchi terrorist organization, Jundullah, having received material support from outside powers.[6] Thus, the sense of threat in Tehran has not subsided regardless of its own growing ability to project influence in neighbouring countries.[7]

Tehran views the United States, more than any other country, as a hegemonic power, one that does not simply want to pursue its own interests but dominate and shape the international order in its own image. Thus, the threat from the United States is more comprehensive and multidimensional than, say, any double dealing on the part of Beijing or Moscow. There is also a sizeable element within the political and security establishment in Tehran that for ideological and domestic political reasons needs the United States to play the role of Iran's foremost deadly threat.

In fact, most inside observers of Iranian foreign and defence policy tend to situate themselves it in the realist camp. The long-time analyst and academic, professor Kayhan Barzegar, refers to the defensive realism school in international relations in order to explain the strategic thinking of the Supreme Leader Ayatollah Ali Khamenei. The emphasis in this understanding of state behaviour is that states foremost want to achieve security and their own survival rather than conquest and hegemony.[8] Offense requires offensive capabilities and the capacity to conquer, something Iran has not shown itself willing or capable of for more than two centuries. Instead, the aim of defensive realism is 'reducing the possibility of war by adopting defensive approaches, and not expressing offensive behaviours'.[9] This includes 'network deterrence' and asymmetric capabilities. Thus, open and full frontal offence is not part of the tool box and the primary focus is on defence.[10] The former aspect still allows for what we define as hybrid warfare, something that has developed more out of the Iraq and Syria campaigns than Iran's original mosaic strategy which was intended as a defence against a possible American attack.

Asymmetric warfare – mosaics and hybridity

More or less since its inception, the Islamic Republic of Iran has had experience of war. Some of the revolutionary groups received guerrilla training from radical Palestinian groups in Lebanon prior to the revolution in 1979. As the revolutionaries were starting to consolidate their rule after the fall of the Shah, Saddam Hussein's Iraq invaded the country in September 1980. The war was first fought on Iranian soil and from 1982 to 1983 increasingly on the border to, and inside, Iraq. The main feature of the war was a barely moving trench frontline war reminiscent of the First World War, but also the use of chemical gas (Iraq) and long-distance missiles primarily aimed at urban centres (Iraq and Iran). The Iranian revolutionaries had alienated just about every regional and global power and therefore suffered under a constant lack of war materiel. This would remain the case for many years. In essence, Iran had no shortage of men, but lacked sorely in technology. Over time improved relations with Russia and China allowed for arms trade and technology transfer. Despite feats of reverse engineering and building domestic arms manufacturing capacity, Iran is still several generations behind in jet fighter technology and its conventional navy is also less developed than that of neighbouring countries and Western powers. However, in view of the US wars against Iraq in 1991 and 2003, the Iranian armed forces are again emphasizing the importance of the human element in the defensive and offensive capabilities, as Iraq's mass of conventional arms and military units had no significant effect on the American juggernaut.[11]

In many ways, Iran's attempt at conventional warfare beyond re-taking territory occupied by Iraq was a failure. Iran did not have the capacity or means to develop a modern army in the conventional technological sense. Yet the harrowing war with Iraq made clear to the new political leadership that future attackers needed to be deterred before they reached the gates of Iran, as it were. From this flow two important strategic decisions and practices: (1) Iran needs to develop allies and capabilities beyond its borders to stave off potential enemies on their own home turf. This is very similar to the centre-periphery model that Israel developed early on after its inception as a way of creating strategic depth. (2) In turn, this requires not the projection of conventional military forces stationed in bases, which Iran could neither produce nor afford, but rather an extended guerrilla-like infrastructure together with local *partners*. These forces were never meant to challenge a foe in open battle as they were not equipped or trained for such warfare; nor would they have fared well in such scenarios. This approach was also reinforced by the nature of most allies and partners Tehran developed in the region. These local groups were usually weak in terms of finances and infrastructure and not in control of state-like institutions. They would build their capacities in the shadow of a, usually weak, central state. This periphery was not necessarily geographical as much as political, since the groups Iran allied itself with tended to be marginalized within their respective political systems.[12]

Partners and allies, not proxies and servants

There is a common misunderstanding that Iran has proxies, that is groups that are beholden to Iran in a direct financial/ideological relationship, which allows Tehran to direct and control them. This misunderstanding is part and parcel of a narrative which blankets out Iranian politics and threat perceptions and posits revolutionary ideology as the prime engine of Iranian behaviour. In reality, the interaction and relationship between Iran and its Iraqi partners, as well as with Hezbollah in Lebanon, is much more complex and two-directional.[13] Iran does support these various groups financially but their staying power in their environment is more tied to their local anchoring than Iranian largesse, real or imagined. Hezbollah is integral to political life in Lebanon and has an important and quite steadfast constituency in the population. In the end, this is more crucial to their survival than Iranian funds.

However, even Hezbollah, which has one of the more capable military forces in the Middle East, adheres to non-conventional military warfare; developing drone, cyber and covert operations capacities rather than trying to acquire the trappings of a conventional standing army. To a large extent this is due to the theatres and terrains where they expect to fight and prefer to confront Israel. When they test the enemy (i.e. Israel) or push the proverbial envelope they prefer to do so by covert and/or non-attributable means, and if they end up fighting an outright war it is primarily defensive, drawing the enemy into, for themselves, familiar ground where Israeli tanks and jet fighters are less effective.

Iraq is the other theatre where Iran has encouraged and supported the combination of political mobilization and military organization. The Popular Mobilization Forces (Hashd al-Shaabi) are a set of military outfits, with various degree of organizational cohesion, that were created as response to the rapid expansion of ISIS in 2014. The larger ones have a history that precedes ISIS and are connected to Iran. They also have political representation in the Iraqi parliament and control government institutions and departments (thus generating income).[14] While they are formally part of the Iraqi state and were decreed to integrate into the regular army in 2019, they are by nature a hybrid phenomenon. Under the leadership of Abu Mahdi al-Muhandis there were efforts to bring greater cohesion to the panoply of groups under the PMF heading. Al-Muhandis was killed in an US airstrike together with the commander of the Iranian Quds forces Qassem Soleimani in January 2020. Soleimani was the pre-eminent Iranian official managing relations with officials and hybrid actors in Syria and Iraq. The net effect of the airstrike has so far not been the weakening of Iran in Iraq as much as an increase in insecurity and chaos. Tellingly, the development that has threatened Iran's political influence in Iraq the most has been the popular dissatisfaction with how the state mismanages its affairs and underperforms.[15] In essence politics and governance rather than military and warfare. With al-Muhandis death the various PMF groups are back to primarily enhancing their own positions thereby making the situation more volatile and unpredictable.[16] Iran used a very conventional means to retaliate against the United States – a missile strike on an air base in Iraq used by US troops. Later, in summer 2020, they used drones strikes and ship mines to reiterate their deterrence capabilities vis-á-vis two important regional US allies: Saudi Arabia and the UAE. Yet this was done with some initial deniability, that is, it was not fully clear who had perpetrated the attacks, Iran or one of its allies.

Necessity is the mother of invention

Iran's hybrid capabilities spring from a defensive tactic, developed in the aftermath of the US invasion of Iraq in the spring of 2003, which has turned offensive. While the US forces quickly vanquished the Iraqi army, they failed to understand the complexities of actually governing a country. The occupation phase was beset by a series of inconceivably stupid decisions, but the one that stands out is the dissolution of the Iraqi army and the wholesale de-Baathification of the state apparatus (compare to the pragmatism of the United States in Germany after the Second World War where general Patton famously refused to let membership in the NSDAP disqualify civil servants from staying in their jobs). Tehran drew several lessons from the quick and ignoble demise of their most immediate and proven deadly foe, Saddam Hussein. First, a top-down hierarchical organization, Soviet style, is useless on the tactical level in modern warfare. The combat units must have greater independence of action to be able to deal with situations where they will have no significant air support and where communications will be unreliable at best – constraints due to US technological superiority that the Iranians have to assume are givens. Thus, in 2005 the Iranian military command structure was radically altered, decentralizing command by creating thirty-one regional commands and giving greater autonomy to brigade level commanders rather than division superiors, thus allowing for a more tactile response to any invading force.[17]

Second, while modern armies like that of the United States can quickly establish control of the skies and intercept/destroy communication lines, their ability to manage close quarter combat in urban areas is less impressive. An invading force will not have the agility of manoeuvre or intelligence to be able to pinpoint the enemy, it will rather rely on fire power and get the intelligence wrong as often as it gets it right. This will turn the local population against them and make their footprint in the local environment heavy and costly. Counter-insurgency tactics will allow them occasionally to capture or kill opponents but it will not enable them to hold territory in any meaningful sense. Like in Vietnam and Iraq, these calculations are as much about political costs and optics as they are about actual military warfare. The aim is to deny the invading force the ability to hold territory and thus establish a baseline of normalcy through a stable foothold. In this war of attrition, the goal is to increase the cost of operations for the invader as much as possible, thus making a sustained presence politically prohibitive.

From these lessons, Tehran developed what is called a mosaic approach to defensive warfare. It is in a sense characteristic of a state that for all its revolutionary rhetoric always falls back on expediency. In the foreseeable future Iran will not have a significant navy or air force and it must therefore rely on a multi-layered and decentralized form of defence that uses the advantages of being on literally familiar ground and various methods of agile and small-scale warfare. The emphasis is on denying access or operability in a specific war theatre using non-direct means of warfare where the objective is as much political as it is military in operational terms.[18] This is the kind of passive resistance that is invoked on the political level, but operationalized: no open and direct engagement with the enemy, instead targeting supply lines and resisting in ways that will wear down the invader – in essence like the kind of attrition warfare and denial of access to geographical space employed by guerrilla forces.

A recent article[19] published in an Iranian defence journal is instructive as to how hybridity is understood and envisioned in the country. The author has conducted a survey among military officers in the regular army on how to better prepare combat units for the kind of warfare that is employed in the region. The primary approach is one of defensive capabilities, and an analysis of Hezbollah serves to illustrate the characteristics of modern warfare and its hybrid element. This is in many ways an apt case to use; it has the kind of ideological cohesion, hybrid political nature and military capabilities that fit the model for a hybrid actor. The author argues that the era of distinguishable military/non-military boundaries is over, and that the means of war and the units involved no longer follow established patterns. This creates extra fluidity in how the situation can change and escalate (compare with Weissmann's reasoning) making initial planning and scenario building essential for the ability of the involved actors to stay on top of the developments if not necessarily controlling it.

But it is also clear that the hybridity is not simply defensive in nature even though that may have been the original purpose. Today Hezbollah is heavily involved in the Syrian civil war and thus it is projecting various forms of military force and capabilities in a theatre that is neither its home turf, nor part of its defensive perimeter. In this regard Iran has followed a similar pattern. The main focus of Iran's mosaic/hybrid capability development has been defensive and the reviewed open access literature from Iran tends to pursue this line. The conflict against ISIS in Iraq and Syria and the support for Bashar al-Assad in the Syrian civil war has forced Iran to further develop its capabilities and tactics. In Iraq Tehran was, like everyone else, surprised at the speed and scale of the ISIS conquest and the fall of Mosul. Tehran then quickly brought in arms to help the Kurdish forces and increased its support of various Shi'a militia groups. In the end it also tacitly worked side by side with the United States in pushing back ISIS, and here the Kurdish and Shi'a militias proved more effective than the regular Iraqi army. Iran has quite successfully switched its asymmetric guerrilla defensive capabilities into an offensive mode. The hybridity spans across the Clausewitzian understanding of war as an extension of politics. Many of the groups supported by Iran in Iraq are not just militarily capable outfits but also political organizations that participate in regular electoral politics and are now nestled in the institutions of the state apparatus. Thus they are not exclusively non-state actors, nor are they fully beholden to the state. Their hybrid nature is as much a political characteristic (proto-state in a manner of speaking) as it is a military capability. From having fought US troops to pushing back Da'esh they operate on all levels of regular and irregular warfare and Iran has exported both the model and its participants to Syria, where some of the groups fighting for Bashar al-Assad are neither regular military nor simple militias but organized and trained by Iran as discreet offensive units.[20]

Conclusion

Iran's threat perception has increasingly considered the United States as a direct threat to the survival of the Islamic Republic. This was especially tangible after the US invasion of Iraq in 2003. As the situation in Iraq deteriorated, Tehran devised a multi-layered non-conventional defensive strategy called mosaic defence. It required a more flexible approach to the defence of the country's territory, utilizing non-conventional arms as well as tactics. Iraq became the battleground where Iran went from defensive measures to deter a potential US invasion to developing offensive capabilities based on the same approach. The offensive mode of the mosaic approach in effect constitutes hybrid warfare (also in a political dimension) and was put to the test in the Syrian civil war. As the political confrontation between the United States and Iran escalated in 2019, Iran decided to employ these hybrid capabilities directly against the United States in order to showcase its ability to defend itself and attack US allies and assets in neighbouring countries. The intended purpose was not to escalate the situation but rather to deter the United States from further confrontation with Iran. In this regard, a hybrid approach with no clear attribution of culpability combined with the employment of advanced technological assets seem to have worked – the Trump administration did not pursue a kinetic response despite heavy political pressure to do so.

Notes

1 Mikael Weissmann, 'Hybrid Warfare and Hybrid Threats Today and Tomorrow: Towards an Analytical Framework', *Journal on Baltic Security* 5, no. 1 (2019): 17–26.
2 See Weissmann, 'Hybrid Warfare and Hybrid Threats', 22–5.
3 This conceptual span is also analysed in Iran, see Q. Qorbanzadeh Savar, H. Nateqi and S. Hosseini Koohkamary, 'Hybrid War: Postmodern Anarchic War', *Quarterly of Passive Defense & Security* 6, no. 22 (2018) [in Persian].
4 It is also clear that as Western societies have become less violence prone internally the phenomenon of violence and war has receded in the general sociological analysis, even to the point of underplaying how central it was to the early-twentieth-century thinkers that defined the field. For a brief summary of this see Siniša Malešević, *The Sociology of War and Violence* (Cambridge: Cambridge University Press, 2012), chs. 1 and 2.
5 For an interesting analysis of Washington DC epistemological myopia on Iran see Negar Razavi, 'The Systemic Problem of "Iran Expertise" in Washington', *Jadaliyya*, 4 September 2019. https://www.jadaliyya.com/Details/39946?fbclid=IwAR2RweuJ8Ry -XCwFIuNeyu-zPBqds8eIo5xIMB8kw7Blg2NExo8tW8ixbOo
6 Muhammad Sahimi, 'Who Supports Jundallah?', *Tehranbureau, PBS Frontline*, 22 October 2009. https://www.pbs.org/wgbh/pages/frontline/tehranbureau/2009/1 0/jundallah.html. For a different theory on the alleged US support to Jundullah, see Mark Perry, 'False Flag: A Series of CIA Memos Describes How Israeli Mossad agents Posed as American Spies to Recruit Members of the Terrorist Organization Jundallah to Fight their Covert War against Iran', *Foreign Policy*, 13 January 2012. https://foreign policy.com/2012/01/13/false-flag/
7 For an article arguing that Saudi Arabia is employing hybrid warfare against Iran see Naser Pourhassan, 'Saudi Hybrid Warfare Components against the Islamic Republic, 2015–2017', *Contemporary Political Queries* 8, no. 4 (Winter 2017) [in Persian].
8 For a quick introduction on the nuances of realism and the sub-schools of offensive and defensive realism see John Mearsheimer, *The Tragedy of Great Power Politics* (New York: W.W. Norton Company, 2001).
9 Kayhan Barzegar and Masoud Rezaei, 'Ayatollah Khamenei's Strategic Thinking', *Discourse: An Iranian Quarterly* 11, no. 3 (Winter 2017): 27–54. For a similar, more recent, assessment see Hadi Ajili and Mahsa Rouhi, 'Iran's Military Strategy', *Survival* 61, no. 6 (2019): 139–52.

10 See also Robert Czulda, 'The Defensive Dimension of Iran's Military Doctrine: How Would they Fight?', *Middle East Policy* XXIII, no. 1 (Spring 2016): 92–109.

11 See Czulda, 'The Defensive Dimension', 5, quoting interview with Brigadier General Ahmed Reza Pourdastan, Commander of the regular military's land forces in 2013.

12 For Lebanon see Joseph Daher, *Hezbollah – the Political Economy of Lebanon's Party of God* (London: Pluto Press, 2016) and Augustus R. Norton, *Hezbollah: A Short History* (Princeton: Princeton University Press, 2007). On the dynamics in Yemen and Iran's role see Thomas Juneau, 'Iran's Policy towards the Houthis in Yemen: A Limited Return on a Modest Investment', *International Affairs* 92, no. 3 (2016): 647–63; and Marieke Brandt, *Tribes and Politics in Yemen: A History of the Houthi Conflict* (New York: Oxford University Press, 2017).

13 Rouzbeh Parsi, 'The US Withdrawal from the JCPOA and the Politics of Iranian Regional Engagement', in *One Year after the Re-imposition of Sanctions: Perspectives on the Strategic Implications of the US »maximum pressure« Campaign against Iran*, eds Achim Vogt and David Jalilvand (Friedrich Ebert Stiftung Analysis, November 2019). http://library.fes.de/pdf-files/iez/15761.pdf.

14 O. Al-Nidawi, 'The Growing Economic and Political Role of Iraq's PMF', Middle East Institute, 21 May 2019. https://www.mei.edu/publications/growing-economic-and-p olitical-role-iraqs-pmf.

15 For an overview of the political challenges see R. Mansour, 'Challenges to the Post-2003 Political Order in Iraq', UI Paper no. 8, 2019. https://www.ui.se/globalassets/ui.se -eng/publications/ui-publications/2019/ui-paper-no.-8-2019.pdf.

16 R. Alaaldin, 'What Will Happen to Iraqi Shiite Militias after One Key Leader's Death?', Brookings Institute, 3 March 2020. https://www.brookings.edu/blog/order-from-cha os/2020/03/03/what-will-happen-to-iraqi-shiite-militias-after-one-key-leaders-de ath/, and R. Mansour, 'In Life and Death, Iraq's Hisham al-Hashimi', *The World Today*, Chatham House, June–July 2020. https://www.chathamhouse.org/publications/twt/life -and-death-iraq-s-hisham-al-hashimi.

17 Czulda, 'The Defensive Dimension', 95. For an overview of the Iranian military development and the Revolutionary Guards in particulars see: Afshon Ostovar, *Vanguard of the Imam. Religion, Politics, and Iran's Revolutionary Guards* (New York: Oxford University Press, 2016); Hesam Forozan, *The Military in Post-revolutionary Iran: The Evolution and Roles of the Revolutionary Guards* (New York: Routledge, 2016).

18 On the specifics of the capabilities and arms utilized in this strategy, see Defence Intelligence Agency, *Iran Military Power: Ensuring Regime Survival and Securing Regional Dominance* (DIA, 2019), esp. 32–3.

19 Davoud Azar, 'Explanation and Analysis of Factors and Indices of the Combat Power of the Iranian Military in Hybrid Warfare', *Quarterly Journal for Military Sciences and Arts* 12, no. 37 (2016). [in Persian]

20 On the composition of the various military units Tehran has created and/or supported in Syria see Ali Alfoneh, *Tehran's Shia Foreign Legions* (Carnegie Endowment for International Peace, 30 January 2018). For an exhaustive analysis of various aspects of Iran's role in the conflict, see Aniseh Bassiri Tabrizi and Raffaello Pantucci, eds, *Understanding Iran's Role in the Syrian Conflict* (RUSI Occasional Paper, August 2016).

16

Information influencing in the Catalan illegal referendum and beyond

Rubén Arcos

Introduction[1]

Intrinsic to the challenge presented by hybrid threats and hybrid warfare is the conscious amplification of political or other divisions already present in targeted societies. The Catalonian issue illustrates how existing vulnerabilities in social cohesion can be exploited though disinformation/misinformation activities; it constitutes a divisive internal political issue that can be utilized by hybrid actors for different aims. These kinds of political issues, highly polarized and that divide societies, can be exploited by external actors in information influencing campaigns, targeting either foreign or domestic audiences. Those issues might be utilized for legitimizing political decisions and actions in the domestic arena, or for conveying distorted representations of foreign political systems and societies for different reasons, including weakening the internal cohesion of those targeted societies or transnational political networks. At the same time, domestic actors can also engage in influence activities, in both legitimate and illegitimate ways, through strategic communication campaigns aiming to manage the perceptions of foreign audiences and produce cognitive, affective and behavioural impacts in domestic stakeholders.

However, conducting post-event analyses of political disinformation campaigns is a difficult endeavour for academics for many reasons: monitoring and gathering data from social media platforms as events unfold usually requires professional social intelligence tools; accounts violating policies of social media platforms may be deleted, data protection regulations prevent the access to data that may identify the perpetrators.[2]

The Spanish Constitutional Court (TC) suspended on 7 September 2017,[3] the Catalan Parliament Law 19/2017, of 6 September, of 'the referendum of self-determination' that called Catalan citizens to a binding referendum to be held on 1 October 2017 with the question 'Do you want Catalonia to be an independent state in the form of a republic?'[4] The Constitutional Court warned of 'the duty to prevent or paralyze any initiative that involves ignoring or avoiding the agreed suspension', and particularly to refrain from initiating actions allowing the preparations and effective holding of such a referendum. The TC warned as well of the possible criminal consequences in case of non-compliance.[5] On 17 October the Constitutional Court sentenced that the Law 19/2017 was illegal and declared its nullity.[6]

Given that the holding of the referendum of 1 October 2017 was against the rule of law, it seems more appropriate here to speak about allegations of external/foreign political meddling than of allegations of foreign electoral interference. Those allegations pointing out to Russia constitute in itself today a controversial issue in Spain. Some of the domestic pro-independence actors were proactively seeking to influence attitudes and behaviours of foreign governments and institutions through strategic communication activities and actions. Generating public expressions of sympathy from abroad to the cause was obviously one of the objectives and consequently domestic actors used communication tactics to that aim. Even if hybrid actors played a role with uncertain effects, much of the information and influence flows can be characterized as well as inside-inside and as inside-out. The Spanish non-profit fact-checking organization Maldita.es has collected cases of disinformation from those days unfavourable to independentism as well.[7] According to Arcos, 'the evolution of events responded to pre-existing internal logics in which the dissemination of inaccurate, biased, purposely deceitful, or partial information, either by external or internal actors, has had the effect of reinforcing pre-existing biased beliefs and attitudes, igniting existing tensions, causing confusion in international audiences, and obstructing the development of a prudent democratic debate.'[8]

This chapter examines information influencing activities and allegations of foreign political meddling in Catalonia associated to the Catalonian illegal referendum of 1 October 2017, as well as developments after 14 October 2019 decision of the Supreme Court of Spain, that sentenced twelve Catalan independentist leaders. First, the allegations of a malign influence operation orchestrated by the Kremlin are examined. The chapter considers agenda-setting, framing and amplification in social media channels as means by which news outlets and communication content can influence the perceptions of individuals about public issues, paying particular attention to the activity of RT and Sputnik, as well as the content produced by Julian Assange and WikiLeaks in support of the independence process. Internet usage data and the new digital media landscape in Spain are also examined in order to acquire a perspective on the potential impact associated to the exposure of publics to contents disseminated by pro-Kremlin digital outlets. Second, the communication and influence activities of domestic pro-independentism players are examined, as well those campaigns conducted by hacktivist group Anonymous. Finally, the chapter addresses the events and developments after 14 October 2019 decision of the Supreme Court of Spain, in particular the conduction of violent actions, disinformation activities and the dissemination of conspiracy theories by different actors.

Allegations of external meddling

On 23 September 2017, the Spanish daily newspaper *El País* published a piece called '*La propaganda rusa sacude el "procés"*', later translated into English as 'Russian meddling machine sets sights on Catalonia' claiming that

The network of fake-news producers that Russia has employed to weaken the United States and the European Union is now operating at full speed on Catalonia, according to detailed analyses of pro-Kremlin websites and social media profiles by this newspaper.[9]

The article, signed by David Alandete, deputy editor by the time, went on stating that

the Kremlin is using the Catalan crisis as a way to deepen divisions within Europe and consolidate its international influence. It appears in the form of websites that publish hoax stories, the activity of activists such as WikiLeaks founder Julian Assange and a legion of bots – millions of automated social media accounts that can turn lies into trending topics.[10, 11]

Articles published by *El País* have also been referenced in the Democrats' report titled 'Putin's asymmetric assault on democracy in Russia and Europe: implications for U.S national security' prepared for the Senate's Committee on Foreign Relations.[12] This January 2018 Minority Staff report quoted a Department of State's report, according to which

Russian state news outlets, such as Sputnik, published a number of articles in the run up to the poll that highlighted alleged corruption within the Spanish government and driving an overarching anti-EU narrative in support of the secessionist movement. These Russian news agencies, as well as Russian users on Twitter, also repeatedly promoted the views of Julian Assange, the founder of WikiLeaks, who has taken to social media to call for Spanish authorities to respect the upcoming vote in Catalonia.

Spanish newspapers have also reported that Russian bots attempted to flood social media with controversial posts in support of Catalonian independence prior to the referendum.[13]

On the likely motives for an alleged malign influence operation there have been different hypotheses, including among others the following: weakening the EU, a sort of vengeance against Europe for the Kosovo issue (although Spain did not recognize the independence of Kosovo), the geopolitical/geostrategic interest of this Mediterranean region and the legitimization of the secessionist Crimean referendum. However, and not surprisingly since denial is a repeated pattern that can be observed in statements from the Kremlin in the face of similar allegations of interference, the official position of the Russian Federation on the *procés* is that 'there is a national legislation and there are some international commitments, and we assume that the internal processes of Spain must be based on these principles'.[14] As reported by EFE, in a June 2019 meeting with the main world news agencies representatives held in San Petersburg, Vladimir Putin declared: 'We have an attitude of utmost respect for Spain, the Spanish people, Spanish history. We have good relations, with historical roots. We are not at all interested in having European countries dismember one after another [. . .] Above all, we pronounce for stability, for the preservation of territorial integrity'.[15] These official public statements challenge the allegations of Russian interference with the obvious effect of producing confusion around the issue. A paper by the Integrative Initiative suggested a route to escape from this sort of 'dead-end street':

> Real leverage over Madrid is precisely what the Kremlin seems to be looking for [. . .] By supporting both sides, Russia is putting itself in a position to try to prevent the Catalan independence crisis moving in an undesirable direction or getting completely out of Moscow's control [. . .] Russia is establishing leverage over both sides; proving it can create/exacerbate problems for both sides too [. . .] It is difficult for either side to deal with this even if they are aware of the manipulation/reflexive control going on. What non-specialists might see as a dichotomy/contradiction (does the Kremlin want to see Catalan independence or not?) is no contradiction at all. All Putin's statements fit if you understand the Russian approach.[16]

An unclassified May 2018 report by the Spanish National Cryptologic Centre (CCN) asserted that 'the presence of activists sponsored by Russian institutions seems to be proven in the media coverage of the conflict in Catalonia during 2017'.[17] However, no additional supporting evidence was provided for this statement in the report. This lack of stronger supporting evidence added to the repeated Kremlin denials of interference in the Catalan crisis, might create a perennial sense of confusion or risks to become a polarizing issue in itself. On 19 December 2017, several witnesses from Spain participated in the fake news inquiry of the Digital, Culture, Media and Sport Committee of the UK Parliament: David Alandete, Francisco de Borja Lasheras and Mira Milosevich-Juaristi.[18] When questioned by the committee member Ian C. Lucas (Labour) about 'evidence that the Russian Government is seeking to interfere with the referendum in Catalonia', David Alandete declared that 'the only evidence that I have as a journalist is that Russian state-affiliated TV organizations have been openly spreading propaganda that benefits those who want independence in Catalonia'.[19]

More recently, El País unveiled that Spain's Audiencia Nacional did open an investigation into the alleged activities of GRU's Unit 29155 in Catalonia 'during the 2017 Catalan breakaway bid'.[20]

> This is not the first time that Russia and its spies have been suspected of influencing the Catalan independence movement. In February, the investigative website Bellingcat published several official documents from the Russian secret service that placed a GRU official named Denis Sergeev in Barcelona on two occasions. Both times, he had traveled under the false name Sergey Fedotov.
>
> On the first trip, Fedotov arrived in the Catalan capital on November 5, 2016, and after spending six days in Spain, returned to Moscow via Zurich. The second trip took place almost a year later on September 29, 2017, just two days before the illegal independence referendum on October 1. On that occasion, the Russian official stayed in Spain until October 9, when he returned to Moscow via Geneva.[21]

One of the effects of targeted disinformation against societies, as part of hybrid threats, as already pointed out in the introduction, is the amplification of political or other existing divisions (evident or latent). The Catalonian issue is obviously an existing cleavage. The surge of far-right political parties in Spain and other more extreme right-wing elements has been driven, at least partially, by tensions and developments in Catalonia.[22]

Issue salience and framing

Agenda-setting and framing explain ways in which news media and communication content can influence the perceptions of individuals about public issues.

According to McCombs, 'through their day-by-day selection and display of the news, editors and news directors focus our attention and influence our perceptions of what are the most important issues of the day. This ability to influence the salience of topics on the public agenda has come to be called the agenda-setting role of the news media.'[23] The daily repetition of the topic issue 'is the most powerful message of all about its importance'.[24] That is to say, news media can potentially influence public opinion by increasing the salience of the issue on the public agenda.[25] This influence is conditioned by the existence or absence of experience that citizens have on the topic issue, being greatest in the case of 'unobtrusive issues' where the public has not direct experience (i.e. foreign policy issues).[26] In the words of Bernard D. Cohen,

> the press is significantly more than a purveyor of information and opinion. It may not be successful much of the time in telling people what to think, but is stunningly successful in telling its readers what to think about. And it follows from this that the world looks different to different people, depending not only on their personal interests, but also on the map that is drawn for them by the writers, editors, and publishers of the papers they read.[27]

On the other hand, frames 'shape what others think of an issue' and the understanding and discussion of the world around us.[28] As defined by Entman,

> To frame is to select some aspects of a perceived reality and make them more salient in a communicating text, in such a way as to promote a particular problem definition, causal interpretation, moral evaluation, and/or treatment recommendation for the item described. Typically frames diagnose, evaluate, and prescribe.[29]

In their comparative study on dissemination of news related to the *procés*, in the period 1 September 2017 to 31 December 2017, through the Facebook post of RT in Spanish, Deutsche Welle, and BBC World, López-Olano and Fenoll found that RT published 236 posts with a coverage closer to Catalan independentism.[30]

An example of this activity is a Facebook post on 28 October 2017, stating 'Civil war in Spain ahoy?' (*Guerra civil en España a la vista?*) linking to a news article in the RT in Spanish portal with the misleading headline: '*Tanques en las calles de Barcelona*': *España y Cataluña al borde de un desenlace violento* ('Tanks in the Street of Barcelona': Spain and Catalonia on the verge of a violent outcome).[31] The article brings to the headline, of what apparently seems to be for the reader a news story, an opinionated quote from a commentator that is included at the end of the full piece stating: 'The analyst says that Spain and Catalonia are clearly heading towards a conflict. To avoid 'tanks in the streets of Barcelona', both sides must step back, he emphasizes.' By sampling the full sentence and bringing its most impactful part (tanks in the street of Barcelona) to the headline, the opinionated original meaning has completely changed. Moreover, by presenting this strong statement in the headline of a news story, even with quotation marks, the reader receives the impression that it is a description of an ongoing situation, especially if the reader came to the story after reading in post 'Civil war in Spain ahoy?'. It could be said that this is a clear example of combustible material for the fire.

The journalist Enric Juliana, in an article published on 1 November 2017 in the newspaper *La Vanguardia*, commented on another example from RT in Spanish, whose misleading headline was 'The new map of Europe. Who supports the independence of Catalonia?' presenting a map of different European countries (Denmark, Switzerland, Norway, Finland, Sweden, Latvia, Lithuania, Estonia, UK, Ireland, Belgium and Slovenia) from which some degree of support (i.e. unofficial statements by some politicians, Parliaments receiving the Catalan government). The RT article was suggesting to the readership that those countries were supporting the Catalan unilateral declaration of independence when the reality was that not a single country in Europe did recognize the 'Catalan Republic' (Juliana 2017).[32] RT later (15 November 2017) published a modified version of the original article with a different headline 'What support has received the Catalan government in Europe?' and added a disclaimer: 'The owner of this news in his first writing was inaccurate so it has been modified. We apologize to our readers for this error. Every day we keep trying because failures like this don't happen again, thanks for your understanding.'[33] The Twitter account of RT still shows the original headline.[34]

Del Fresno and Manfredi (2018) analysed the content produced by Julian Assange and WikiLeaks in support of the independence process in the period 25 September to 15 November, finding that Assange adhered 'to the narrative and pro-independence worldview, equating it with all of Catalonia and ignoring the existence of the other half of society, which is also Catalan and not pro-independent' and that constructed 'the perception of Spain as a dictatorship or non-democratic state'.[35]

Amplification through bots and fake accounts

On 27 March 2018, an article on 'How Twitter Bots Help Fuel Political Feuds' published in the *Scientific American* referenced the joint research conducted by researchers at Fondazione Bruno Kessler in Italy and at the University of Southern California, on the use of social bots related to the Catalonian referendum. The authors identified two polarized factions of Twitter users as Independentist and Constitutionalist and quantified 'the structural and emotional roles played by social bots'.[36] According to their findings:

Our results demonstrate that bots sustain each faction from the periphery of the online social network structure by mainly targeting human influencers. Bots tend to target human Independentists with messages evoking negative sentiments and associating hashtags with negative connotations. Importantly, we show that bots provide semantic associations, in messages directed to the Independentists, that inspire fight, violence, and shame against the government and the police. In addition to promoting target-specific content generated by human hubs, social bots achieved social contagion also by fabricating automated content within specific communities of humans.[37]

The researchers conducted the following collection strategy:

we manually selected a set of hashtags and keywords to collect messages (tweets) posted to a microblogging platform (Twitter). The list contains various general Catalan issue-related terms: #Catalunya, #Catalonia, #Catalogna, #1Oct, #votarem, #referendum, #1O. We monitored the Twitter stream and collected data by using the Twitter Search API, from September 22, 2017 to past the election day, on October 3, 2017: this allowed us to almost uninterruptedly collect all tweets containing any of the search terms. The data collection infrastructure ran inside FBK servers to ensure resilience and scalability. We chose to use the Twitter Search API (https://dev.twitter.com/rest/public/search) to make sure that we obtained all tweets that contain the search terms of interest posted during the data collection period, rather than a sample of unfiltered tweets: this precaution avoids incurring in known sampling issues related to collecting data using the Twitter Stream API (https://dev.twitter.com/streaming/overview) rather than the Twitter Search API.

This procedure yielded a large dataset containing approximately 3.6 million unique tweets, posted by 523 thousand unique users.[38]

However, neither the research paper nor the supporting material mentions links of bots to Russia or to any state-sponsored operation.

On 14 December 2017, Janis Sarts, Director of the NATO STRATCOM Centre of Excellence, spoke before the Spanish Mixed Commission on National Security.[39] Sarts pointed out that for the majority of governments the key area was defending elections from external interferences (using massive disinformation campaigns and amplification through the use of botnets in the cyberspace). Regarding Catalonia, according to the news agency Europa Press, Sarts explained that the Centre did not monitor the situation in Spain, but that from a certain moment, botnets that spread pro-Russian narratives on the internet began to tweet about Catalonia.[40]

On June 2019, Twitter make a disclosure of 'Information operations on Twitter' in its blog informing on the suspension of fake accounts in Spain linked to pro-secessionist political parties:

Earlier this year, we suspended 130 fake accounts originating in Spain. These accounts were directly associated with the Catalan independence movement, specifically Esquerra Republicana de Catalunya. They were primarily engaged in spreading content about the Catalan Referendum. The network includes fake accounts which appear to have been created with the intent to inorganically influence the conversation in politically advantageous ways. Setting up fake accounts is a violation of the Twitter Rules, full stop.[41]

Disinformation messages and malicious narratives can be further amplified through botnets and fake personas, creating a false impression of veracity in audiences exposed to those contents. However, as explained elsewhere,[42] neither the dissemination of correct information and sound judgements, nor the propagation of fake news and biased opinions for influence purposes, guaranteed that targeted publics are exposed to them. The more people watching a TV programme or following a specific Twitter account, the more people are likely to be exposed to persuasive messages. Similarly, the exposure of target audiences to persuasive communications does not guarantee an effective influence on attitudes and behaviour. From a processual perspective, to be influenced the recipients of persuasive communications 'must make the preliminary responses of paying attention to the message, comprehending its contents, accepting the conclusions advocated, and rehearsing this acceptance sufficiently to permit later expression of the induced change'.[43]

Social networks and digital media ecosystem

According to IAB Spain's Annual Social Networks Study (IAB Spain 2019), in Spain an 85 per cent of internet users (between sixteen and sixty-five years) use social media networks, representing a total amount of 25.5 million users, being WhatsApp (88 per cent) and Facebook (87 per cent) the networks with greater penetration among users, followed by YouTube (68 per cent), Instagram (54 per cent), and Twitter (50 per cent) as the top 5 social media. Spain is a top 10 Twitter market (ninth) with 8.3 million active users on Twitter, as of April 2018 (Statista 2018).[44]

The number of digital news media in Spain has experienced an important growth, from 1,274 digital media identified in 2005 to 3,431 in March 2018.[45] According to Salaverría et al., 3,202 were active by 31 May 2018 (1,229 of which are news media born digital), with Madrid and Catalonia being the regions with a higher number of digital news media.[46] The existence of co-official languages in specific regions like Catalonia, Valencia, Galicia and the Basque Country seems to be a factor driving the growth of digital news media.[47] A total of 1,334 of the above-mentioned 3,202 active digital news media only used the internet for the dissemination of content, while a majority of 58.3 per cent combine this with other platforms for the dissemination of content, more specifically, digital media with radio broadcasting (n = 872), with printed media (n = 795), television (n = 238) and with apps (n = 444).[48]

According to the information from the internet portal of RT in Spanish, the state-funded Russian TV channel in Spanish started broadcasting from Moscow in December 2009 and has an audience of eighteen million people that see RT every week in ten countries in Latin America. The signal is available in Spain and the United

States as well. Regarding the internet portal, 'RT in Spanish is at the top among the international informative web pages' and 'according to data from SimilarWeb, for several consecutive months the Spanish version of RT exceeded in visits to the Spanish portals of BBC, CNN, Euronews, France 24 and the Latin American channel TeleSur'.[49]

The Facebook page of RT in Spanish has 7.5 million followers while RT Play in Spanish has 3.3 million followers. The YouTube channel has 2.84 million subscribers and RT live has 103,000 followers. The Twitter account @ActualidadRT has 3.13 million followers.

On the other hand, Sputnik Mundo, the Spanish version of the other main state-funded platform, is followed on Twitter by 101,048 accounts (October 2019), and it has 379,000 followers on Facebook. A search in the Sputnik Mundo portal with the keyword 'Cataluña' provides a considerable number of results (n = 1.426) for the period 1 September to 21 December 2017, given an idea of the salience of the issue in this digital news outlet.

Key non-state independentist players and Catalonian public diplomacy organizations

In his work on the Catalan independentist process, the historian Jordi Canal highlights the key role played in the *procés* by 'parainstitutional' organizations like the Catalan National Assembly (ANC) and Òmnium Cultural (Canal 2018: 169–77).

ANC declares itself to be 'a strictly non-partisan civil organization' that 'does not receive any governmental funding'.[50] According to its by-laws, ANC

a) Promotes the creation of the political and social conditions necessary for the achievement and constitution of the independent Catalan state of right, social and democratic.
b) Brings together all the people that work with objectives similar to those of the Catalan National Assembly, either from all kinds of groups, entities, movements, political parties, or individually.[51]

In their website, they provide an essentials section in which visitors can download logos, digital postcards, posters and other communication products to be used in grassroots campaigns.[52]

Carme Forcadell was a former president of ANC and she later became president of the Catalonian Parliament in 2015.

On the other hand, Òmnium Cultural, with over 125,000 members, declared itself to have 'worked for over fifty years as a civil society agency to promote the Catalan language and culture and also to disseminate Catalonia's will for freedom. In recent years one of Òmnium's aims has been to assist Catalonia in its quest to become a new independent state'.[53] According to the information published by the digital newspaper El Confidencial, these organizations have been receiving public funding by the Catalonian government,

Between 2008 and 2010 it received one and a half million euros in aids. In 2006, it received 661,000 euros for the acquisition of its headquarters in Barcelona [. . .] That same year it received 1.1 million euros. Between 2011 and 2013, with Artur Mas as head of the presidency, he would also have obtained public aid of almost one and a half million euros. During those years and until the appointment of Cuixart, the deputy and activist Muriel Casals was in charge of the association (2010–2015). One of its most important partners is the Barcelona coach, Pep Guardiola, who has already released his three sons.[54]

The Public Diplomacy Council of Catalonia, DIPLOCAT, was a public-private consortium aimed at promoting 'initiatives which allow for a direct knowledge of Catalonia in the international field'

> The PCM – DIPLOCAT has to contribute to this objective furthering the image, reputation, and international promotion of Catalonia via the exporting of the best knowledge of the reality of the country and its unique assets and values, so as to aid the internationalization of Catalonia. Fulfilling this objective offers direct repercussions such as an increased attraction of investments, knowledge, institutions, and people, and contributes to generating positive public opinion abroad and establishing relations of trust with the rest of the world.[55]

The Spanish government closed the DIPLOCAT, as part of the measures adopted after the application of article 155 of the Spanish Constitution. According to a report released by Spain's Court of Auditors on the economic resources for foreign relations activities by the Catalan Autonomous Community fiscal years (2011–2017), from the analysis of the activities carried out by DIPLOCAT between 2013 and 2017, it is observed that 558 activities out of 751 were aimed at publicizing, promoting and fostering the *procés*.[56] DIPLOCAT received over EUR 12 million from public funds.
According to the Professor of Political Sciences Joan Antón,

> the secessionist communicative strategy has been a success because it has counted on the autonomic means of communication, fundamentally TV3 and Catalunya Radio, and because its communicative offer had an enthusiastic and growing social demand. At the same time, the political errors of the central government (not recognizing the problem, belittling, disproportionate repression) have multiplied the problem and given credibility to the independence story.[57]

Hacktivism and #OpCatalunya

The Spanish Department of Homeland Security (DSN) warned on 20 October 2017 that 'the hacktivist group Anonymous, through associated twitter accounts, is announcing a massive cyberattack campaign for tomorrow day 21 under the name of "#OpCatalunya" and "#FreeCatalunya". The last weeks, state pages have received different cyberattacks under these same slogans'.[58] On 21 October the website of the Constitutional Court and other services experienced a denial of service attack.[59] The different DDoS attacks were headed by the release of an Anonymous video on 24 September.[60]

National security strategy and legislative action

On 1 December 2017, the Spanish government approved the new National Security Strategy 2017. The document states:

> To a large extent, technology has given pride of place to connectivity, to the detriment of security. Acts such as the theft, use, and dissemination of information and sensitive data, and hostile actions that include disinformation activities and interference in electoral processes represent a huge challenge today, for both governments and citizens.[61]

The Strategy includes as well references to hybrid influencing and disinformation:

> Traditional armed conflicts are being compounded by additional forms of aggression and influence, threats associated with the proliferation of weapons of mass destruction, and other forms of hostile acts. Sophisticated high-precision systems are combined with the functional fatality of cyberattacks, influence campaigns and acts of disinformation. Ambiguity and the difficulty of attribution are constant factors of what are known as hybrid conflicts: those that incorporate operations combining information, subversion, economic and financial pressure and military actions. These actions, perpetrated both by State actors and by non-State actors, aim to mobilize public opinion and create political destabilization.[62]

Similarly, the 2019 National Cybersecurity Strategy affirms that 'cyberspace should be considered as a strategic communication vector that can be used to influence public opinion and how people think by manipulating information, disinformation campaigns or hybrid actions'.[63]

Operation Judas

On 23 September 2019, Guardia Civil arrested nine people in the province of Barcelona within the framework of a police investigation led by the National Court 'aimed at clarifying alleged criminal activities planned by members of the CDR' resulting in the seize of precursors susceptible to be used in the manufacture of explosive artefacts.[64]

According to news reports, the Prosecutor's Office of the National Court considered that they formed 'a terrorist group of a Catalan secessionist nature' and attributed them 'crimes of terrorism and/or rebellion'.[65] A lieutenant prosecutor's note, that was leaked to the media, asserted that

> given the certainty that the actions were to be carried out taking advantage of the period between the anniversary of the illegal 1st of October referendum and the publication of the [Supreme Court] decision on the procés judgement, it was decided to proceed to the arrest of those involved to abort the project that could have caused irreparable damage due to the progress of their preparations.[66]

According to later news reports by El País, two of the members alleged to belong to a violent branch of the CDR (Committees for the Defense of the Republic[67]) 'have confessed to making explosives and testing them', and quoting 'sources from the investigation', explained that 'the officers have video recordings that show some of the detainees testing the explosives, as well as testimony from witnesses who recognized several group members who purchased chemical substances that can be used to make explosives'.[68]

This obviously represents an important radicalization step forward within a part of the whole secessionist movement.

14 October 2019

On 13 October 2019 the Twitter account @YourAnonXelj published a video on Twitter together with the following message: '#Anonymous message for the Spanish state and the world. Tomorrow the #OpCatalonia2019 will officially begin. We are anonymous. We are one'.[69] The English Tweet was preceded by a similar previous Tweet in Spanish published at 2.46 pm 'Mensaje de #Anonymous para el estado español y el mundo. Mañana se iniciará oficialmente la #OpCatalonia2019. We are anonymous. We are one'.[70] This tweet was followed by another one on 14 October 2019 by the account @Spanglish__Tea:

> #OpCatalonia2019 #OpCatalonia #Catalonia #GlobalRevolution #Anonymous
> #AnonFamily #AnonymousUnited #WeAreLegion #WeAreNation #WeDecided
> No me van a callar, esto no es suficiente!!!
> They can't shut us down, that's not enough!!!
> Visca Catalunya!!! Viva Catalonia!!!

Powering up political influencing and civil disobedience with the means of the digital era

The events following the 14 October 2019 decision of the Supreme Court of Spain, regarding the Catalonian illegal referendum of 1 October 2017 and the subsequent unilateral declaration of independence, that sentenced twelve Catalan independentist leaders for offenses of sedition, misuse of public funds, or disobedience, illustrate how cyber and digital communication tools can be used to challenge the domestic status quo, support the disruption of the public order and create urban chaos, and influence events for political purposes.

The website of Tsunami Democràtic was used to provide access to an app claiming to be 'a platform for the coordination of peaceful actions of civil disobedience', as well as access to communication materials to be used in those actions, and provided legal advice to individuals intending to participate in the protest through a 'Guia bàsica de consells legals'.[71, 72]

The URL was blocked 'by provision of the Judicial Authority' during the afternoon of 18 October 2019.[73] However, during a period it was still possible to access a similar content under the URL https://tsunamidemocratic.github.io.

The application of Tsunami Democràtic 'can only be used if someone in your trusted circle gives you a QR code. Once you have read the QR code with the app you will already be part of the Tsunami!'[74] The text of a humorous defying banner on the need for the QR code required to use the Tsunami D app stated 'Intelligence services here is the QR code'.[75] Moreover, the app did not require to disclose any personal data and claimed to grant anonymity.

Tsunami Democràtic made public call on 14 October to collapse the two major airports in Spain, the airport of El Prat and Madrid-Barajas. This resulted in over a hundred cancelled flight due to the impossibility of airline crews to access the airport.[76]

The Twitter account of the Chinese outlet China Daily published a propaganda, which is a thirty-six-second video on 15 October 2019 misleadingly comparing events in Hong Kong and Catalonia using several images of the El Prat Airport and the following text:

> On October 14, 9 Catalonia pro-independence leaders were sentenced between 9 and 13 years. In Barcelona, thousands of people protested on the streets, and some of them wore masks. Riot police responded and the two sides clashed. Protesters threw fire extinguishers and random objects at police. Police used batons to disperse demonstrators and fired rubber bullets. Separatism will not be tolerated in any countries. Separatism will face punishments. This is an alarm call to all Hong Kong rioters![77]

Of course, the opportunity presented by this piece of propaganda was seized and the tweet was later amplified by pro-independence influencers to discredit Spain as an authoritarian country.[78]

Disinformation narratives, conspiracy theories and violence

On 18 October 2019, during a press conference, the Minister of Interior, Fernando Grande-Marlaska, highlighted that

> The diffusion of narratives aimed at manipulating and polarizing the audience continues through the transmission and attribution of actions of violence

provocation to the State Forces and Security Corps (Mossos, Police, Guardia Civil) by the means of infiltrated individuals, different from the CDR, with supposed video and testimonial evidences [. . .] and massive re-diffusion of images from altercations with the pretention of smearing the reputation of police officers.[79]

An example of this disinformation activity attributing violent actions of provocation to infiltrated police officers within the so-called Committees for the Defense of the (un-existing Catalan) Republic has been analysed by the Spanish fact-checker Maldita .es.[80],[81]

Violent actions by insurgents during the first week of protest resulted in the injury of over 300 police officers; according to the Minister of Interior the riots on 18 October resulted in the injury of 101 police officers and damage of 264 vehicles.[82] According to Ignacio Cembrero, an estimated number of 4,500 activists participated in violent action against the police, of which 500 were from abroad.[83] The news agency Efe claimed that experts and police sources who were consulted 'have no doubt that leaders of ultra-left and European anarchist groups are actively participating in the riots of these days, with "extensive experience" in violent altercations in recent years in Greece, France, Germany or Italy'.[84]

The catalogue of violent actions included the launching of stones and other harmful objects like steel balls, Molotov cocktails, acid, firing barricades using trash containers and even the launch of a pyrotechnic rocket against a police helicopter.[85]

Paradoxically, one of the most visible political leaders of the independentist movement, ERC's Gabriel Rufián, was received in the demonstration of 19 October with shouts of 'botifler' (traitor) after he tweeted: 'Call to all groups, entities and people of peace to defend the legitimate right to protest and to reduce the tension of these days. Against the violence of baton and barricade, human barrier of civil society'.[86]

Commenting on the violent protest, the president of ANC, Elisenda Paluzie, stated that

the altercations and riots between protesters and police 'make the Catalan conflict visible', so that 'it is these incidents that make us present in the international press continuously' and 'make the conflict visible'.[87]

Conclusion

Information influencing and strategic communication in the context of the Catalan illegal referendum is a very complex issue involving many different actors. There are clear examples of 'pro-Kremlin disinformation' related to Catalonia identified by the East Stratcom Task Force, in addition to the examples covered in this chapter of misleading news stories and posts from state-funded Russian outlets. However, there are also important information gaps, including those related to the attribution of some activities reported by the media, that should prevent from extracting definitive conclusions.

The AMEC Integrated Evaluation Framework for measurement and evaluation, for example, clearly differentiates between outputs (i.e. reach, visitors, number of posts, tweets or retweets, readers), out-takes (response from target publics), outcomes (cognitive, attitude and behavioural effects) and overall impact of communication.[88] Exposure to tweets, post and misleading stories is not the same as outcomes or results.

Domestic pro-secessionist actors also developed a strong communication activity targeting foreign audiences and portraying secessionism as a fully peaceful movement. However, recent developments including violent protest and sabotage against railroads by some groups evidence that the movement is not uniform.

Actions aimed at blocking transport infrastructures and regular working routines are also part of a deliberate communication strategy aiming at keeping the *procés* salient in the agenda.

The highly polarizing nature of the issue constitutes a societal vulnerability that can be exploited in hybrid influencing operations by hostile foreign actors.

Notes

1   This chapter partially draws on previous research presented by the author as a research paper prepared for presentation at CATS intelligence workshop, 16–17 May 2018, Stockholm. It also draws partially on the authors' research published in the Hybrid CoE strategic analysis paper *Post-Event Analysis of the Hybrid Threat Security Environment: Assessment of Influence Communication Operations* (October 2018).
2   Franziska B. Keller, David Schoch, Sebastian Stier and JungHwan Yang, 'Political Astroturfing on Twitter: How to Coordinate a Disinformation Campaign', *Political Communication* 37, no. 2 (2019): 256–80. DOI: 10.1080/10584609.2019.1661888.
3   Spanish Constitutional Court, *Recurso de inconstitucionalidad n⁰ 4334-2017, contra la Ley del Parlamento de Cataluña 19/2017, de 6 de septiembre, del Referéndum de Autodeterminación*, 8 September 2017. https://www.boe.es/boe/dias/2017/09/08/pdfs/BOE-A-2017-10287.pdf.
4   Generalitat de Catalunya, *Ley 19/2017, de 6 de septiembre, del referèndum de autodeterminación*, 6 September 2017. https://portaldogc.gencat.cat/utilsEADOP/PDF/7449A/1633376.pdf.
5   Spanish Constitutional Court, *Recurso de inconstitucionalidad n⁰ 4334-2017*.
6   Spanish Constitutional Court, *STC 114/2017*, 17 October 2017. https://www.boe.es/buscar/doc.php?id=BOE-A-2017-12206
7   Maldita.es, 10 bulos sobre el 1-O: Cataluña, campo de batalla de la desinformación, 1 October 2018. https://maldita.es/malditobulo/10-bulos-sobre-el-1-o-cataluna-campo-de-batalla-de-la-desinformacion/
8   Rubén Arcos, *Post-event Analysis of the Hybrid Threat Security Environment: Assessment of Influence Communication Operations* (Hybrid CoE Strategic Analysis, October 2018), 5.
9   David Alandete, 'Russian Meddling Machine Sets Sights on Catalonia', *El País*, 28 September 2017. https://elpais.com/elpais/2017/09/26/inenglish/1506413477_994601.html.
10 Alandete, 'Russian Meddling Machine Sets Sights on Catalonia'.

11 An example of the activity of the account @JulianAssange is the following
    11 September 2017 tweet: 'If today is a guide on Oct 1 Europe will birth a new 7.5m
    nation or civil war. Front page news English media hide.' See: https://twitter.com/
    DefendAssange/status/907295818637606912.

12 U.S. Senate, Committee on Foreign Relations, *Putin's Asymmetric Assault on
    Democracy in Russia and Europe: Implications for U.S. National Security*, 10 January
    2018. https://www.foreign.senate.gov/imo/media/doc/FinalRR.pdf.

13 US Department of State, quoted in US Senate, Committee on Foreign Relations,
    Putin's Asymmetric Assault, 135.

14 Serguéi Lavrov, quoted in Marc Sarginedas, 'Rusia no reconocerá el referéndum
    unilateral catalán', *El Periódico*, 7 June 2016. https://www.elperiodico.com/es/politica/
    20170607/rusia-no-reconocera-referendum-catalan-independencia-6090182.

15 Vladimir Putin, quoted in EFE, 'Putin sobre Cataluña: "No queremos que se
    desmorone ningún Estado europeo"', 6 June 2019. https://www.efe.com/efe/espana/
    mundo/putin-sobre-cataluna-no-queremos-que-se-desmorone-ningun-estado-euro
    peo/10001-3994465.

16 The Integrity Initiative, *Framing Russian Meddling in the Catalan Question*, October
    2017. https://www.stopfake.org/en/framing-russian-meddling-in-the-catalan-qu
    estion/.

17 Translated by the author from the original in Spanish: 'parece demostrada la
    presencia de activistas patrocinados por instituciones rusas en la expresión
    mediática del conflicto derivado de la situación creada en Cataluña durante 2017,
    como consecuencia del alejamiento de la legalidad constitucional vigente de ciertas
    instituciones autonómicas catalanas.' National Cryptologic Centre, *Ciberamenazas y
    tendencias, Edición 2018* (May 2018): 10.
    https://www.ccn-cert.cni.es/informes/informes-ccn-cert-publicos/2835-ccn-cert-ia-09
    -18-ciberamenazas-y-tendencias-edicion-2018-1/file.html.

18 House of Commons, Digital, Culture and Sport Committee, *Oral Evidence: Fake News,
    HC 363*, 19 December 2017. http://data.parliament.uk/writtenevidence/committe
    eevidence.svc/evidencedocument/digital-culture-media-and-sport-committee/fake
    -news/oral/74926.html.

19 House of Commons, Digital, Culture and Sport Committee, *Oral Evidence: Fake News,
    HC 363*.

20 Óscar López-Fonseca and Fernando Pérez, 'Spain's High Court Opens Investigation
    into Russian Spying Unit in Catalonia', *El País*, 21 November 2019. https://english.elpa
    is.com/elpais/2019/11/21/inenglish/1574324886_989244.html.

21 López-Fonseca and Pérez, 'Spain's High Court Opens Investigation into Russian
    Spying Unit in Catalonia'.

22 It is worth mentioning that the ideas of Aleksander Dugin are being introduced
    in Spain through translations of his books by publishers in the sphere of far-right,
    together with works by Alain de Benoist among others.

23 Maxwell McCombs, *Setting the Agenda: The Mass Media and Public Opinion*
    (Cambridge: Polity Press, 2004), 1.

24 McCombs, *Setting the Agenda*, 2.

25 Maxwell McCombs, R. Lance Holbert, Spiro Kiousis and Wayne Wanta, *The News and
    Public Opinion: Media Effects on Civic Life* (Cambridge: Polity Press, 2015).

26 McCombs, Holbert, Kiousis and Wanta, *The News and Public Opinion*, 81.

27 Bernard C. Cohen, *The Press and Foreign Policy* (Princeton: Princeton University
    Press, 1965), 13.

28 James N. Druckman, 'Foreword', in *Doing News Framing Analysis: Empirical and Theoretical Perspectives*, eds Paul D'Angelo and Jim A. Kypers (New York: Routledge, 2010), xiv.

29 Robert M. Entman, 'Framing: Toward Clarification of a Fractured Paradigm', *Journal of Communication* 43, no. 4 (Autumn 1993): 52.

30 Carlos López-Olano and Vicente Fenoll, 'Posverdad, o la narración del procés catalán desde el exterior: BBC, DW y RT', *El profesional de la información* 28, no. 3 (May–June 2019): 11.

31 RT, '"Tanques en las calles de Barcelona": España y Cataluña al borde de un desenlace violento', Facebook, 28 October 2017. https://www.facebook.com/ActualidadRT/po sts/10156317026373273/ See also: RT, '"Tanques en las calles de Barcelona": España y Cataluña al borde de un desenlace violento', 28 October 2017. https://actualidad .rt.com/actualidad/253812-espana-cataluna-violencia-conflicto?fbclid=IwAR3CR3 HPTUslfGIYPbpx6nWtknNmiHV2woEGUo3LPyZZ23Q0dDct6g4eppg.

32 Enric Juliana, 'Los rusos', *La Vanguardia*, 1 November 2017. https://www.lavangua rdia.com/politica/20171101/432516055884/los-rusos.html.

33 RT, 'Qué apoyos ha recibido el gobierno catalán en Europa?', 11 October 2017. https:// actualidad.rt.com/actualidad/252564-nuevo-mapa-europa-apoyo-cataluna.

34 RT, (@ActualidadRT), 'El nuevo mapa de Europa: Quiénes apoyan la independencia de Cataluña?', *Twitter*, 11 October 2017. https://twitter.com/ActualidadRT/status/ 918176742119964672.

35 Miguel Del-Fresno-García and Juan-Luis Manfredi-Sánchez, 'Politics, Hackers and Partisan Networking. Misinformation, National Utility and Free Election in the Catalan Independence Movement', *El profesional de la información* 27, no. 6 (November–December 2018): 1230.

36 Massimo Stella and Emilio Ferrara and Manlio De Domenico, 'Bots Increase Exposure to Negative and Inflammatory Content in Online Social Systems', *Proceedings of the National Academy of Sciences* 115, no. 49 (December 2018): 12435.

37 Stella, Ferrara and De Domenico, 'Bots Increase Exposure to Negative and Inflammatory Content in Online Social Systems', 12439.

38 Stella, Ferrara and De Domenico, 'Bots Increase Exposure to Negative and Inflammatory Content in Online Social Systems'.

39 Congreso de los Diputados, 'Comisión Seguridad Nacional 12 – Janis Sarts, Director of the NATO STRATCOM Center of Excellence', *YouTube*, 1 January 2018. https://ww w.youtube.com/watch?v=nxfb6q3ig_w.

40 Europapress, 'Un centro de la OTAN detectó que "bots" que difundieron narrativas prorrusas tuitearon también sobre Cataluña', 14 December 2017. http://www.euro papress.es/nacional/noticia-centro-otan-detecto-bots-difundieron-narrativas-pror rusas-tuitearon-tambien-cataluna-20171214165935.html.

41 Yoel Roth (@yoyoel), 'Information Operations on Twitter: Principles, Process, and Disclosure', *Twitter*, 13 June 2019. https://blog.twitter.com/en_us/topics/company /2019/information-ops-on-twitter.html.

42 Arcos, *Post-event Analysis*.

43 William J. McGuire, 'Order of Presentation as a Factor in "conditioning" Persuasiveness', in *The Order of Presentation in Persuasion*, ed. Carl I. Hovland (New Haven and London: Yale University Press, 1966), 98–9.

44 See 'Leading Countries Based on Number of Twitter Users as of January 2020', *Statista*, accessed 16 September 2018. https://www.statista.com/statistics/242606/nu mber-of-active-twitter-users-in-selected-countries/.

45 See Ramón Salaverría, María del Pilar Martínez-Costa Pérez and James Breiner, 'Mapa de los cibermedios de España en 2018: análisis cuantitativo', *Revista Latina de Comunicación Social* 73 (2018): 1034–53.

46 Ramón Salaverría et al., 'El mapa de los cibermedios en España', in *Ecosistema de ciber medios en España: tipología, iniciativas, tendencias y desafíos*, eds Carlos Toural -Bran and Xosé Lopéz-García (Salamanca: Comunicación Social, 2019), 25–49.

47 Salaverría et al., 'El mapa de los cibermedios en España', 27.

48 Salaverría et al., 'El mapa de los cibermedios en España', 31.

49 See 'Quiénes somos', RT, accessed 8 April 2020. https://actualidad.rt.com/acerca/qu ienes_somos.

50 See 'Organisation', Assemblea Nacional Catalana, accessed 8 April 2020. https://as semblea.cat/index.php/organisation/?lang=en.

51 See Assemblea Nacional Catalana, *Estatus de L'Assemblea Nacional Catalana*, 10 March 2012. https://assemblea.cat/wp-content/plugins/download-attachments/inc ludes/download.php?id=714.

52 'Materials de les Campanyes', Assemblea Nacional Catalana, accessed 8 April 2020. https://assemblea.cat/index.php/materials/?lang=en.

53 Òmnium Cultural, https://www.omnium.cat/ca/.

54 El Confidencial, 'Así son la ANC y Òmnium: grandes soberanistas, opacas y con subvenciones', 15 July 2017. https://www.elconfidencial.com/espana/2017-07-15/o mnium-cultural-asamblea-nacional-catalana-entidades-independentistas_1414974/.

55 Public Diplomacy Council of Catalonia, *Statutes of Patronat Catalunya Món – Consell de Diplomàcia Pública de Catalunya*, accessed 8 April 2020. https://web.archive.org/w eb/20170928224150/http://www.diplocat.cat/en/about-us/statutes.

56 See: Tribunal de Cuentas, Oficina de Prensa, *El Tribunal de Cuentas aprueba el Informe de fiscalización relativa al destino dado a los recursos asignados a la ejecución de políticas de acción exterior de la Comunidad Autónoma de Cataluña, correspondientes a los ejercicios 2011-2017*, 2 April 2019. https://www.tcu.es/tribunal -de-cuentas/es/sala-de-prensa/noticias/El-Tribunal-de-Cuentas-aprueba-el-Informe -de-fiscalizacion-relativa-al-destino-dado-a-los-recursos-asignados-a-la-ejecucion-de -politicas-de-accion-exterior-de-la-Comunidad-Autonoma-de-Cataluna-correspondi entes-a-los-ejercicios-2011-2017/.

57 Joan Antón interviewed by author, 17 March 2018.

58 Translated by the author. See original note in Spanish at 'Seguridad Nacional – Última hora', Seguridad Nacional, 20 October 2017. https://www.dsn.gob.es/es/actualidad/seg uridad-nacional-ultima-hora?page=183, Last updated 26 February 2020.

59 El País, Anonymous ataca la página web del Tribunal Constitucional, 21 October 2017. https://elpais.com/politica/2017/10/21/actualidad/1508574710_898791.html.

60 'Anonymous Operation Free Catalonia', *YouTube*, 24 September 2017. https://www.you tube.com/watch?v=f4cAkfTYDrA.

61 Government of Spain, *National Security Strategy 2017* (1 December 2017), 34.

62 Government of Spain, *National Security Strategy 2017*, 57–8.

63 Government of Spain, *National Cybersecurity Strategy 2019* (1 April 2019), 15.

64 See press release: Guardia Civil, 'Noticia', 23 September 2019. http://www.guardiacivil .es/es/prensa/noticias/7123.html.

65 Ángeles Vázquez, Juan José Fernández, Antonio Baquero and Guillem Sànchez, 'Detenidos 9 miembros de los CDR acusados de querer atentar con explosivos', *El Periódico*, 24 September 2019. https://www.elperiodico.com/es/politica/20190923/r edada-guardia-civil-cdr-7647000.

66   Vázquez, Fernández, Baquero and Sànchez, 'Detenidos 9 miembros de los CDR acusados de querer atentar con explosivos'.

67   Independentist activist groups.

68   Óscar López-Fonseca and Fernando J. Pérezei, 'Two Catalan Separatists Confess to Making and Testing Explosives', *El País*, 26 September 2019. https://elpais.com/elpais /2019/09/26/inenglish/1569483015_617275.html?rel=mas.

69   Account @YourAnonXelj, '#Anonymous Message for the Spanish State and the World. Tomorrow the #OpCatalonia2019 Will Officially Begin. We Are Anonymous. We Are One', *Twitter*, 13 October 2019. https://twitter.com/YourAnonXelj/status/1183498913 636110336.

70   20 hours later the tweet had 2,3 K Retweets and 3,1 K Likes. See: 'Tweet Engagement Stats', *Twitter*, 13 October 2019. https://www.trendsmap.com/twitter/tweet/118336334 8714397696.

71   'Guia bàsica de consells legals', Tsunami Democràtic, accessed 18 October 2019. http:/ /tsunamidemocratic.cat/wp-content/uploads/2019/09/consells_legals.pdf.

72   #Tsunami Democràtic, https://tsunamidemocratic.cat/.

73   http://82.223.97.47.

74   Translation from the original text in Catalan. See: 'Descarrega't l'app del Tsunami Democràtic', Tsunami Democràtic, accessed 8 April 2020. https://tsunamidemocratic .github.io/app.html.

75   See the account @serfmar: 'per si us demanen el QR', Twitter, 18 October 2019. https:/ /twitter.com/serfmar/status/1185193256184897537.

76   Dani Cordero and Alfonso L. Congostrina, 'Las protestas independentistas colapsan el aeropuerto de Barcelona', *EL País*, 14 October 2019. https://elpais.com/ccaa/2019/10 /14/catalunya/1571042788_418131.html.

77   China Daily (@ChinaDaily), 'Separatism will not be Tolerated in Any Countries', Twitter, 15 October 2019. https://twitter.com/ChinaDaily/status/11841104274977382 40.

78   See for example the account @aleixsarri, 'La premsa oficial de la Xina pren com a exemple la resposta espanyola contra Catalunya per amenaçar Hong Kong. Queda clar, oi?', Twitter, 18 October 2019. https://twitter.com/aleixsarri/status/118504803227 6090881.

79   Translated by the author. See: La Moncloa (@desdelamoncloa), 'Rueda de prensa del ministro de @interiorgob, Fernando Grande-Marlaska, tras la reunión del Comité de Seguimiento de la situación en #Cataluña', 18 October 2019. https://twitter.com/desde lamoncloa/status/1185131577547902977.

80   Maldito Bulo (@malditobulo), 'Qué sabemos sobre las fotos de supuestos policías infiltrados que se harían pasar por "CDR quema contenedores"? Las imágenes son de 2011', Twitter, 18 October 2019. https://twitter.com/malditobulo/status/11850961970 41725441.

81   Maldita.es, 'Qué sabemos del vídeo en el que un hombre grita "¡Que soy compañero, coño!" a un grupo de policías? Fue grabado en 2012 en Madrid', 17 October 2019. https://maldita.es/maldito-bulo/que-sabemos-del-video-en-el-que-un-hombre-grita- que-soy-companero-cono-a-un-grupo-de-policias-fue-grabado-en-2012-en-madrid/.

82   Javier Munder, 'Gerard Melgar, Marifé Velasco, Carlos Garcés, Última hora en Barcelona: Los incidentes se extienden a la Rambla y los Mossos disparan proyectiles de foam', *El Mundo*, 20 October 2019. https://www.elmundo.es/cataluna/2019/10/19 /5daabddafc6c83927b8b45ae.html.

83   Ignacio Cembrero for the TV channel La Sexta, 19 October 2019.

84 Sagrario Ortega, 'El núcleo duro de los disturbios en Cataluña: 500 radicales con apoyo exterior', 19 October 2019. https://www.lavanguardia.com/internacional/20 191019/471058073263/el-nucleo-duro-de-los-disturbios-en-cataluna500-radicales-co n-apoyo-exterior.html.

85 See, e.g., El Periódico, 'Así lanzaron los manifestantes un cohete al helicóptero de Mossos', 16 October 2019. https://www.elperiodico.com/es/politica/20191016/cargas -mossos-conselleria-interior-barcelona-7686079.

86 Gabriel Rufián (@gabrielrufian), 'Ante las manifestaciones de hoy', *Twitter*, 19 October 2019. https://twitter.com/gabrielrufian/status/1185532934863949824.

87 Luis B. García, 'Paluzie sostiene que las imágenes violentas en Catalunya "hacen visible el conflicto"', *La Vanguardia*, 28 October 2019. https://www.lavanguardia.com/ politica/20191028/471238447665/elisenda-paluzie-anc-violencia-cataluna-visible-co nflicto.html.

88 AMEC, accessed 8 April 2020. https://amecorg.com/amecframework/.

Part IV

Conclusions

17

Moving out of the blizzard

Towards a comprehensive approach to hybrid threats and hybrid warfare

Mikael Weissmann, Niklas Nilsson and Björn Palmertz

Water is fluid, soft, and yielding. But water will wear away rock, which is rigid and cannot yield. As a rule, whatever is fluid, soft, and yielding will overcome whatever is rigid and hard. This is another paradox: what is soft is strong.

Lao Tzu

The unifying purpose of this volume has been to address the array of security challenges arising in the contemporary volatile security environment, characterized above all by an increasingly blurred distinction between war and peace. In this inherently complex and increasingly ambiguous environment, the concepts of hybrid threats and hybrid warfare, henceforth HT&HW, are helpful in both structuring an understanding of the nature of the threats we are facing and the strategy and modus of potential adversaries. Thus, the volume has pursued a comprehensive view of the threats as well as the existing tools and means to counter them.

This focus puts the spotlight on the nature of the threats and adversaries and the challenges they pose to Western democracies. However, it fundamentally boils down to the question of the capacity in Western-style democracies and Western security institutions to confront HT&HW, by comprehending the particular vulnerabilities in their societies and addressing them, as well as devising responses to hostile measures by external actors. The particular vulnerabilities and limitations, as well as advantages of Western democracies, call for particular approaches in this environment. Open societies built on the normative foundations of the rule of law, human rights and democracy, necessarily protective of the freedoms of speech, association and the press, need to devise solutions that not only preserve these fundamental freedoms but also draw on their particular strengths. As has been demonstrated in previous chapters, this work is well underway, in the form of numerous entities tasked with analysing and addressing the problem.

Against the backdrop of the existing overload of overlapping concepts coined or reintroduced to capture the nature of the contemporary security environment, and the controversy surrounding their use, the volume has refrained from attempts to invent new labels or engage at length with the conceptual debate. Instead, we have settled for the use of HT&HW as unifying themes for the volume in an attempt to move the discussion away from how phenomena are supposed to be termed to how they can be understood and addressed. As demonstrated by the range of contributions, there is undoubtedly much to be said on this topic. In this light, a particular contribution of the volume is the unified effort of academic scholars and practitioners, from different fields, to provide a common perspective on HT&HW, based on experiences from a wide set of empirical contexts.

For this purpose, the volume was structured into three parts, each providing a distinct perspective on HT&HW. This was intended not only to allow scholars and practitioners, as well as thematically and area-focused authors, equal chance to present their perspectives in their own right. The aim was also to create synergy effects between the different areas of expertise.

The first part gathered perspectives of key Western collective security actors represented by the two international organizations with primary responsibility for upholding the Western security community, NATO and the EU, as well as the single largest and most influential security actor, the United States. With a common point of departure in Russia's 2014 annexation of Crimea, all three actors have faced a necessary reevaluation of their conceptualizations of adversaries, threats and countermeasures. Indeed, the key challenge posed by the events in 2014 was the ambiguity and obscurity of events taking place on the ground, raising serious questions regarding if, when and how to respond to similar attacks against NATO or EU members, below the threshold of actual armed attack. Both NATO and the EU have since devised a series of detection and response mechanisms focused on providing early warning and attribution of aggressive actions, as well as deterrence and retaliation. The reactions can be summarized as a common realization of previously unidentified weaknesses in Western societies and joint efforts to close these gaps.

Given the composite nature of the threats at hand, the responses need to be organized according to the same principles, integrating societal sectors as well as states. Another important takeaway from these chapters is the importance of knowing your adversary. Whereas identifying and attributing threats produces reactive responses, proactively addressing existing vulnerabilities in order to build resilience requires awareness not only of what an adversary does but also why. In this regard, it becomes pertinent to view the world through the adversary's eyes in order to identify strategic objectives and ways to achieve them as well as the adversary's vulnerabilities.

The validity of this perspective becomes particularly salient in the second part focused on the tools and means employed to conduct and counter-hybrid warfare. Indeed, the analyses of the approaches of major actors associated with HT&HW in a Western perspective, Russia and China, reveal that the conceptual overstretch accompanying these labels, considered a problem in the Western debate, instead functions as an asset in the strategic thinking of these challengers to the Western security order. In Russia, *gibridnaya voina*, with its inherent assumption that most of the West's international activity aims to undermine Russia one way or another, functions as a rhetorical device for identifying domestic or external threats and interpreting these as parts of the West's concerted offensive against Russia. In Chinese writings on the topic, the range of methods associated with HT&HW amount to a comprehensive, cross-domain spectrum denoting perceptions on threat, response and operationalization of hybrid warfare. These increasingly fluctuating borders between the different means associated with HT&HW are apparent in the analyses of information, cyber, intelligence capabilities and the military – indeed, it is questionable to what extent binary divisions into military/non-military or kinetic/non-kinetic means make sense in the current security environment. All the more so since binary thinking regarding the threat risks reproducing itself into the response, thus counteracting the proactive, comprehensive societal approaches deemed necessary to counter HT&HW.

This point is further validated by the contributions in the third section, presenting case studies of the United States, Taiwan, the Baltic States, Ukraine, Iran and Catalonia – demonstrating how the tools and means of HT&HW have been put to use and countered in a diverse set of empirical contexts. The problem of defending against adversaries and hostile actions that – very consciously – operate in the grey zone, below the threshold of actual war, is a recurring theme in these studies. And even if deterrent capabilities in the sense of military force may be very strong, as in the case of the United States, divided responsibilities between civilian agencies and the military, based on perhaps outdated understandings of war and peace, place limitations on the ability to respond. The contrast could not be more apparent when compared to China's policies against Taiwan, which amount to a concerted, sophisticated and strategic combination of means, which nevertheless does not (presently) include the active use of military force.

The point that strategies involving HT&HW are enacted out of a perceived necessity to challenge Western military supremacy by other means is underscored by the example of Iran, which has, due to the perceived existential threat posed by the United States, devised a strategy of guerrilla warfare, in large part performed by proxy forces and in areas outside Iran's territory. In Spain, a concerted Russian information campaign aiming to fuel and broaden national divisions over the Catalonian referendum is a clear example of how actors employing HT&HW seek out and attack vulnerabilities in target countries that are nevertheless pre-existing and do not emerge primarily as an effect of external influence or aggression.

Finally, the case studies also include (at least partially) successful examples of countermeasures against hybrid warfare. In the Baltics, the relatively low level of Russian hybrid activity is attributed partially to the low priority given to the Baltic States in Russian foreign policy, but also to a largely successful deterrence strategy combining military means and broad deterrence by denial below the threshold of an armed attack. Ukraine has, in the midst of an armed but covert attack against the country, proved capable of combining a conventional military response with a sustained informational campaign that has, despite the severe losses incurred, served to expose Russia as the aggressor and consolidated domestic cohesion as well as international support for the country.

The result is a comprehensive view of what may be termed 'hybridity' that, rather than a static picture of actions and responses, provides a cross-sectional and cross-temporal understanding of the interaction between actors, threats, responses and results. Hybridity is a suitable label, having been used in the social sciences 'to designate processes in which discrete social practices or structures, that existed in separate ways, combine to generate new structures, objects, and practices in which the preceding elements mix'.[1] Modelled below, the Hybridity Blizzard Model provides a picture of how ongoing or potential adversarial hybrid measures and responses to these dynamically impact long-term societal vulnerabilities and resilience.

Towards a model of hybrid threats and hybrid warfare

As has been evident in this book, to fully comprehend and counter hybrid threats and warfare is a complex task, but also a very important one. Further on we will outline a schematic model for how to comprehend HT&HW: the 'Hybridity Blizzard Model'. The model comes in three versions, of which the first presents a simplified picture of the dynamics of and between HT&HW, as well as responses and countermeasures. The second version adds a temporal dimension to this relationship, demonstrating how short-term actions and responses relate to long-term vulnerabilities and resilience. The third version, in contrast, aims to provide a more accurate picture of the complex real-world situation. The aim of the model is to enable not only a better understanding of the dynamics themselves but also how to identify, comprehend and act against HT&HW.

The Hybridity Blizzard Model (simplified version)

The simplified Hybridity Blizzard Model outlines a schematic model of the dynamics of the interrelated relationship between defender and attacker in the short-term as well as long-term perspective, and how the different time and actor dimensions interact (see Figure 17.1). Figure 17.1 depicts these interactive and temporal relationships as

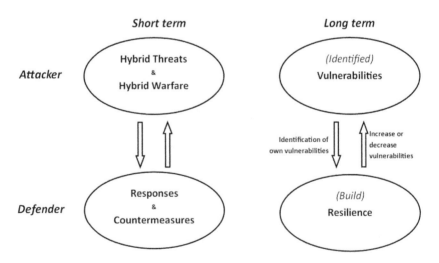

Figure 17.1 Hybridity Blizzard Model, simplified version. Source: Authors.

an ecosystem, which we believe is a good analogy for understanding the dynamics of hybridity, ecosystem being defined as 'all the living things in an area and the way they affect each other and the environment'.[2] While admittedly not alive in a traditional sense, 'living' is an excellent way to model the intelligent social actors on the battlefield and their use, deception, and denial of using different means and tools in hybrid conflicts. It is also a beneficial way of thinking about the relationship between HT&HW, responses and countermeasures, as well as long-term vulnerabilities and resilience. In short, as an environment where all parts affect each other, all parts are actively affected by intelligent social actors aiming to defeat the opponent.

The simplified Hybridity Blizzard Model includes the time and actor dimension. Both of these are important, as HT&HW is neither a one-off event, nor possible to temporally separate from its context. In this model, we include two actors, the defender and the attacker, along with two temporal dimensions, 'short-term' and 'long-term'. In the short-term perspective, the battle consists of an ongoing reciprocal process between HT&HW conducted by the attacker, and the defender's different responses and countermeasures in the duel. This is a continuous and ongoing process with no predetermined beginning or end.

In the long-term perspective, the competition is between the defender's vulnerabilities and the resilience built to ameliorate them. The attacker is expected to identify vulnerabilities in order to exploit them. Vulnerabilities identified by the defender – 'identification of own vulnerabilities' – helps to build the defender's resilience. Efforts to build resilience will logically imply a change in vulnerabilities. Hopefully, the vulnerabilities will decrease, however, change on the defender's side may theoretically open up new vulnerabilities to be identified and exploited by the attacker – 'increase or decrease vulnerabilities' in Figure 17.1. There is also a relationship between the short-term and long-term perspectives (see Figure 17.2). When the

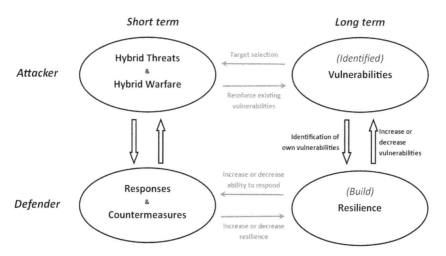

Figure 17.2 Hybridity Blizzard Model, simplified version, temporal dimension. Source: Authors.

attacker considers how to deploy hybrid warfare against the defender, the identified vulnerabilities are key in the 'target selection'. Also, by targeting weaknesses, *ceteris paribus*, the existing vulnerabilities will be reinforced (and then probably targeted again, and so on and so forth).

There is also a relationship on the defender's side between short-term responses and countermeasures on the one hand, and the building of long-term resilience on the other hand (see Figure 17.3). Existing resilience affects the defender's ability to respond and execute countermeasures towards attacks and threats ('increase or decrease ability to respond'). In turn, responses and countermeasures will increase or decrease the defender's resilience. In short, there is a back and forth process between the long term and short term on both sides.

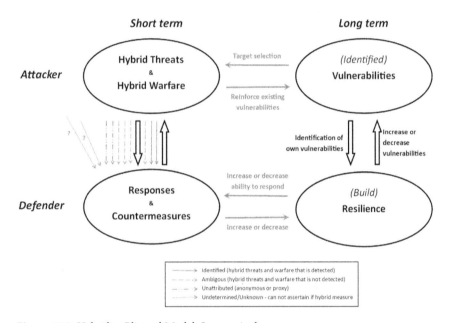

Figure 17.3 Hybridity Blizzard Model. Source: Authors.

The Hybridity Blizzard Model

One problem with the simplified model is that while it provides a schematic picture of hybrid conflicts, it fails to account for the chaos, deception and denial aspects of real-world HT&HW. While the simplified model is analytically sound, it simply does not fully account for the mess out there. In order to provide a complementary and more accurate view of the complex security environment, we propose a more complex version of the 'Hybridity Blizzard Model'. The imagery of a blizzard is useful to depict a situation where the target of HT&HW will be blindly attacked from all possible angles all the time by innumerous small attacks, which cannot be separated from one another or localized, rendering the defender unable to respond and act.

In principle, we could probably add several arrows in Figure 17.3 between all parts. However, this would be of little use to enhance our understanding. Instead, we have focused on the short-term side, outlining the crucial components that best link hybrid conflicts with a blizzard. What makes the situation so messy is the fact that the threats and warfare targeting the defender is not always 'identified', but 'ambiguous', often 'unattributed' and sometimes even 'undetermined or unknown'. As outlined in Figure 17.3, HT&HW are frequently ambiguous and undetected. Adding to the complexity is the risk of false-positives, which not only pose a problem in their own right (crying wolf); they may also in themselves be part of a larger hybrid strategy.

Moreover, HT&HW may be unattributed – inherent in the deception and denial of hybridity – where the origins are either anonymous or covered through the use of proxies.

As if not enough, observed actions or events can be undetermined or unknown, where you do not know if you are observing a hybrid measure or something else. For example, are you observing someone's proxy, or is the 'proxy' in fact the origin and not part of someone's larger strategy/plan? Are the problems with the electricity grid or the glitch in your banking system a manifestation of hybrid warfare, or simply a 'glitch'. Is the threat you perceive against medical or food supply chains a hybrid threat, or is it simply a 'threat' but with no actor origin?

In short, hybridity is depicted not as two schematic arrows back and forth, but as the base of a blizzard of events and actions where the 'normal situation you were supposed to be a part of is now so totally screwed up as to turn the entire scenario into a farce'. And this farce is the reality we live in and have to learn to manage. Sometimes a tale is told of the man who was lost somewhere in Scotland, who asked a farmer if he could tell him the way to Edinburgh. 'Oh sir', the farmer replied, 'if I were you, I shouldn't start from here!' It is not the best joke, but nevertheless a reasonable metaphor for the situation of Western democracies today.[3] We may not be where we want to be, but it is where we are. If we are to be successful in countering HT&HW while at the same time upholding our values and norms, there is no other option than to accept the place we are at.

Conclusion

It should by now be without doubt that HT&HW needs to be addressed through a comprehensive, all-inclusive approach. There is no one threat, no correct answer on how to counter and respond to HT&HW, nor how to build resilience. Nor is there one actor or structure that can succeed both today and tomorrow. As outlined earlier, there is a blizzard out there that needs to be handled. We have to take it for what it is, and adapt and re-adapt when the opponent and the threat constantly changes.

In the Introduction, we used a quote from Sun Tzi as a way to understand the purpose of hybrid warfare – 'The greatest victory is that which requires no battle.' How then do we avoid losing the war? The best solution is not to seek battle, but to find ways to be the one achieving such a victory. One way to get there is to think about HT&HW in the same way as Lao Tzu thought about water.

Water is fluid, soft, and yielding. But water will wear away rock, which is rigid and cannot yield. As a rule, whatever is fluid, soft, and yielding will overcome whatever is rigid and hard. This is another paradox: what is soft is strong.

The paradox of soft as strong is a good guide when thinking about HT&HW and its responses and countermeasures, as well as about resilience and vulnerabilities. In order to be successful, one cannot focus only on hard defence or hard security issues, nor to seek battle. This would risk resulting in the wearing away as a result of the opponent's hybrid warfare; the hybrid measures are fluid, soft and yielding and will overcome whatever is rigid and hard. The opponent will identify soft targets, work opportunistically to target identified vulnerabilities, seeking ways to avoid or circumvent your detection mechanism, neutralizing your ability to respond and retaliate. This is outlined in Figure 17.3, where the attacker seeks to avoid detection of attacks, using proxies and other means to remain anonymous. Threats may even be undetermined or unknown to you, where you may not know that you are targeted or that there is a threat. This is how rigidity and hardness will be overcome. In a similar way, your defence also needs to be fluid, soft and flexible. That is the only way to achieve victory against an opponent disregarding peace and war, using the full scale of hybrid means.

Applying a cost benefit analysis to the targets of an opponent may not place core government agencies and coordination centres at the top of the list. Indeed the benefit in disrupting them would be great, but as they are most likely also prepared and skilled in averting threats against their area of responsibility a positive outcome becomes uncertain and the risk for rapid exposure great. Instead, this analysis may benefit areas that fall in between the responsibility of agencies, blind spots where threats may be identified slowly and a response take some time to sort out. The local government level may be easier to approach through middlemen or proxies as they are not as used to apply a national security filter to new venture proposals or offers to purchase land or assets. The private sector may be easier to influence since they seldom have access to the same intelligence as core agencies and operate based on business aims that may not take the long-term strategies of a foreign state into account. Any situation where the actor utilizing hybrid means can stay undetected, deflect the perception of what is going on, while continuing to inject uncertainty is potentially beneficial. Even if many efforts fail and each victory is small, the limited cost per operation compared to employment of traditional military means makes it a highly attractive alternative. In addition, it offers a greater degree of deniability, opportunity to evaluate and redirect on short notice, and grow a freedom of action without considerable response from the opponent.

Practical advice

But how do we manage these challenges in practice? The key is to develop a detection system that is simultaneously aware of false-positives and false-negatives. There is a need for pragmatism, flexibility and inclusiveness of actors, sectors and levels – within and between countries. The hybrid measure will not come where you expect it, at least not all the time. When countermeasures are successful, the opponent will change its pattern of attack. All actors need to be included, and both short- and long-term perspectives need to be attended to. The response cannot be divided; long-term vulnerabilities are the target for hybrid warfare, and resilient societies will enhance the effect of responses and countermeasures. The idea of building a total- or comprehensive defence is, at least in principle, a good model to succeed with this.

More concrete, it is crucial that key international organizations such as NATO and the EU work together with different states both within and outside international organizations. It is also important to include dedicated organizations such as the Hybrid CoE and the different NATO centres of excellence. In addition, though also part of NATO and many of the dedicated centres, the US is a key actor that is of foremost importance to the protection of Western democracies against HT&HW. HT&HW should be countered through the overlap of capabilities and experiences of the collective that, symbolized in the intersection in Figure 17.4.

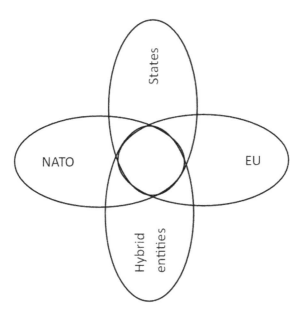

Figure 17.4 International collaboration. Source: Authors.

It is also essential to collaborate across sectors and levels and to avoid allowing traditional borders to hinder collaboration. This is never as important as when countering HT&HW, as vulnerabilities tend to exist precisely in the border areas between sectors and levels, and this is what the opponent will target. This requires collaboration between the military, political, economic, civilian and informational spheres, which needs to evolve across the public and private sectors, as well as from the local and regional levels, through the national to the international level.

Notes

1 Nestor García-Canclini, 'Hybridity', in *International Encyclopedia of the Social & Behavioral Sciences*, ed. Neil J. e. Smelser and Paul B. e. Baltes (Amsterdam: Elsevier, 2001), 7095.
2 Definition from Cambridge Dictonary.
3 Hedley Bull, *The Anarchical Society: A Study of Order in World Politics* (Basingstoke: Palgrave Macmillan, 2012), 285.

Selected bibliography

1 Security challenges in the grey zone: Hybrid threats and hybrid warfare

Dr Niklas Nilsson, Dr Mikael Weissmann, Björn Palmertz, Per Thunholm, Henrik Häggström

Heinrich Brauss, Kalev Stoicescu and Tony Lawrence, *Capability and Resolve: Deterrence, Security and Stability in the Baltic Region* (Tallinn: International Centre for Defence and Security, 2020).

Ofer Friedman, *Russian 'Hybrid Warfare': Resurgence and Politicisation* (London: Hurst & Company, 2018).

Mark Galeotti, 'Hybrid, Ambiguous, and Non-Linear? How New is Russia's "New Way of War"?', *Small Wars & Insurgencies* 27, no. 2 (2016): 7.

Hall Gardner, *Hybrid Warfare: Iranian and Russian Versions of 'Little Green Men' and Contemporary Conflict* (Rome: NATO Defence College, Research Division, December 2015).

Keir Giles, 'Russia's "New" Tools for Confronting the West: Continuity and Innovation in Moscow's Exercise of Power', Chatham House, 21 March 2016. https://www.chathamhouse.org/publication/russias-new-tools-confronting-west

Frank G. Hoffman, 'Hybrid Threats: Reconceptualizing the Evolving Character of Modern Conflict', *Strategic Forum*, no. 240 (Washington, DC: Institute for National Strategic Studies, National Defense University, April 2009). https://www.comw.org/qdr/fulltext/0904hoffman.pdf.

Frank G. Hoffman, 'Hybrid Warfare and Challenges', *JFQ* 52 (1 quarter 2009): 34–9.

Robert Johnson, 'Hybrid War and Its Countermeasures: A Critique of the Literature', *Small Wars & Insurgencies* 29, no. 1 (2018): 143.

Alexander Lanozska, 'Russian Hybrid Warfare and Extended Deterrence in Eastern Europe', *International Affairs* 92, no. 1 (2016): 178.

MCDC, Countering Hybrid Warfare Project, summary. https://www.gov.uk/government/publications/countering-hybrid-warfare-project-understanding-hybrid-warfare

Sean Monaghan, 'Countering Hybrid Warfare: Conceptual Foundations and Implications for Defence Forces', *Multinational Capability Development Campaign (MCDC)*, Information note, March 2019. https://assets.publishing.service.gov.uk/government/uploads/system/uploads/attachment_data/file/840513/20190401-MCDC_CHW_Information_note_-_Conceptual_Foundations.pdf

Williamson Murray and Peter R. Mansoor, eds, *Hybrid Warfare: Fighting Complex Opponents from the Ancient World to the Present* (Cambridge: Cambridge University Press, 2012).

James Pamment, Howard Nothhaft, Henrik Agardh-Twetman and Alicia Fjällhed, *Countering Information Influence Activities: The State of the Art*, version 1.4 (Lund University, 1 July 2018). https://www.msb.se/RibData/Filer/pdf/28697.pdf

Nicu Popescu, 'Hybrid Tactics: Neither New nor only Russian', European Union Institute of Security Studies, January 2015. https://www.iss.europa.eu/sites/default/files/EUIS SFiles/Alert_4_hybrid_warfare.pdf

Bettina Renz, 'Russia and "Hybrid Warfare"', *Contemporary Politics* 22, no. 3 (2016): 283–300.

Timothy Thomas, 'The Evolution of Russian Military Thought: Integrating Hybrid, New-Generation and New-Type Thinking', *The Journal of Slavic Military Studies* 29, no. 4 (2016): 557–9.

Rod Thornton, *Asymmetric Warfare: Threat and Response in the Twenty-First Century* (Cambridge: Polity, 2007).

Gregory F. Treverton, Andrew Thvedt, Alicia R. Chen, Kathy Lee and Madeline McCue, *Addressing Hybrid Threats* (Stockholm: Swedish Defence University, 2018), 10 ff.

Frans-Paul van der Putten, Minke Meijnders, Sico van der Meer and Tony van der Togt, eds *Hybrid Conflict: The Roles of Russia, North Korea and China* (The Hague: Clingendael Institute, 2018).

Mikael Weissmann, 'Hybrid Warfare and Hybrid Threats Today and Tomorrow: Towards an Analytical Framework', *Journal on Baltic Security* 5, no. 1 (2019): 17–26.

Part I The view of practitioners

2 NATO and hybrid warfare: Seeking a concept to describe the challenge from Russia

Dr G. Alexander Crowther, Research Professor, Florida International University, former Special Assistant to the Supreme Allied Commander, Europe and former researcher in the Strategic Studies Institute and the US National Defense University.

Jānis Bērziņš, *Russia's New Generation Warfare in Ukraine: Implications for Latvian Defense Policy* (Riga: National Defence Academy of Latvia, Center for Security and Strategic Research, Policy Paper, no. 2, April 2014), 5. https://www.sldinfo.com/wp-con tent/uploads/2014/05/New-Generation-Warfare.pdf

Ofer Fridman, *Russian 'Hybrid Warfare': Resurgence and Politicisation* (Oxford: Oxford University Press, 2018).

Valery Gerasimov, 'The Value of Science Is in the Foresight: New Challenges Demand Rethinking the Forms and Methods of Carrying out Combat Operations', original in Russian *VPK News*, no. 8 (476), 5 March 2013. https://vpk-news.ru/sites/default/files/ pdf/VPK_08_476.pdf. English version in *Military Review*, January–February 2016. https://www.armyupress.army.mil/Portals/7/military-review/Archives/English/Milit aryReview:20160228_art008.pdf

Lee Litzenberger, 'Beyond Zapad 2017: Russia's Destabilizing Approach to Military Exercises', *War on the Rocks*, 28 November 2017. https://warontherocks.com/2017/11/ beyond-zapad-2017-russias-destabilizing-approach-military-exercises/

NATO, *Chicago Summit Declaration*, 20 May 2012. Available at https://www.nato.int/cps/ en/natohq/official_texts_87593.htm?selectedLocale=en

NATO, *NATO's Response to Hybrid Threats*, 8 August 2019. https://www.nato.int/cps/en/na tohq/topics_156338.htm?

NATO, 'Readiness Action Plan', NATO. https://www.nato.int/cps/en/natohq/topics_119 353.htm

NATO, *Wales Summit Declaration*, 5 September 2014. 'Russia's Aggressive Actions' in Paragraph 1, 'Hybrid' in Paragraph 12. Available at https://www.nato.int/cps/en/na tohq/official_texts_112964.htm

NATO Defense College, *Research at the NDC*. Available at http://www.ndc.nato.int/resear ch/research.php?icode=3

NATO Multimedia Library, *Hybrid Warfare Article Archive*. Available at http://www.nato libguides.info/hybridwarfare/articles/archives

Vladimir Putin, 'Speech and the Following Discussion at the Munich Conference on Security Policy', 10 February 2007. http://en.kremlin.ru/events/president/transcr ipts/24034

3 An American view: Hybrid threats and intelligence

Dr Gregory F. Treverton, University of Southern California, former Chair of the US National Intelligence Council

Christopher Andrew, *For the President's Eyes Only: Secret Intelligence and the American Presidency From Washington to Bush* (New York: HarperPerennial, 1996).

Richard K. Betts, *Enemies of Intelligence: Knowledge and Power in American National Security* (New York: Columbia University Press, 2007).

For how we got here: National Security Council Report 68 (NSC 68), at URL: http://www.trumanlibrary.org/whistlestop/study_collections/coldwar/documents/ pdf/10-1.pdf

Harold P. Ford, *Estimative Intelligence: The Purposes and Problems of National Intelligence Estimating*, rev. edn (Lanham: University Press of America, 1993).

Roger Z. George and James B. Bruce, eds, *Analyzing Intelligence: National Security Practitioners' Perspectives*, 2nd edn (Washington, DC: Georgetown University Press, 2014).

Peter Gill, Stephen Marrin and Mark Phythian, eds, *Intelligence Theory: Key Questions and Debates* (London: Routledge, 2009).

Michael Herman, *Intelligence Power in Peace and War* (Cambridge: Cambridge University Press, 1996).

Roger Hilsman, Jr., 'Intelligence and Policy-Making in Foreign Affairs', *World Politics* 5, no. 1 (October 1952): 1–22.

Robert Jervis, 'Why Intelligence and Policymakers Clash', *Political Science Quarterly* 125, no. 2 (2010): 185–204.

David Kahn, 'The Intelligence Failure of Pearl Harbor', *Foreign Affairs* 70, no. 5 (Winter 1991–2): 138–52.

Sherman Kent, *Strategic Intelligence and American Foreign Policy* (Princeton: Princeton University Press, 1949), 3–7, 69–77, 151–8.

Jeffrey Richelson, *The U.S. Intelligence Community*, 5th edn (Boulder: Westview Press, 2007).

Abram N. Shulsky, *Silent Warfare: Understanding the World of Intelligence*, 3rd edn (Washington, DC: Brassey's, 2001).

Russ Travers, 'The Coming Intelligence Failure', *Studies in Intelligence*, 1997, at URL: https ://www.cia.gov/library/center-for-the-study-of-intelligence/csi-publications/csi-studies /studies/97unclass/failure.html

Gregory F. Treverton, *Reshaping National Intelligence for an Age of Information* (Cambridge: Cambridge University Press, 2001).

4 A perspective on EU hybrid threat early warning efforts

Dr Patrick Cullen, Senior Research Fellow, Norwegian Institute of International Affairs (NUPI) & member of the 'Countering Hybrid Warfare' component of the Multinational Capability Development Campaign (MCDC)

Michael Aaronson, Sverre Deisen, Yves de Kermabom, Mary Beth Long and Michael Miklaucic, 'NATO: Countering the Hybrid Threat', *PRISM* 2, no. 4 (2011): 111–24.

Atlantic Council, 'Breedlove: NATO have Begun Shaping Rapid Response Force', *Commanders Series*, 17 September 2014.

Jānis Bērziņš, *Russia's New Generation Warfare in Ukraine: Implications for Latvian Defense Policy* (Riga: National Defence Academy of Latvia, Center for Security and Strategic Studies, 2014). https://www.sldinfo.com/wp-content/uploads/2014/05/New-Generation-Warfare.pdf

Patrick Cullen and Njord Wegge, *MCDC Countering Hybrid Warfare Project: Countering Hybrid Warfare* (MCDC, March 2019). https://assets.publishing.service.gov.uk/gove rnment/uploads/system/uploads/attachment_data/file/784299/concepts_mcdc_cou ntering_hybrid_warfare.pdf

Margriet Drent, Rob Hendriks and Dick Zandee, 'New Threats, New EU and NATO Responses', *Clingendael Report*, July 2015, 38–43.

EEAS, 'Food for thought paper "Countering Hybrid Threats"', 13 May 2015. https://www .statewatch.org/news/2015/may/eeas-csdp-hybrid-threats-8887-15.pdf

European Commission, 'EU Playbook: Operational Protocol for Countering Hybrid Threats', Brussels, 5 July 2016. https://www.statewatch.org/media/documents/news/20 16/jul/eu-com-countering-hybrid-threats-playbook-swd-227-16.pdf

European Commission, 'Joint Framework for Countering Hybrid Threats', 6 April 2016. https://eur-lex.europa.eu/legal-content/EN/TXT/?uri=CELEX%3A52016JC0018

Daniel Fiott and Roderick Parkes, 'Protecting Europe: The EU's Response to Hybrid Threats', *EUISS Challiot Paper* 151, April 2019.

Patryk Pawlak, 'Countering Hybrid Threats: EU-NATO Cooperation', *European Parliamentary Research Service*, March 2017. https://www.europarl.europa.eu/RegData /etudes/BRIE/2017/599315/EPRS_BRI(2017)599315_EN.pdf

Jens Stoltenberg, keynote speech, NATO Transformation Seminar, 25 March 2015. https:// www.nato.int/cps/ic/natohq/opinions_118435.htm

Jan Jakub Uzieblo, 'United in Ambiguity? EU and NATO Approaches to Hybrid Warfare and Hybrid Threats', *EU Diplomacy Paper*, College of Europe, Brugge, May 2017, 22.

Part II Tools and means

5 Conceptualizing and countering hybrid threats and hybrid warfare: The role of the military in the grey zone

Dr Mikael Weissmann, Associate Professor, Head of Research / Deputy Head at the Land Operations Section and Co-Convener of the Hybrid Warfare Research Group (HWRG), Department of Military Studies, Swedish Defence University.

John Chambers, 'Countering Gray-Zone Hybrid Threats: An Analysis of Russia's "New Generation Warfare" and Implications for the US Army' (Modern War Institute at West Point, 2016). https://apps.dtic.mil/dtic/tr/fulltext/u2/1020295.pdf

Ofer Friedman, *Russian 'Hybrid Warfare': Resurgence and Politicisation* (London: Hurst & Company, 2018).

Mark Galeotti, *Hybrid War or Gibridnaya Voina? Getting Russia's Non-Linear Military Challenge Right* (Prague: Mayak Intelligence, 2016).

Frank G. Hoffman, *Conflict in the 21st Century: The Rise of Hybrid Wars* (Arlington: Potomac Institute for Policy Studies, 2007). https://potomacinstitute.org/images/stories /publications/potomac_hybridwar_0108.pdf

Frank G. Hoffman, 'Examining Complex Forms of Conflict: Gray Zone and Hybrid Challenges', *PRISM* 7, no. 4 (2018): 30–47.

Sean Monaghan, 'Countering Hybrid Warfare: Conceptual Foundations and Implications for Defence Forces', *Multinational Capability Development Campaign (MCDC)*. https ://assets.publishing.service.gov.uk/government/uploads/system/uploads/attachment _data/file/840513/20190401-MCDC_CHW_Information_note_-_Conceptual_Foun dations.pdf

Lyle Morris et al., *Gaining Competitive Advantage in the Gray Zone: Response Options for Coercive Aggression below the Threshold of Major War* (RAND Corporation, 2019). https://doi.org/10.7249/RR2942

Nupi, 'Multinational Capability Development Campaign 2015–18 (Countering Hybrid Warfare)', Nupi. Accessed 17 March 2020. https://www.nupi.no/en/About-NUPI/P rojects-centres-and-programmes/Multinational-Capability-Development-Campaign -2015-18-Countering-Hybrid-Warfare

Erik Reichborn-Kjennerud and Patrick Cullen, 'What Is Hybrid Warfare?', Norwegian Institute of International Affairs (NUPI), Policy Brief, January 2016. http://hdl.handle .net/11250/2380867

Rod Thornton, *Asymmetric Warfare: Threat and Response in the Twenty-First Century* (Cambridge: Polity, 2007).

Mikael Weissmann, 'Hybrid Warfare and Hybrid Threats Today and Tomorrow: Towards an Analytical Framework', *Journal on Baltic Security* 5, no. 1 (2019): 17–26.

James J. Wirtz, 'Life in the "Gray Zone": Observations for Contemporary Strategists', *Defense & Security Analysis* 33, no. 2 (2017): 106–14.

6 Understanding Russian thinking on *gibridnaya voyna*

Dr Markus Göransson, Assistant Professor and project leader of the Russia programme, Swedish Defence University

A. A. Bartosh, 'Hybrid Warfare: "Friction" and "Wear and Tear"', *Military Thought* (English edition) 1 (2018): 27.

A. A. Bartosh, 'Smysly gibridnoy voyny', (The Meanings of Hybrid War), *Vestnik akademii voennykh nauk* 59 (2017): 2.

A. A. Bartosh, 'Strategy and Counterstrategy in a Hybrid War', *Military Thought* (English edition) 4 (2018): 27.

Ofer Fridman, *Russian 'Hybrid Warfare': Resurgence and Politicization* (London: Hurst & Company, 2018).

V. V. Gerasimov, 'Organizatsiia oborony Rossiiskoy federatsii v usloviiakh primeneniia protivnikom "traditsionnykh" i "gibridnykh" metodov vedeniia voyny' (The organization of the defense of the Russian federation under conditions of the employment by the adversary of 'traditional' and 'hybrid' methods of waging war), *Vestnik akademii voyennykh nauk* 2 (2016): 55.

V. A. Kiselyov and I. N. Vorobyov, 'Hybrid Operations: A New Type of Warfare', *Military Thought* (English edition) 2 (2015): 24.

Marina Evgen'evna Kuchinskaia, 'Politika sderzhivaniia Rossii: "novaia norma" (a new normal) dlia NATO' (The politics of deterrence of Russia: 'a new normal' for NATO), *Problemy natsional'noi strategii* 1 (2017): 40.

I. M. Popov and M. M. Khamzatov, *Voyna budushchego. Kontseptual'nye osnovy i prakticheskie vyvody* [War of the Future. Conceptual foundations and practical conclusions] (Moscow: Kuchkovo Pole, 2018).

Damien van Puyvelde, 'Hybrid Wr – Does It Even Exist?' *NATO* (2015).

Aleksandr Ivanovich Vladimirov, *Osnovy Obshchey Teorii Voyny. Chast' I-III* [Foundations of a General Theory of War, Volumes I-III] (Moscow: Universitet Sinergiia, 2016).

7 China and its hybrid warfare spectrum

Dr Lora Saalman, Senior Fellow, EastWest Institute; Associate Senior Fellow, Stockholm International Peace Research Institute

段君泽 [Junze Duan], '俄式"混合战争"实践及其影响' ['Russian-style "Hybrid Warfare" Practice and Impact'], 现代国际关系 [*Modern International Relations*], no. 3 (2017): 31–6.

高凯、赵林 [Kai Gao and Lin Zhao], '"混合战争" 俄罗斯新战略博弈手段' ['"Hybrid Warfare" Russia's New Strategic Game'], 军事文献 [*Military Literature*], July 2019, 10–13.

归泳涛 [Yongtao Gui], '"灰色地带"之争: 美日对华博弈的新态势' ['"Gray Zone" Controversy: New Trends in the U.S.-Japan Game Against China'], 日本学刊 [*Japan Studies*], no. 1 (January 2019): 45–69.

胡欣 [Xin Hu], '"混合战争"终结混乱的方程式?' ['"Hybrid Warfare" The Formula to End Chaos?'], 世界知识 [*World Affairs*], 2 April 2018, 74.

李炳彦 [Bingyan Li], '"智战时代"与东方兵学智慧' ['"Intelligent Warfare Era" and Eastern Military Science Wisdom'], 孙子研究 [*Sun Zi Studies*] 16, no. 4 (April 2017): 81–3.

李元斌、何昊宸 [Yuanbin Li and Haochen He], '混合战争视角下的美国极限施压与"颜色革命"' ['U.S. Extreme Pressure and "Color Revolutions" from the Perspective of Hybrid Warfare'], 军事文献 [*Military Literature*], September 2019, 7–10.

刘纪未、张畅 [Jiwei Liu and Chang Zhang], '"混合战争"理论视阈下：俄罗斯军事战略调整探析' ['Analysis of Russian Military Strategy Adjustment from the Perspective of "Hybrid War" Theory']. 江南社会学院学报 [*Journal of Jinan Social University*] 21, no. 2 (June 2019): 47–52.

马瑾、舒正平、穆歌、张富雪 [Jin Ma, Zhengping Shu, Ge Mu and Fuxue Zhang], '混合战争条件下的无人系统作战能力分析' ['Analysis of Unmanned Systematic Combat Capability under Mixed War Conditions'], 第六届中国指挥控制大会论文集 (上册) [*Proceedings of the 6th China Command and Control Conference (Volume 1)*], 2016, 410–14.

潘乐天 [Letian Pan], '美军"多域战"的实质及启示' ['Substance and Inspiration behind the U.S. Military's "Multi-Domain" Warfare'], 科技导报 [*Science and Technology Review*] 35, no. 21 (31 May 2017): 125–30.

Liang Qiao and Xiangsui Wang, *Unrestricted Warfare* (Beijing: PLA Literature and Arts Publishing House, February 1999). https://archive.org/stream/Unrestricted_Warfare

_Qiao_Liang_and_Wang_Xiangsui/Unrestricted_Warfare_Qiao_Liang_and_Wang_Xi
angsui_djvu.txt

秦安 [An Qin], '"震网"升级版袭击伊朗，网络毁瘫离我们有多远' ['An Upgraded
Version of "Stuxnet" Hits Iran, How Far Away Is Destruction from Us'], 网路空间安全
[*Cyberspace Security*] 09, no. 11 (November 2018): 41–3.

Lora Saalman, 'Little Grey Men: China and the Ukraine Crisis', *Survival – Global Politics
and Strategy* 58, no. 6 (December 2016). http://www.tandfonline.com/doi/abs/10.1080
/00396338.2016.1257201?needAccess=true&journalCode=tsur20

司光亚、张阳、王艳正 [Guangya Si, Yang Zhang and Yanzheng Wang],
'网电空间作战建模仿真研究综述' ['Review on Modeling and Simulation in
Cyberspace Operations'], 系统仿真学报 [*Journal of System Simulation*] 30, no. 2
(February 2018): 386–97.

唐永胜、李薇、沈志雄 [Yongsheng Tang, Wei Li, and Zhixiong Shen], '因势利导:
把握中美竞争的战略主动权' ['Take Advantage of the Situation: Grasping the
Strategic Initiative in China-U.S. Competition'], 国际观察 [*International Review*], no.
3 (March 2019): 22–40.

王宝付 [Baofu Wang], '"混合战争": 战争演进的新形态' ['"Hybrid Warfare": A New
Form of Warfare Evolution'], 光明日报 [*Guangming Daily*], no. 11 (6 April 2016):
1–3.

王湘穗 [Xiangsui Wang], '混合战：前所未有的综合' ['Hybrid Warfare: Unprecedented
Synthesis'], *PLA Daily* [解放军报], no. 7 (23 May 2019): 1.

叶秋玲、王玉琨 [Qiuling Ye and Yukun Wang], '日本发布新版《防卫计划大纲》
寓意为何?' ['What Is the Meaning of Japan's New Version of its Defense Plan
Guidelines?'], 军事文献 [*Military Literature*], no. 3 (March 2019): 33–5.

袁艺、李志飞、朱丰 [Yi Yuan, Zhifei Li and Zhu Feng], '无人机与未来作战刍议'
['Unmanned Vehicles and Future Combat Operations'], 国防 [*National Defense*], no. 5
(May 2019): 36–50.

赵时轮 [Shilun Zhao], '无人机危害及恐怖行为反制对策研究' ['Countermeasure
Research Against Unmanned Vehicle Harm and Terrorist Acts'], 中国军转民 [*China
Military to Civilian*], Issue Unavailable, Date Unavailable, 15–20.

朱星平 [Xingping Zhu], '混合战争背景下我国人防工程的使命' ['Mission of China's
Civil Air Defense Engineering in the Context of Hybrid Warfare'], 国防科技 [*National
Defense Technology*] 40, no. 1 (February 2019): 73–7.

8 Influence operations and the modern information environment

Björn Palmertz, Senior Analyst, CATS, Swedish Defence University

Marie Baezner and Patrice Robin, *Cyber and Information Warfare in the Ukrainian
Conflict* (Zürich: Eidgenössische Technische Hochschule Zürich, 2018).

Pascal Brangetto and Matthijs Veenendaal, *Influence Cyber Operations: The Use of
Cyberattacks in Support of Influence Operations* (NATO CCD COE, 2016). https://cc
dcoe.org/uploads/2018/10/Art-08-Influence-Cyber-Operations-The-Use-of-Cyberattac
ks-in-Support-of-Influence-Operations.pdf

Elizabeth Bodine-Baron, Todd C. Helmus, Andrew Radin and Elina Treyger, *Countering
Russian Social Media Influence* (RAND Corporation, 2018). https://www.rand.org/pubs
/research_reports/RR2740.html

Canadian Security Intelligence Service, *China and the Age of Strategic Rivalry: Highlights
from an Academic Outreach Workshop* (2018). https://www.canada.ca/content/dam/c

sis-scrs/documents/publications/CSIS-Academic-Outreach-China-report-May-2018
-en.pdf

Robert B. Cialdini, *Influence: The Psychology of Persuasion*, rev. edn (New York: Collins, 2007).

Daniel Cohen and Ofir Bar'el, *The Use of Cyberwarfare in Influence Operations* (Tel Aviv University, Yuval Ne'eman Workshop for Science, Technology and Security 2017). https ://icrc.tau.ac.il/sites/cyberstudies-english.tau.ac.il/files/media_server/cyber%20center/ cyber-center/Cyber_Cohen_Barel_ENG.pdf

Renee DiResta, Kris Shaffer, Becky Ruppel, David Sullivan, Robert Matney, Ryan Fox, Jonathan Albright and Ben Johnson, *The Tactics & Tropes of the Internet Research Agency* (New Knowledge, 2018).

Keir Giles, *Countering Russian Information Operations in the Age of Social Media* (Council on Foreign Relations, 2017).

Keir Giles, *The Next Phase of Russian Information Warfare* (NATO StratCom COE, 2016). https://www.stratcomcoe.org/next-phase-russian-information-warfare-keir-giles

Emilio J. Iasiello, 'Russia's Improved Information Operations: From Georgia to Crimea', *Parameters* 47, no. 2 (2017): 51–63.

J.-B. Jeangène Vilmer, A. Escorcia, M. Guillaume and J. Herrera, *Information Manipulation – A Challenge for Our Democracies* (CAPS/IRSEM, 2018). https://www.diplomatie.gouv .fr/IMG/pdf/information_manipulation_rvb_cle838736.pdf

Daniel Kahneman, *Thinking, Fast and Slow*, 1st edn (New York: Farrar, Straus and Giroux, 2011).

David M. J. Lazer et al., 'The Science of Fake News', *Science* 359, no. 6380 (9 March 2018): 1094–6.

James Pamment, Howard Nothhaft, Henrik Agardh-Twetman and Alicia Fjällhed, *Countering Information Influence Activities: The State of the Art* (Lund University, 2018). https://www.msb.se/RibData/Filer/pdf/28697.pdf

Anton Shekhovtsov, *Russia and the Western Far Right* (New York: Routledge, 2018).

Swedish Civil Contingencies Agency, *Countering Information Influence Activities – A Handbook for Communicators* (2018). https://www.msb.se/RibData/Filer/pdf/28698 .pdf

Gregory F. Treverton, Andrew Thvedt, Alicia R. Chen, Kathy Lee and Madeline McCue, *Addressing Hybrid Threats* (Center for Asymmetric Threat Studies and Hybrid CoE, 2018). https://www.hybridcoe.fi/wp-content/uploads/2018/05/Treverton-Addressi ngHybridThreats.pdf

UK Government Communication Service, *RESIST Counter Disinformation Toolkit* (2019). https://gcs.civilservice.gov.uk/publications/resist-counter-disinformation-toolkit/

9 Hybrid threats and new challenges for multilateral intelligence cooperation

Henrik Häggström, Senior Analyst, Center for Asymmetric Threat Studies (CATS), Swedish Defence University

Olga Abilova and Alexandra Novosseloff, *Demystifying Intelligence in UN Peace Operations: Toward an Organizational Doctrine* (New York: International Peace Institute, July 2016).

Wilhelm Agrell, *The Black Swan and its Opponents – Early Warning Aspects of the Norway Attacks on 22 July 2011* (Stockholm: National Defence University, CATS, 2013).

Jan Ballast, 'Merging Pillars, Changing Cultures: Nato and the Future of Intelligence Cooperation within the Alliance', *International Journal of Intelligence and CounterIntelligence* 31, no. 4. (2018): 720.

Walter Dorn, 'The Cloak and the Blue Beret: Limitations on Intelligence in UN Peacekeeping', *International Journal of Intelligence and CounterIntelligence* 12, no. 4 (1999): 417–47.

Walter Dorn, 'Intelligence at UN Headquarters? The Information and Research Unit and the Intervention in Eastern Zaire 1996', *Intelligence & National Security* 20, no. 3 (September 2005): 440–65.

Walter Dorn, 'United Nations Peacekeeping Intelligence', in *The Oxford Handbook of National Security Intelligence*, ed. Loch K. Johnson (Oxford: Oxford University Press, 2010), 275–95.

European External Action Service, 'EU Intelligence Analysis Centre (EU INTCEN): Fact Sheet. Accessed 20 January 2020. https://www.asktheeu.org/en/request/637/respo nse/2416/attach/html/5/EU%20INTCEN%20Factsheet%20PUBLIC%20120618%201 .pdf.html

Arnt Freytag von Loringhoven, 'Adapting NATO Intelligence in Support of "One NATO"', *NATO Review* 8, September 2017. https://www.nato.int/docu/review/2017/Also-in -2017/adapting-nato-intelligence-in-support-of-one-nato-security-military-terrorism/ EN/index.htm

Roger Z. George, *Meeting 21st Century Transnational Challenges: Building a Global Intelligence Paradigm* (Washington, DC: CIA Center for the study of intelligence, 2007), 151. https://www.cia.gov/library/center-for-thestudy-of-intelligence/csi-publica tions/csi-studies/studies/vol51no3/building-a-global-intelligenceparadigm.html

Henrik Häggström and Filip Ahlin, *Det nya normala – studie om hot mot den kärntekniska industrin* (Swedish Defence University, CATS, 2017).

Erik D. Jens, 'Human Intelligence Operations in ISAF', *American Intelligence Journal* 13, no. 1 (2013): 21–8.

John Kriendler, 'NATO Intelligence and Early Warning', *Conflict Studies Research Center Special Series*, 13 June (Swindon: Conflict Studies Research Center, 2006).

Stéphane Lefebvre, S., 'The Difficulties and Dilemmas of International Intelligence Cooperation', *International Journal of Intelligence and CounterIntelligence* 16, no. 4 (2003): 527–42.

Janine McGruddy, 'Multilateral Intelligence Collaboration and International Oversight', *Journal of Strategic Security* 6, no. 3 (2013): 214–20.

Steven Metz, *Rethinking Insurgency* (Carlisle: Strategic Studies Institute, 2012).

Sebastiaan Rietjens and A. Walter Dorn, 'The Evolution of Peacekeeping Intelligence: The UN's Laboratory in Mali', in *Perspectives on Military Intelligence from the First World War to Mali – between Learning and Law*, ed. Floribert Baudet, Eleni Braat, Jeoffrey van Woensel and Aad Wever (The Hague: Asser Press, 2017).

Adriana N. Seagle, 'Intelligence Sharing Practices Within NATO: An English School Perspective', *International Journal of Intelligence and CounterIntelligence* 28, no. 3 (2015): 560.

James Igoe Walsh, *The International Politics of Intelligence Sharing* (New York: Columbia University Press, 2010).

10 Cyberwarfare and the internet: The implications of a more digitalized world

Anne-Marie Eklund Löwinder, Head of Security, The Swedish Internet Foundation and Cryptographic Officer at the Internet Corporation for Assigned Names and Numbers (ICANN) Anna Djup, Analyst, Information Assurance, Center for Asymmetric Threat Studies (CATS), Swedish Defence University

Ben Buchanan, *The Cybersecurity Dilemma: Hacking, Trust and Fear between Nations* (London: C. Hurst & Co, 2016).

Gordon Corera, *Intercept: The Secret History of Computers and Spies* (London: Weidenfeld & Nicolson, 2016).

G. Dileep Kumar, *Network Security Attacks and Countermeasures* (IGI Global, 2016).

Andy Greenberg, *Sandworm: A New Era of Cyberwar and the Hunt for the Kremlin's Most Dangerous Hackers* (New York: Doubleday Publishing, 2019).

C. P. Gupta and K. K. Goyal, *Cybersecurity: A Self-Teaching Introduction* (Stylus Publishing, LLC, 2020).

Eric D. Knapp and Joel Thomas Langill, *Industrial Network Security*, Second edn (Waltham: Syngress Media, 2014).

Kai-Fu Lee, *AI Superpowers: China, Silicon Valley and the New World Order* (Houghton Mifflin: Harcourt Publishing Company, 2018).

Joseph Menn, *Cult of the Dead Cow: How the Original Hacking Superbroup Might Just Save the World* (Hachett Book Group, Inc., 2019).

Robert Radvanovsky and Jacob Brodsky, *Handbook of SCADA/Control Systems Security* (Taylor & Francis Inc., 2016).

P. W. Singer and Allan Friedman, *Cybersecurity and Cyberwar: What Everyone Needs to Know* (Oxford: Oxford University Pres, 2014).

Nicole Starosielski, *The Undersea Network* (Durham: Duke University Press, 2015).

Kim Zetter, *Countdown to Zero Day: Stuxnet and the Launch of the World's First Digital Weapon* (New York: Crown Publishing Group, 2014).

Part III Cases

11 The US and hybrid challenges: Past, present and future

Jed Willard, Director of the Franklin Delano Roosevelt Center for Global Engagement, Harvard University

Joseph F. Dunford, Jr, 'Remarks and Q&A at the Center for Strategic and International Studies' (speech, Washington, DC, 29 March 2016). https://www.jcs.mil/Media/Spee ches/Article/707418/gen-dunfords-remarks-and-qa-at-the-center-for-strategic-and-international-studi/

Frank G. Hoffman, 'The Contemporary Spectrum of Conflict: Protracted, Gray Zone, Ambiguous, and Hybrid Modes of War', in *2016 Index of U.S. Military Strength*, ed. Dakota L. Wood (The Heritage Foundation, 20 June 2015). https://s3.amazonaws.com/ims-2016/PDF/2016_Index_of_US_Military_Strength_ESSAYS_HOFFMAN.pdf

Frank G. Hoffman, 'Examining Complex Forms of Conflict: Gray Zone and Hybrid Challenges', *PRISM* 7, no. 4 (8 November 2018). https://cco.ndu.edu/News/Article/16 80696/examining-complex-forms-of-conflict-gray-zone-and-hybrid-challenges/

Nicholas Kristof, 'This Is How a War With China Could Begin', *New York Times*, 4 September 2019. Accessed 12 September 2019. https://www.nytimes.com/2019/09 /04/opinion/china-taiwan-war.html

Michael Matlaga and John Schaus, 'Competing in the Gray Zone' (CSIS, 24 October 24 2018). https://www.csis.org/analysis/competing-gray-zone-0

Michael C. McCarthy, Matthew A. Moyer and Brett H. Venable; *Deterring Russia in the Gray Zone* (Carlisle: Strategic Studies Institute, 2019).

Michael O'Hanlon, 'A Report From NATO's Front Lines', *The National Interest*, 10 June 2019. Accessed 20 June 2015. https://nationalinterest.org/feature/report-natos-front -lines-62067

RFE/RL, 'Putin Tells FT: "The Liberal Idea Has Become Obsolete"', *Radio Free Europe / Radio Liberty*, 28 June 2019. https://www.rferl.org/a/putin-tells-ft-the-liberal-idea-has- become-obsolete-/30026237.html

12 China's political warfare in Taiwan: Strategies, methods and global implication

Dr Gulizar Haciyakupoglu, Research Fellow, the Centre of Excellence for National Security (CENS), S. Rajaratnam School of International Studies (RSIS), Nanyang Technological University (NTU), Singapore.

Dr Michael Raska, Assistant Professor, Coordinator of Military Transformations Programme, IDSS, RSIS, Singapore

Dean Cheng, 'Winning Without Fighting: Chinese Legal Warfare', *The Heritage Foundation*, 21 May 2012. https://www.heritage.org/asia/report/winning-without-fi ghting-chinese-legal-warfare

'Chinese Public Diplomacy in Taiwan', in *Hybrid Threats: A Strategic Communications Perspective*, ed. Sean Aday, Māris Andžāns, Una Bērziņa-Čerenkova, Francesca Granelli, John-Paul Gravelines, Mils Hills, Miranda Holmstrom, Adam Klus, Irene Martinez-Sanchez, Mariita Mattiisen, Holger Molder, Yeganeh Morakabati, James Pamment, Aurel Sari, Vladimir Sazonov, Gregory Simons and Jonathan Terra (NATO Strategic Communications Centre of Excellence (NATO StratCom COE), 8 April 2019). Retrieved from https://www.stratcomcoe.org/hybrid-threats-strategic-communi cations-perspective

Paul Huang, 'Chinese Cyber-Operatives Boosted Taiwan's Insurgent Candidate', *Foreign Policy*, 26 June 2019. https://foreignpolicy.com/2019/06/26/chinese-cyber-operatives -boosted-taiwans-insurgent-candidate/

Huang Jaw-Nian, 'The China Factor in Taiwan's Media: Outsourcing Chinese Censorship Abroad', *China Perspectives* 3 (2017). http://journals.openedition.org/chinaperspect ives/7388

Mallory King, 'New Challenges in Cross-Domain Deterrence', *RAND Perspective*, no. 259. Available at: https://www.rand.org/content/dam/rand/pubs/perspectives/PE200/PE259 /RAND_PE259.pdf

Rebecca Lin and Felice Wu, 'Taiwan's Online "Opinion War" Arrived', *The Common Wealth*, 27 April 2019. https://english.cw.com.tw/article/article.action?id=2375

Thomas Mahnken, 'Thinking about Competitive Strategies', in *Competitive Strategies for the 21st Century*, ed. Thomas Mahnken, 3–11 (Stanford: Stanford University Press, 2012).

Nicholas J. Monaco and Google Jigsaw, 'Computational Propaganda in Taiwan: Where Digital Democracy Meets Automated Autocracy', Computational Propaganda Research

Project, Working Paper No. 2017.2 (2017). http://blogs.oii.ox.ac.uk/politicalbots/wp-co ntent/uploads/sites/89/2017/06/Comprop-Taiwan-2.pdf

Mark Stokes and Russell Hsiao, 'The People's Liberation Army General Political Department: Political Warfare with Chinese Characteristics', *Project 2049* (14 October 2013): 4. Retrieved from: https://project2049.net/2013/10/14/the-peoples-liberation-ar my-general-political-department-political-warfare-with-chinese-characteristics/

13 Hybrid warfare in the Baltics

Dr Dorthe Bach Nyemann, Associate Professor in International Relations, Institute for Strategy, Royal Danish Defence College

Lucan Ahmad Way and Adam Casey, 'Is Russia a Threat to Western Democracy? Russian Intervention in Foreign Elections, 1991–2017' (Draft Memo for Global Populisms as a Threat to Democracy, 3 November 2017).

Leva Berzina, *The Possibility of Societal Destabilization in Latvia: Potential National Security Threats* (National Defence Academy of Latvia, Center for Security and Strategic Research, 2016).

MCDC Countering Hybrid Warfare Project: Countering Hybrid Warfare (MCDC, March 2019).

Henrik Praks, 'Hybrid or Not: Deterring and Defeating Russia's Ways of Warfare in the Baltics – the Case of Estonia'. *Research Paper* (Research Division – NATO Defense College, Rome, December 2015).

Toms Rostoks and Nora Vanaga, *Creating an Effective Deterrent against Russia in Europe: Military and Non-Military Aspects of Deterrence* (Riga: Friedrich Ebert Stiftung, November 2018).

Alexander Sergunin, *The Baltic Sea Region after the Ukraine Crises and Trump – A Russian Perspective* (DIIS, 2019).

Andrei Soldatov and Irina Borogan, 'Russia's Approach to Cyber: The Best Defence Is a Good Offence', in *Hacks, Leaks and Disruptions - Russian Cyber Strategies* (Chaillot Papers, no. 148, 2018).

Heine Sørensen and Dorthe Bach Nyemann, *Deterrence by Punishment as a Way of Countering Hybrid Threats: Why We Need to Go beyond Resilience in the Gray Zone*, 2019, www.gov.uk/government/publications/countering-hybrid-warfare-information-notes

Anna Tiido, *Russians in Europe: Nobody´s Tool – The Examples of Finland, Germany and Estonia* (Tallinn, Estonia: International Centre for Defence and Security, September 2019).

Martin Zapfe, 'Deterrence from the Ground Up: Understanding NATO's Enhanced Forward Presence', *Survival* 59, no. 3 (July 2017): 147–60.

14 De-hybridization and conflict narration: Ukraine's defence against Russian hybrid warfare

Dr Niklas Nilsson, Assistant Professor, Co-Convener of the Hybrid Warfare Research Group, Department of Military Studies, Swedish Defence University

Heinrich Brauss, Kalev Stoicescu and Tony Lawrence, *Capability and Resolve: Deterrence, Security and Stability in the Baltic Region* (Tallinn: International Centre for Defence and Security, 2020).

Ofer Friedman, *Russian 'Hybrid Warfare': Resurgence and Politicisation* (London: Hurst & Company, 2018).

Mark Galeotti, 'Hybrid, Ambiguous, and Non-Linear? How New Is Russia's "New Way of War"?', *Small Wars & Insurgencies* 27, no. 2 (2016): 282–301.

Hall Gardner, *Hybrid Warfare: Iranian and Russian Versions of 'Little Green Men' and Contemporary Conflict* (Rome: NATO Defence College, Research Division, December 2015).

Keir Giles, 'Russia's "New" Tools for Confronting the West: Continuity and Innovation in Moscow's Exercise of Power', Chatham House, 21 March 2016. https://www.chathamhouse.org/publication/russias-new-tools-confronting-west

Frank G. Hoffman, 'Hybrid Threats: Reconceptualizing the Evolving Character of Modern Conflict', *Strategic Forum*, no. 240 (Washington, DC: Institute for National Strategic Studies, National Defense University, April 2009). https://www.comw.org/qdr/fulltext/0904hoffman.pdf

Frank G. Hoffman, 'Hybrid Warfare and Challenges', *JFQ* 52 (1 quarter 2009): 34–9.

Robert Johnson, 'Hybrid War and Its Countermeasures: A Critique of the Literature', *Small Wars & Insurgencies* 29, no. 1 (2018): 143.

Alexander Lanozska, 'Russian Hybrid Warfare and Extended Deterrence in Eastern Europe', *International Affairs* 92, no. 1 (2016): 178.

MCDC, Countering Hybrid Warfare Project, summary. https://www.gov.uk/government/publications/countering-hybrid-warfare-project-understanding-hybrid-warfare

Sean Monaghan, 'Countering Hybrid Warfare: Conceptual Foundations and Implications for Defence Forces', *Multinational Capability Development Campaign (MCDC)*, Information note, March 2019. https://assets.publishing.service.gov.uk/government/uploads/system/uploads/attachment_data/file/840513/20190401-MCDC_CHW_Information_note_-_Conceptual_Foundations.pdf

Williamson Murray and Peter R. Mansoor, eds, *Hybrid Warfare: Fighting Complex Opponents from the Ancient World to the Present* (Cambridge: Cambridge University Press, 2012).

James Pamment, Howard Nothhaft, Henrik Agardh-Twetman and Alicia Fjällhed, *Countering Information Influence Activities: The State of the Art*, version 1.4 (Lund University, 1 July 2018). https://www.msb.se/RibData/Filer/pdf/28697.pdf

Nicu Popescu, 'Hybrid Tactics: Neither New nor only Russian', European Union Institute of Security Studies, January 2015. https://www.iss.europa.eu/sites/default/files/EUISSFiles/Alert_4_hybrid_warfare.pdf

Bettina Renz, 'Russia and "Hybrid Warfare"', *Contemporary Politics* 22, no. 3 (2016): 283–300.

Timothy Thomas, 'The Evolution of Russian Military Thought: Integrating Hybrid, New-Generation and New-Type Thinking', *The Journal of Slavic Military Studies* 29, no. 4 (2016): 557–9.

Rod Thornton, *Asymmetric Warfare: Threat and Response in the Twenty-First Century* (Cambridge: Polity, 2007).

Gregory F. Treverton, Andrew Thvedt, Alicia R. Chen, Kathy Lee and Madeline McCue, *Addressing Hybrid Threats* (Stockholm: Swedish Defence University, 2018).

Frans-Paul van der Putten, Minke Meijnders, Sico van der Meer and Tony van der Togt, eds *Hybrid Conflict: The Roles of Russia, North Korea and China* (The Hague: Clingendael Institute, 2018).

Mikael Weissmann, 'Hybrid Warfare and Hybrid Threats Today and Tomorrow: Towards an Analytical Framework', *Journal on Baltic Security* 5, no. 1 (2019): 17–26.

15 Iran's hybrid warfare capabilities

Dr Rouzbeh Parsi, Head of the Middle East and North Africa Programme, Swedish Institute of International Affairs

E. Abrahamian, *A History of Modern Iran* (Cambridge: Cambridge University Press, 2018).

H. Ajili and M. Rouhi, 'Iran's Military Strategy', *Survival* 61, no. 6 (2019): 139–52.

M. Axworthy, *Revolutionary Iran: A History of the Islamic Republic* (Penguin, 2019).

K. Barzegar and M. Rezaei, 'Ayatollah Khamenei's Strategic Thinking', *Discourse: An Iranian Quarterly* 11, no. 3 (Winter 2017): 27–54.

A. Bassiri Tabrizi and R. Pantucci, eds, *Understanding Iran's Role in the Syrian Conflict* (RUSI Occasional Paper, August 2016).

M. Boroujerdi, *Iran: A Political Handbook* (Syracuse: Syracuse University Press, 2018).

M. Brandt, *Tribes and Politics in Yemen: A History of the Houthi Conflict* (New York: Oxford University Press, 2017).

R. Czulda, 'The Defensive Dimension of Iran's Military Doctrine: How Would They Fight?', *Middle East Policy* XXIII, no. 1 (Spring 2016): 92–109.

J. Daher, *Hezbollah – The Political Economy of Lebanon's Party of God* (London: Pluto Press, 2016).

D. Esfandiary and A. Tabatabai, *Triple-Axis: Iran's Relations with Russia and China* (London: Bloomsbury Publishing, 2018).

H. Forozan, *The Military in Post-revolutionary Iran: The Evolution and Roles of the Revolutionary Guards* (New York: Routledge, 2016).

J. M. Goodarzi, *Syria and Iran: Diplomatic Alliance and Power Politics in the Middle East* (London: I.B. Tauris, 2009).

K. Lim, 'National Security Decision-Making in Iran', *Comparative Strategy* 34, no. 2 (2015): 149–68.

J. A. Lynn, *Battle: A History of Combat and Culture* (Cambridge, MA: Westview Press, 2003).

S. Malešević, *The Sociology of War and Violence* (Cambridge: Cambridge University Press, 2012).

R. Mansour, 'Challenges to the Post-2003 Political Order in Iraq', UI Paper no. 8 (2019). https://www.ui.se/globalassets/ui.se-eng/publications/ui-publications/2019/ui-paper-no.-8-2019.pdf

A. R. Norton, *Hezbollah: A Short History* (Princeton: Princeton University Press, 2007).

A. Ostovar, *Vanguard of the Imam: Religion, Politics, and Iran's Revolutionary Guards* (New York: Oxford University Press, 2016).

R. K. Ramazani, *Independence without Freedom: Iran's Foreign Policy* (Charlottesville: University of Virginia Press, 2013)

N. Razavi, 'The Systemic Problem of "Iran Expertise" in Washington', *Jadaliyya*, 4 September 2019. https://www.jadaliyya.com/Details/39946?fbclid=IwAR2RweuJ8Ry-XCwFIuNeyu-zPBqds8eIo5xIMB8kw7Blg2NExo8tW8ixbOo

S. Ward, *Immortal: A Military History of Iran and Its Armed Forces* (Washington: Georgetown University Press, 2014).

16 Information influencing in the Catalan illegal referendum and beyond

Dr Rubén Arcos, Rey Juan Carlos University

Rubén Arcos, 'Disarming Disinformation: EU Response to Russian Disinformation Picks Up Pace', *Jane's Intelligence Review* (October 2020): 30–3.

Rubén Arcos, *Post-event Analysis of the Hybrid Threat Security Environment: Assessment of Influence Communication Operations* (Hybrid CoE Strategic Analysis, October 2018). https://www.hybridcoe.fi/wp-content/uploads/2018/11/Strategic-Analysis-2018-10-Arcos.pdf

Rubén Arcos, 'Pushing Back: EU and NATO Confront Hybrid Threats in Centre of Excellence', *Jane's Intelligence Review* (March 2019): 28–33.

Bernard C. Cohen, *The Press and Foreign Policy* (Princeton: Princeton University Press, 1965).

Miguel Del-Fresno-García and Juan-Luis Manfredi-Sánchez, 'Politics, Hackers and Partisan Networking: Misinformation, National Utility and Free Election in the Catalan Independence Movement', *El profesional de la información* 27, no. 6 (November–December 2018): 1230. http://www.elprofesionaldelainformacion.com/contenidos/2018/nov/06.html

Robert M. Entman, 'Framing: Toward Clarification of a Fractured Paradigm', *Journal of Communication* 43, no. 4 (Autumn 1993): 52.

Government of Spain, *National Cybersecurity Strategy 2019* (1 April 2019). https://www.dsn.gob.es/es/file/2989/download?token=EuVy2lNr

Government of Spain, *National Security Strategy 2017* (1 December 2017). https://www.dsn.gob.es/2017-spanish-national-security-strategy

Hybrid CoE, *Hybrid CoE Trend Report 4: Trends in the Contemporary Information Environment. Hybrid CoE Expert Pool Meeting on Information* (May 2020). https://www.hybridcoe.fi/wp-content/uploads/2020/05/Hybrid-CoE-Trend-Report-4.pdf

Carlos López-Olano and Vicente Fenoll, 'Posverdad, o la narración del procés catalán desde el exterior: BBC, DW y RT', *El profesional de la información* 28, no. 3 (May–June 2019): 11. https://recyt.fecyt.es/index.php/EPI/article/view/epi.2019.may.18/44237

Maxwell McCombs, *Setting the Agenda: The Mass Media and Public Opinion* (Cambridge: Polity Press, 2004).

Maxwell McCombs, R. Lance Holbert, Spiro Kiousis and Wayne Wanta, *The News and Public Opinion: Media Effects on Civic Life* (Cambridge: Polity Press, 2015).

William J. McGuire, 'Order of Presentation as a Factor in "conditioning" Persuasiveness', in *The Order of Presentation in Persuasion*, ed. Carl I. Hovland (New Haven and London: Yale University Press, 1966), 98–9.

National Cryptologic Centre, *Ciberamenazas y tendencias, Edición 2018* (May 2018). https://www.ccn-cert.cni.es/informes/informes-ccn-cert-publicos/2835-ccn-cert-ia-09-18-ciberamenzas-y-tendencias-edicion-2018-1/file.html

Massimo Stella, Emilio Ferrara and Manlio De Domenico, 'Bots Increase Exposure to Negative and Inflammatory Content in Online Social Systems', *Proceedings of the National Academy of Sciences* 115, no. 49 (December 2018): 12435. https://www.pnas.org/content/115/49/12435

Part IV   Conclusions

17 Moving out of the blizzard: Towards a comprehensive approach to hybrid threats and hybrid warfare

Dr Mikael Weissmann, Dr Niklas Nilsson, Björn Palmertz

NO BIBLIOGRAPHY FOR CONCLUSION

Index

CPSIA information can be obtained
at www.ICGtesting.com
Printed in the USA
BVHW041441200322
631476BV00002B/4